WEYERHAEUSER ENVIRONMENTAL BOOKS

PAUL S. SUTTER, EDITOR

Weyerhaeuser Environmental Books explore human relationships with natural environments in all their variety and complexity. They seek to cast new light on the ways that natural systems affect human communities, the ways that people affect the environments of which they are a part, and the ways that different cultural conceptions of nature profoundly shape our sense of the world around us. A complete listing of the books in the series appears at the end of the book.

NATIVE SEATTLE

Histories from the Crossing-Over Place

COLL THRUSH

Foreword by William Cronon
with a new preface by the author

Second Edition

UNIVERSITY OF WASHINGTON PRESS *Seattle & London*

Native Seattle is published with the assistance of a grant from the Weyerhaeuser Environmental Books Endowment, established by the Weyerhaeuser Company Foundation, members of the Weyerhaeuser family, and Janet and Jack Creighton.

University of Washington Press
www.washington.edu/uwpress
ISBN 9780295741338 (hardcover)   ISBN 9780295741345 (paperback)
The Library of Congress has catalogued the earlier edition as follows:

Thrush, Coll-Peter, 1970–
Native Seattle : histories from the crossing-over place / Coll Thrush.
    p. cm.—(Weyerhaeuser environmental books)
Includes bibliographical references and index.
ISBN: 978-0-295-98700-2 (cl. : alk. paper)
ISBN: 978-0-295-98812-2 (pbk. : alk. paper)
1. Indians of North America—Washington (State)—Seattle—History.
2. Indians of North America—Washington (State)—Seattle—Antiquities.
3. Indians of North America—Washington (State)—Seattle—Social life and customs.
4. Seattle—(Wash.)—History.   5. Seattle (Wash.)—Antiquities.
6. Seattle (Wash.)—Social life and customs.   I. Title.
E 78.W3T47   2007
979.7'77200497—dc22   2006034199

CONTENTS

FOREWORD

Present Haunts of an Unvanished Past
William Cronon

MONG THE OLDEST, most powerful, and most pernicious of
all ideas associated with the American frontier is the Myth of
the Vanishing Race. The story it tells is of settlers from across
the ocean or from far corners of the continent coming to
a new land and finding there an abundant Eden, rich in resources and
inhabited by native peoples enjoying nature's bounty in harvests that
entailed little labor to improve the soil. Sometimes the myth portrays
these native inhabitants as savages who for no good reason seek to
destroy their new neighbors with unjustified acts of wanton violence.
Sometimes the myth presents Indians far more favorably, as a noble
race choosing to live lightly on the land, behaving with great honor and
generosity toward new arrivals whom they could easily have viewed as
invaders but whom instead they supported with gifts of food and other
necessities of life, only turning to violence after provocations so awful
that no reasonable person could expect anyone to endure them. But however the frontier myth portrays American Indians, whether negatively
or positively, it almost always ends in a transformed landscape in which
wilderness has given way to civilization, and, strikingly, native peoples
have vanished from the scene. Poignant though this narrative may sometimes seem, it has always been a cruel lie, distorting the actual lives and
histories of peoples who remain fully present in the transformed landscape despite the failure of historical narratives to notice their ongoing
presence in it.

Scholars and activists have been critiquing the Myth of the Vanishing Race for decades, so by now its many distortions of American Indian
history should hardly come as a surprise. Yet it persists for many reasons. Its oldest ideological purpose was undoubtedly to help forgive the

invaders their invasion—by implying that whatever the intentions on either side, an "uncivilized" people could not survive their encounter with the "civilized" people who would replace them. Sad though their vanishing might be, no one was really to blame for it—or so the story would have us believe. Subtler aspects of the myth reinforce this message. By casting frontier settlement in heroic terms, with honorable men and women on both sides coming into tragic conflict in the struggle to build a new nation, Indians and settlers alike can be represented as grander, nobler, larger than life. To the extent that the frontier has served as a defining feature of American nationalism since the nineteenth century, this heroic tale has proved to be an enduring resource for American national identity. Furthermore, the American devotion to romantic nature that emerged simultaneously as part of the same nation-building process had the consequence of tying Indians to a wilderness landscape that came to symbolize an older, simpler, purer world that a fallen humanity could now no longer inhabit. Strikingly, the movement to set aside national parks and wilderness preserves was nearly simultaneous with the movement of Indian tribes onto reservations, so that human inhabitants were made to vanish from the American wilderness as a self-fulfilling prophecy of its unpeopled nature.

YET THERE IS A LESS-NOTICED ASPECT of the Myth of the Vanishing Race that is arguably just as problematic. Perhaps in part because Indian peoples have long been associated with "nature," it has been remarkably easy not to notice their presence in places that are marked as "unnatural" in American understandings of landscape. Chief among these are urban and metropolitan areas, which for more than a century have provided homes for people of American Indian descent to a much greater degree than most people realize. Although there is a widespread assumption that most Indians live on reservations, in fact, many more live outside the boundaries of those legal homelands, with a substantial fraction living in cities. In the U.S. Census for the year 2000, for instance, New York City was home to 106,444 full or mixed-blood American Indians, Alaskan Natives, and Native Hawaiians, compared with 66,236 in Los Angeles,

25,513 in Chicago, and comparably large numbers in most other cities.[1] To the extent that actual Indians did indeed "vanish" from various parts of the continent, it wasn't because they had ceased to exist; they had simply migrated elsewhere—often, like so many other Americans, to urban areas. Perhaps most strangely of all, when native peoples occupied sites where the forces of urbanization were greatest, they found themselves becoming invisible—not to themselves, of course, but to their new neighbors—in the very places that had always been their homes.

It is this ironic story—almost never told by scholars precisely because the Myth of the Vanishing Race has been so pervasive—that Coll Thrush brilliantly narrates in his remarkable and beautifully written book, *Native Seattle: Histories from the Crossing-Over Place*. Beginning with the observation that few cities in the United States have placed greater emphasis on their native heritage than Seattle, he then points to the subtle and tragic processes that gradually marginalized and obscured Indian people residing in that city. Even as totem poles and Northwest Coast Indian artworks were coming to symbolize Seattle's special regional identity, native inhabitants were being assigned their traditional roles in the narrative of the vanishing race: as poignant icons of a lost past, as images of timeless beauty, but not as living residents. In a city where so many streets and sites bear Indian names and where, as Thrush wryly notes, totem poles until only recently outnumbered cell phone towers, it has been all too easy for non-Indian inhabitants and visitors to miss the fact that thousands of native people still live within the boundaries of the city.

One strand of Thrush's narrative, then, is a series of ghost stories: tales of how Seattle became a city haunted with evocative images of its native past. Among its many Indian ghosts, none has played a more prominent role than Chief Seattle himself, or Seeathl as this book prefers to call him as a reminder of his actual historical identity. Chief Seattle is associated with what is arguably the single most famous piece of

---

1. Mark Fogarty, "Stats say Big Apple has most urban Indians," *Indian Country Today*, February 25, 2003; on-line at http://www.indiancountry.com/content.cfm ?id=1046182689.

Indian oratory in all of American history, a text that most Americans have encountered many times without giving much thought to its origins or authenticity, both of which are murky at best. Its closing lines explicitly describe cities like Seattle as places still perennially visited by the shades of departed peoples who still hold them dear:

At night when the streets of your cities and villages will be silent and you think them deserted, they will throng with returning hosts that once filled and still love this beautiful land. The white man will never be alone. Let him be just and deal kindly with my people, for the dead are not powerless. Dead—did I say? There is no death, only a change of worlds.

It is hard not to be moved by the poetry of these lines (see pp. 5–6), which no doubt accounts for the frequency with which they are quoted—and yet it would also be hard to imagine a passage that more unambiguously affirms the Myth of the Vanishing Race. That is why it is so unsurprising to learn that we have no real authority for believing that Chief Seattle actually spoke these words, or that he so easily imagined a future time when his still-living people had ceased to dwell in their homeland.

This, then, leads to the second major theme of Coll Thrush's book. Tacking back and forth between myth and reality, he painstakingly demonstrates the ongoing presence of Duwamish, Suquamish, and other native residents of Seattle who have always been present, always part of its history, even as the myth was doing its work of reinventing a supposedly vanished Indian landscape to fit the frontier and regional narrative of the emerging city on the shore of Puget Sound. In so doing, he effectively turns the myth on its head by showing how intimately Seattle's native residents were involved in every stage of the city's historical evolution. Far from vanishing, they were present at the creation, they continued to make essential contributions as the city grew to metropolitan status, and they persisted in maintaining their special relationships with the local landscape right down to the present. Over and over again, Thrush discovers a geography of native use and native dwelling that the modern cityscape obscures without quite eliminating altogether. Some places in this intricate web of native relationships with the local environment eventually came to be highlighted in the imagined geography of modern Seattle, while others found no place in that geography. Among its many accomplishments, *Native Seattle* offers quiet but irresistible proof that any full understanding of the city's history must incorporate all aspects of native history and geography, not just the ones selectively celebrated by the Myth of the Vanishing Race.

The result is a history with implications far beyond Seattle. No other book does what this one does. In a world where many modern people too easily lose track of the natural ecosystems they inhabit, preferring instead to seek out "nature" in remote corners of the globe, it is useful to be reminded that even a great city has a long history of human habitation that is intimately and inextricably bound to the local lands and waters and creatures that help define such places. By seeking out the myriad ways that Seattle's native peoples related to the world around them, Thrush offers modern city dwellers an unexpectedly powerful way of seeing aspects of the urban landscape that might otherwise be entirely invisible to them. And by showing readers how human beings in the past have related to the local ecosystems even of great metropolitan areas in profoundly different ways, he reminds us not to be taken in by the seductive but all-too-selective appeals of our mythic imaginations. Just as Seattle's native peoples have never vanished from the city, neither have the geographies—natural and historical and imagined—that made those people native to this place. By helping us see the modern city at least a little through the eyes of people whose presence might otherwise be too easy to ignore, Coll Thrush invites us to revisit the histories and geographies of our own home places as well.

PREFACE TO THE
SECOND EDITION
Coll Thrush

NATIVE SEATTLE was always about place: the power that places hold over our lives, the traditions within which our cultures interact with places, and the ways that we dwell concretely and often conflictedly with each other in those places. It was also always about stories: stories that were almost lost, others that have dominated popular historical memory, and the larger narrative of the interactions between the two. "Place-story" was a term I used to try and capture the conjunction between sites of history and the accounts we make of them, whether we are Native or newcomer. These stories necessarily braid together, they interact, and they entangle and inform each other in ways that are often difficult to make sense of.

Place-stories, meanwhile, are inherently plural. The subtitle of this book, *Histories from the Crossing-Over Place*, was intentional: there are multiple histories at play here. The first is the experience of the Duwamish, in whose territory the city sprang up. Accounts of local women and men living within the increasingly tight fabric of the city's urbanizing landscape in the early twentieth century, for example, provide a link between ancient Duwamish presence on the land and their ongoing efforts for federal recognition, as well as kinship connections to other tribes in the region. Second, there is the history of Native migrations to the city: Makah encampments adjacent to what would become known as Pioneer Square at the turn of the twentieth century, Haida people living in Interbay in the 1930s, or the diverse occupiers of Fort Lawton in 1970. These other Indian histories in Seattle speak not just to the ways in which Native people and peoples made use of the city and its regional networks, but limn the very reaches of those networks to illustrate Seattle's growing influence on the Northwest Coast. And lastly, there are the histories of the uses of Indian imagery in Seattle. These place-stories invariably use the Native to make sense of the urban. Pioneer daughters lamenting urban growth by using the Whulshootseed language, the imposition of north coast-style totem poles as civic icons, and of course the various non-Native deployments of the Chief Seattle Speech all speak to the ways in which, rather than being mutually exclusive, urban and Native histories in Seattle are in fact mutually constitutive. They have been created in conversation each other. They are the same place-story.

It is also a story that is ongoing. In the ten years since *Native Seattle* was first published, many of the themes and trends that I tried to bring together in the book have continued and in some cases deepened. That is to say, while the book ended with the sesquicentennial of the city's founding, Seattle's Native history has not come to an end. This new preface is an attempt to bring the story up to the present by first focusing on some of what has happened in Native Seattle since the beginning of the twenty-first century and then setting Seattle's history in the context of the stories of other cities. An increasingly visible Native community in Seattle and a growing literature on Indian histories in urban places illustrate how the city's place-stories continue to be told and to tell themselves in the inescapable histories of this city and others.

First, though, a comment on terminology. In *Native Seattle*, I deliberately oscillated between "Native," "Indian," and specific tribal designations to illustrate the fact that no single term holds unchallenged hegemony over discourse about the history of colonialism in what became the city. Upon moving to British Columbia in 2005, I encountered another set of terms: Aboriginal, First Nations, and others, specific to the history and nature of colonialism in that country. In the years since, consensus has begun to grow around another term: Indigenous (sometimes capitalized, sometimes not). Scholars, especially those who themselves identify as Indigenous, have in many cases settled on this word, and it has become the identifying term for major organizations in the field such as the Native American and Indigenous Studies Association. Meanwhile, on-the-ground activists have increasingly begun to use the word. For example, as I write this in the fall of 2016, land and water defenders from many tribes and nations are involved in a standoff against an oil pipeline at the Standing Rock reservation in North Dakota, and in the very active social media landscape attendant to the action, #IndigenousRising is one of the many hashtags. The language also appears in the United Nations Declaration of the Rights of Indigenous Peoples, enacted in 2007 after decades of global activism and organizing.[1]

Today, I use Indigenous, signifying both the direction of the field and my own commitments to supporting the broader Indigenous rights movement. This is at odds with how the term appears in the original text of *Native Seattle*: there, it appears uncapitalized and refers only to traditional ways of living on the land in and around the city. Capital-I Indigenous, meanwhile, is a far more capacious term, one that speaks not only to traditional practices but to the ongoing presence and cultural and political vitality of Native communities in Seattle and across the world. It does not imply, as my earlier use of "indigenous" might be understood, that such things came to an end. Instead, "Indigenous" reflects the energy of a new turn in academic research and writing, and mirrors the rise of the modern global Indigenous rights movement. If I were to write *Native Seattle* again, it would be my term of choice, as it would demand not only an Indigenous past for the city, but also an active present and open future.

I T WOULD BE TEMPTING with Seattle's Indigenous history to focus only on Duwamish place-stories like those that are featured in its atlas. Sites such as Rids the Cold, Herring's House, and Tucked Away Inside speak to the ecological and other intimacies of life in Duwamish territory, while names like Greenish-Yellow Spine, Serviceberry, and Place of Waterfalls are virtual photographs of that territory. (For another mapping project that incorporates many of these places

---

1. For some of the foremost thinkers and writers in the field, see *Critical Indigenous Studies: Engagements in First World Locations*, ed. Aileen Moreton-Robinson (Tucson: University of Arizona Press, 2016). For a history of the global Indigenous rights movement, see Sheryl Lightfoot, *Global Indigenous Politics: A Subtle Revolution* (London: Routledge, 2016).

into a handy foldout map of the city's Duwamish landscapes and environmental history, see the Burke Museum's Waterlines Project at www.burkemuseum.org/static/waterlines.) Certainly, these are in many ways the most compelling place-stories in the city, having emerged out of thousands of years of inhabitance. However, there are additional maps we might create, relating to other Indigenous place-stories. Following a single Indigenous man's life through the city, for example, emplaces another geography on the city. His name was John.

John T. Williams was a Ditidaht man from the west coast of Vancouver Island. As such, his story reflects the long history of non-Duwamish Indigenous presence in the city: Ditidaht people and their relatives, the Nuu-chah-nulth and Makah, have been coming to Seattle since the late nineteenth century. Indeed, Williams's family had been in Seattle since the very beginning of the twentieth century, when his grandfather Samuel Williams carved for Ye Olde Curiosity Shop on the waterfront. John Williams was an eighth-generation carver, meaning that his profession's genealogy ran at least as deep in time as the whole history of Seattle. He was a well known fixture of Victor Steinbrueck Park at the Pike Place Market, where he, his brother, and other Indigenous artists worked and interacted with tourists and locals. The Pike Place Market, then, holds a place-story of Indigenous migration, of the continuation of Ditidaht artistic traditions and the enfoldment of those traditions into an urban sense of place.

There is another place associated with Williams, however: the corner of Boren and Howell, just uphill from downtown, near I-5. It was there, on August 30, 2010, that Williams was killed by a Seattle police officer named Ian Birk. From his squad car, Birk had noticed Williams walking with a piece of carving cedar and his unopened working knife, the tool of his trade. Quickly exiting his vehicle, Birk shouted at the half-deaf Williams, and within seconds let loose a volley of bullets that hit the carver in the back and side. Williams died soon after.

Williams's killing—or, as many described it, murder—shocked Seattle's liberal sensibilities and galvanized the Indigenous community, who linked his death to much longer histories of violence and dispossession, as well as to the issue of police brutality against Indigenous people, people of color, and the poor more broadly. Hundreds of Indigenous Seattleites and their allies marched through the city in protest against the killing, calling for criminal charges against Burk and a review of the use of lethal force by Seattle police. A civil lawsuit, meanwhile, was brought by Williams's family. Williams's life and death also inspired new creative works both in and far beyond Seattle: Choctaw-Alutiiq artist Storme Webber performed poetry devoted to Williams at the Seattle Arts Festival while holding a talking stick crafted by John's brother Rick, and the Canadian First Nations hip–hop group A Tribe Called Red released the song "Woodcarver" on their eponymous 2012 album. As for Ian Birk, a Seattle Police Department firearms review board ruled the shooting unjustified and a federal investigation drew attention to systemic problems in the police force. In the end, the Williams family received a large settlement from the city, and Birk resigned from the force without facing any charges.

But the story did not end there, and there is a third Seattle location associated with Williams's life. In 2011, Williams's brother Rick and other artists set to carving a memorial pole for the lost member of their family and community. The pole, featuring ravens and eagles and other important representations of genealogy and connections to traditional territories, was carried through the city and erected at Seattle Center near the iconic Space Needle. The pole, Alutiiq scholar Thomas Michael Swenson argues, "recuperates Seattle as an indigenous space that recognizes Williams's social value as a member of the city's community."[2] Pike Place Market, Boren and Howell, the Seattle Center: John T. Williams's life marks a Ditidaht transect across the urban landscape, constellating place-stories of grief, anger, injustice, and healing.

The events surrounding John T. Williams's death and memorial came at a time when Indigenous people and issues in Seattle achieved levels of public prominence and attention higher than at any point since the early 1970s. Local federally recognized tribes like the Muckleshoot

2. Thomas Michael Swensen, "Forever Crossing Over: At the Intersection of John T. Williams's Life and Memorial," *American Indian Culture and Research Journal* 39:4 (2015), 1-18.

and Suquamish continued to assert their treaty rights over fisheries and other elements of the urban environment, strengthening the government-to-government relationships that had developed in the decades since the Boldt Decision. The Suquamish, whose reservation is located across Puget Sound but whose members include some Duwamish descendants, also reclaimed part of their material heritage from the city. In 2013, they brought home cultural belongings from Old Man House, the location of Seeathl's grave, which had languished at the Burke Museum since they were excavated some six decades earlier. As the objects' human protectors carried them across the Sound on a Washington State ferry, a large pod of orcas circled the ship, which the Suquamish understood as a blessing. Meanwhile, local tribes have welcomed participants in the annual Canoe Journey, in which many tribes and First Nations, from up and down the Northwest Coast, visit the shores of Seattle as part of their weeks-long mobile celebrations throughout the region.

Beyond the federally recognized tribes, Seattle's urban Indigenous community has also become increasingly visible in the decade since *Native Seattle* was first published. Performers like Red Eagle Soaring, a dance and theatre ensemble made up of Indigenous youth of many backgrounds, took stages across the city. Artists such as Seminole-Choctaw filmmaker Tracy Rector, whose "You Are On Indigenous Land" photography installation, made up of intimate portraits of members of her community taken by her and her colleagues, received praise from the local press. And in 2015, Blackfeet legal advocate and jurist Debora Juarez successfully campaigned for the city council, representing the city's northernmost district. A far cry from the place of Indigenous people in the city's consciousness in earlier eras—symbols of a vanishing race or threats to urban order—Indigenous women and men have become important players in the city's cultural and political landscape.

Indigenous institutions are also on the rise. Daybreak Star cultural center, located in Discovery Park and founded by the activists who took over Fort Lawton in 1970, remains a crucial resource for many people in Seattle's Indigenous community, including hosting the annual Seafair Days powwow. At the University of Washington, meanwhile, wəɬəbʔaltxʷ (Intellectual House) opened in 2015, after years of organizing by activists both within and outside the UW community. It serves as a center for Indigenous concerns on campus and is already a much-sought-after venue for academic and other events. But wəɬəbʔaltxʷ's place-story goes deeper than that. According to Tseshaht Nuu-chah-nulth professor Charlotte Coté, "when you walk into Intellectual House, you really do feel the spirits of their ancestors. This is not just a building." Designed by Cherokee-Choctaw architect Johnpaul Jones in a style reminiscent of the longhouses that once graced the nearby Duwamish community of Little Canoe Channel, wəɬəbʔaltxʷ was described by organizing committee member Denny Hurtado of the Skokomish Tribe as "a home where we can share our culture with the non-natives, and build bridges amongst us."[3] And down at the Pike Place Market, Nooksack artist and entrepreneur Louie Gong has opened the famed market's first Indigenous-owned business, Eighth Generation. Together, all of these new additions to Seattle's Indigenous landscape speak to the ongoing work of the city's Indigenous community to be seen, to create, and to flourish.

Seattle's Indian-inflected self-image has also continued to grow and change. In 2008, for example, the city unveiled a new trail circling Lake Union that was named after Cheshiahud, the Duwamish man who had once lived on the lake's shoreline. Nearby, at the Museum of History and Industry's new location, the 1950s diorama of the Denny Party no longer serves as the starting point of the city's history; instead, a gallery curated under the guidance of local tribal members reminds visitors that they, as was Denny, are on Indigenous land. In 2014, meanwhile, the city council ruled unanimously to rename Columbus Day as Indigenous Peoples Day, making Seattle one of the first cities to reorient itself in relation to a long-honored and much-excoriated commemoration of colonialism's ultimate bête noir. That same year, the Seattle Seahawks won the Super Bowl, and even that victory was framed in part through Indigenous imagery: the Burke Museum displayed a Kwakwaka'wakw

3. "Faculty Friday: Charlotte Coté," www.washington.edu/wholeu/2016/07/22/faculty-friday-charlotte-cote/ [accessed 10/5/2016].

eagle transformation mask thought to the be the inspiration for the football team's logo, while during the team's victory parade, running back Marshawn Lynch received a drum from Lummi tribal member John Scott. Lynch's beating of the drum received worldwide attention and once again highlighted Indigenous presence in the city. Finally, in the years to come, the city's much-debated redevelopment of the waterfront will feature the work of Puyallup artist Qwalsius (Shaun Peterson), whose Coast Salish–style works will push back against the North Coast imagery so associated with Seattle's public image.

In the midst of all this, with the deepest place-story of all, the Duwamish remain. Despite being denied federal recognition yet again in 2015—a decision the Department of the Interior described as "final"—the tribe's members continue to fight for legal and cultural recognition. In the wake of the 2015 ruling, more than fifty Duwamish people and allies protested at the West Seattle home of Interior Secretary Sally Jewell, and in one newspaper account of the decision, tribal chairwoman Cecile Hansen stated firmly, "we're not invisible."[4] This is true. As they had during the 2001 sesquicentennial of the Denny Party's landing at Alki Beach, the Duwamish continue to make their presence known in very public ways while attending to their own cultural revival. Former tribal council member James Rasmussen, for example, is one of the leaders of the Duwamish Cleanup Coalition, whose goal is to continue the work of remediating the Superfund site that is Seattle's only river, while the tribe's dance group T'ilibshudub (Dancing Feet) often performs around the city and elsewhere. Most notably, the Duwamish opened their long-planned longhouse and cultural center in 2009, just across West Marginal Way from the site of their ancient town of Crying Face. The tribe has also been involved in documenting its own history, perhaps most importantly through the work of University of Victoria graduate student and Duwamish descendant Julia Allain

4. Paige Cornwell, "Duwamish Denied Federal Recognition but Vow to 'Fight On,'" *Seattle Times*, 8 July 2015.

who collected stories of many of the tribe's leading families.[5] These activities and others show that federal recognition, as a colonial legal framework, does not necessarily determine Indigeneity: as Indigenous people around the world have asserted, they can exist regardless of someone else's rules.

None of the events described above have happened without significant Indigenous activism, as has been always been the case throughout Seattle's history, in which Native people have had to struggle to claim a place in the city and to combat the stereotypical images of the doomed, vanished Indian. In doing, so, they have exhibited what Ojibwe journalist and scholar Gerald Vizenor has called "survivance." Survivance, a neologism that connotes both survival and resistance, speaks to something beyond simple persistence:

Theories of survivance are elusive, obscure, and imprecise by definition . . . but survivance is invariably true in native practice and company. The nature of survivance is unmistakable in native stories . . . and is clearly visible in narrative resistance and personal attributes, such as the native humanistic tease, vital irony, spirit, cast of mind, and moral courage.

The character of survivance creates a sense of native presence over absence, nihility, and victimry. Survivance is a continuation of stories, not a mere reaction . . . survivance is greater than the right of a survivable name.[6]

Nothing captures this notion of survivance more than the 2015 protests against oil giant Shell, whose enormous drilling rig was anchored for a time in Elliott Bay. Hundreds of "kayaktivists" took to the water to speak out against drilling and block aquatic access to the rig, but this was more than the usual Seattle environmentalist action. There, among the brightly colored plastic watercraft, were tribal canoes, leading the

5. Julia Allain, "Duwamish History in Duwamish Voices: Weaving Our Family Stories Since Colonization," Ph.D. dissertation, University of Victoria, 2014.

6. Gerald Vizenor, "Aesthetics of Survivance: Literary Theory and Practice," *Survivance: Narratives of Native Presence*, ed. Gerald Vizenor (Lincoln: University of Nebraska Press, 2008), 1.

charge in defense of the earth. Such is survivance; such is the truth that Seattle's Indigenous history is far from over.

"EVERY AMERICAN CITY was built on Indian land, but few advertise it like Seattle." With that opening line, I wanted to point out something quite unique about the city: it is the largest urban center in the United States that sells itself using Indigenous imagery. Certainly, other places in the region—Spokane, Tacoma, Yakima—carry Native monikers, but it is Seattle that most fully embraces Indigenous history and imagery as central to its self-fashioning. Certainly, Seattle contrasts with other West Coast cities such as Portland, where Indian imagery is rarely used and is overshadowed by the ghosts of Lewis and Clark and the Oregon Trail, or San Francisco or Los Angeles, with their mythology of the Spanish colonial past.

Then I moved to Vancouver, a city that, even more than Seattle, has created an Indigenized identity for itself. Vancouver sits on the traditional and ancestral territories of three First Nations: the Musqueam, the Squamish, and the Tsleil-Waututh. More than just traditional and ancestral, though, these lands are also unceded: Indigenous title has never been extinguished by law. Instead, the land was simply taken via settler force of will. This is a key difference from Seattle, where the Treaty of Point Elliott is the law of the land and undergirds government-to-government relations between the city and the federally recognized tribes. At the same time, local First Nations in Vancouver have been able to wrest a significant amount of recognition from the city: at the 2010 Olympics, all three—plus a fourth First Nation, the Lil'wat—welcomed the world to Vancouver at the opening ceremonies as official hosts to the games. And in 2014, the city council officially acknowledged the Musqueam, Squamish, and Tseil-Waututh nations and the fact of the city's presence on unceded land.

There are many similarities between Seattle's Indigenous history and that of Vancouver, however. The dispossession of Indigenous land in British Columbia's largest city often runs parallel to that of the American Northwest's primary metropolis. For example, during the same decade that the Lake Washington Ship Canal was finished, lowering the lake and destroying the Black River where many Duwamish people lived, Vancouver city leaders "liquidated" the Kitsilano Indian Reserve adjacent to downtown (and five blocks from where I live). And popular imagery of Native peoples—in particular North Coast–style totem poles, which once again overshadow the artistic traditions of local Coast Salish peoples, and the inukshuk, a cairn-like stone figure appropriated from Inuit culture—has often threatened to overshadow the lived experience of Indigenous people in the city. For example, in the years running up to the Olympics, dozens of women, most of them Indigenous, disappeared from the Downtown Eastside, and were eventually discovered to have been murdered at a farm in the suburbs. It is this tension, between Indigenized urban self-images and the real experiences of Indigenous people, that often energizes Indigenous activism such as the Idle No More movement that sprung up across Canada in 2012. As in Seattle, urban and Indigenous histories, whether in the United States or in Canada, are intimately intertwined, and separating the two is an act of willful narrative violence.[7]

Beyond the shores of the Salish Sea, other urban Indigenous histories are beginning to emerge as scholars, both Indigenous and settler, go into the archives and engage oral tradition armed with new questions about the relationship between cities and Indigenous peoples. In Los Angeles, for example, researchers including Seneca Indigenous studies scholar Mishuana Goeman have been developing an interactive map of Indigenous LA, drawing both on the extensive records of the Spanish missions and the oral testimony of Tongva and other local peoples. This mapping parallels—and outdoes—the atlas to *Native Seattle*.[8] In

---

7. For accounts of Indigenous history and urban dispossession in Vancouver, see Jordan Stanger-Ross, "Municipal Colonialism: City Planning and the Conflict over Indian Reserves, 1928-1950," *Canadian Historical Review* 89:4 (December 2008), 541-580; Jean Barman, "Erasing Indigenous Indigeneity in Vancouver," *BC Studies* 155 (Autumn 2007), 3-30. For the Musqueam Nation's perspectives on Vancouver, see The City before the City (www.thecitybeforethecity.com) and the Nation's website (www.musqueam.bc.ca).

8. Mapping Indigenous LA website, mila.ss.ucla.edu [accessed 10/18/2016].

Chicago, meanwhile, historians John Low, Rosalyn LaPier, and David Beck have been reclaiming a particularly rich history of Indigenous activism going back more than a century. For example, Potawatomi chief Simon Pokagon famously critiqued the 1893 World's Columbian Exposition, demanding that his people be allowed to represent themselves at the fair. Coming less than a decade after the Chief Seattle Speech, Pokagon's statement is not so much elegy as it is activism, and later decades of organizing by the city's multiethnic Indigenous community would build upon the work of Pokagon and others.[9] Others have made comparisons between far-flung settler cities. For instance, Penelope Edmonds's work on Victoria, British Columbia, and Melbourne, Australia, outlines methods of dispossession that would be familiar to anyone who knows Seattle's history. In both cases, whether in the territory of the Songhees First Nation or that of the Kulin Alliance, racist discourses of civilization and savagery, stories about Indigenous threats to hygiene and morality, and even the material consequences of urban forms such as the street grid dramatically shaped both Victoria and Melbourne and look very similar to what happened in Seattle.[10] Meanwhile, Maori researcher Melissa Matutina Williams's work on migrants to Auckland in New Zealand/Aotearoa resonates closely with stories of Indigenous people who settled in Seattle, from similar governmental policies of relocation to the work of keeping traditional culture alive in an urban setting far from home.[11] Back in the United States, Ho-Chunk scholar Renya Ramirez has collected stories in the Bay Area to describe the "hubs" created by a diverse Indigenous population that includes both

9. For two accounts of Indigenous history in Chicago, see John M. Low, *Imprints: The Pokagon Band of Potawatomi Indians and the City of Chicago* (East Lansing: Michigan State University Press, 2016); Rosalyn R. LaPier and David R. M. Beck, *City Indian: Native American Activism in Chicago, 1893-1940* (Lincoln: University of Nebraska Press, 2015).

10. Penelope Edmonds, *Urbanizing Frontiers: Indigenous Peoples and Settlers in 19th-Century Pacific Rim Cities* (Vancouver: UBC Press, 2010).

11. Melissa Matutina Williams, *Panguru and the City: Kainga Tahi, Kainga Rua: An Urban Migration History* (Wellington: Bridget Williams Books, 2015).

descendants of local tribes as well as immigrants from Latin America.[12] Other researchers have pushed urban Indigenous studies even further, taking it to the centers of empire: Nancy Van Deusen's work on Indigenous legal activism in sixteenth-century Spain or my own recent work on Indigenous travelers to London prove that urban Indigenous history can be found even in the most unlikely of places.[13]

Other projects are scheduled to appear in the years to come: at least two studies of Detroit, one focused on the fur trade era and another on twentieth-century intersections of Indigenous and Black history; a history of Indigenous presence in the suburbs of Minneapolis and St. Paul; an in-depth and wide-ranging account of urban relocation across the country; and an Indigenous-centered history of Washington, DC, a city that played a central role in diplomacy between Indigenous nations and the government of the United States. Taken together, these studies, like the ones that have come before them, challenge the notion that Indigenous peoples represent the past and cities represent the future, and never the twain shall meet. Instead, they show how the urban influenced the Indigenous and vice versa. Like *Native Seattle*, they attempt to undo one of the most powerful storylines in world history.

Since publishing *Native Seattle*, I have often been asked about my position on the Chief Seattle Speech. Was it truly a powerful statement made by an Indigenous leader in response to settler incursion on Duwamish territories? Or was it primarily a fiction created by a Seattle doctor, which trafficked in the mythology of the vanishing Indian? My position, as was also stated in the original edition, is that it is somewhere in between. There is no question that Seeathl was a powerful orator, and other speeches he gave around the time of the 1855 treaties that have come down through oral

12. Renya Ramirez, *Native Hubs: Culture, Community, and Belonging in the Bay Area and Beyond* (Durham: Duke University Press, 2007).

13. Nancy E. Van Deusen, *Global Indios: The Indigenous Struggle for Justice in Sixteenth-Century Spain* (Durham: Duke University Press, 2015); Coll Thrush, *Indigenous London: Native Travelers at the Heart of Empire* (New Haven: Yale University Press, 2016).

tradition attest to this. I have no doubt that he said *something* that resonated long past his death in 1866. At the same time, the speech as written by Henry A. Smith in 1884, does indeed sound much like other Victorian accounts of a dying race that was doomed to haunt white society. In this sense, I think it is a situation of both-and rather than either-or. Like Seattle's urban and Indigenous histories more generally, Duwamish oration and American fiction are deeply imbricated with each other in this almost singular text of Indigenous-settler relations.

At the end of many versions of the Speech, Seeathl is described as saying, "There is no death, only a change of worlds." Whether he actually said those words or not, they are particularly apt for thinking about urban Indigenous histories in Seattle and beyond. While places like Seattle have been the site of enormous Indigenous suffering, they are also places of Indigenous survivance, of a vibrant community that continues to claim its place within the city's political and cultural landscapes. In a broad sense, there is no death here. Meanwhile, sometime in the years immediately after the publication of *Native Seattle*, the world officially became urban: the majority of the Earth's population now resides in cities. Indigenous people across the world are part of this story; in the United States, Canada, Australia, and New Zealand, for example, the majority of Indigenous people in each country now live in urban areas. Indigenous migration patterns around the world confirm this, whether in Latin America or northern Europe or Africa. In that sense, then, there has been a "change of worlds." But despite powerfully influential ideas that Indigeneity cannot withstand urban modernity, that change has not erased Indigenous people from local places or global spaces. Whether in the form of traditional sites that continue to inform Indigenous identities, the movement of Indigenous people to (and from) urban places, or the uses of Indigenous imagery, urban Indigenous history across the planet, as in Seattle, continues apace. My hope is that, over the past ten years, *Native Seattle* has contributed to that continuation, and in doing so, has helped provide a context for urban Indigenous futures.

PREFACE TO THE ORIGINAL EDITION

ONCE UPON A TIME—meaning in the early phases of graduate school—I had the idea that I was going to have to write about everything that ever happened to every Indian person in Seattle, but I soon realized that this was neither possible nor would it make a book anyone wanted to read. The stories included in this book, then, are intended simply as examples of the kinds of experiences Native people have had in the city and its hinterland and, just as important, how those experiences have intersected with larger questions about urban development and urbanity itself. As with the Duwamish and their struggle for recognition, I hope that this book will create new opportunities for Indian people in Seattle to speak about their lives and be heard, even if the stories they tell differ markedly from, or even contradict, the broader urban narrative I have written.

And the narrative is indeed intended to be a broad one, stretching from before the landing of the "Denny Party" at Alki Beach in 1851 to the beginning of the twenty-first century. Chapter 1 sets the stage by examining the current state of Seattle's "place-story," which is dominated by metaphorical Indians and the notion—promulgated both by scholarly literature and by popular culture—that urban and Native histories are somehow mutually exclusive. The narrative then continues with two chronological chapters. Chapter 2 retells the founding of Seattle as a complex historical process, a *longue durée* rather than a snapshot singularity, which took place within a dynamic landscape whose indigenous inhabitants shaped the founding process in important ways. Chapter 3 examines the even greater role that indigenous people such as the Duwamish played in the creation of an urban frontier on

Puget Sound. Throughout Seattle's "village period," the 1850s through the 1870s, the Duwamish and other Indian people literally made Seattle possible through their labor and their participation in town life, even as they were scapegoated as symbols of urban disorder.

Chapter 4 is the first of two "hinges" in the narrative, both focusing closely on Seattle's Indian landscapes during narrowly defined but critically important periods of change in Seattle's urban Native histories. The first hinge, in the 1880s, uses the federal census and other fine-grained sources to show a nascent city in which multiple kinds of Indian history—of local indigenous people, Native migrants to the city, and Indian images in the "urban vocabulary"—began to intersect in complicated ways. The second hinge, Chapter 8, focuses on the 1930s, when these three histories had matured into dominant facets of Seattle's urban story and when the city stood poised for the transformative experience of the Second World War.

Chapters 5–7, instead of proceeding chronologically, each look at one of these three Native histories in the period between the two "hinges" of the 1880s and the 1930s. Chapter 5 examines the experiences of local indigenous people through Seattle's massive environmental transformations and their near-total dispossession from the urban landscape through the seemingly self-fulfilling prophecy of the "vanishing race." Chapter 6 is about the creation of a vast Native hinterland woven together by the movement of Indian people and things to and from Seattle and places along the broader Northwest Coast. Non-Indians' use of Indian imagery to tell (and sell) Seattle's story, and contention over what exactly that story was, are the subjects of Chapter 7.

After the second "hinge" of Chapter 8, the final two chapters examine the postwar period through two related but distinct stories. Chapter 9 is about the multiethnic, pan-Indian urban community that took shape in the postwar years, while Chapter 10 is about the resurgence of local tribes such as the Duwamish in the arena of civic discourse. Both chapters illustrate the ongoing legacies of earlier periods in Seattle's Native pasts, the ways in which Indian people have claimed space and authority within the city, and how these legacies and claimings continue to interact with Seattle's Native symbolism and urban storyline.

The idea that Indians and cities are mutually exclusive—or, more to the point, that Native people do not "belong" in urban places—is, in addition to being an outgrowth of broader American ideas about progress, also a result of the simple fact that Indian people can be very hard to find in cities. Collecting the histories included in this book was at times like looking for a handful of needles in an even greater number of haystacks. I always operated, however, under the axiom that "absence of evidence is not necessarily evidence of absence," and so made few assumptions about what kinds of sources might include references to Native people. I used the sources typical of any ethnohistorical project such as anthropologists' field notes, oral tradition, Indian agents' reports, and archaeological studies. I also mined standard sources of urban social and cultural history—memoirs, newspapers, locally produced neighborhood studies, federal censuses, and subscription histories—for any mention of Native people. In many cases, these sources had to be analyzed on two levels: I used them both to establish the presence of Native people and to assess non-Indian attitudes about the presence of Native people in the city. Lastly, I spent a great deal of time examining urban sources such as engineers' reports that made no mention of Indians at all. It was here that absences turned into evidence: by triangulating between these sources, Native sources such as oral tradition or indigenous topographical names and sources speaking to the environmental consequences of urban transformation, I was able to link both engineers and elders—and thus urban and Indian histories—through close attention to place and environmental change. The highly interdisciplinary, even omnivorous, methodologies of environmental history were thus critical to unearthing Seattle's Native pasts.

Unearthing those pasts also involved resurrecting the racism of the past. While looking for non-Indian narratives about Indian people in the city, I all too often encountered words and phrases that have been used to demean, marginalize, and even kill Native men and, especially, women. Some people fear that repeating such racist language perpetuates racism. I am of the belief, however, that the only way that we can talk critically about racism is to understand—and see clearly—the language that reinforced it. I hope that the reader will understand that my use of quotations that include words such as "squaw" or "savage" was done with the goal of laying bare the ignorance and racism of the past. I also hope that this book will contribute to the ongoing struggle against the ignorance and racism of the present, which, if often masked, run surprisingly deep.

Writing Native histories in English is by definition an imprecise art. Scholars and tribal people have come up with many ways, for example, to write down Whulshootseed words. (Even the name itself is up for debate. Some call it Puget Sound Salish, while others call it Lushootseed; Whulshootseed is the southern, Seattle-area dialect version of the name.) With nonspecialist readers in mind, in the main text of this book I have used indigenous names for local places only in English translation. Readers interested in more detailed information on these places, including the Whulshootseed versions of their names, should visit the atlas at the back of the book. There, the Whulshootseed names are spelled using a practical orthography developed by atlas coauthor Nile Thompson. Within the main text, I have chosen to spell individual Native people's Indian names—Whulshootseed or otherwise—using English approximations. At times, these spellings differ from those in most historical sources. For example, the man after whom Seattle is named is referred to in this book as Seeathl rather than as Seattle—or Sealth, another common anglicization of his name—both to distinguish the individual from the city (and the Chief Seattle Speech attributed to him) and to suggest a pronunciation as close as possible to the Whulshootseed original. (It should be pronounced something like "see-ahthl," with the break between syllables like the break in "uh-oh" and the final sound like the Welsh "ll.") I hope that any loss of linguistic integrity will be compensated for by greater readability.

WITHOUT A DOUBT, the most important collaborators in a project like this are Native people themselves. There is no longer any reason (or excuse) for a scholar to write Indian history without the active participation of tribal people. The Muckleshoot Indian Tribe in my hometown of Auburn, Washington, granted me access to oral histories dealing with Seattle and supported my interest in publishing the material included in this book's atlas. I especially want to thank the members of the tribe's Culture Committee, tribal staff members, and archaeologist Lynn Larson, who suggested that I talk to the Muckleshoot in the first place. Without the accounts of Ollie Wilbur, Art Williams, and other Muckleshoot community members, this would have been a very different, and much less interesting, book.

The Duwamish Tribe of Seattle, on the other hand, chose to participate only indirectly in this project. I am grateful for the suggestions they did make and have done my best to incorporate them and to include Duwamish voices past and present, garnered from archival and press sources, wherever possible. Based on what I know of the tribe's archives and oral tradition through conversations with other researchers, I am not convinced that the overall shape of this book would have been radically different had the Duwamish participated more directly. It might have included some additional specific information on the mixed-race families of "Seattle Illahee," a few more details about the 1916–25 "break" in Duwamish leadership, and a clearer picture of what Duwamish community members were doing between that alleged break and their new visibility beginning in the 1970s. But my portrayal of the roles that their ancestors played in early Seattle history and the part present-day tribal members have played in reshaping the city's narrative would likely change little. My hope is that this book will spark even greater public interest in the Duwamish and their stories, and I wish them the best in their continued search for federal recognition and in their efforts to build a longhouse on the river that bears their name.

Because this book is not only about the indigenous peoples of Seattle and their descendants, it was important to gain insights from within the multiethnic, pan-tribal, urban Indian community in the city. I especially want to thank Teresa BrownWolf Powers, and indirectly the American Indian Women's Service League, for granting me access to hours of unedited interviews Teresa taped with Service League members. As with the tribal oral histories, these interviews filled what would have otherwise been silence. Sandy Osawa, Roger Fernandes, and Jeanette Bushnell also helped me think about present-day urban Native issues, and my interview with former "Skid Road queen" Bill Regan provided a window into a community that left virtually no records behind. If nothing else, these people proved just how diverse and complex Seattle's urban Indian community is.

There is also a person whose life and history sit at the crossroads of almost all of Seattle's various Indian histories and who deserves special praise for her generosity and insightfulness. Although a member of the Muckleshoot Tribe, where she also works as a grant administrator, Jackie Swanson is also the great-granddaughter of Chesheeahud, a Duwamish man who figures prominently in Seattle's early history. She was also deeply involved in the American Indian Women's Service League in the 1970s and, through that experience, knew intimately the now-largely-disappeared world of Indian Skid Road. Whether sharing her own writings about the history and significance of the Service League, inviting me to examine old photos of powwows and other events, or showing me the baskets made by Chesheeahud's daughter Julia Siddle (her grandmother), Jackie helped me see just how closely interwoven these histories are and offered insights in a truly compassionate, helpful way.

Several remarkable scholars have been generous guides along the way to this book. John Findlay took great interest in my personal and professional development, reeled me in during some of my more excessive flights of fancy, and helped me understand what the word "edit" really means. Richard White quietly encouraged me to say what I mean and do it clearly, and his willingness to continue advising this project after his departure from the University of Washington to Stanford University speaks volumes about his commitment to students. Gail Dubrow reminded me to connect the work to the concerns of real people and supported my interests in public history. If Sasha Harmon was an invaluable resource for her expertise in local Indian affairs, then she has also proved an excellent trimmer of awkward prose. Suzanne Lebsock and Jim Gregory, both members of my PhD committee, provided important insights as well despite the fact that urban Indian histories are far removed from their own areas of interest.

The support of my fellow graduate students improved this work nearly as much as the advice I received from my faculty. I began graduate school with a cohort of Americanists whose names will no doubt become well known within the discipline in years to come: Jen Seltz, Roberta Gold, Andrea Geiger, Michael Witgen, Connie Chiang, Jeff Brune, and Liz Escobedo. The hours that I—the "local guy"—spent with them in readings courses and research seminars kept me from being provincial. Ray Rast joined us later and was a kindred spirit thanks to his interests in place, landscape, and memory. I also received encouragement and criticism—as well as lessons on writing for audiences who do not spend their days thinking about Native issues—from Susan Smith, Ali Igmen, Michael Reese, David Biggs, and Joe Roza, among others. Ned Blackhawk, Pam Creasy, and Pauline Escudero Shafer kept me honest as a white guy doing Indian history. When my own writing bogged down, I often turned to Kate Brown's beautiful study of the Ukrainian borderlands for inspiration. Matt Klingle, however, deserves more credit than any other graduate colleague. While writing his "companion volume"— an environmental history of Seattle—Matt was both big brother and research assistant, offering personal and professional guidance while also keeping an eye out for Native people in the archives. I look forward to seeing his book next to this one on the shelf.

Lisa Scharnhorst, Sandra Kroupa, Carla Rickerson, Gary Lundell, and the other staff of the University of Washington Special Collections deserve praise for their tolerance, interest in my research, and deep knowledge of the trove they guard. Beyond the University of Washington, many other people made this book possible. John Lutz, of the University of Victoria, helped me flesh out the British Columbia side of things, while Paige Raibmon, now a colleague at the University of British Columbia, offered important insights arising from the intersections between our two projects. Carolyn Marr and Howard Giske guided me through the Museum of History and Industry's collections, while Greg Lange and the staff of the Puget Sound Branch of the Washington State Archives in Bellevue suggested sources I never would have thought to examine. Miriam Waite and the Daughters of the Pioneers honored me both with a small scholarship and with an afternoon among the descendants of people who appear herein. Local historian David Buerge deserves credit for writing a series of *Seattle Weekly* articles that inspired my interest in Seattle's indigenous history in the first place. Peripatetic anthropologist Jay Miller helped with insights into local oral tradition and language. And with one eye on the local details and the other on the broader scholarship, Lorraine McConaghy was a compatriot in civic iconoclasm and a counselor in times of academic insecurity. Her passion and rigor helped to make this a better book and me a better scholar. Local historical and ecological activists such as David Williams, Valerie Rose, Tom Dailey, Monica Wooton, Paul Talbert, Georgina Kerr, and others proved to me that there was an audience for this history. To some degree, this book was written for people like them. I hope it inspires them to continue their efforts to engage the places where they live and the histories to which they are party.

As editor of the Weyerhaeuser Environmental Series, of which this book is the first Indian-centered volume, Bill Cronon encouraged me to rethink whether this book belonged in the series and provided nothing but enthusiasm along the way. Julidta Tarver, meanwhile, kept me on track for publication, showed great warmth during some trying times, and paid me a great deal of attention despite the fact that she is semiretired from the University of Washington Press. Two anonymous reviewers also provided critically important feedback on the manuscript, seeing things I no longer could after all the years of living with this project. Pam Bruton deserves credit for the thankless task of copyediting, and Marilyn Trueblood oversaw the production of the book at the Press.

Two collaborators deserve their own paragraph. Nile Thompson, a gifted linguist with an eye for detail (to say the least), has made an irreplaceable contribution through his work on the "Atlas of Indigenous Seattle" at the end of this book. I dread to think what might have ended up in print without his expertise in Salish linguistic structure and worldview, his working knowledge of Whulshootseed, and his attention to fine nuances of logic and evidence. Now I truly understand why linguistics is its own discipline, and why historians should keep to their own turf. Amir Sheikh, who designed the maps for the atlas, was both a stalwart friend and an intellectual co-conspirator. As he pursues graduate studies of his own, I only hope I can contribute as much to Amir's future scholarship as he has already contributed to mine.

Finally, this book is dedicated to three people who have shaped my life in profound ways. First, Robert H. Keller Jr., the resident historian at Western Washington University's Fairhaven College, saved me from law school and showed me that all the things I cared about in fact counted as history. It is difficult to imagine having been anything other than a historian, and I have Bob to thank for that. Second, my husband, Simon Martin, has been my therapist, keel, and accountant through the neuroses and vagaries of graduate school and the academic life. Over the past dozen years, he has sacrificed a great deal in my pursuit of a career, but I think he would agree that it's been worth it. Lastly, this book is dedicated to my mother, Paula Thrush, who died of cancer in February 2005 and thus never had the chance to see this published or even to know that I'd been offered a position at the University of British Columbia. She made me who I am through her utter inability to sit still and do nothing, through her passion for place and the environment, and through her unswerving (if not always uncritical) support of her only child. I wish I could talk to her again.

NATIVE SEATTLE

1 / The Haunted City

EVERY AMERICAN CITY is built on Indian land, but few advertise it like Seattle. Go walking in the city, and you will see Native American images everywhere in the urban landscape. Wolf and Wild Man stalk the public spaces of downtown in the form of totem poles. Tlingit Orca totems adorn manhole covers, and a bronze Indian chieftain raises a welcoming hand as the monorail hums past. Street musicians, protestors, and holiday shoppers move across a plaza paved with bricks laid in the pattern of a cedar-bark basket. Souvenir shops hawk dreamcatchers and sweatshirts with totemic Frogs, while only doors down, a high-end gallery sells argillite totem poles, soapstone walruses, and Earthquake spirit masks carved by modern masters. Massive car ferries with names like *Klickitat* and *Elwha* slide across Puget Sound, passing an island where, since the 1962 world's fair, Kwakwaka'wakw performers have welcomed visitors and world leaders to a North Coast–style longhouse. Out in the neighborhoods, schoolchildren have adorned bus shelters with Haida designs of the Salmon spirit, and Coast Salish spindle whorls have been soldered into a sewage treatment station's security gates. And then there are the names on the land itself: one park named for a red paint used in traditional ceremonies and another for an ancient prairie; a marina called Shilshole and an industrial waterway known as Duwamish; the lakefront enclave of Leschi, named for an executed indigenous leader. Seattle, it seems, is a city in love with its Native American heritage.[1]

Indeed, it is the totem poles, motifs of the Salmon spirit, and ferries with Indian names that tell you where you are: without them, Seattle would somehow be less *Seattle*. Every carved image, every statue of an Indian, every indigenous name on the land implies that you are here in this place and not in another. They are part of how you know you are not in New York or New Orleans, London or Los Angeles. They are what we expect from Seattle. They are stories about place.

Iconic western writer William Kittredge has described how stories and places are connected:

Places come to exist in our imaginations because of stories, and so do we. When we reach for a "sense of place," we posit an intimate relationship to a set of stories connected to a particular location, such as Hong Kong or the Grand Canyon or the bed where we were born, thinking of histories and the evolution of personalities in a local context. Having "a sense of self" means possessing a set of stories about who we are and with whom and why.

In Seattle, visitors and residents alike tell and are told stories about this city: that it is built on Indian land, that that land was taken to build a great metropolis, and that such a taking is commemorated by the city's Native American imagery. These stories in and of place, these place-stories, define Seattle as a city with an indigenous pedigree.[2]

But Seattle is also a haunted city. In a metropolis built in indigenous territory, and where cellular phone towers only recently outnumbered totem poles, it comes as no surprise that Seattle has Indian ghosts. There is the tale of Joshua Winfield, a settler who built his home on an Indian cemetery near Lake Washington, only to be frightened into eternity by indigenous revenants one night in 1874. The spectral pleas of another Indian ghost, allegedly that of a murdered Native prostitute, have been heard since the Prohibition era in a rambling Victorian home near the Duwamish. At a nearby golf course, a naked Indian described as a shaman has been seen since the 1960s, dancing at night on what is rumored to be another indigenous burial ground. And at Pike Place Market, the apparition of an Indian woman in a shawl and floor-length skirt has appeared for generations in the windows of the magic shop and in the aisles of the bead store. Meanwhile, members of the local tribes pray for the dead on the banks of the industrial river named for their people, and Native storytellers lead purification ceremonies in the underground streets and storefronts beneath Pioneer Square, in hopes of bringing peace to wandering indigenous specters.[3]

By far, though, the most famous haunting of Seattle is accomplished by the city's namesake, a man called Seeathl. A local indigenous leader of Duwamish and Suquamish heritage who facilitated the city's founding, Seeathl is best known for words he is said to have spoken during treaty discussions in the 1850s, when Seattle's urban promise seemed to require the dispossession of local Native peoples:

Your religion was written on tablets of stone by the iron finger of an angry God lest you forget. The red man could never comprehend nor remember it. Our religion is the tradition of our ancestors, the dreams of our old men, given to them in the solemn hours of the night by the Great Spirit, and the visions of our leaders, and it is written in the hearts of our people.

Your dead cease to love you and the land of their nativity as soon as they pass the portals of their tomb; they wander far away beyond the stars and are soon forgotten and never return. Our dead never forget this beautiful world that gave them being. They always love its winding rivers, its sacred mountains, and its sequestered vales, and they ever yearn in the tenderest affection over the lonely-hearted living and often return to visit, guide, and comfort them.

We will ponder your proposition, and when we decide, we will tell you. But should we accept it, I here and now make this the first condition, that we will not be denied the privilege, without molestation, of visiting at will the graves where we have buried our ancestors, and our friends, and our children.

Every part of this country is sacred to my people. Every hillside, every valley, every plain and grove has been hallowed by some fond memory or some sad experience of my tribe. Even the rocks, which seem to lie dumb as they swelter in the sun along the silent seashore in solemn grandeur, thrill with memories of past events connected with the lives of my people.

And when the last red man shall have perished from the earth and his memory among the white men shall have become a myth, these shores will swarm with the invisible dead of my tribe; and when your children's children shall think themselves alone in the fields, the store, the shop, upon the highway, or in the silence of the pathless woods, they will not be alone. In all the earth there is no place dedicated to solitude.

At night when the streets of your cities and villages will be silent and you think them deserted, they will throng with returning hosts that once filled and still love this beautiful land. The white man will never be alone. Let him be just and deal kindly with my people, for the dead are not powerless. Dead—did I say? There is no death, only a change of worlds.

According to *Seattle Times* writer Eric Scigliano, the Chief Seattle Speech, as it has come to be known, is a "ghost story like no other." It represents not just the words of one man but also "the innumerable souls who fished and sang and made art along these shores and had no inkling of cities." Seeathl gave voice to those "wraiths," and the city's modern residents, Scigliano warns, should "tread lightly and treat the land softly. You never know who might be watching—from above, or even nearer."[4]

But like any good haunting, the authenticity of the speech cannot be proven. It first appeared in print more than three decades after Seeathl put his mark on the Treaty of Point Elliott, and it bears a suspicious resemblance to Victorian prose lamenting the passing of the "red man." There is no question that Seeathl spoke eloquently at the treaty proceedings—he carried Thunder, which gave skills of oratory, as one of his many spirit powers—but his exact words are lost. What we do know, however, is that the speech has become a key text of both indigenous rights and environmentalist thinking, with some of its adherents going so far as to call it a "fifth Gospel." Simultaneously urtext and Rorschach test, the words of Seeathl haunt Seattle, telling stories of Native nobility, American colonialism, and longing for a lost environmental paradise. Somewhere between fiction and fact, these place-stories haunt any history of Seattle. But they often have little to do with the more complicated story of the real Seeathl, who died in 1866 on a reservation across Puget Sound from Seattle and was buried in a grave bearing his new Catholic name: Noah. Instead, these ghost stories of Seeathl have far more to do with the people telling them.[5]

This is the power of ghost stories, of phantoms at the Market, and the sage wisdom of dead chiefs: they tell us more about ourselves, and about our time, than they tell us about other people or the past. In writing of the role of ghosts in medieval European society, historian Jean-

Claude Schmitt has claimed that "the dead have no existence other than that which the living imagine for them," and recent scholarship on American ghosts has shown that hauntings are among the most telling of cultural phenomena, expressing powerful anxieties, desires, and regrets. As Judith Richardson has illustrated in her work on ghosts in New York's Hudson Valley, hauntings are in fact social memories inspired by rapid cultural and environmental change, arising not so much from moldering graves as from the struggle to create a meaningful history. Ghosts are also rooted in places, perhaps none more so than the ghosts of Indians. In her analysis of hauntings in American literature, Renée Bergland has argued that stories of Indian ghosts are also place-stories about what happened in particular places and what those happenings meant. "Europeans take possession of Native American lands, to be sure," Bergland writes, "but at the same time, Native Americans take supernatural possession of their dispossessors." Thence springs the resonance of the Chief Seattle Speech, which is not easily separated from the winding rivers and sequestered vales it mourns. It is a story about a place as much as it is a story about a people, and it is a story about us in the present as much as it is about historical actors.[6]

There is also an intimacy to Seattle's ghost stories. Among the indigenous people of Puget Sound, the phantasms most feared were those of the recent dead and of kin; these sorts of ghosts vexed the living and put them in great danger, particularly in the rainy winter months. The ghosts of strangers were far less dangerous. The greater its entanglement with the living, it was thought, the greater a phantom's power. And so it is in Seattle's ghostly history: the closer we have lived to each other, the more we have been haunted.

At the same time, the problem inherent in Seattle's Indian ghost stories—indeed the central problem of Seattle's Native American history—is that none of these imagined Indians was ever real. While there may be some kernel of historical truth to some of them, for the most part they are historical creations, both because they spring out of the city's past and because they are ways to make sense of that past. The danger in this, however, is that they all too often tell us exactly what we expected to hear. The restless Indian dead confirm the city's storyline, which is this: Native history and urban history—and, indeed, Indians and cities—cannot coexist, and one must necessarily be eclipsed by the other. The standard story told about Seeathl and the city named for him is perhaps the best example of this narrative; take, for example, *New York Times* correspondent Tim Egan's version. In his bestselling meditation on Pacific Northwest history and landscape, *The Good Rain*, Egan writes of kayaking on Elliott Bay and pondering the connections between Seeathl and Seattle. Looking back and forth between the modern urban skyline and the site of the indigenous leader's grave across Puget Sound, Egan summarizes the story of the man and the city: "He lived to be a very old man, going from aboriginal king of Elliott Bay and the river that drained into it, to a withered curiosity on the muddy streets of what would become the largest city in the country named after a Native American." To understand Seeathl and Seattle, it seems that this is all you need to know, and it tells us what we knew all along: that the Native past must give way to the urban future. The place-story of Chief Seattle is about the change from one world to another, with Native history surviving only as a prophetic shadow, a disturbing memory, an instructive haunting.[7]

This is not to say that Indian people do not exist in the urban present. Of course they do—in the thousands. Some of them, in fact, have also become part of the city's narrative. Along with totem poles and Seeathl, the homeless street Indian completes the city's trinity of Native imagery. This third kind of Indian place-story, however, is less often an indictment of the injustices of the urban political economy than it is a tale about racial inevitability. In short, stories about Native people on Seattle's streets are also a kind of ghost story. In Jack Cady's murder mystery *Street*, for example, the shape-shifting narrator takes on the form of "an aging Tlingit seduced south from Alaska" who dreams of killer whales and talking salmon, while in *Still Life with Woodpecker*, Tom Robbins's heroine Princess Leigh-Cheri wanders through downtown, noticing that "Indian winos, in particular, were unhurried by the weather." Both Robbins and Cady conflate street Indians with the very atmosphere of the city: Robbins cloaks his version of Seattle in a "shamanic rain" that whispers "like the ecstasy of primitives," while Cady's city hun-

8

kers down under weather systems "more gray and ancient than a soli-
tary old Indian." Meanwhile, in *Hunting Mr. Heartbreak*, Jonathan Raban
recalls seeing homeless Native people sprawled in a bricked-over doorway in Belltown on his first visit to Seattle. They were "like sacks of
garbage waiting for collection by the early-morning truck. I tiptoed past
them," he notes, "as one walks needlessly quietly in the presence of the
dead."[8]

And so here is the moral of the urban Indian story as we think we
know it: that Native people in the city are barely people; they are instead
shades of the past, linked almost mystically to a lost nature. Cady spells
it out directly: one of his characters, a homeless Haida-Filipino man
named Jimmy, is described as "turning into a ghost right before our
eyes. That's not a white man's metaphor," Cady's narrator tells us. "It's
an Indian fact." It is as though the returning hosts, those phantoms
prophesied in the Chief Seattle Speech, have turned out to be nothing
more than homeless Indians. Even Seattle resident Sherman Alexie,
the Spokane–Coeur d'Alene Indian author rightly lauded for the complicated humanity of his Native characters, slides effortlessly into this
urban parable. In his novel *Indian Killer*, in which "every city was a city
of white men," racist cops and a serial killer share Seattle with a troupe
of Indians living under the Alaskan Way Viaduct, all dampening in that
same rain, here an "occupying force." But his hero, John Smith, who
may or may not be the murderer scalping white men throughout the
city, has nothing to fear from the rain: "He was aboriginal," Alexie writes.
"He stepped through this rain and fog without incident." Even in *Indian
Killer*, otherwise a powerful meditation on what it means to be both modern and Indian, cities are somehow places where Native people cannot
belong except as half-fulfilled people or as ciphers for nature. Being a
metaphor in Seattle, it would seem, is an Indian fact.[9]

And if cities indelibly mark their Indian inhabitants in urban ghost
stories, then these homeless Indians also mark the city in return, and
not just in fictional accounts. Although more than ten thousand people
of indigenous ancestry—including lawyers and activists, bus drivers
and artists, bankers and newspaper editors—now call Seattle home, it
is the homeless Indians who are most visible in Seattle's urban land-

scape and who in fact seem to make Seattle *Seattle*. They make Pike Place Market's public restrooms one of the city's "true" landmarks according to one local alternative weekly, because the toilets are "the one place where bustling tourists, drunken Indians, and desperate junkies come together . . . in a sort of cultural nexus, representing all that is truly great about this fine city." For some like local essayist Emily Baillargeon, Native people on the streets signify urban inequality. "As new corporate legions rush home or to their after-hours playgrounds," she wrote during the high-tech boom of the 1990s, "they brush past alcoholic Native Americans camped out on rain-slicked corners." Even among the homeless themselves, Native people are part of Seattle's geography: one white street kid in the University District, for example, noted that "downtown it's all drunk Indians." So while we can infer from some ghost stories that Native people are somehow incapable of being fully human in Seattle—that the urban and the Indian are somehow antonyms—we also learn more about this place through stories about Indians: what kind of city Seattle is, and who belongs where.[10]

None of this is to say that homelessness and other, more subtle forms of dislocation are not central to the urban Indian experience. On the contrary, loss of cultural identity, debilitating poverty, and institutionalized racism have each shaped the lives of many Native people throughout Seattle's history. The history that follows makes this clear. The problem with stories about metaphorical urban Indians, however, is that they allow us to imagine only certain kinds of Native history in the city: the parts we are prepared to see by the stories we tell. These stories mask more complicated experiences: the surprising opportunities offered by urban life, the creative struggles to carve out Indian spaces in the city, and, most importantly, the ways in which Native women and men have contributed to urban life. Stories of ghosts and totem poles and dispossessed chieftains cast Indians only as passive victims of, rather than active participants in, the urban story. These place-stories are the easy way out, allowing us to avoid doing our homework. In other words, they make appealing fiction but bad history.

If the prophetic chieftains and totem poles, like the shamanic rains and homeless ghosts, are all supposed to make Seattle somehow unique (and each of these stories is tied closely to urban boosterism and marketing, as we shall see), then it is surprising how closely Seattle's stories track with national narratives. Our city's place-stories and those of our nation mirror each other—Indians and cities exist at opposite ends of the American imaginary; one represents the past, while the other represents the future. For all their differences, last Mohicans, final showdowns at Wounded Knees, and lone Ishis wandering out of the California foothills are variations on the same theme: the inevitable disappearance of indigenous peoples before the onslaught of American progress. Cities, on the other hand, are the ultimate avatars of that progress, representing the pinnacle of American technology, commerce, and cultural sophistication. It comes as no surprise, then, that many nineteenth-century representations of American expansion show Indians watching forlornly as townscapes appear on the horizon. John Gast's famous *American Progress* (1872), for example, shows Progress embodied as an enormous (and, dare we say it, ghostly) white woman floating westward over the continent, trailing telegraph wire. Behind her, a locomotive steams across the plains and a great city of bridges and smokestacks sprawls in the sunrise, while ahead of her Indians and buffalo flee into the shrinking darkness. Seattle's counterpart is a 1906 brochure selling real estate on the tideflats south of downtown; it features figures that look suspiciously like Hiawatha and Pocahontas gazing over placid waters toward a belching urban skyline. These are place-stories, telling us how the nation became what it is and who belongs where—and when.[11]

If popular culture has placed cities and Indians at two ends of the nation's historical trajectory, then academic scholarship has given that place-story its legitimacy. The connections between urban and Indian histories—both in Seattle and across the nation—have yet to be made, even in studies of the American West, a region defined both by its urban nature and by the persistence of Native peoples. From the Allegheny Mountains to the Pacific Coast, towns and cities were the vanguards of American conquest, appearing (and sometimes disappearing again) with stunning rapidity. The survival of western cities hinged on their ability to control hinterlands of people, places, and things—loggers, goldfields, water—and so the consolidation and conquest of the American West were urban phenomena. In urban histories, however, Indians all too often appear only in the introduction or first chapter, then exit stage left after a treaty or a battle. Its regional mythology, and much of its scholarship, still defined by the battle between civilization and savagery, the American West seems to have room for either cities or Indians but not both.[12]

Meanwhile, the vast literature on Native peoples in the American West has uncovered the economic, political, cultural, and social components of Indian dispossession, as well as the diverse ways in which Native people responded, ranging from accommodation to resistance. Much of this western Indian history has focused on reservations, and for a good reason: these are the places where colonial policies created long paper trails, and these are the places where indigenous and tribal ways of life have remained most visible. In cities, Indians are harder to find, and as a result, among the thousands of books, monographs, and articles on Indian history in the West, only a scant few focus on urban places.[13]

When scholars do study Indians in cities, their research falls into two camps. First, there are studies of the problems facing Native people in urban places, often focusing on the notion of "disaffiliation." While offering insights into the experiences of Native people in cities, such studies (including many conducted in Seattle) often pathologize their subjects and take for granted the alleged inability of many Native people to cope with urban (and, by association, modern) life. The second kind of scholarship about urban Indians, based in the New Social History inspired by the civil-rights movements of the 1960s and 1970s, focuses on the development of urban Indian organizations in cities throughout the country. More than simply institutional histories, these works also examine the role such organizations have played in the creation of new Indian, and especially pan-Indian, identities. Increasingly, they are written by Native people themselves. But virtually none of these works of recent urban Indian history include the deeper, indigenous histories of the places where those organizations took form. If urban and Native histories rarely speak to each other, then the histories of indigenous peoples on whose lands cities were built and the histories of present-day urban Indian communities are also estranged.[14]

In *Native Seattle*, I bring together multiple kinds of Native history in order to challenge the assumption that Indian and urban histories are somehow mutually exclusive. I include histories of the indigenous people of Seattle—of the Duwamish and Shilshole and Lake peoples who helped birth the city and yet who bore its greatest burdens. I also include histories of the many Indian migrants, from dozens of tribes and communities, who have been coming to this place for much longer than most of us realize. Lastly, I include the Chief Seattle Speech and other Indian imagery that has often been closely linked to debates about who belongs in the city and what it has meant to live in a place that has been transformed so quickly and so utterly.

Throughout Seattle's past, the strands of urban and Indian history have been entwined, and there is very little distance, in either space or time, between the dispossession of local indigenous people, the rise of an urban pan-Indian community, and the development of urban narratives populated with Indian metaphors. At almost every turn, what it meant to be urban and what it meant to be Native have been inextricably linked in Seattle.

The histories in these pages are drawn not just from the mythic narratives of Seattle's received history but from archival materials and oral traditions. They are linked to particular places in the city, and to the dramatic changes that have, quite literally, *taken place* on Seattle's shores and hills and streets. While not as explicitly an environmental history as other studies, *Native Seattle* nonetheless combats the urban-Indian-as-metaphor stereotype by not only describing the lived experiences of Native people in the city and its hinterland but by grounding the city within particular Native places ranging from a fishing camp buried beneath fill in the heart of the city to a British Columbia village linked to Seattle by trade and migration. By examining the environmental transformations of these places and the movement of people, things, and symbols between and among them, this book links Seattle's urban Native pasts to the broader scholarship regarding the resettlement of indigenous territories, the ecology of cities and their hinterlands, and narratives regarding nature, culture, and history.

One place where these kinds of histories come together is Pioneer

Place Park at the corner of First Avenue and Yesler Way, where a long-vanished sawmill once powered Seattle's commercial beginnings. Here, a Tlingit totem pole, a bronze bust of Seeathl, and an art installation calling attention to the struggles of homeless Indians represent the three facets of Seattle's Native iconography: the exotic aesthetics of the northern Northwest Coast, the noble urban namesake, and the pathetic Indian of the streets. Pioneer Place Park, like the historic Pioneer Square neighborhood that surrounds it, is an archive of urban narratives. But in Whulshootseed, the indigenous language of Puget Sound country, neither carries the name "Pioneer," a word that reflects only one version of history. In Whulshootseed, it is "Little Crossing-Over Place." Long before Henry Yesler set up his sawmill, this was a tidal lagoon tucked behind a small island. It was home to great cedar longhouses, whose residents fished for flounders in the lagoon, gathered berries and bulbs in nearby prairies, drank clear water from springs in the hillside, and buried their dead on a bluff overlooking Elliott Bay. Before it was a place of narratives *about* Indians, then, this was a place inhabited *by* Indians. And long after Yesler's sawmill had burned, Pioneer Place became, for a while at least, the heart of an urban Indian community whose members eked out a living in the district of flophouses and taverns that birthed the term "skid road." Different places with the same set of coordinates, Little Crossing-Over Place, Skid Road, and Pioneer Place Park are three layers in an urban palimpsest, a gathering of place-stories. In between them lie ashes and sawdust, brick and asphalt, opportunity and misery—in other words, the detritus of Seattle's Native multiple pasts.

There is Little Crossing-Over Place, where an indigenous community gave way to sawmills and single-resident occupancy hotels, but there is also the larger crossing-over place of Seattle as a whole. Go virtually anywhere in Seattle, and you are close to it. Among the bungalows and beachside biking trails are the home of a sacred horned serpent, the site of a burning longhouse, and an upland clearing full of marsh tea and cranberries. Between and behind the art galleries and gas stations are the first Indian Center, the riverside studio of a Native artist hired to carve totem poles, and the apartment of a woman down from Juneau to get an education. The entire city is a palimpsest, a text erased only partially and then written over again. It is a landscape of places changed by power, of Indian places transformed into urban ones and sometimes back again. Or, to borrow the words of historian James Ronda, the story of Seattle is "a story about power and places, and what happens when power changes places, and then how places are in turn changed." Seattle's past is rich with these kinds of crossings.[15]

Native Seattle is also intended as a crossing of different kinds of history. Beyond bringing together urban and Indian histories, it also brings cultural, social, and environmental histories into conversation with each other. Literary criticism and postcolonial studies have emphasized the power of narrative to define, debase, and control the Other, and Seattle is no exception. The place-stories told in this city were a key method of dispossession and discrimination, and in trying to understand them, *Native Seattle* is a cultural history. But as Cole Harris, the elder statesman of Canadian geography, has shown, it is not enough to merely tell stories about stories: we must look beyond the literary and cultural forms of colonialism to examine the material conditions that ultimately implemented those stories. We need to examine the roles that physical power, the state, flows of capital, and technologies like law and mapping played in turning indigenous territory into a modern metropolis. I accomplish this here through the lenses of social history—the unearthing of the lived experiences of ordinary people—and environmental history. Nature may not have agency in this story as clearly as it does in most works of environmental history, but the irruptions of unfinished history, so common in Seattle's urban story, are grounded in place. As the land is transformed, it gives up new stories and reveals new layers of the past, and in those new stories can be found the agency of ancient, inhabited natures. Finally, it should not be forgotten that all environmental history in the Americas, by definition, is Native history, because it has all happened on Indian land.[16]

With these multiple Native histories in mind, then, Seattle's story can offer insights into other places. For all its uniqueness (again, few large American cities have so consistently used Indian imagery to define their own image), Seattle's history suggests that other cities may have urban Indian stories of their own. In Chicago, with its origins in the

Fort Dearborn "massacre," or in New York City and its "$24 Question," as Edwin G. Burrows and Mike Wallace have called the Dutch purchase of indigenous Manhattan, the opportunities exist for a new kind of urban history that begins with those cities' place-stories. Meanwhile, bringing the benevolent friars and pious neophytes who haunt the place-stories of Californian cities into conversation with Native social history might reorient the meaning of places like San Francisco and Los Angeles. Every American city—Boston, Omaha, Honolulu, Savannah—has the potential for this kind of history, as do places like Vancouver or Veracruz, Sapporo or Sydney, or any other place shaped by encounters between the urban and the indigenous.[17]

In the end, though, all history is local, and so I limit my view to one city, and in doing so reorient Seattle's urban story by placing its Native histories at the center. I challenge narratives of civic progress by focusing on the costs, both planned and unforeseen, of urban development. This is not always a happy story. In his classic, remarkable study of the Marquesas, Greg Dening describes the metaphorical islands and beaches—the categories of "we" and "they" and the boundaries between them—that shaped the history of real islands and beaches in the Pacific. He notes that, for the people who experienced them, and to some extent for the people who study them, "the remaking of those sorts of islands and the crossing of those sorts of beaches can be cruelly painful." This is certainly true of Seattle's history or, in the words of poet Colleen McElroy, "Seattle's awful history, where all that is breathtaking is breath taking." This is not always a happy story, but perhaps more importantly, it is rarely a simple one either.[18]

Seattle is haunted by urban conquest and by its many Native pasts. But put the ghost stories aside, and see what happened here before the ghosts came. Begin at the supposed beginning, at the moment when the first breath was taken: in Seattle's version of the encounter between Pawtuxet and Plymouth, between indigenous and European worlds. On a beach, to be precise.

2 / Terra Miscognita

N THE WORDS OF ONE DESCENDANT of the Denny Party, as Seattle's founders are typically called, the story of the city's origin "is an oft-told tale yet is ever new." Indeed. In the century and a half since the landing of Arthur Denny and his compatriots on the beach at Alki Point on 13 November 1851, Seattle's creation story has been reduced, reused, recycled, and reenacted in books, plays, speeches, and art. Often, the telling of the story says more about the moment of the telling than about the event itself; we will encounter many such recountings throughout Seattle's Native histories. The basic story, however, has remained the same. Seattle historian Murray Morgan captured the scene best in his 1951 "history from the bottom up," *Skid Road*. In this perennially popular tale of the politics and personalities of Seattle's first century, Morgan described the arrival of the twenty-four settlers on a rainy beach:

Three of the four women cried when the brig's boat put them ashore on the salt-smelling beach. Portland had been rude and the ship awful, but this was worse: the only habitation was a log cabin, still roofless, and the only neighbors a host of bowlegged Indians, the men wearing only buckskin breechclouts, the women skirts of cedar bark, the children naked. The sky was low and gray, the air sharp with salt and iodine, the wind cold; but soon the women were too busy to weep.

Morgan's version of the story has it all: the miserable passage on the schooner *Exact*, the dismal weather, the crying women, the unfinished cabin. And most importantly, the story has Indians. Possibly dangerous, certainly alien, their presence makes the story all the more dramatic. It is in this moment—in the tense introduction between two peoples—that Seattle's urban history begins. And to no small extent, it is the moment when, according to the standard version of Seattle's storyline, local Indian history begins to end.[1]

Seattle's creation story is not even really a story at all, but rather a snapshot. Certainly, the Denny Party's overland journey from Illinois is part of the back-story, but it is really the singularity of the landing at Alki Point, across Elliott Bay from present-day downtown, that is the mythic point of beginning, in which longer processes are collapsed into a frozen moment in time. In this respect, Seattle's creation story is like many others. In a 1991 essay about evolution and baseball, for example, natural historian Stephen Jay Gould argued that stories about beginnings "come in only two basic modes. An entity either has an explicit point of origin, a specific time and place of creation, or else it evolves and has no definable moment of entry into the world." In his account of the differences between the sport's gradual evolution from a "plethora of previous stick-and-ball games" and the more mythic story of Cooperstown, Gould noted that "we seem to prefer the . . . model of origin by a moment of creation—for then we can have heroes and sacred places." The same is true for American history more broadly: we love our Mayflowers, Lexingtons, and Fort Sumters. They are discrete moments chosen out of the complexity of the past and designated as the place where one thing is said to end and another to begin.[2]

In Seattle, where the heroes are the Denny Party and the sacred place is Alki Point, that snapshot in place and time has literally been turned into a shrine of sorts. At the Museum of History and Industry, the city's official repository of its past, a diorama displays the events of that blustery November day. Comprising wax figures, handmade miniature clothing, shellacked greenery, and a painted beachscape backdrop, the diorama was created in 1953 by local doll maker Lillian Smart to commemorate Seattle's recent centenary and to celebrate the museum's opening. It includes all the stock characters and props of the city's founding myth: a roofless cabin at the forest's edge, tiny handkerchiefs lifted to wax faces, and children's heads turned warily toward Chief Seattle and a few other Indian men. The tableau made manifest the story that Seattle residents had already been telling themselves for decades, and within a few months of the diorama's unveiling, its sponsors—the Alki Women's Improvement Club and the West Seattle Business Association—claimed that "thousands of Seattle residents, tourists, and school children have stood in front of it, admiring its beauty and realism, and paying silent homage to Seattle's founders." For more than two generations of Seattleites, visiting the diorama has been a kind of urban pilgrimage. Still on display at the beginning of the twenty-first century, Smart's powerful visual distillation of the city's creation story is the image that most likely comes to many local residents' minds when they think of Seattle's founding.[3]

Not unlike baseball's creation story or the origin myth of the nation itself, with its providential Pilgrims landing in that single sacred moment at the place they named Plymouth, Seattle's creation story is also one of predestination. For all the drama of crying women, threatening skies, and strange Indians, Seattle's future seems a done deal. Civic booster and local historian Welford Beaton, for example, reiterated the title of his book *The City That Made Itself* by claiming that "Seattle started deliberately." Nearby titles on any local library shelf express the same sense of nascent destiny, of future greatness born in those first moments at Alki. Outdoing Beaton, Mayor George Cotterill's *Climax of a World Quest* reads Seattle's twentieth-century future back onto the voyages of explorers like Vancouver, Cook, and even Magellan. In local mythology, the arrival of "Seattle's Pilgrims" is deliberate, planned, and preordained, sprung like Athena from the collective forehead of Arthur Denny and the other members of his party. As for the indigenous people encountered in the creation moment at Alki Point, their future was also foretold, written in disease and dispossession. The powerful story of the "vanishing red man," as we shall see, both informed the Denny Party's journey to Puget Sound in the first place and has informed the telling of their landing at Alki ever since. It is one of the foundational pillars of Seattle's standard civic narrative, in which one kind of history (Indian) begins to decline the moment another history (urban) starts its ascent.[4]

But beginnings and endings are rarely clear in history, and the events that we call history were rarely as deliberate or discrete as we imagine them to be from our vantage point in the present. Like most creation stories, whether of a sport or of a nation, Seattle's origin myth obscures more about actual historical events than it reveals. First, it renders invisible a complex local indigenous landscape of stories reaching back to the ice age, of villages made wealthy by river and prairie and tideflat, and of numinous forces beyond human understanding. Second, by compressing the landing of 1851 into a single moment, it ignores earlier processes of empire and ecology that set the stage for city making on Puget Sound. Third, it obscures the ambitions and imaginations of the Denny Party themselves, ascribing to them motivations and knowledge that are more ours than theirs. Finally, it sets urban founders and indigenous people—and, through them, urban and Indian history—in opposition, as seemingly alien to each other as the two groups that met on the beach that November in 1851.

But if we widen our view beyond that one day of that one year on that one beach, Seattle's creation story takes on a very different form, looking more like Gould's blurry account of baseball's actual evolution. Rather than a single moment of creation, in this version of the story urban founding on Puget Sound becomes a complex, contingent process in which indigenous worlds are misapprehended, empires vie for dominance, and future city fathers change their minds and make mistakes. And most importantly, in this other kind of creation story indigenous people and places are at the center of the telling and have everything to do with getting to the place called Seattle. Well before the city's mythic moment of birth, Seattle's urban and Indian histories were already being bound together in a landscape rich with contested meanings and possibilities.

BEFORE THE ARRIVAL OF THE *EXACT* and the Denny Party, perhaps in the 1830s, a young man named Wahalchoo was hunting sea ducks off a promontory of open grassy spaces among wind-stunted trees, known to him as Prairie Point. He was looking for more than scoters and scaups; Wahalchoo had been fasting and was also in search of spirit power. He found it there near

Prairie Point, if only briefly. While retrieving spent arrows, he spied a vast longhouse deep in the green waters, surrounded by herds of elk and with schools of salmon swimming over its cedar-plank roof. This, Wahalchoo knew, was the home of a power that brought wealth, generosity, and respect to those who carried it. With its help, Wahalchoo could become a great leader. He went home to find his father, who could help him obtain the power, but the older man was away, and when Wahalchoo returned to Prairie Point, the waters were clear but empty. The longhouse beneath the waves had disappeared, and Wahalchoo was left to seek power elsewhere.[5]

Indigenous people like Wahalchoo (who would, some twenty-five years later, make his mark on a treaty under the Christian name Jacob) moved through landscapes that were dense with meaning. The proof is in the names. Prairie Point, which would become Alki Point in 1851, was but one named place on a peninsula bordered on the west and north by deep salt water and on the east by a meandering river and its estuary. The headland that brooded to the east of Prairie Point was Low Point, while to the south along the outer shore, a creek called Capsized came pouring out of the forest near a place called Rids the Cold; south of there were headlands called Tight Bluff and Place of Scorched Bluff. Together, these place-names map the indigenous landscape: open places among the forest, cliffs tightly crowded with brush or blackened by mineral deposits. They are also the closest things we have to photographs of the pre-urban world; by the time landscape photographers arrived in Seattle, most of these places had been utterly transformed.

But photographs, like dioramas, are static, and the world around Prairie Point was not. Thrust out into the currents and storm paths of Puget Sound, the point's sand and stone were built up in one season, then swept away in another; before the seawalls and bulkheads of the modern era, the promontory constantly shifted, sometimes subtly and at other times abruptly. Similarly, the indigenous landscapes of what would come to be known as Puget Sound country were changing long before the arrival of the Denny Party in 1851. Some of these changes were slow, others catastrophic, as Prairie Point snagged overlapping nets of power, knowledge, and ecology over the course of centuries. When

Arthur Denny and the rest came to Alki Point, which they called New York, they intruded upon a world already in the midst of profound changes. New networks of trade, imperial reconnaissance, and, most important of all, epidemic disease each served as preludes to the founding of an American city.

The first written records of the lands and waters around the future Seattle come from 1792, when British explorer George Vancouver and his crew sailed into the inland sea aboard the *Discovery*. Like most European explorers, Vancouver spent little time trying to ascertain indigenous peoples' own knowledge of their world. His journals contain few Native words and say little of the region's indigenous geography; instead, they are filled with names like Whidbey and Rainier. They are examples of what geographer Daniel W. Clayton has called "imperial fashioning," in which indigenous places were reinscribed with European nomenclature and incorporated into the colonial geographies of European nation-states. Even the name for the sea itself—given in honor of Vancouver's subordinate Peter Puget, who had diligently surveyed so much of it—transformed the inland sea, whose indigenous name simply meant "salt water," into a British waterway with an Anglo-Norman pedigree. It transformed the undifferentiated space of *terra incognita* into place, or "space with a history," emptying it of its indigenous history— at least on official maps—and making it part of a North America littered with historical references to European people and places. This was also one of Seattle's first kinds of urban history, in its linking of indigenous places like "Puget Sound" to imperial centers such as London. But underneath this refashioned landscape lay another geography; for virtually every imperial Puget there was an indigenous counterpart, even if Vancouver and his men simply could not, or would not, see it. It was less *terra incognita* than it was *terra miscognita*.[6]

For the *terra* here already included an urban history of its own. When Wahalchoo returned home for help in obtaining wealth and power, he went, not to some hovel in the wilderness, but to a proud village called Place of Clear Water, with a great cedar longhouse that was one of the largest indigenous structures in North America. Not far away, just around Low Point from the place where Wahalchoo had gone diving for power, was another settlement: Herring's House, made up of several longhouses and a larger house used for winter ceremonies. Neither settlement was just a "village," a term that may connote primitiveness and transience. Instead, these were places where elite families coordinated social alliances, religious observances, and resource distribution. Although not large in terms of population—both Herring's House and Place of Clear Water likely had only several scores of residents each—they and other indigenous winter settlements functioned as towns in relationship to their territories. Natural resources, political power, and spiritual force circulated through these settlements in ways reminiscent of the networks enmeshing larger urban places in other parts of the world—Captain Vancouver's London included.[7]

Each of these winter towns, along with nearby seasonal camps, resource sites, and sacred places, was linked into a broader geographic community through webs of kinship, trade, and diplomacy. Throughout Puget Sound, these larger communities (many of which would become known as tribes through relations with the American federal government in the nineteenth century) were typically organized around watersheds, and there were three such groups in the territories that would someday become Seattle. Herring's House, for example, was part of a larger constellation of communities whose members called themselves the People of the Inside Place, after the location of their main settlements inland from the Sound. Their name for themselves would be anglicized as "Duwamish." A second group, known as the Hachooabsh, or Lake People, and usually described as a band of the Duwamish, lived in towns ringing a vast, deep lake behind the hills fronting Puget Sound. A third group, with connections to the first two as well as to the people of Place of Clear Water (who are now known as the Suquamish), was the Shilshoolabsh, the People of Tucked Away Inside, who took their name from their main settlement on the tidal inlet that the Americans would call Salmon Bay. These three indigenous communities—the Duwamish, the Lakes, and the Shilsholes—each had their own towns, with names like Place of the Fish Spear and Little Canoe Channel, and each town in turn had its own hinterland of prairies and cemeteries, fish camps and hunting grounds. These local geographies were themselves connected through trade and kinship to communities as far away as the arid interior plateau of the Columbia River and the coast of Vancouver Island, knitting the entire region together in a complicated indigenous weave of towns and territories.[8]

When *Discovery* came into Salt Water in June of 1792, that weave was already fraying. With few exceptions, Puget Sound country seemed "nearly destitute of human beings" to the Englishmen. Vancouver wrote that "animated nature seemed nearly exhausted; and her awful silence was only now and then interrupted by the croaking of a raven, the breathing of a seal, or the scream of an eagle." After several encounters with Native people, one reason for the silence became clear: smallpox. "This deplorable disease," Vancouver wrote, "is not only common, but it is greatly to be apprehended is very fatal among them, as its indelible marks were seen on many." Blind eyes, pockmarked skin, and other ravages familiar to any urban European were clear evidence that the scourge of *Variola* had visited the local people, and indeed, at least one major epidemic had already swept through the region. Likely extrapolating from his own experiences in the great cities of Europe, Vancouver imagined what had been lost as his expedition came upon the remains of Native communities where "since their abdication, or extermination, nothing but the smaller shrubs and plants had yet been able to rear their heads." Vancouver and other Europeans tended to see indigenous North Americans as "people without history," but the evidence of that history, in the form of fallen-in roofs and prairies unburned by their cultivators and reverting to forest, was everywhere.[9]

Dramatic changes like those caused by Comes Out All Over, as smallpox was known in the local language, were nothing new to the indigenous people of "Puget's Sound." Their ancestors had arrived some ten millennia earlier, just as vast glaciers were retreating from the region, and their creation stories describe a chaotic post–ice age world where rivers flowed in both directions, the earth shifted, and brutal cold harassed the people until Dookweebathl, the Changer, brought order to things. It would take millennia for the climate to stabilize and for salmon and cedar, the two most important benefactors of later indigenous life, to colonize the region, while volcanic eruptions, massive earthquakes, and catastrophic mudflows routinely punctuated Native history with episodes of devastation. For the hierarchical societies living on the shores of Salt Water, change produced anxiety: the word *dookw*, "to change" or "transform," is the root for a host of concepts including worry, dissatisfaction, anger, infirmity, and ferocity. At the same time, it is also the root of the words for "yesterday" and "tomorrow"—an indication that change was a constant in indigenous life before the arrival of Europeans and that the "people without history" were people with a past.[10]

Few of these changes, however, had consequences as dramatic, widespread, and permanent as the introduction of smallpox and other diseases into the local ecology. The microbial intrusion, followed not long after by that of Vancouver and his crew, presaged—indeed, facilitated—the coming of an even greater change: the settlement of the country by people of European descent. The voyage of the *Discovery* had little direct impact on the people of Salt Water, but in places like London and Boston and Washington, Vancouver's accounts inspired ambitious Britons and Americans to establish a permanent presence in the region, encouraged by accounts of a dwindling indigenous population. The first Americans came in 1841, when the United States Exploring Expedition, led by Lieutenant Charles Wilkes, sailed up the Sound. The "Ex. Ex.," as the expedition was known, was among other things tasked with strengthening American claims to lands north of the Columbia River, still held jointly by Britain and the United States. Not surprisingly, the mission included naming. As the crews of Wilkes's sloop of war *Vincennes* and its attendant brig *Porpoise* carefully mapped the bays and inlets, they added a new set of names to Puget Sound's growing imperial geography. That summer, Prairie Point obtained its first English-language name when it was christened Point Roberts after the Ex. Ex.'s physician.[11]

Like Vancouver, Wilkes found that the landscapes of Puget Sound "savoured of civilization." As for the indigenous residents, their apparently small numbers suggested that the "Indians of Puget Sound," as they had been named, were unlikely to stand in the way of white settlement, and even if they did, new waves of disease were "rapidly thinning them off." The real threat for Wilkes and for the Congress that sent him came not from indigenous people but from the British, who were establishing a year-round presence at Fort Nisqually on the southern Sound. As facilitators of the highly dynamic fur trade, Fort Nisqually's Hudson's Bay Company factors were always looking for new places to build, and for a short time Prairie Point was a candidate for one of these outlying bastions of mercantile capitalism. An 1833 survey by Fort Nisqually physician William Tolmie provided the first written description of the point ("flat and dotted with small pines, and the soil . . . mostly sand") and the first mentions of its surrounding environs and the "Tuomish" Indians, who he noted were "miserably poor and destitute of firearms." But despite the apparent friendliness of the local people—some surely led by Seeathl—it was a bad place for an outpost, with poor soil and no freshwater. With the signing of a treaty between Britain and the United States in 1846, the issue became moot; British influence at Fort Nisqually faded, although the fort's presence continued to have far-reaching consequences. During an outbreak of dysentery and measles in the winter of 1847–48, Native people from all over Puget Sound, including the territories in and around the future Seattle, traded there and took the microbes home with them.[12]

Despite wave after wave of disease—at least five separate epidemics by 1850—indigenous people remained the dominant presence around Salt Water, as Samuel Hancock, one of the first American settlers on Puget Sound, learned when he stopped at Prairie Point in 1849. "A great many Indians came from their houses to the beach here, to ascertain where we came from," he wrote, adding that they seemed "well disposed" toward him. Hancock traded with the people, exchanging tobacco and looking glasses for clams and salmon. Although buffeted by strengthening storms of change during the early nineteenth century, symbolized by new place-names, new diseases, and new things to buy and sell, Prairie Point was still very much an indigenous place when Hancock visited. The place where the *Exact* would drop anchor two years later was still more Salt Water than Puget Sound. Nothing illustrates this more than the word Hancock used to describe the growing number of white settlers in the region: he called them Whulgers, using the indigenous word for Salt Water to describe those who thought they were coming to Puget's Sound.[13]

WHILE ARTHUR DENNY IS UNANIMOUSLY credited with being the father of Seattle, that title could just as easily go to a forgotten figure named George Brock. A resident of the Willamette Valley at the western end of the Oregon Trail, Brock appears only briefly, not unlike one of Shakespeare's plot-driving apparitions, in the story of the Denny Party's journey west. When the Denny and Boren families arrived at the confluence of the Burnt and Snake rivers, Brock was there, and in the shadow of bunchgrass-covered hills blackened by summer wildfires, he warned Arthur Denny that the best Willamette land was already spoken for but that another region ideal for settlement lay just to the north. In his memoirs, Denny recalled that his attention "was thus turned to the Sound, and I formed the purpose of looking in that direction." Brock's bit of rumor and speculation—he apparently had never seen Puget Sound—effectively and suddenly diverted the two Illinois families. As they labored up the difficult Burnt River Canyon toward the Columbia, they were now on their way not to the oak-dotted prairies of the Willamette but to the timber-shadowed shores of Salt Water.[14]

But if Arthur Denny seems to have been easily swayed by the shadowy Brock, his group did not rush headlong into unknown territory. Instead, their tentative, incremental steps toward settlement reflect the cautious, mindful demeanor for which Seattle's founders were renowned. In September 1851, as family members lay bedridden with fever in Portland hotel rooms, Arthur Denny interviewed Thomas Chambers, a Puget Sound settler in town on business. Chambers provided Denny with his first firsthand account of the territory to the north, including the indigenous inhabitants, who he said were "friendly and they were glad to have the Bostons—as they called the Americans—to come." Chambers's testimony cemented Denny's intentions to lead the group to the Sound. Meanwhile, Arthur's brother David and new compatriot John Low headed to Olympia, a tiny settlement built around tideflats at the head of the Sound. There, they met two men who would make the landing at Alki Point possible: Leander Terry, who was also looking to settle on the inland sea, and Captain Robert Fay, a retired whaling captain who wanted to hire local Indians to catch salmon, preserve it at Point Roberts, and load it onto ships bound for San Francisco. Fay offered Denny, Low, and Terry seats in his open scow, and on 25 September, the four men came ashore just inside Low Point, around the headland from where Wahalchoo had dived for power years before. There, they found scores of Indians waiting. Among them was the headman who had agreed to procure indigenous workers for the venture: Seeathl.[15]

His business arrangements complete, Fay left Terry, Denny, and Low to explore the area. Land reconnaissance was largely out of the question thanks to a bewildering landscape of tideflats, salt marshes, and dense forest, so after hiring two indigenous men from the camp to serve as guides, the three Americans headed up the Duwamish River by canoe. Had Low, Terry, or Denny been able to converse with their guides in Whulshootseed instead of a crude combination of hand signs and Chinook Jargon, they might have learned the ancient and practical names of landmarks on the river: shortcuts, trailheads, backwaters. They might have learned the names for the river's abundance: salmon-drying frames, duck nets stretched between tall poles, fine carving wood. Their guides might not, however, have told them of the numinous places along the river and its delta: a boulder carved with shamanic power spirits, the home of a malevolent spirit that took the form of a fingerless hand rising from the water, the ruins of an ancient fish weir dating to the time of the Changer. More than just a resource territory, the valley of the Duwamish was also a place rich with stories and powers, but the guides apparently shared none of this knowledge with their charges, and even if they had, they would likely have been misunderstood. This was not only because of the vast differences between English and Whulshootseed, but because the settlers and their guides also spoke two mutually unintelligible languages of landscape. Where indigenous people saw spirits and nets and carving wood—the wealth of the land as it was and had been—Denny and the others saw the wealth of the land as it could and would be, expressed in words like "arable," "improvement," and "export." And so after their reconnaissance was complete, David Denny penned a note to his brother, decreeing that the valley of the Duwamish had "room enough for one thousand travelers." The decision to found a city had been made, and Low caught Captain Fay's next scow back to Olympia, on his way to Portland with the news. If any moment must be named as the birth of Seattle, then surely this was it.[16]

In fact, though, some of those thousand travelers had already arrived, and they and their indigenous neighbors helped prepare the way for the rest of the Denny Party. A month before Denny, Low, and Terry arrived at Seeathl's fishing camp, Luther Collins, Henry Van Asselt, and Jacob and Samuel Mapel had joined some seven hundred Indians camped at Low Point before setting out to stake claims in the valley of the Duwamish. While Denny and Terry set to building a cabin, with Native workers paid in bread for their assistance, local Indians and whites made their presence known. On one day, for example, Collins and a Native man known as Nisqually John drove a team of oxen past on the beach; on another, "Old Duwampsh Curley" and several other Indians came to visit, offering Denny and Terry a meal of roast duck. Not long after, Terry hitched a ride to Olympia in Collins's scow to gather the rest of the party in Portland. David Denny was left "alone" to continue work on a cabin for his family and their cohort.[17]

When the thousand-travelers note arrived in Portland, Arthur Denny and the rest of his party, healed from their bouts of ague and joined by the Bell family from Indiana, booked passage on a two-masted schooner called the *Exact*. On 5 November, they left Portland, crossed the Columbia's murderous bar, and headed north along the coast. Along with the families bound for David Denny's cabin at Alki, the *Exact* carried other settlers hoping to establish homes on Puget Sound and miners, many straight from the California goldfields, on their way to the Queen Charlotte Islands far to the north. More than a week later, on 13 November, the twenty-four "Pilgrims" made landfall at Prairie Point and were greeted by a very grateful David Denny, who was suffering mightily from a fresh axe wound on his foot. Then came the famed moment of creation: the crying, the rain, the anxious meeting with Seeathl and his people.[18]

The date may be the same, but the historical circumstances of this urban founding bear few similarities to the singular, deliberate, and pre-ordained landing described in Seattle's traditional creation story. Instead, the story of the Denny Party's arrival at Alki Point is one of rumors and abrupt changes in plans; of illness and accidents; of Native towns and other settlers who got there first. Most importantly, the story has active Indian players: the labor contractor Seeathl, the guides who took the first members of the Denny Party up the river, even Nisqually John and Old Duwampsh Curley. Their presence and agency set the story, not in an emptied-out wilderness, but in a still densely populated indigenous world. The process of getting to Alki—of founding an American city on Salt Water—had depended in no small part upon indigenous people and places. The process of getting along *at* Alki would as well. This would prove to be the greatest mistake made in apprehending the topography of *terra miscognita*: the idea that founding a city could take place without the presence—indeed, the tolerance—of indigenous people.

WHEN THE DENNY PARTY LANDED at the point, they called it neither Prairie Point nor Seattle. Instead, the tiny American outpost was christened New York. Over time, it would come to be known as New York–Alki, a moniker meaning "New York by-and-by" or "New York eventually" in the local lingua franca of Chinook Jargon. In the middle of the nineteenth century, the metropolis at the mouth of the Hudson River was the *ne plus ultra* of American aspiration, the model to which new cities on the nation's urban frontier aspired. It was the commercial capital of the nation and reached out with steamers, railways, newspapers, and retail houses into the rapidly expanding antebellum nation. More than simply the economic center of the country, though, New York was also its cultural hearth. While some critics had begun to describe New York as a "wicked city," it was more commonly lauded as the driver of American progress, its success the result of a refined, cultured urban environment that stimulated the nation's intellectual and social development. The founders might have chosen a different name for their hopeful settlement just three or four decades later, after waves of immigration, exposés of urban violence, and new attitudes about the perils of modern urban life had changed the meaning of New York. But to a tiny clutch of families in a half-finished cabin on a Puget Sound beach in 1851, Gotham must have seemed the apotheosis of urban ambition.[19]

Leander Terry and his younger brother Charles were from upstate New York and had likely had firsthand experiences with America's premier city. But for the majority of Seattle's founders, the frontier towns of Illinois shaped their vision for Puget Sound's New York in ways a distant Gotham never could have. In 1850, when the Denny and Boren families left home for Oregon, Knox County, Illinois, was in the midst of an urban revolution. Permanent white settlement in the area had begun only in the 1830s, but by midcentury the forests of sugar maple, basswood, and wild cherry were giving way as families headed by men with stolid biblical names like Israel and Azel and Hiram established farms and feedlots. Life on the farms revolved around the young town of Abingdon, whose limestone buildings and prim grid of streets sat on high rolling ground above a tributary of the Spoon River. Town life in Abingdon, a satellite of St. Louis, was orderly: liquor violations, morals charges, and murders were virtually unheard of, and judges handed out one hundred percent conviction rates for such disorderly acts as "wantonly" burning prairies. (We might ask if it was the fire itself or the wantonness with which it was lit that was so criminal.) "Court days" were a primary form of entertainment in this straitlaced town, and the Cherry Grove Seminary, founded by Cumberland Presbyterians, was the dominant cultural institution. It was from this buttoned-up Protestant world that Seattle's "Pilgrims" came.[20]

But if Knox County seems to us almost stereotypically midwestern, it was in fact part of the "Old Northwest," and its orderliness and peace stood on foundations of chaos and war. In 1850, Abingdon was on St. Louis's urban periphery, but only twenty years earlier, it had been at the edge of the *pays d'en haut*, a vast region crisscrossed by trade networks. These networks, along which furs and other commodities made their way, reached between the centers of European and Asian society and indigenous communities like those of the Coiracoentanon, who lived along the banks of what they called the Amaquonsippi and what Americans would call the Spoon. By the eighteenth century, what had been a "middle ground" of accommodation had become what historian Richard White has called a "world of fragments," as European empires and indigenous nations vied for power. The violence of the period led many Coiracoentanon to leave the valley of the Amaquonsippi for refugee settlements to the south. The last local conflict, known as the Black Hawk War, saw the end of indigenous tenure in what could then become Knox County. With treaties only a quarter century old nullified by war, the surviving Coirancoentanon had by 1832 "disappeared forever from this locality" according to one early writer, with "none of the whites knowing when or where they went."[21]

The result was that the Dennys and other settlers of 1840s Knox County had very little contact with Native people, although evidence of the indigenous past lay all around them. Settlers regularly came across earthen mounds, flint arrowheads, and the ruins of wigwams as they plowed and felled. Indians also remained part of local memory in accounts of war. Social power in Knox County typically sprang out of the Black Hawk War, whose veterans and organizers translated their military leadership into civilian political careers, and so the foundations of Abingdon's new urban order actually lay in chaos and violence. The Lows, from nearby Bloomington, Illinois, and the Bells, from more distant Edwardsville, Indiana, had all likely had similar experiences in American towns built in the former *pays d'en haut;* William Bell's father, for example, had been a ranger during the wars of American expansion. The Denny Party brought with them both visions of urban order (and perhaps resigned expectations of war with a "doomed" race) and very little firsthand experience with Native people.[22]

On Puget Sound, those visions and expectations collided with the realities of settling in Puget Sound. They collided, first, with the fact that Indian people were not about to disappear with the arrival of the urban frontier and, second, with the dawning reality that, while war was always a possibility, for the most part indigenous people were planning to participate in the creation of that frontier. Founding a city in the Pacific Northwest meant living alongside Native men, women, and children. Almost immediately after the *Exact* put the settlers ashore, for example, Indians came to live with them. Arthur Denny recalled the scene:

Soon after we landed and began clearing the ground for our buildings they commenced to congregate, and continued coming until we had over a thousand in our midst, and most of them remained all winter. Some of them built their houses very near to ours, even on the ground we had cleared, and although they seemed very friendly toward us we did not feel safe in objecting to their building thus near to us for fear of offending them, and it was very noticeable that they regarded their proximity to us as a protection against other Indians.

Denny's account paints a radically different picture from Lillian Smart's creation story diorama. Instead of twenty-four settlers on an empty beach, with perhaps a handful of Indians on hand, we see those same twenty-four whites as pale faces among hundreds of darker ones. Denny's account also speaks to the reasons Native people came to New York–Alki—out of curiosity, to trade, or in fear of increasingly common raids from northern Indians. Regardless of the reasons, by a few weeks after the founding, New York–Alki was no longer just an American settlement. It was also an indigenous one.[23]

Arthur Denny and the others should not have been surprised. Although they had had only one direct interaction with Indians on the overland journey, a furtive skirmish with some Shoshoni men on the Snake River, other experiences farther west made it clear that city founding in the Northwest would include Indians. The early growth of Portland, for example ("quite a thriving town . . . even at that early period" in Arthur Denny's own words), was fueled largely by its new sawmill. When the mill opened in 1850 on the bank of the Willamette, local indigenous people established a new settlement adjacent to it within weeks, where they made up a significant portion of Portland's population and the mill's labor force. Similarly, the "embryo city" of Olympia at the head of Puget Sound consisted of "about a dozen one-story frame cabins, covered with split cedar siding, well-ventilated and healthy, and perhaps twice as many Indian huts near the custom house" when David Denny and John Low met Lee Terry there.[24]

Within a few weeks of its founding, New York–Alki looked much the same. It was a biracial place. To use the language of the day, it was a place of Bostons and Siwashes, the former a reference to the city of origin of many of the first Americans on Puget Sound and the latter a derogatory term derived from the French word *sauvage*. With little experience other than tales of war, the settlers were forced to amend their ambitions in light of their new, and seemingly precarious, circumstances. Likewise, indigenous people who had left for Prairie Point but who had arrived in New York–Alki had to come to terms with the new rules of engagement represented by white settlement. Facing each other across linguistic and cultural chasms, the indigenous and white residents of Prairie Point/New York–Alki mystified each other. Native practices were often inexplicable to the settlers: despite complaints from one of the settler wives, for example, one elderly indigenous woman insisted on throwing her used tea leaves at table legs whenever she visited the cabins. Meanwhile, settler children caught herding garter snakes into a brush fire were sharply admonished by Indian neighbors, who said it would bring a flood. (Soon after, according to a Denny descendant's own account, there was in fact a downpour.) Indigenous men and women found the newcomers, and in particular the Boston women, equally strange. They crowded into the crude cabins to watch the women cook and clean; several memoirs tell of Mary Denny and Lydia Low enlisting harsh words or a hot skillet to maintain some semblance of privacy. During those first few weeks, Americans and Indians each made attempts to reach across divides of language, belief, and etiquette.[25]

Sometimes, it worked. When some laundry disappeared soon after the setters arrived, Arthur Denny spoke to Seeathl, who admonished the other Indians present and oversaw the swift return of the missing garments. On another occasion, one of the white women fed a sick indigenous child, whose father, a "hard case" dubbed Old Alki John, gave her a tin pail in return. Although she refused his gift—more likely an actual payment, and her refusal thus a minor affront to Native ideals of reciprocity—the two families had nonetheless established a bond. Also during that first winter, a woman named Ooyathl, one of the wives of Seeathl, died suddenly. David and Arthur Denny built a cedar coffin for her body, which was "wrapped . . . in so many blankets that it would not go in." Helping give Ooyathl the high-class burial her status demanded helps explain the close connections between the Denny families and the families of Seeathl in decades to come, with David Denny a particular favorite of many Native people in and around Seattle.[26]

But attempts at accommodation did not mean there were no tensions. The male members of Denny Party in particular saw themselves as the intellectual and moral leaders of New York–Alki, no matter the number of their indigenous neighbors. During that first winter, they made it clear that a new political order, with them at the top, was emerging at Prairie Point. When a "very white" Indian woman named Seeayay came to the settlement to escape an abusive husband on the Puyallup River to the south, David Denny advocated on her behalf. She later married the son of Old Alki John (just plain Alki John), and as a result, David Denny became known as the "Law-Man" among local indigenous communities. Meanwhile, when an altercation between Indians visiting from the Green River and the Cascade foothills threatened to turn violent, Arthur Denny stepped in and kept them apart until tempers died down. (While the indigenous disputants likely saw him as an impartial outside moderator, in keeping with local legal tradition, Denny surely interpreted their acquiescence as a sign that the Indians sought order—in particular, *his* order.) Other performances of white authority were less subtle. When the *Vincennes*, the same ship that had been part of Wilkes's expedition, arrived at New York–Alki during that first winter, it repeatedly fired cannon that had once been used in a massacre in the South Pacific. The booming reports made "a strong and respectful impression upon the hundreds of Indians . . . while to the settlers, noticing the effect upon the Indians, it was music of a delightful character." During the same months that an American minority learned to live among an indigenous majority, that minority made it clear who planned to be in charge in the years ahead.[27]

At the same time, indigenous people exerted their own influences over the urban beginnings of New York–Alki. When the brig *Leonesa* arrived, exchanging staples like flour and sugar for wooden piles to help build San Francisco, it was Native men who cut most of the trees and floated the lumber out to the ship. Indians also brought bushel after bushel of potatoes to the settlement as supplies ran low during the winter, gathering them from gardens in their own towns. And just as the name New York was followed by a Chinook Jargon suffix, the first commercial venture in the settlement, set up by John Low and Charles Terry in November, had a name drawn from the hybrid trade language. The New York Markook House (*markook* or *makook* meaning "trade") kept "constantly on hand and for sale at the lowest prices all kinds of merchandise usually required in a new country." Indeed, New York–Alki was a new country, for Native and settler alike.[28]

DESPITE THE SYMBOLISM of events like Ooyathl's burial and the firing of the ship's cannon, both intended to make lasting (if conflicting) impressions upon local Indians, the founding of New York–Alki does not register prominently in the oral tradition of local Native peoples. In fact, it does not register at all. Among the many indigenous accounts of nineteenth-century history in central Puget Sound, there are virtually no stories about the Denny Party and the little settlement on the point. Clearly, what is so important to Seattle's civic place-story is much less so in Indian country. Perhaps the landing at Alki was just one more arrival of settlers during a period when similar foundings were taking place on the shores of Salt Water; perhaps it is overshadowed by other events of the 1850s: the treaties and the resulting conflict that settlers would name an "Indian War." And of course, not all stories survive. Nor do their keepers.

But perhaps the most obvious reason that the Alki landing is not part of local indigenous oral tradition is because the settlement of New York–Alki was a temporary arrangement. And so in the late winter of 1852, Arthur Denny, Carson Boren, and William Bell set out to circumnavigate Elliott Bay in search of a permanent location for their homesteads. Since selling piles and timbers to passing ships was "the only dependence for support in the beginning" as far as Denny could see, "it was important to look well to the facilities for the business." The new site had to meet four requirements: a deep harbor, a supply of freshwater, fine stands of timber close to the shore, and feed for stock. As the three men explored the shores of Elliott Bay, they circulated through another arc of the landscape, but the indigenous places around Elliott Bay were largely invisible—save one. One Denny descendant described their arrival at the spot, using modern landmarks to orient her readers:

In the afternoon as they paddled south, the explorers discovered that the high bluff gradually dropped from a height of forty feet to the level of a little tide stream with meadow grass on its banks, which we know as Yesler Way. North of this was a knoll at the foot of Cherry Street. South of the stream was a low wooded section, and half hidden therein were the ruins of an Indian hut. The distinct shore line ended rather abruptly and merged into tide flats at what is now the foot of King Street, making a point at low tide and an island at high tide.

The three men decided that this place, known as Little Crossing-Over Place to Seeathl and his people because of a trail leading into the backcountry, was to be their new home.[29]

Soon, it would become Seattle. On 23 May 1853, plats for the town of Seattle were officially filed. By then, the settlement had grown into a small hamlet, including figures like Henry Yesler and David "Doc" Maynard who would become key players in Seattle's urban drama. Although the Whulshootseed name for the site was now familiar to many of the settlers, the "awkward and meaningless" word meaning Little Crossing-Over Place was never considered as a name for the town, while Duwamps and Duwamish River, two other options used briefly during 1852, were considered ugly and unflattering.[30] Instead, the community leaders chose to name their town after Seeathl, who had played such a vital role in life at New York–Alki. Historians have debated Seeathl's reaction to this; some say that he was indifferent, others that he was horrified by the decision and even went to Olympia to protest it, and still more suggest that he may have given the name willingly as he approached the end of his life. Regardless of what he thought, the naming of Seattle is typically portrayed in civic historiography as a critical turning point: a handing over from the indigenous to the urban.[31]

Indeed, well before the day when Bell, Boren, and Denny decided that Little Crossing-Over Place would be their new home, the indigenous world of the Duwamish, Lakes, and Shilsholes had been irrevocably transformed. The ruined longhouse at Little Crossing-Over Place, overgrown with wild roses (and, according to oral tradition, only one of several that had once stood there), spoke to the abandonment of towns in the wake of epidemics and slave raids. In Whulshootseed, similar words described both houses and human bodies: house posts were limbs, roof beams were spines, walls were skin. Just as sweeping a house and healing a body could be expressed with the same verb, related words spoke of illness and the falling down of a home, and so the ruins were testaments to loss. Meanwhile, on a nearby bluff above Elliott Bay at what is now Spring Street, a cemetery adorned with tin and trade beads spoke of the epidemics and the traders who had brought them. Read like a text, the landscape seemed to tell of the passing of Indians from Puget Sound, and so the naming of Seattle seems the end of an era.[32]

But, of course, the story is much more complicated than that. When the plat for Seattle was filed in May 1853, it showed a grid of straight lines not unlike the layout of Abingdon or one of the other towns from which the Bostons had come. On the ground, however, the landscape would not be easily transformed into a model of Cartesian harmony. Arthur Denny could attest to that. "The front of our territory was so rough and broken as to render it almost uninhabitable at that early time," he recalled. "I dug a well forty feet deep in the bottom of the gulch and only got quick sand with a very limited amount of water. Direct communication with the bay, by which we received all our supplies at that time, was next to impossible, owing to the height of the bluff." *Terra miscognita*, in the form of gullies and springs, sand and slopes, would exert its own agency over Seattle's growth, forcing urban visions to accommodate local realities.[33]

So would the people of Little Crossing-Over Place and Herring's House and Clear Water and all the other Native towns. Just as Vancouver's Puget

Sound had not erased Salt Water, just as Wilkes's Point Roberts and the Denny Party's New York–Alki had only partially obscured Prairie Point, Seattle would not entirely replace Little Crossing-Over Place. In naming settlements like Seattle, Europeans and Americans sought to claim them and turn the abstract spaces of wilderness into places—into Home. But such efforts were never completely successful. Instead, the day-to-day realities of settlers and Natives meant that the newcomers would have to contend with the people and places they sought to replace. Rather than being emptied of their meanings, places in and around the young town would collect new meanings as settlers accreted their own experiences onto sites with existing indigenous histories. For Seattle, that meant that the coming years would be a time of gathering—of new stories about place, about race, and about the boundaries between cooperation and conflict. Seattle's urban Indian history was just beginning.

3 / Seattle Illahee

N 1858, HEARING that indigenous people had been trading gold at forts on the Fraser River north of Puget Sound, hopeful hundreds ventured into the Fraser's deep canyons, home to the Stó:lō and Nlaka'pamux peoples, in search of the yellow metal. Within a year, more than twenty thousand prospectors, many of them American, had overrun the Fraser. Unattached women were few and far between in the diggings, and life there was a heady mix of longing and libido. Folk songs on the Fraser included a randy little ditty about a place on Puget Sound known for its good food and good women. Sung in a mixture of English and Chinook Jargon, it painted a vivid, if vulgar, picture of Seattle's attractions:

There'll be mowitch [venison]
And klootchman [Indian women] by the way
When we 'rive at Seattle Illahee [Seattle country].
There'll be hiyu [many] clams
And klootchman by the way
Hiyu tenas moosum [Many "little sleeps" (sex)]
Till daylight fades away.
Kwonesum kwonesum cooley [Always always run]
Kopa nika illahee [To that place]
Kunamokst kapswalla moosum [To steal sleep together]
As the daylight fades away.
Row, boys, row!
Let's travel to the place they call Seattle
(That's the place to have a spree!)
Seattle Illahee![1]

While magazines and newspapers enticed overlanders to Puget Sound with stories of arable land and a salubrious climate, "Seattle Illahee" was another kind of public relations altogether, and likely did as much to establish Seattle's reputation throughout the Northwest as any emigrant handbook.

That the miners sang of Seattle Illahee is fitting. On a literal level, it was the name of one of the town's primary economic ventures: the Illahee was a brothel staffed mostly by Native women, many of them most likely from British Columbia. On a more symbolic level, however, *illahee*, a Chinook Jargon term meaning "country" or "place" or "home," suggested a truth about everyday life in early Seattle: it was as much an indigenous place as a settler one. David Kellogg, who arrived in Seattle in the 1850s, could have told you that. Decades later, he described early Seattle as "a very small village, really more Indian than White!" It was a place where Indians dominated the young urban landscape. "Along the beach stretched the shanties with the inevitable canoes," wrote Kellogg, "some hauled high onto the beach and covered with mats while the smaller ones lay idly at the water's edge, ready for immediate use. Every polackly [night] the singing and pounding in the shanties was the mighty orison."[2]

During its "village period," an era stretching from the Denny Party's move to Little Crossing-Over Place in 1852 to the coming of the railroad in 1883, Seattle was indeed a Native place. Indigenous people came to town throughout those decades both to continue long-standing traditions and to make bids for inclusion in urban life. Perhaps most importantly, they came to work, and Indian labor would facilitate much of Seattle's early development. It would also challenge federal Indian policy, as civic leaders enacted Indian policies of their own that often ran counter to the ambitions of a weak national government. Well after the treaties and the "Indian War" that would erupt between some settlers and some Native people in 1855 and 1856, the presence of Native people in town continued to shape civic politics, as Indians became signifiers of urban disorder in the eyes of many of Seattle's leading citizens. Seattle Illahee was a perfect name for a place where indigenous people—both as participants in the town's successes and as scapegoats for its problems—were at the core of life on the urban frontier.

WHEN NEW SETTLERS ARRIVED in the little mill town on Elliott Bay, they were often shocked by the large numbers of Duwamish, Lake, and Shilshole people in and around Seattle. Alonzo Russell came in 1853 and recalled years later that "like any boy of fourteen my first impressions of Seattle were of the Thousands of Indians standing by." Caroline Leighton, the wife of an early customs collector, came in 1866, and in a florid diary entry from April of that year wrote "the frogs have begun to sing in the marsh, and the Indians in their camps. How well their voices chime together." She also described a small stream of freshwater that cascaded down a gully into the lagoon at Seattle. Once, that stream had been a water source for the longhouses of Little Crossing-Over Place. Fifteen years later, the stream still served Native people, as they came to town and replaced Little Crossing-Over Place with a bustling new community that existed alongside, and enmeshed with, the Bostons. Only a "small and insignificant village" in the eyes of 1859 arrival Dillis Ward, Seattle was dominated by indigenous people, who made it their own, using the new proto-urban venue, with its connections to new trade networks, new forms of political and spiritual power, and new audiences, to enact and even enhance economic, political, religious, and social traditions. Continuous streams of both water and history flowed here.[3]

All around the fledgling town, Indian people insisted on inclusion in settler society. When a wedding united the Mapel and Van Asselt families in 1862, Seeathl and several hundred of his people arrived to observe the festivities along the Duwamish River. After dinner, the newlyweds stood on display while Native men and women filed by to look at them. Afterward, Seeathl and others began a celebration of their own on a sandspit at the mouth of the Duwamish, and Mapel recalled that "all that was good in the power of the spirits was called upon and invoked as a blessing for Henry Van Asselt." More than simply the marriage of two settlers, the wedding was a meeting of two cultures, with both making a performance out of it. In allowing the Indians to gaze "in awe" at the "white Klootchman," the settlers defined themselves as superior newcomers in a land of primitives. Meanwhile, in their finery and solemnity, Seeathl and his retinue similarly defined themselves as high-class people. And the Mapel–Van Asselt wedding was not unusual; indigenous ceremony was a key element of Seattle's urban scene during its first decades, linking Native tradition with new circumstances. Caroline Leighton described a gathering to sing and dance spirit powers on the Seattle shoreline in 1866:

A little, gray old woman appeared yesterday morning at our door, with her cheeks all aglow, as if her young blood had returned. Besides the vermilion lavishly displayed on her face, the crease at the parting of her hair was painted the same color. Every article of clothing she had on was bright and new. I looked out, and saw that no Indian had on any thing but red. Even old blind Charley, whom we had never seen in any thing but a black blanket, appeared in a new one of scarlet.

This example of Native people maintaining traditional cultural practices in the new setting of a mill town is a powerful challenge to the notion that Seattle's Indian history was coming to a close. When half the town showed up dressed in red, it was clear that Seattle was still a good deal indigenous.[4]

But if some indigenous people pursued traditional ceremonies in town, others came to Seattle to access the new spirit power that lived there: Jesus Christ. One Native woman named Sally, said to be a sister of Seeathl, was well known around town for her church attendance and in fact strove to build friendships only with churchgoing white women. Meanwhile, Ben Solomon, born at Little Crossing-Over Place before the longhouses were abandoned and the wild roses took over, became a figure in the local Roman Catholic congregation and after his first communion built a chapel near the large Native towns on the Black River south of Seattle.[5]

Weddings and other ceremonies offered venues for cultural encounter in Seattle, but all too often the collision of indigenous religious observance with the norms of settler society highlighted the differences between Seattle's two peoples. For many pioneers, Native ceremonies in town created lasting and deeply unsettling memories. David Kellogg recalled vividly the year 1862, for example, when he heard that a "Klale Tomaniwous"—a Chinook Jargon term that Bostons typically translated as "black magic"—was going to take place along the waterfront. Arriving at a small house made of cedar-bark mats and lumber from Henry Yesler's sawmill, Kellogg witnessed the initiation of a man known as Bunty Charley; "the pounding against the roof with poles and on the circle of stones around the fire was deafening," Kellogg recalled. The proceedings soon moved outside, with participants tossing Charley's rigid body into the air and spraying it with mouthfuls of what appeared to be blood. Soon after, Charley began behaving like the Bear power that had possessed him, walking on all fours among the driftwood before shambling off toward the river. The next morning, he was seen in town wearing the badge of his new status: a dusting of white duck down on his head and shoulders. This was a traditional initiation into a secret society, and its staging on the Seattle waterfront was in keeping with the ritual's logic. Such practices were not just religious rituals but social performances, designed specifically to shock and impress observers and to cement the status of the secret society's members. It certainly worked in Kellogg's case. "Holy smoke but it was a sight," he wrote years later, his shock still resonating decades later.[6]

The ducks that provided Bunty Charley's dusting of down likely came from the Duwamish River's estuary, which had been the source of other such emblems of status for centuries. But like new kinds of spiritual power, novel objects that could express social standing—old blind Charley's scarlet blanket, for example—could now also be procured in Seattle. Indian people visited Louisa Boren Denny to buy strips of silk cut from old dresses, and she reminisced that the men in particular "looked very fine with them around their waists, knotted at the side." Meanwhile, Native women made use of that most cherished of pioneer symbols, the patchwork quilt, to highlight the status of their menfolk. Another Denny kinswoman described how the Indians' quilts of blue and pink on white groundwork were made into shirts, and how "when dressed in a pair of blue trousers and with a bright red scarf tied around

Seeathl, photographed by E. M. Sammis in 1864, played a crucial role in the founding of the sawmill town named for him, even if his death in 1866 merited no mention in Puget Sound newspapers. UW NA1511

This 1906 real estate brochure reflected dominant perceptions of the relationship between cities and Indians in American history: the two were considered mutually exclusive. UW MSCUA

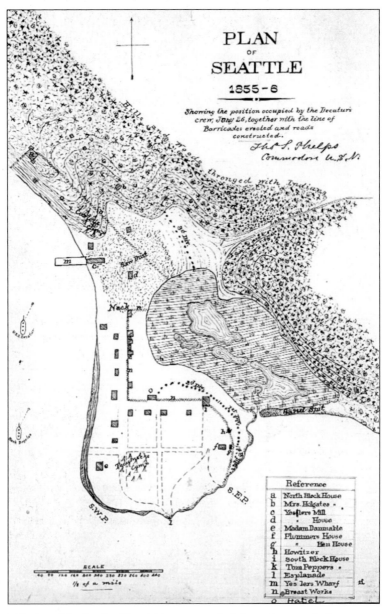

This plan of the "Battle of Seattle" in January 1856, drawn by a naval officer involved in the conflict, shows the lagoon where Little Crossing-Over Place once stood. It also shows indigenous settlements in and around town, depicted with marks that look suspiciously like Plains-style tipis, as well as the "woods thronged with Indians" on the slopes above the settlement. UW4101

These Native men, likely employees at Henry Yesler's sawmill, were photographed standing in front of Yesler's cookhouse in 1866. Their labor, like that of many other local indigenous people, made Seattle's early survival possible. UW5870

Julia Yesler, daughter of Henry Yesler and a Duwamish woman, represented the "Seattle Illahee" of mixed-race families, which both illustrated the importance of Native people to town life and caused consternation among some white settlers. Photo courtesy of Kathie Zellerberg.

SMALL POX !

CITY ORDINANCE NO. 30.

The City of SEATTLE does Ordain as follows:

SECTION 1. It shall be the duty of every practising physician within the limits of this city to report within six hours in writing, to the Mayor or Health Officer every case of contagious or infectious disease which has come to his knowledge. For every violation of this duty the offender shall be subject to a penalty of not more than one hundred and not less than fifty dollars.

SEC. 2. It shall be the duty of every owner or occupant of any house, store or other building within the limits of this city, to report to the above-named officers, every case of a like nature within six hours after the same has come to his knowledge, under a like penalty as above expressed.

SEC. 3. It shall be the duty of every owner or occupant of any store, house or other building where a case of contagious or infectious disease exists, to forthwith place on such building in a conspicuous place a yellow flag, and to keep the same thus exposed until permitted to remove it by order of the Mayor or Health Officer. Every violation of this section shall subject the offender to the payment of a fine of one hundred dollars. It shall be the duty of the Health Officer to compel the enforcement of this section, and in case of neglect or refusal of any such owner or occupant to provide and place such flag, to place one there himself.

SEC. 4. Any person who has any such contagious or infectious disease, who shall leave the house where he is ordered to remain by the Mayor or Health Officer, and go upon the streets, or go from house to house, or in any public place whatever, or in any way put himself in contact with persons not properly in attendance upon him, until he is fully discharged under the written order of the Health Officer, shall suffer a penalty of not more than five hundred nor less than one hundred dollars.

It shall be the duty of the City Marshal to enforce this provision.

SEC. 5. All clothing and bedding used by or about any person who may have any contagious or infectious disease, shall be burned under the direction of the Health Officer. Every person who shall neglect or refuse to obey the order of such officer, in this regard, shall suffer a penalty of one hundred dollars.

SEC. 6. The corporate limits of the city of Seattle shall and hereby is constituted a Health District, and the Mayor, and two Councilmen who shall be appointed by the Mayor, shall constitute a Board of Health, under whose direction all steps shall be taken for the enforcement of this ordinance.

SEC. 7. A Health Officer shall be elected by the Council, whose compensation shall be fixed before he enters upon the discharge of his duties.

SEC. 8. No vessel, whether propelled by steam or sail shall be permitted to land at the piers or at any point within the city, unless the Master of such vessel shall report first to the Health Officer that there are no cases of infectious or contagious disease on board of such vessel, and such Master then have permission from such officer to land.

Any Master or other person in command of such vessel, who shall violate this section shall suffer a penalty of not more than five hundred dollars nor less than one hundred dollars.

SEC. 6. It shall be the duty of the Board of Health to provide a Pest House, to which all persons who may have any contagious or infectious disease shall be removed, if so ordered by the Health Officer. The said Board are hereby empowered to contract with some competent Physician to vaccinate all persons who in his opinion may require it, the expense thereof to be a charge upon the city.   JOHN T. JORDAN, Mayor,
GEO. N. McCONAHA, Clerk.

July 23, 1872.

Board of Health,

J. T. JORDAN, Mayor, C. P. STONE,
F. MATTHIAS, Councilmen.
Health Officer—Dr. G. A. WEED.

This 1872 handbill warning of smallpox, the oldest extant piece of printed material from Seattle, does not directly mention Native people but nonetheless exhibits the intense anxiety about urban disease outbreaks, for which Indians were often blamed. UW4095

CITY OF SEATTLE,

Puget Sound, Washington Territory, 1878.

This 1878 bird's eye view of Seattle, created by a man named Glover, includes a tiny flotilla of Native canoes and an Indian encampment, marked here with a black box. It does not, however, show the many other kinds of Native presence in and immediately around Seattle. UW14531

When Native men and women provided a salmon feast for the 1883 Railroad Jubilee, they may not have known the effect that the railroad and the immigration that followed soon after would have on their lives. Photograph by Theodore Peiser. UW NA1390

Kikisebloo ("Princess Angeline"), the daughter of Seeathl, is pictured here in 1890 on the front porch of her home near the Seattle waterfront. Although she was revered by many as "Indian royalty," Kikisebloo was also mocked and maligned, and her "shanty" was seen by some as evidence that Seattle needed to "clean up" its urban landscape. UW NA1521

Chesheeahud and Tleebooleetsa, also known as Lake Union John and
Madeline, were among the handful of Duwamish people who obtained
homesteads in and around Seattle in the late nineteenth century. Like
Kikisebloo, they were often portrayed as remnants of a "vanishing race."
However, this photograph shows the persistence of some indigenous people
in traditional places as well as the continued connections between indigenous and pioneer families. Photograph by Orion Denny. UW NA590

Indigenous dispossession in 3 acts

Act 1: In 1905, the home of Hwelchteed and Cheethlooleetsa stands on the shoreline, across Salmon Bay from the Seattle suburb of Ballard, which supplanted Hwelchteed's ancestral community of Tucked Away Inside. Hwelchteed's canoe is moored nearby. Photograph by Webster and Stevens. MOHAI 1983.10.9067

Act 2: Just a few years later, most likely in 1913, Hwelchteed is pictured during his eviction. The three white men are unidentified but are almost certainly linked in some way to the construction of Lake Washington Ship Canal, which required the clearance of indigenous people and others whose homes were in the way of progress. Photograph by C. Langstaff. Magnolia Historical Society Collection, UW Special Collections

Act 3: Construction of the locks for the Lake Washington Ship Canal. Hwelchteed's home, where Cheethlooleetsa appears to have died sometime around the time of eviction, stood just to the right of this view. By the time construction began, Hwelchteed was living on the Port Madison (Suquamish) Reservation across Puget Sound. Photograph by Webster and Stevens. MOHAI 2002.3.2022

The completion of the Lake Washington Ship Canal was the final straw for many indigenous people. When Lake Washington (in the background) dropped and became level with Lake Union (foreground), the Black River, where many Duwamish people continued to live, ceased to exist. UW SEA1102

Seetoowathl, who lived in a floathouse on the Duwamish River just below the view in the postcard on the facing page, was an important source of information about indigenous geography in the Seattle area. He and his wife starved to death during the winter of 1919-20.

The Seattle waterfront, including Ballast Island, was sometimes described as the Venice of the Pacific because of the many Native canoes moored there. Some were Duwamish; others belonged to people from far away. Photograph attributed to John P. Soule, 1891. UW NA680

Encampments of Native migrants, like this one just south of the downtown business district (but incorrectly labeled as Ballast Island), were common sights in Seattle during the late nineteenth and early twentieth centuries. Photograph by Anders B. Wilse. MOHAI 1990.45.14

This Native woman, photographed at an encampment near First Avenue and King Street in 1898, is most likely Nuu-chah-nulth, from the west coast of Vancouver Island. Journeys like hers, often taken annually, linked Seattle to Native communities as far away as southeast Alaska. Photograph by Oliver Phelps Anderson.

Just as Native people moved in Seattle's "Indian hinterland," so too did Native imagery. The Chief-of-All-Women Pole, stolen from an Alaskan Tlingit community in 1899, is shown here being erected in Pioneer Square as Seattle's first official piece of public art. Photograph by Anders B. Wilse. MOHAI 1988.33.146

The Tilikums of Elttaes, shown here on parade during the Golden Potlatch of 1912, enthusiastically adopted "savage" symbolism for their displays of civic boosterism, illustrating the extent to which the "Indian hinterland" also transformed Seattle's urban vocabulary. UW313

Indian Basket Sellers
Seattle

Native vendors of "curios" were a common sight on Seattle streets,
as this 1912 postcard shows, and sometimes even within the aisles of
department stores. Along with agricultural labor in the fields of western
Washington, such urban entrepreneurship became part of an annual
routine for many Northwest Coast families. MOHAI 2002.50.41.1

Taken in 1911, this photograph captures the interaction between a white woman and a Native basket vendor, most likely Makah or Nuu-chah-nulth. Photograph by Webster and Stevens. MOHAI *1983.10.7929*

Baskets and other objects purchased from Native vendors often ended up in the curio corners of elite Seattle homes, as in this mill owner's parlor. Photograph by Anders B. Wilse. MOHAI 1988.33.60

AUTHORIZED BIRDS EYE VIEW OF THE ALASKA-YUKON-PACIFIC EXPOSITION

SEATTLE, U.S.A. 1909

OPENS JUNE 1ST   CLOSES OCT. 16TH

The Alaska-Yukon-Pacific Exposition (AYPE) was Seattle's "coming out party" and an articulation of the city's urban identity. Not surprisingly, the million or so visitors to the fair encountered many kinds of Native imagery—and sometimes even real Indians. UW AYP462

Native people from Siberia and Labrador, like Native people from North
America, the Philippines, and elsewhere, were displayed at the AYPE. While
typically portrayed in racist terms, many of these people came to the fair of their
own accord. Here, Frederick W. Seward, nephew of the more famous Seward
who purchased Alaska, gingerly holds a young Inuit boy named "Seattle" and
is flanked by the "Eskimo Belle" Columbia and Seattle's unidentified mother.
UW AYP545

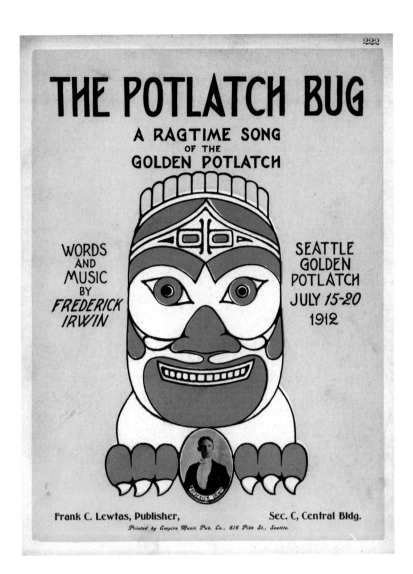

The "Big Bug," official mascot of Seattle's Potlatch festivals, drew on racist caricatures of Northwest Coast art, just as those who organized the Potlatches conducted "cannibalistic" ceremonies to initiate new members into their "tribe." UW Ashford Collection

While Potlatch organizers drew on totem poles and other northern imagery to create an urban vocabulary, pioneers such as these photographed in 1905 by Theodore Peiser at the Alki landing monument, crafted an entirely different kind of urban narrative. Instead of using Indian imagery to advertise a bright future, pioneers often used Indian imagery to lament a disappearing past. MOHAI Peiser 10088

Although they had little say in the creation of urban narratives, local Native communities did participate in urban commemorations and told their own stories of Seattle. Here, Suquamish tribal members perform at Chief Seattle Day festivities in 1912. UW NA1950

In 1948, Ernest Bertelson took this photograph of several unidentified Native people in the heart of Pioneer Square. As early as the 1930s, this neighborhood—the original Skid Road—was already home to an urban Indian community. UW NA1678

In the late 1950s, the American Indian Women's Service League was created to help address the needs of Seattle's urban Indians and to rehabilitate the public image of Native people. Members shown here in 1960 include Pearl Warren, Martha John, Leona Lyness, Hazel Duarte, Ella Aquino, and Dorothy Lombard. Photograph by Harvey Davis. MOHAI PI 1986.5.30279

Inspired by the work of the Service League but informed by a new, more radical approach to activism, Colville tribal member Bernie Whitebear was one of the leaders of the occupation of Fort Lawton by the United Indians of All Tribes in 1970. Photograph by Cary Tolman. MOHAI PI 1986.5.55140.1

The descendants of Seattle's indigenous people—the Duwamish, the Suquamish, and the Muckleshoot—began making public claims on the urban landscape in the late twentieth century. Here, Muckleshoot tribal members march through South Seattle to protest the criminalization of Indian fishing. MOHAI PI 1986.5.4450

his waist and a gaudy red bandanna handkerchief . . . around his head, his feet encased in bead-embroidered moccasins, a siwash was a 'hyas tyee' (very fine chief)." Indigenous women were also regular patrons at C. C. Terry's store, where they bought tin cups to beat into ornaments, and it was not uncommon to see them dressed in hoopskirts and carrying parasols. As commerce with places like San Francisco grew in the 1850s and 1860s, such consumer goods provided yet another reason for indigenous people to visit. Along with dentalium-shell chokers and blankets woven from mountain-goat wool, now hoopskirts and parasols purchased in town could reflect their owners' prestige.[7]

Prestige and power could also be found in meetings of the mind between settler and Native leaders. In the 1850s, for example, Saneewa, a Snoqualmie headman from an important indigenous town at the foot of the Cascades, came every autumn with his family, his ponies, and his dogs to camp in Arthur Denny's pasture. Like Seeathl, Saneewa saw Denny, arguably the most powerful man in town, as a strategic ally, but the relationship was mutually beneficial. As the leader of a community located at the western entrance to the lowest pass across the central Cascades, which Denny coveted for a wagon road, Saneewa provided crucial information about the route through the mountains. A few years later, Denny would be among the surveyors to map what they called Snoqualmie Pass. And as for Saneewa, many of his people and their descendants were able to remain in the valley where they had always lived, rather than removing to reservations, in part because of the relationships they built with settler "headmen" like Denny. Here, urban and indigenous ambitions coincided, with trips to town reinforcing one Native leader's territorial prerogatives while also facilitating the opening of new routes for American settlement of the region.[8]

Hoopskirts and duck down, ponies in pastures and wedding parties near sandspits—each of these things highlighted the ways in which settlers and Indians encountered each other as indigenous men and women participated in town life during Seattle's first decades. Social status, religious observance, and political alliance were all part of the urban indigenous frontier on Puget Sound and offered means for Native men and women to participate in urban society. But throughout Seattle's village period, each of these reasons for coming to town was overshadowed by another: Indians came to Seattle (or, in some cases, never left the place that became Seattle) for jobs. As they contributed to the town's economy, they would prove all too well that Seattle's Indian history was nowhere close to ending. Indeed, indigenous people saw Seattle as more than a settler community: it was *their* community, since they had been partners in its creation. The question was what, if anything, the Bostons, their civic leaders, and their federal government were going to do about it.

N THE EARLY-MORNING HOURS of 26 January 1856, the U.S. Navy's sloop of war *Decatur* opened fire on the *illahee* called Seattle. Its targets were not the fifty or so white residents huddling in a tiny blockhouse at the corner of Front and Cherry; rather, the *Decatur* was gunning for the estimated one thousand "hostiles" in the woods behind town. They had come from indigenous communities in southern Puget Sound and the far side of the Cascade Mountains to sack Seattle, traveling down the old trail from Lake Washington to Little Crossing-Over Place and taking up positions beyond the cleared yards at the edge of town. They had already burned many outlying homesteads and now seemed about to raze what little existed of central Puget Sound's urban potential. Throughout the day, settlers and marines exchanged fire with the attackers, and by ten o'clock that evening, the enemy had retreated back to Lake Washington. No bodies were ever found, but some settlers estimated that as many as two hundred Native warriors had died; among the settlers, one man and a teenage boy had been killed. In less than twenty-four hours, the "Battle of Seattle" was over.[9]

Enshrined in local mythology as the ur-travail of early Seattle—a violent inverse of the Chief Seattle Speech—the Battle of Seattle is like countless other events held to have occurred in what historian Patricia Nelson Limerick has called the "empire of innocence," in which blameless white pioneers earn honor and success by surviving threats from nature, Indians, or a corrupt government. But what on its surface might seem like a showdown between savagery and urbanity was in reality a much messier affair, illustrated by a map of the conflict drawn by the

Decatur's Colonel George S. Phelps. It shows a handful of streets and landmarks such as the blockhouse and the hotel belonging to Mary Ann "Mother Damnable" Conklin; above and to the right are the "hills and woods thronged with Indians." But at the edges of the little town, we also see two clusters of cross-hatchings—almost like Plains tipis— representing Indian encampments. On the slope above Henry Yesler's mill sits "Curley's Camp," and the other, named "Tecumseh's Camp," stands across a dirt street from Mother Damnable's. Distinguished from the Native attackers, these were indigenous people who had come to Seattle, but not to destroy it. Many of them had come to build it.[10]

Let there be no mistake: without the labor of Indians, Seattle would have been stillborn. As lumbermen and laundresses, hunters and haulers, indigenous men and women made the city possible. But at the same time, their presence also brought the needs of an "embryonic town" into conflict with the larger aims of federal policies designed to segregate and manage Native communities. Civic leaders challenged the remote federal government and created a local Indian policy based on the needs of urban communities like Seattle and predicated upon a weak federal presence in the region. Not everyone felt that "Siwashes" belonged in town, though, and a series of legal restrictions placed on indigenous people reflected settlers' deep ambivalence about the place of Indians in urban life. As at Alki Point that first winter, the presence and persistence of Indians simultaneously facilitated and challenged Seattle's urban ambitions.

Seattle's indigenous workers included the men employed at Henry Yesler's sawmill, the primary engine of commercial development for the first two decades of the town's existence. In the early 1850s, nearly every white man in town worked in the mill, but its output of some eight thousand board feet of lumber on a good day required the additional labor of Native men. Edith Redfield, an early settler, described sawmills like Yesler's as "little kingdoms, a law unto themselves . . . here white men, Indians, Chinamen, and Kanakas [indigenous Hawai'ians] worked side by side and boarded at the Company's cook-house." Indians and settlers may have worked and boarded together, but Natives also had particular contributions to make. John M. Swan recalled how indigenous men, seasoned by regular bathing in the Sound, were well suited for rafting lumber out to arriving ships. Remembering the loading of the *Orbit* for the San Francisco market, for example, Swan recalled that "several of us that were looking at them were shivering with the cold." Indian mill workers were especially crucial during the Fraser River gold rush, when, in the words of settler William Ballou, "workmen could not be hired for love nor money on Puget Sound" as settlers hied off to the diggings. And as Indians carted sawdust away from Yesler's mill, they dumped it along the shoreline, filling the lagoon of Little Crossing-Over Place and destroying the flounder fishery for which it had been known. Indigenous labor, then, obliterated an indigenous place.[11]

Mill work was only part of the contribution Indians made to Seattle's livelihood. With supplies hard to find or outrageously priced, settlers depended on Native subsistence networks to survive. J. Thomas Turner told historian Hubert Howe Bancroft a quarter century later that whites in early Seattle "awaited upon the ebb and flow of the tides for their principal food . . . we were largely dependent upon the Native inhabitants . . . for our potatoes and food products of forest and Sound." Jane Fenton Kelly, the daughter of a Duwamish Valley family, recalled that Native people made domestic life possible among the marshes and dense timber:

Mother would send us out to watch for a canoe and we would hail them and give them a written order to the grocery man. He would fill it, and they would bring it out to us. They charged twenty-five cents or "two-bits" as they called it, for each article they brought, large or small. I can remember after we were on the homestead one-half mile up the hill, an old Indian by the name of Jake carried a five-gallon keg of New Orleans molasses to us and charged us but twenty-five cents.

In this way, the duck nets and salmon-drying frames of Seattle's indigenous geography fed its immigrant population. The arrangement benefited Indians as well; hunters who brought mallards and other waterfowl to white families were typically paid a quarter dollar for each bird. These coins, along with pelts of bears and other animals, often changed hands on "whiskey boats" that plied the Sound with cargoes of flour, tobacco, beads, and liquor.[12]

Indigenous work went beyond mill labor and subsistence provision; Indians participated in almost every aspect of the Seattle economy, successful or otherwise. They packed hundreds of barrels of salmon for David "Doc" Maynard in the fall of 1852, a venture abandoned after the fish spoiled before arriving in San Francisco. They used traditional methods to render dogfish oil, the primary lubricant for sawmill equipment in Puget Sound until the 1890s. Native men cleared land and helped build homes on the slopes above Elliott Bay, and Native women did the washing within those homes. Indians paddled the canoe that carried the U.S. mail, and shoreline-hugging "Siwash buggies," as canoes were sometimes called, were often the only way to travel from one place to another. And of course there were the women celebrated by the ditty "Seattle Illahee." We can now only imagine the mix of limited opportunities and male coercion that led those women and girls from British Columbia or elsewhere to the Illahee, but their contributions to the economy and reputation of Seattle easily rivaled those of Yesler's mill employees. With the exceptions of banking, American-style medicine, and a handful of other settler-dominated vocations, Indians made Seattle work in the 1850s, and their efforts helped settlers distinguish "good" Indians from "bad." Walter Graham, whose Lake Washington farm had burned during the Battle of Seattle, nonetheless recalled that the Indians he knew were "good workers" and that one had worked for him for three years.[13]

But if settlers and Indians forged everyday relationships through work, tensions between indigenous people and the newcomers could also flare into violence. Well before the attack on the town in January 1856, violence between Indians and whites had been a regular, and deeply distressing, occurrence. One such case was that of an Indian called Mesatchie ("Wicked" in Chinook Jargon) Jim, who killed his Native wife near Seattle in 1853. As punishment, Luther Collins and several other settlers lynched Jim on Front Street. That lynching precipitated the slaying of a white man named McCormick near Lake Union; in return, two more Native men were hanged in town. Such spirals of violence took place when indigenous notions of justice, which often mandated retaliation, coincided with a powerful strain of vigilantism in settler society. That same year, preacher's wife Catherine Blaine recorded a similar cycle of killings that took the lives of two white men and as many as a dozen Indian men, inspiring settlers to organize a militia to take care of the "problem" Natives. Had cooler heads not prevailed, the militia's offensive against indigenous people would have taken place, not out in the woods or on a river somewhere, but right in the heart of town where the Indians in question were staying. "We feel considerably alarmed for ourselves," the consistently timorous Mrs. Blaine wrote, and her anxiety reflected that of many of her neighbors, Boston and Native alike.[14]

Compared with the attempts at understanding that had taken place at Alki Point only a few years earlier, these events illustrate just how dry the tinder was as more settlers moved in on indigenous lands near Seattle. And, in fact, many settlers did connect white emigration to violence, if only to blame each other. Recalling the Mesatchie Jim case, for example, mill owner Henry Yesler described the effects of "lower class" emigrants on Indian-white relations, noting that "whenever there was trouble it was the fault of some worthless white man." In what would become one of the most important patterns of conflict in Seattle in the coming decades, Yesler identified class as a key element of race relations. Tensions between the "law and order crowd," represented by Yesler, Arthur Denny, and other civic leaders, and the "worthless," less orderly elements of urban society would shape life in Seattle for years to come. While Yesler blamed interracial violence on the wrong kind of emigrants, many indigenous people knew that low-class settlers were only part of the problem.[15]

And so within just a few short years of Seattle's founding, both settlers and Natives were calling for a new sort of order. That new order came in the form of treaties designed to mitigate interracial violence by creating new boundaries between white and Indian communities and settling—pun intended—the question of indigenous title to the land. Much of the run-up to the signings took place in urban outposts. Seattle was the site of one such proceeding on 12 January 1854, when Isaac

Ingalls Stevens, the new territorial governor and Indian superintendent, introduced himself and the treaty process to more than a thousand Indians and some ten dozen settlers gathered in front of Doc Maynard's office. One year, ten days, and many speeches later, Seeathl and other headmen signed the Treaty of Point Elliott.[16]

In towns throughout Puget Sound, settlers celebrated the treaty process; one Native elder, in a particularly eloquent choice of words, described Seattle settlers' reaction to the treaty as "hooraying." There was some cause for optimism among Indians as well. Among other things, the treaty ensured that indigenous people would have the right to camp, hunt, fish, and harvest berries and roots at the "usual and accustomed stations and grounds." But despite the promises of the treaty, few Indians were hooraying. In fact, significant factions in Native communities on Salt Water and beyond took offense at the treaty agreements, and some did not hesitate to express their indignation. In late 1855, for example, a shaman named Chaoosh visited David and Louisa Denny at their cabin on Lake Union after a government "potlatch" at Tulalip north of Seattle. Enraged at the agent's offers of cheap needles and strips of blankets, he warned them that whites were few in number and could be easily wiped out. The condescending gifts, paltry compared to what could be found in any town's shops, only added to growing Native outrage at the hubris of the Bostons.[17]

As tensions grew, urban settlements, beachheads of the American invasion of Puget Sound, were obvious targets for the indigenous uprising that seemed increasingly inevitable. In response, white officials began with what seemed like the most obvious first step: removing Indians from the towns. Indian agent Michael T. Simmons, however, found that doing so was no simple task. A month before the attack on Seattle, after several attacks had already taken place elsewhere in the region, Simmons reported finding among Seattle's indigenous residents "a strong determination . . . not to cross over to their reservation. . . . I informed them that they must go over or they should receive nothing. Finally they obeyed my wishes and those of the head chief." Removal, however, could not only not prevent war but might actually lead to it; Henry Yesler and several other Seattleites, for example, warned that forcing Indians onto the reservations "was to all appearance tantamount to a declaration of war against them."[18]

But many did not leave, and, in fact, when the Battle of Seattle finally came, it was Indians who saved the day and the settlement. On the eve of the conflict, several hundred Native people remained in and immediately around the town, including Curley, who had close connections both with Henry Yesler and with Leschay (Leschi), a Nisqually militant who was allegedly organizing the attack. Curley met with Leschay to call for peace, but the warrior would not be swayed. And so, along with several other Duwamish people and a number of white men who lived with Indian women, Curley brought warning of the attack to the settlers, giving them just enough time to make haste to the tiny blockhouse. Connections between settlers and Native people, forged through everyday life, had saved Seattle. (Leschay would be hanged in 1858 for the murder of an American soldier, a highly controversial punishment that divided settler opinion and ultimately resulted in Leschay's unofficial exoneration in 2004.)[19]

Despite the role that "friendlies" had played in mitigating the attack by "hostiles" on Seattle, once the smoke had cleared, settler leaders quickly labeled all Indians potentially dangerous and renewed their efforts to get Indian people out of town. For settlers unfamiliar with the complicated alliances and enmities that linked indigenous communities in Puget Sound, segregation seemed the way to proceed, especially with territorial newspapers warning that "the savage war-whoop, as it were, [is] at the doors of every town and settlement within our borders." But it was as difficult a task now as before the attack. In July 1856, for example, Henry Yesler, now Indian agent for the Seattle area, reported to Governor Stevens that a number of Native people were fishing, clamming, and harvesting berries at Salmon Bay. Yesler also wrote of two Indian families who were still in the "off-limits" area of Lake Washington because one of their men, mortally wounded by a faulty musket, wanted to die and be buried on his *"illahee."* Meanwhile, George Paige, another Indian agent, complained that Doc Maynard had been treating Native people like Seeathl's churchgoing sister Sally and filling prescriptions for them without first applying to Paige for authorization.

Their faith in traditional medicine shaken by epidemics, some indigenous people saw visiting American doctors as a way to stay alive. (That is, if they could get past Duwamish Valley settler Luther Collins, who shot at Seattle-bound Indians so often that it merited a letter of complaint from one naval commander to Governor Stevens.)[20]

Work remained the primary reason Native people stayed in town after the attack, and Paige complained about this issue more than any other. His threats to withhold government rations from Indians living in town fell flat, as they were "mostly in the employ of whites, consequently etc. do not require feeding." The source of the problem, Paige wrote, was the "intermedling" businessmen who needed workers; Doc Maynard was particularly guilty of having "tampered" with the agent's charges. This was ironic, considering that Maynard had complained about the very same issue only two months earlier when he briefly served as an Indian agent. While overseeing the relocation of Seattle's indigenous residents to remote West Point in the late summer of 1856, Maynard was confronted by Henry Yesler, who "wanted a portion of them to work for him & it would cause him much trouble to go to the said encampment after them." Enlisting the support of Arthur Denny and other town leaders, Yesler convinced many of the Indians to stay put and encouraged others to come in from the Lake Washington backcountry. Those who did follow Maynard's orders, referred to by Yesler and Arthur Denny as "fools," struggled through a series of brutal winter storms on the exposed and isolated spit. The reservations were no better. In November 1856, an Army captain at the Muckleshoot Agency in the Cascade foothills wrote to his superiors on behalf of Duwamish headman William that "on the reservation, they were furnished with a little flour daily by the Indian Agent, Page [sic], that they could get no clams there, and the consequence was that many died of hunger, and unless a number had gone to their old ground to procure Salmon, they should all have died on the reservation." The point had been made: life in town was better for Indians, just as Indians in Seattle were often better for the town.[21]

By the end of 1856, it was clear that agents' efforts to vacate indigenous settlements in and around Seattle had not worked. Four separate bands of Native people remained in the Seattle vicinity at the end of the year. One small group of thirty or so, under the leadership of a man known to settlers as Cultus ("Worthless") Charley, was camping just north of town along the beach, and more than a hundred remained directly across the bay at Herring's House. Meanwhile, Curley's band of forty had settled in behind Mother Damnable's in the heart of town. And even Native people who had gone to the reservations would return, if only seasonally; by midsummer of 1857, some three hundred Indians were camped at the mouth of the Duwamish River opposite Seattle, likely at an ancient settlement and stockade called Little-Bit-Straight Point.[22]

By not moving, Native people continued both to play a central role in Seattle's fledgling economy and to vex many of their non-Indian neighbors, and the tensions between these two facts were expressed in a series of policies enacted in Seattle during the 1860s. The first came in 1865, when Seattle officially incorporated. Among the first ordinances passed was one decreeing that "no Indian or Indians shall be permitted to reside, or locate their residences on any street, highway, lane, or alley or any vacant lot in the town of Seattle." But it also demanded that "all persons having in their employ any Indian or Indians within the corporate limits of said town shall provide lodgments or suitable residences for the said Indians during the time of said employment, on, or immediately attached to their own places of residence." Signed by Charles Terry, Ordinance No. 5 tried to codify a middle road between segregation and integration. Set alongside ordinances dealing with taxes, sidewalks, and magistrate fees, the "Removal of Indians" ordinance—which was really only about the removal of certain kinds of Indians and the retention of others—highlighted just how central Indians were to urban life on Puget Sound.[23]

A second ambivalent document appeared a year later, in 1866, in the form of a petition protesting a proposed reservation for Duwamish Indians along the Black River south of Seattle, the "inside" place that gave the Duwamish their name. Citing that the sixteen Native families living there had been "justly and kindly protected" by the settlers, the 156 signatories—virtually every white man in King County—argued that a reservation would be an "injury . . . to the quiet and flourishing settlements along the Black and Duwamish rivers." Moreover, it would be "unnecessary to the aborigines and injurious to your constituents." Indigenous people working in town or living along the river were one thing; for Arthur and David Denny, Henry Yesler, Doc Maynard, and the other petitioners, the imposition of a reservation close to Seattle was quite another. The settlers preferred their own system of managing Indian-white relations, and so the proposed reservation was never established, an outcome that would have significant consequences for Duwamish legal status decades later.[24]

The absence of a federal government capable of consistently enforcing its own Indian policies, along with the necessity of Indian labor, meant that the people of Seattle—settler and indigenous alike—had to craft their own strategies for dealing with each other in the first years of the town's existence. Men like George Paige tried to enforce reservation policy, while others like Henry Yesler actively thwarted it, and still others like Doc Maynard seemed to change strategy depending on their circumstances. Meanwhile, some indigenous people like Seeathl went along with the treaties and left Seattle, while others like his sister Sally insisted on continuing to come to town. And still others such as Leschay were driven by the American government's proposals to try to burn the settlers' urban outpost to the ground.

In later years, it would be this last indigenous strategy that would most commonly be used to explain why Seattle seemed to stall in the years after the "Indian War." Arthur Denny, for example, painted a bleak picture of the Battle of Seattle's long-term effects, noting that "those who remained . . . were so discouraged, and so much in dread of another outbreak, that they were unwilling to return to their homes in the country . . . as a consequence it was years before we recovered our lost ground to any great extent." Certainly, burned homesteads on the outskirts of town had frightened some settlers away, but other forces—the Fraser River gold rush, an economic depression, the Civil War, and the lack of a railroad—did more to retard Seattle's growth during the 1850s and 1860s than the brief indigenous uprising. And in fact, much of the growth that did take place during those lean years was thanks to

Indian labor. In the form of logs shipped, fish caught, laundry washed, and mail delivered, Native people had kept Seattle from becoming yet another failed urban vision. But even as the "woods thronged with Indians" faded into clear-cuts and memories, indigenous people remained a threat to many Bostons' visions of urban destiny—if not from outside Seattle, then from within it.[25]

S EATTLE MADE ITS TELEVISION DEBUT during the Vietnam War, when *Here Come the Brides* first aired on 25 September 1968. With its theme song claiming "the bluest skies you've ever seen are in Seattle," *Brides* fictionalized one of Seattle's most beloved stories—the importation of dozens of white women to Seattle during and just after the Civil War—for a national audience. It was inspired by the story of Asa Shinn Mercer, twenty-five years old and the newly elected president of the territorial university. Of all his accomplishments, Mercer is most remembered as the entrepreneur who brought eleven unmarried women to the men of Seattle in 1864. Mostly Unitarians from the industrial town of Lowell, Massachusetts, the women, who would come to be known as "Mercer Girls," either married white bachelors or became schoolteachers. Lauded for his effort, Mercer brought a second installment, of thirty-four "girls," in 1866. Their story, fraught with just the right mix of adventure and romance, has been part of Seattle's place-story ever since. The 1960s television version was a balm against the growing horror of televised war in Southeast Asia, and in the 1860s, the real Mercer Girls were a balm as well, not against the horrors of that decade's own terrible war, but against something that seemed more immediately threatening to many settlers: the mixed-race world of Seattle Illahee.[26]

When he went to the cities of the East seeking young women, Asa Mercer went with a blessing in the form of a letter of recommendation from William Pickering, Washington territorial governor. Both Mercer and Pickering saw this as a missionary enterprise; in a circular distributed ahead of his visits, Mercer cautioned that "we only wish a class of emigrants who will improve the religion, morals, and tone of society in the T[erritory]." Mercer, and by proxy certain elements of Seattle society, were not interested in recruiting the East's urban rabble; rather, they wanted upstanding young women who could serve as social housekeepers, transferring the civilizing institutions of marriage and education to the savage West. As women signed on, the travails ahead worried many of their families; some wrote letters describing the "ignorance, coarseness, and immorality" of Seattle and claiming that Washington Territory was "the last place in the world for women." In a sense, they were right: Seattle was a far cry from Lowell or New York. When those first eleven women disembarked from the sloop *Kidder* on 16 May 1864, they joined an ongoing struggle to establish urban order, and not surprisingly in Seattle Illahee, indigenous people were at the center of the debate. What was at stake, at least in the minds of some Seattleites, was the town's very survival.[27]

As he traveled through New England and New York, Mercer described the challenges American civilization faced in the Northwest. He was particularly concerned about relations between white men and Indian women, which purportedly threatened the moral tone of a place where, according to one settler, "it required a combination of all the towns . . . to muster enough white women to make up three of four sets at a dance." With those demographics, the companionship of Native women, like the labor of Native people more generally, was part of everyday life in Seattle and had been since the town's beginning. The story of early Seattle is the story of intimate encounters. "Indian Jennie," a niece of Seeathl, married African American settler John Garrison "according to the Indian custom" in the 1850s, around the time that Matthew Bridges married his Native wife, Mary, who had been born at Little Crossing-Over Place. Rebecca FitzHenry was born in town to a white father and Duwamish mother in 1862. Six years later, the Duwamish woman Kalaeetsa gave birth to her son Charles, whose father was settler Michael Kelly. Mill owner Henry Yesler recalled how many unmarried white men working in local sawmills had Native women as companions, and Yesler himself had fathered a child named Julia with the fifteen-year-old daughter of Curley, despite the fact that his wife, Sarah, was still alive and well and living in Ohio. Through these new relations, a whole generation of mixed-race children called Seattle their *illahee* by the 1860s.[28]

For Asa Mercer and others, this was a dire problem in need of fixing. Minister's wife Catherine Blaine wrote home in 1853, for example, about the doomed marriage of a settler named Joe Foster to Betsy, the grand-daughter of Seeathl. Infamous for being "unkind" to his wife, Foster's behavior eventually led Betsy to hang herself in their small house in town. Her Indian relatives demanded the body for burial, while Foster pleaded with settlers to allow her to be interred in the town cemetery. They acquiesced, but Blaine's husband refused to officiate at the funeral, which was attended only by a few "squaw men" and their Native com-panions. "Now, what a situation he is in," Catherine Blaine penned to her kin back East, "with his little half-breed child and despised by whites and hated by the Indians. . . . He is, I believe, the son of a minister and well brought up." Blaine's portrayal of the Foster family's tragedy is telling. While clearly identifying Foster's abuse as the proximal cause of Betsy's suicide, it also hinted at a deeper problem in the minds of many Seattleites. On an urban frontier with few white women, settler men could be "tempted" into liaisons with indigenous women, and even a minister's son could be dragged down into the chaos that misce- genation brought. In another letter, Blaine bemoaned "the degradation men bring on themselves" in Seattle through their relationships with Native women, who were "but little better than hogs in human shape." The children of such unions were a problem as well in the eyes of some Bostons; settler and historian Charles Prosch condemned mixed-race couples for "giving birth to a class of vagabonds who promised to become the most vicious and troublesome element in the population." The situation seemed to threaten the whole region; according to mis-sionary Charles Huntington, race mixing cast a pall of "moral dark-ness" over Puget Sound, against which the Mercer Girls shone as beacons of light.[29]

Asa Mercer's importation of white women was just one means of rectifying the problem; the law was another. In 1855 the territorial leg-islature had passed the Color Act, which voided solemnized marriages between whites and Indians in Washington State. Three years later, that law was amended to nullify all *future* interracial marriages as well, and in 1866 the legislature would enact a new Marriage Act denying even common-law legitimacy to indigenous-white relationships. Meanwhile, Superintendent of Indian Affairs W. W. Miller published an editorial in the *Washington Standard* in 1861 calling for an end to the "degrading" practice of "open prostitution and concubinage" between settlers and Indians, which was "so utterly subversive of good order." Revealing that there were also economic motives behind such a call for order, the 1866 Legitimacy Act barred mixed-race children from inheriting their father's estate if children existed from a previous marriage to a white woman. Unless white control of land and political power was protected by legislative means, many proponents of miscegenation laws feared that thousands of acres would be handed down to a generation of "mongrels" and that the "half-breed vote" would prove an embarrassment to ambitions toward statehood. (During his tenure in the territorial legislature, for example, Arthur Denny himself would advocate tirelessly against giving mixed-heritage people the vote.) For all their scope and number, though, the laws were often difficult to enforce; historian Charles Prosch complained that during the 1860s and 1870s it was difficult to find jurors and attorneys who did not have Indian family members and who were not therefore "in sympathy with the delinquents." Just as the presence of Indians thwarted some settlers' urban visions, everyday life in Seattle Illahee resisted the "civilizing" efforts of racist laws.[30]

As moralizers fretted and lawmakers legislated, life went on in Seattle Illahee, including at the namesake Illahee itself. Opened in 1861 by John Pinnell, who had previously run brothels on San Francisco's Barbary Coast, the Illahee appeared the same year that Superintendent Miller's miscegenation editorial appeared in the local press. It was one of the largest buildings in Seattle, with a dance floor, a long bar, and a series of private rooms. Described in the 1870 census as "Hurdy-Gurdies," the Indian women employed there (few if any of them from local tribal communities) were also called "sawdust women" after the Illahee's location on the fill that had obliterated Little Crossing-Over Place and its lagoon. One typically pious memoir described "bawdy houses" and "squaw brothels" resounding with the "the frantic cries of those whose sin had brought them to the verge of madness and despair," suggesting that such institutions were well known even to those who would never consider darkening their doors.[31]

On the streets and alleys south of Mill Street, the mad houses (another nickname for establishments like the Illahee), saloons, and gambling parlors of Seattle were known collectively as the Lava Beds, a name with both infernal and libidinal connotations. In Seattle's new place-story, the "sawdust women" were the antitheses to the "Mercer Girls," and the mad houses stood in opposition to the orderly world north of Mill Street. Even the landscape reflected the difference: prim houses among cleared woods on the hills versus shanties on the sopping tideflats. At the same time, the Lava Beds fueled the urban economy, and despite all their moral outrage, critics of the Illahee lived in a town whose growth was driven by the engines of "moral darkness." Asa Mercer, John Pinnell, and "their" women represented a kind of urban symbiosis; after all, it was not far from one side of Mill Street to the other.

Never mind symbiosis, though: to the enforcers of moral authority in Seattle, the Lava Beds and the people who frequented them were threats to urban order. For newspaper editors, Christian religious leaders, and others, the presence of Indians in Seattle seemed to threaten not just the town's moral fiber but its very existence. Native people and the settlers who "sided" with them—for this struggle was very definitely perceived as having two sides—were portrayed as having the potential to quite literally destroy Seattle. Two vectors of destruction, almost apocalyptic in their scope, were of particular concern: disease and fire. In the minds of many influential Seattleites, both contagion and conflagration had their origins—and scapegoats—in the town's mad houses and sawdust women. Long after the Battle of Seattle, it seemed that indigenous people could still sack the place.

The earliest extant text printed in Seattle, dating from 1872, is a handbill warning of an impending visitation by the dread smallpox, which remained a potent reality in Puget Sound a century after its first terrible appearance. This was especially true in the filthy, congested cities Americans and Canadians had built. In the early 1860s, for example, another wave of Comes Out All Over had traveled from town to town, arriving in Seattle from San Francisco via Victoria, British Columbia.

As before, indigenous communities bore the brunt of the microbes, which killed hundreds (if not thousands) of Indians in 1862 alone. Native people were at a loss as to how to stop it. Settler Joseph Crow, for example, recalled the unsuccessful efforts of a Native doctor to heal patients in a house at Front and King Streets on the Lava Beds during an outbreak in 1864—after which the doctor, his skills now seen as useless, disappeared. But if Indians were the primary victims of epidemics, they were also the primary scapegoats. Between the lines of the handbill warning of disease lay powerful ideas about race, sex, and urban destiny.[32]

In January 1876, for instance, two Native women died of smallpox in Seattle. What to us seems like a small outbreak inspired the *Seattle Daily Intelligencer* to decry a much more pressing issue: the traffic in "miserable prostitutes" by men like the "vile wretch" who had brought the two women from Victoria. And so when a Native woman died of smallpox in a building south of Mill Street and another was found to be infected, the press placed the blame squarely on the residents of the Lava Beds and their supposed moral failings:

It is not generally deemed advisable to mention the presence of this loathsome disease in a city, but we believe that to be . . . an injustice to the public, who should be seasonably apprised of contagion in any quarter and thus be enabled to guard against it. Aside from this, we have another reason for alluding to the subject, and that is to call immediate attention to the necessity of our city authorities taking prompt steps to provide for the care of other cases, which must occur from exposure to this, and to adopt some stringent regulations relative to allowing any Indians from British Columbia and elsewhere, to be landed at this port, or to visit or reside in this city. As yet nothing has been done in the way of preventing these filthy animals from visiting our city at will, and bringing . . . what may become a pestilence in our midst.

Adding "beastly squaws" and "filthy animals" to a racist lexicon already inhabited by "sawdust women" and "squaw men," the editorial also posed a central question about urban progress: were Seattle's legal and medical establishments mature enough to deal with this crisis? Law enforcement were still in its infancy and Bostons still regularly died during epidemics; those facts, combined with still-fresh memories of vast mortality among the Indians, put very real fear in the hearts of settlers. If ecological imperialism—the introduction of new species like smallpox to new worlds like Salt Water—had made Seattle's founding possible, the fear now was that it could unmake it as well.[33]

In response to this new outbreak, the city council ordered the mayor to pass laws preventing the spread of contagion to other Seattleites. If the official urban powers could not deal with the problem, the *Daily Intelligencer* warned, other forces might be brought to bear. Concerned citizens, the paper suggested, might, "regardless of our authorities so-called, take the matter in their own hands and adopt that vigorous course in the premises which is needed." The heated rhetoric of the *Daily Intelligencer* reflected the near hysteria that swept Seattle during smallpox visitations. In March 1877, for example, some "evil disposed person" raised the standard of contagion, a yellow flag, in the window of a tenement on Mill Street. The paper described what happened next: "several timid persons . . . plunged off the sidewalk into the mud, and shied away like young fillies in their first hurdle." Even a false alarm, as this turned out to be, could disrupt town life.[34]

Meanwhile, real outbreaks continued. In May 1877, Mayor Gideon Weed, a physician by training, received a report of smallpox at Salmon Bay. He went to investigate and discovered that one Native woman had already died. Her relatives had buried her, burned her clothing and bedding, and then "quit the locality," but Weed located them the next day along the Duwamish and had them placed under armed guard in a "pest house" on the ridge between Seattle and Lake Washington. Their fate is lost to history, but the incident was a great boost to the reputation of Mayor Weed, who was lauded in the press as having done "much more than could even have been asked or expected of him in that official capacity." It also inspired a new policy: during smallpox outbreaks, the police would prevent all Indians from entering Seattle "so far as is practicable." But quarantines and exclusion did not prevent Native communities from carrying more than their share of smallpox's burden. In the twelve months leading up to July 1877, for example, there were eighteen cases of the disease in Seattle, twelve white and six Indian; nine of the whites recovered while only one Indian did. More indigenous people living in and around Seattle died in the next twelve months; the encampment at Smith's Cove was hit particularly badly. Settlers discovered a number of Indian bodies there, buried in shallow graves with their broken guns. Not long after, the remains of a man identified as "the son of Old Moses" were found jammed in a trunk north of town, spurring another round of vaccinations among settlers who "may have fooled around the tainted spot." Although smallpox was heading into decline as a major cause of mortality among both Indians and settlers, it remained on many Bostons' minds in the late 1870s as one of the gravest dangers presented by indigenous people in the urban landscape.[35]

Smallpox was one danger; fire was another. In the nineteenth century, fire was perhaps the ultimate urban fear: again and again, cities throughout the industrializing world had experienced devastating fires that often changed the course of their history in profound ways. In Seattle Illahee, fears of fire combined with anxieties about Indians to spawn a second apocalyptic discourse. In short, many settlers—and in particular, those in charge of the newspapers—were convinced that Native people were going to burn the town down. One 1878 editorial, for example, described the Lava Beds as a "tinder box, all primed and charged as it were, and ready to explode without a moment's warning in a wholesale conflagration." After a "narrow escape" in September, the *Daily Intelligencer* posited that "in time of peace it is best to prepare for war" and called for the building of water tanks and the hiring of night watchmen to patrol the Lava Beds and Indian camps. But for some, the best way to deal with the fire danger was simply to get rid of the Native encampments on the flats near Main Street. Not only were their inhabitants "an element too indecent to be tolerated within the city limits," said one editorial, but their bonfires threatened the "whole business portion of town." "There is also an old 'siwash' shanty situated further down the reef, and near the old Pinnell house," the article continued, "which should be razed to the ground and occupants driven off to the reservation where they belong." The author then demanded that the chief of police take responsibility for keeping Indians out of the city; if he did not, the result was sure to be catastrophic. Once again, the danger was not just material; it was also moral. Never mind that other Native people lived in town as family members and employees; it was these "threats" who warranted the most public attention and who became an integral part of the young city's new place-story.[36]

In the end, neither of the fires that swept Seattle—one in 1879 and the "Great Fire" of 1889—had anything to do with Indians. The first started in a middle-class hotel, and the second, which destroyed most of the business district, began in a cabinetmaker's shop. Other fires, meanwhile, targeted Indian people. On the night of 7 May 1878, for example, someone burned down the Illahee. The *Daily Intelligencer* celebrated the blaze, which "swept off a fusty obstruction to progressive improvements in that quarter." "Citizens and firemen stood about watching the fire," one settler recalled, noting that "not a pint of water was thrown upon the fire, nor an effort made to save any part or article." Throughout Puget Sound, laws and torches became weapons in the battle between two urban orders, one symbolized by the Mercer Girls and the other by the Lava Beds. In the decades to come, two competing urban visions—an "open town" that actively encouraged its red-light district and a "closed town" with zero tolerance for vice—remained at the core of Seattle politics. What would be forgotten in the future, though, was that such debates had their roots in earlier conflicts over the role of Native people in town life and over who belonged in this new place called Seattle.[37]

SOMETIME IN THE 1870S, a Chinese man named Ling Fu was brought before Judge Cornelius Hanford in Seattle's courthouse, accused of not having the proper citizenship papers. Facing deportation, Ling Fu argued that he did not need to carry papers: he had been born on Puget Sound. To test him, Judge Hanford quickly shifted his inquiry into Chinook Jargon, which had become nearly as common as Whulshootseed or English in Puget Sound country. "Ikta mika nem? Consee cole mika?" (What is your name? How old are you?), he demanded of Ling, who in turn replied, "Nika nem Ling Fu, pe nika mox tahtlum pee quinum cole" (My name is Ling Fu, and I am twenty-five years old). Clearly surprised, the judge responded,

"You are an American, sure, and you can stay here." He then turned to the bailiff and decreed, "Ling Fu is dismissed."[38]

Ling Fu's brief trial symbolizes the ways in which settlers—Boston, Chinese, and others—had been transformed by their life in Seattle Illahee. Accounts of Seattle's "village period" are full of settlers speaking Chinook Jargon and sometimes even Whulshootseed; of white men and women learning indigenous subsistence practices from their Native neighbors and employees; and of people from places like Illinois and Ireland, Gloucester and Guangzhou, learning to accommodate Indians' insistence on participation in urban life. Nearly thirty years after Seattle's founding, Native people were still in town, and their participation in urban life had changed the Bostons as well. The mad house known as the Illahee might have been destroyed, but the larger Seattle Illahee, in which indigenous lives were woven into the urban fabric, remained, even as Seattle stood perched on the brink of an urban revolution.

4 / Mr. Glover's Imbricated City

I N THE SPRING OF 1878, the *Seattle Daily Intelligencer* announced that a certain Mr. Glover, after making sketches the previous winter, had completed a drawing of Seattle "supposed to be taken from a considerable elevation." According to the newspaper, the resulting bird's-eye view of the town was "at once a map and a picture," portraying "every street, public building and private residence . . . with extraordinary accuracy." Nearly three feet wide, the drawing included not just the city but its surroundings, "Lakes Washington and Union basking in the summer sunlight, and the Cascade range towering over all." The *Daily Intelligencer* also reported that Glover and his business partner planned to embark on a campaign to print and distribute lithographs of the panorama, to specific ends:

To those who subscribe liberally a very liberal allotment of pictures will be made, and as they convey a truthful and accurate portrait of our city and harbor, they will prove invaluable to friends afar off anxious to know what Seattle is like. To property owners the picture will also prove of the greatest value for circulation amongst investors. There are hundreds of capitalists who would be only too glad to know of so genial a clime and so many natural advantages for a commercial city, and where they could invest their money in good paying railroads and real estate. The promoters of the view should be encouraged to perfect their arrangements immediately, as the city never needed the picture more than at the present time.

In an era of intense competition among young northwestern cities, Glover's portrait and its counterparts representing Port Townsend, Tacoma,

Portland, and other towns played critical roles in urban image making and in the pursuit of immigration and investment.[1]

But panoramic city views from the nineteenth century usually bore little resemblance to the actual places they marketed. Instead, in the words of one urban historian, they "depart from reality so as to emphasize and exaggerate order, progress, prospects for future unlimited growth, and other themes dear to the hearts of urban boosters." Thus, one might expect Seattle's 1878 portrait to be a vision of the city as it wished itself to be: a pastoral landscape surrounding an orderly grid of streets and a bustling harbor, with little evidence of streets filled with thigh-deep mud, stump-cursed lots, noxious effluents from mills and canneries, or undesirable populations. True to the genre, the 1878 panorama did offer a pleasant, idealized image of Seattle that gave little indication of muck, clear-cuts, fish guts, or Chinese boarding houses. But look closely: there, along the waterfront, among the steamers and the tall ships, a small flotilla of dugout canoes approaches a Native encampment on the shoreline at the heart of the city. Glover's bird's-eye-view Indians were matter-of-fact parts of the urban landscape, neither elided nor elevated. And in fact, as their inclusion in Glover's urban imagination suggests, real Indian people still had a place in Seattle's social and economic life in 1878. Despite the Bostons' efforts to craft boundaries between Indians and settlers through laws, lynch mobs, and torches, Seattle remained a landscape where Indians and settlers lived alongside each other, their lives still woven tightly together.[2]

When Charles Kinnear and his parents and siblings arrived a few months after Glover unveiled his panorama, they saw this shared landscape firsthand. After buying a salmon from a Native vendor for five cents through the window of their room in the Occidental Hotel, Kinnear and his brother went out to explore their new home. They soon came across an Indian encampment with canoes pulled ashore and racks of salmon eggs curing over small fires, stretching for more than three blocks along the waterfront. As the boys watched, more canoes arrived "in a constant stream," filled with freshly caught coho salmon, and the indigenous men commenced to play *slahal,* the "bone game" of strategy and sleight of hand known throughout the Northwest.

Just beneath our station on the high bank were sixty-three long-haired, nude Indians (all their clothes in one pile) sitting in two lines facing each other, boards on their laps, stones in their hands beating the boards as they sang. . . . In the middle of each line was an Indian Chief with nothing on but a big red handkerchief around his neck. In one hand was a pair of carved bones which—placed under the handkerchief—were changed from one hand to the other, the closed fists then swinging outward, again under the handkerchief, back and forth, and the opposing chief designated the hand supposed to be holding the bones. Both hands were then thrown upward, the bones going from the hand not guessed, and the score keep deposited a stone indicating the loss. The bones then went to the opposite chief who made his trial. Bye and bye all arose, the losing side sneaking along the beach to their wigwams . . . the stack of clothes divided into as many piles as there were victorious Indians.

Thus the Kinnear boys, who would later become two of Seattle's most prominent citizens, encountered the urban indigenous frontier of Seattle Illahee, where fine hotels existed alongside racks of curing salmon roe and where a growing urban skyline contrasted with an old-fashioned bone game on the cobbles in front of it.[3]

In Whulshootseed there is a word, *yiq,* that describes the process of working designs of bear grass, maidenhair fern, or wild-cherry bark onto the stunning woven baskets for which Duwamish, Lake, and Shilshole women were renowned. Imbrication, as anthropologists have named this process in English, is by nature forceful, with deer-bone awls pressing into watertight cedar bark or spruce root to create images—mountain ranges, men, rain—passed down through generations of weavers. But the word has a second meaning as well; *yiq* can also describe the process of working something into a tight place or, as one elder described it, "worrying" something into place. What an apt metaphor, then, for the process by which the urban and indigenous worlds interacted within the landscape framed by Glover's drawing, with Native and Boston places and peoples woven together in a shared geography, with a weave that was often disturbingly tight. Seattle was an imbricated place.[4]

It was also a place on a threshold. Before 1880, many indigenous people with roots in the landscape that was becoming Seattle had remained there, continuing to pursue subsistence activities and traditional cultural practices in and around town. After 1880, the remaining Duwamish, Lake, and Shilshole people would face increasing pressures to leave the city, both because of Seattle's sudden expansion around the turn of the century and because of federal allotment policy that encouraged them to move to area reservations. Meanwhile, a new kind of Native community would take shape in the city. Indigenous people from beyond Puget Sound, having occasionally visited Salt Water in the past, would now make Seattle part of an annual cycle of migration, leading to the formation of a multiethnic urban Indian community outnumbering the local indigenous population. The year 1880 was also a turning point in the rhetorical place of Native people in white Seattle's civic consciousness. Despite their portrayal as markers of urban disorder, real Indians played an important role in daily life during the "village period." But in the urban revolution that would take place between 1880 and 1930, actual Native people would be overshadowed by symbolic Indians in Seattle's urban imagination. The matter-of-fact canoes on Glover's waterfront would be replaced by imagined savages, noble or otherwise, and Indian images would receive far more attention than Indian people. The moment captured by Mr. Glover holds elements of both the past and the future, weaving together two periods in Seattle's urban Indian story.[5]

On the ground, the warp and woof of Native and Boston lives created a shared landscape. Not just on Seattle's waterfront but throughout the young city, along the rivers and shorelines around it, and just over the encircling hills, Seattle Illahee was growing, and the shared world that characterized the village period remained part of daily life. Nowhere is this clearer than in that record of all but the most invisible lives: the federal census. As intrepid enumerators moved through Seattle and its environs in the spring and summer of 1880, just two years after Mr. Glover unveiled his drawing, they captured in their forms and tables some of the details behind those canoes pulling up to the lithographed beach. They gave voices, if only muffled ones, to Native people who called Seattle home, and their records, along with other accounts of this moment in Seattle's history, highlight the diversity of Native experiences within the urban weave and provide a glimpse into the complexities of a developing urban Indian population.[6]

In the 1880 census, Indians tend to appear in groups, suggesting that attempts to create spatial boundaries between whites and Natives, if not successful in banishing Indians from the city altogether, had at least resulted in a handful of small enclaves within Seattle's urban geography. One such enclave existed along the waterfront near the city's center and was home to several families of local indigenous people. John and his wife, Stosach, lived with the elderly Goleeaspee; the men both fished for a living, while Stosach was a washerwoman. Samson, another fisherman, lived with his wife, Julia, while their neighbor Moses (likely the man whose son had died of smallpox three years before, his body discovered in a tree trunk on the outskirts of town) hunted to support his wife, Quitsalitsa, and their daughters, Julia and Amelia. The best-known resident of this enclave was Kikisebloo, or "Princess Angeline," the eldest daughter of Seeathl and mother of Betsy, the woman who had committed suicide to escape her husband's abuse back in the 1850s. Together, these families represented the continued presence of local indigenous people in an urbanizing landscape, who combined traditional resource use with opportunities afforded by the new urban economy. One Seattle resident recalled Indian traders and vendors in the 1870s, writing of "many Indian canoes landing at the foot of Seneca Street and Madison Street, and many Indian women [who] brought us 'oolalies' [berries] and clams and mallard ducks." The small settlement where Kikisebloo and the others lived was one site for these activities, allowing local Native people to maintain connections to places and resources that reflected pre-urban patterns of settlement.[7]

Meanwhile, on the tidelands just south of Yesler's sawmill and the Lava Beds, another small enclave of Indians reflected a growing pattern in Seattle. At the beginning of the 1880s, the Puget Sound hops industry was reaching international prominence, thanks in part to a devastating blight in Europe. In a seasonal circuit that would become part of Seattle's urban cadence in the years to come, Native people from British Columbia, Alaska, and elsewhere in Washington Territory traveled to the fields of hops ripening in the valleys around Seattle and typically included a stay in Seattle. Listed mostly as laborers (with the women listed, significantly, as "keeping camp" rather than keeping house), the people the enumerator found on the tideflats were likely partway through this seasonal round. Indian Wallace lived with Indian Jennie, Indian Jack lived with Indian Sallie, and Indian Peter and Indian Annie shared their camp with their son Indian Sam; all were from British Columbia. Nearby, young indigenous Alaskan women named Indian Kitty and Indian Rose camped with Kitty's infant son, Indian Tommy, while a camp close by sheltered Indian Jennie and Indian John. Not unlike the "Chinaman John" system of nomenclature that rendered Asian immigrants anonymous in many historical records, this "Indian" naming practice relegated many Native people—particularly those not connected to local families or communities—to anonymity, lacking even a tribal designation. But their origins far from Seattle suggested that a new kind of urban development, the creation of a far-reaching Indian hinterland, was under way.[8]

And, of course, there were the Lava Beds. Here, mixed-race households of white men and Indian women existed among the saloons, brothels, and Chinese hostels. Two such households were those of cook William Milton, who lived with British Columbia Native Mary Murphy, and sailor George Hill, whose wife, "Indian Mary," also hailed from the north. As Milton's and Hill's occupations suggest, many of the white men in such relationships were on the lower rungs of the urban economy. Sometimes, economic circumstances required mixed-race couples to share homes, as unemployed laborer Thomas Scott and "Indian Jennie" did with out-of-work Canadian James Holt and Ellen Dillon, Holt's Indian-Hawai'ian partner. Others, such as Julia Lowar, the daughter of an indigenous woman from Washington Territory and a French father, who lived on the Lava Beds with Joseph Francis, a Hebridean laborer, could afford to keep their own homes. The backgrounds of couples like these also reflect patterns associated with the fur trade of previous decades; many of the men were from Canada or Scotland, while most of the women were of mixed parentage, their fathers from France, Hawai'i, Canada, or the Celtic fringe.

While some of the mixed-race households on the Lava Beds in 1880 appear to have been marriages (if only *à la façon du pays*, considering the miscegenation laws of the time), others hint at the reason this district was called the Lava Beds in the first place. Nova Scotian barkeeper Thomas Asgood, for example, rented rooms to Nancy McCarthy, the daughter of a Frenchman and a Washington Indian, and to another "Indian Mary," this one a full-blood member of an unspecified Native community. Nearby, Louisé Woolene, Annie Powers, and Maggie Murphy—all young, mixed-race women, likely from British Columbia—lived above a tavern owned by Welshman Richard Prichard and his partner, William Cheney. Nearby, twenty-five-year-old Indian Katie Hays boarded with barkeep George Behan and his bartender, Thomas Barry; and Native seventeen-year-old Nellie Hilton roomed at the establishment of German immigrants Jacob and Mattie Wirtz. Meanwhile, Cecilia Thomas, a twenty-nine-year-old woman of Hawai'ian and British Columbian Indian descent, was listed as the sole occupant of her household. While specifics about each of these women's lives are lost to history, it is quite possible that some or all of them participated, at least casually, in the sex trade for which the Lava Beds was reviled by Seattle's voices of urban order. Surely, a number of Indian women working in the sex trade were missed by the enumerators, having avoided the census taker or having been hidden by their employers. Pinnell's Illahee may have burned in 1878, but the "sawdust women"—whether prostitutes or not—were still around.

Urban Indian enclaves along the waterfront and on the Lava Beds reflected civic leaders' desires to segregate indigenous people from "respectable" settler society, but the distinction between them broke down as Native men and women went uptown to work in the homes of middle-class and elite white families. In particular, Indian women played an important role as domestic servants and live-in laborers in 1880. Throughout Seattle, enumerators found young Indian women living and working in the homes of white families. Fourteen-year-old, mixed-race Hannah Benson helped minister's wife Mary Whitworth keep house for her husband, their civil-engineer son Fred, and their daughter Etta. Meanwhile, nineteen-year-old Lois Hilderbidle, also the daughter of a white father and Indian mother, worked as a servant in the home of physicians Alvin and Herman Bagley and Herman's wife, Kitty. However, Indian servants could also be found in more modest homes: Irish laborer John Christopher and his wife, Bridget, employed fifteen-year-old boarder Lizzie Whitney, a full-blood Washington Territory Indian; and single-mother Henrietta Minks, a resident of the Lava Beds, received much-needed assistance from a British Columbian woman known as "Indian Kate." Nothing remains to illuminate why Elizabeth FitzPatrick, a young mixed-race woman, chose to live with and work for mill owner George W. Stetson's family, but we might guess: money, a bit of prestige, and a ticket off the reservation. Even a handful of young Native men took advantage of such arrangements: Willie Henry, the fourteen-year-old son of a Nova Scotian father and a local Indian mother, was living with James Carpenter and family when the enumerator came to visit in 1880.

Writing in the 1920s, Mrs. E. E. Heg, a member of the Trinity Church congregation, emphasized the importance of these Indian domestic laborers to the white women of Seattle during this time. Noting that the only kind of domestic help available in Seattle came from Native women, she pointed out that such workers freed her and other Episcopalian women to help organize Seattle's first parish. High-status Indian women, meanwhile, were sometime employed by high-status white families, as in the case of Kikisebloo, who did laundry at the parsonage of the First Presbyterian Church throughout the 1870s and whose impatience with the minister's young children became something of a running joke in town. Her regular journeys between the indigenous enclave on the waterfront and the parsonage up the hill illustrate just how permeable boundaries were between white and Native Seattle. It also suggests a certain kind of congruency between two status-conscious societies: high-class Duwamish working for high-class Boston.[9]

Indigenous fishermen, hop pickers from Alaska and British Columbia, the saloon crowd, and domestic servants—these were the roles into which Seattle's urban Indians were expected by their Boston neighbors to fit. Each category came with its own respective space on the margins of society: waterfront, tideflat, Lava Bed, laundry room. However, few spatial expressions of power are pure or complete, and elsewhere in Seattle, other Indians, and Indian women in particular, had become part of settler society, not as washerwomen or camp-keepers or Lava Bed wives, but as members of mixed-race families scattered throughout Seattle. There was Jacob Harding's wife, Lucy, the daughter of Washington Territory and British Columbia Indians, and Jennie, the British Columbian wife of German immigrant John Drummerhouse. An eight-year-old mixed-race Indian child named Hattie, perhaps adopted (or perhaps a disturbingly young house servant), lived with the logger Francis Guye and his wife, Eliza, both of them white; and Andrew Castro, sixty years old, shared a home with his twenty-two-year-old Native sister-in-law Annie and her son John, age five. The occasional marriage between a white man and a Native woman appears in King County's official records as well. The 1876 wedding between Peter Brown and an anonymous "Indian woman," Robert M. Stewart's 1878 marriage to "Helen, an Indian," and the 1881 nuptials of Louie Henry and Ellen Hatlepoh suggest that the antimiscegenation laws of the 1850s and 1860s were only haphazardly implemented. Even though enumerators' schedules and marriage records tell us little about these people, these brief glimpses of lives, and perhaps even loves, nonetheless speak to the ways that Native and settler histories had become intimately interwoven.[10]

Pioneer daughter Sophie Frye Bass recalled another mixed-race family enumerated in the 1880 census, that of John and Mary Kelly and their daughter Maria. Living in an immaculately kept little house on Fourth Avenue between Pike and Pine streets, Washington Territory–born Mary did laundry at home for her white neighbors, while Irish immigrant John was a skilled blacksmith. Maria, fourteen in 1880, was a schoolmate and friend of young Sophie Frye and other settler children, once holding a "potlatch" by handing out candy hearts bearing inscriptions such as "Do you love me?" and "Be my girl." Like Mr. Glover's bird's-eye view of Seattle, in which indigenous people were a part of everyday urban life, memories of families like these attested to the ways in which everyday relations between Indian and settler called into question those very categories. The mixed-race family of Maria Kelly was just as much a part of settler society as that of Sophie Frye.[11]

While Indian and non-Indian lives interwove at the fine-grained level of the census schedule, on a larger scale Indian and non-Indian spaces beyond the city limits were also beginning to interweave in 1880. After the slumps of the 1860s and early 1870s, Seattle at last began to grow in accordance with its founders' imaginations, leapfrogging over enclosing hills, marshes, and waterways in the late 1870s. One newspaper editor described Seattle's growth spurt in a call for any doubters to "go out over the hills to the real front of action and progress," where they would see the signs of urban development: "fires smoking in the distance on every hill, new roofs peeping out through vistas of vanishing foliage, trim garden fences routing out the old logs and debris." These changes in the landscape told "the story of extending dominion, and the beginning of the new regime of solid growth for Seattle." Residents living "on the outskirts this year," noted one observer, "find themselves next year right in town." This was no less true for Native people living in and immediately around Seattle. As the city spread across the rugged landscape between Puget Sound and Lake Washington, outlying settlements—indigenous and settler alike—were imbricated into the urban fabric.[12]

Seattle's sudden expansion in the late 1870s took place on many fronts and often uncovered glimpses into the indigenous landscape it would soon obliterate. To the south, a terrible beach road, "broken and demoralized" after each winter's rains, made its sloppy way past the oxbows and marshes of the river valley to the settlement of Duwamish, which had recently celebrated the opening of a lyceum, a sure sign that change was on the way. Not far away, county officials had chosen "one of the finest pieces of land in the county . . . over one hundred and sixty acres of land of a black alluvial character" as the site of a farm and hospital for the poor and indigent. Previously leased by Illahee entrepreneur John Pinnell to several Chinese truck farmers, the farm stood on deep shell middens created by generations of indigenous harvests, which explained the remarkably fertile soils.[13]

Meanwhile, to the north, urban outposts seemed to be springing up everywhere. In 1878 Belltown, immediately north of Seattle along Elliott Bay, boasted sixty-eight houses, one school, a grocery, and a boarding-house for shipbuilders, while more houses were under construction. As the townscape took form, builders often unearthed bodies wrapped in cedar bark, the remains of an indigenous cemetery. At Lake Union, "quite a town" now surrounded David Denny's sawmill, with close to two hundred residents. After a sidewalk was built to the lake from Seattle's northern city limit in 1879—following the route of an indigenous trail—residents expected streetcars, water lines, and "the villas of our wealthy townsmen" to follow in short order. To the northwest, families had begun clearing land around Salmon Bay in 1877, and by 1879 farms could be found along both sides of the bay, with a population "sufficiently numerous to sustain a district school." And to the northeast, along the no-longer-distant shores of Lake Washington, families began staking claims—and more importantly, moving to them—in the late 1870s, banking on an eventual canal connecting the lake with Puget Sound.[14]

Here was Seattle's first urban sprawl, and it caught both Native people and Native places in its weave. The Duwamish River offered evidence of an indigenous past in the middens at the County Farm, but it also offered evidence of an indigenous present in the form of several large indigenous settlements along its banks. In Belltown, where growth disturbed graves, living Native people camped along the beach near where longhouses had once stood amid gardens of salal. At Salmon Bay, where a dozen Shilshole families had been living in the 1850s, some still remained. Doctor Jim, "manly, fine-looking, and intelligent," according to one observer, lived at the mouth of the bay near where Hwelchteed, known to most settlers as Salmon Bay Charlie, owned ten acres. Meanwhile, in the Salmon Bay settlement itself, Alonzo Hamblet managed the West Coast Improvement Company while his Tsimshian daughter-in-law Mary concerned herself with the local church; and the Scheurmann family's ten children—along with those of other mixed-race families like the Ryersons and Tollens—helped fill the seats at the small schoolhouse. To the east on Lake Washington, Native people camped on Union Bay with the permission of settler Joe Somers, while close by, Chesheeahud, called Lake Union John, and Dzakwoos, also known as Indian Jim Zackuse, worked their respective five and ten acres at the eastern end of Lake Union. And south of there, "Indian Jack" and his wife, Eliza, owned an acre in Columbia City, a new suburb at the head of a slough along the lake.[15]

Some of these Native men and women, like Mary Hamblet or those camping in West Seattle on their way to the hop fields, were new to Seattle, themselves emigrants in search of urban opportunity. Others, like Chesheeahud and Dzakwoos, were local people with attachments to local places. These were the Indians that an 1879 *Daily Intelligencer* reported "had severed their tribal relations, taken homesteads, quit their nomadic life and gone to farming, and who didn't care to lose their places on account of unpaid taxes." Far from vanishing, these were indigenous people who had chosen to stay near traditional territories and make a go of it in an urbanizing landscape. And although they had "severed tribal relations" according to American law, they and their homes would remain important landmarks for indigenous people traveling to and from the city.[16]

However, staying in the old places was getting more and more difficult in 1880. The urban imbrication was getting tighter, as indigenous towns turned into poor farms, burial grounds became basements, and fishing sites became waterfront real estate. For some Native people, the pressures were simply too much. Doctor Jim, the healer living at the mouth of Salmon Bay, was one of these. Like many other indigenous doctors in Puget Sound, much of his social standing had been swept away by epidemics and American medical practices; unlike some, though, Doctor Jim had become fluent in English and had chosen to live close to the settlers. But things reached a breaking point for Doctor Jim one morning in 1880, when he hanged himself in his house, within sight of the old Shilshole town of Tucked Away Inside.[17]

As bad as things had gotten for Doctor Jim, the challenges facing indigenous people in and around Seattle were small in comparison to what was to come. In many ways, 1880 was a brief interlude between two dark periods in Seattle's Indian history. The chaotic violence of earlier decades had largely quieted, the epidemics had waned, and the legality of Native homesteading allowed for some semblance of independence and economic stability. But the urban ambition reflected in Mr. Glover's bird's-eye drawing of Seattle, and the changes attendant to it, were about to reach new heights, and indigenous people who had worried themselves into the tight weave of the city's rapidly urbanizing landscape would face challenges on a completely new scale. Fire, water, and iron would soon change everything.

5 / City of the Changers

W HEN OLLIE WILBUR WAS A LITTLE GIRL living on the cusp of the nineteenth and twentieth centuries, the horse and buggy ride from the Muckleshoot Reservation to Seattle was a long one and, in her words, "awful, you know—have to go uphill, downhill, we'd all get off and walk." Even so, her family went every year to visit her grandmother's brother, who lived in a ramshackle floating house near the mouth of the Duwamish. Seetoowathl—or Old Indian George, as his neighbors called him—still lived where he had been born, in a place known in his language simply as Tideflats. He shared the house with his wife, who was either "quite insane" or "the meanest old . . ." depending on whom you talked to, and he made a living by catching dogfish and rendering their oil for local sawmills. ("That's all he does, is fish, the old man," Ollie recalled.) The monotony of fishing was broken every September when Ollie and her parents came with canned berries from the foothills. Their journey linked Seetoowathl, who refused to speak English with visiting ethnographers, and his prickly wife to a reservation some thirty miles distant. Long past the treaty and the Battle of Seattle, indigenous people whose ancestors once lived in Duwamish, Shilshole, and Lake communities like Little Crossing-Over Place and Herring's House still lived in Seattle, even as many of their kin found homes far from the city.[1]

Between 1880 and 1920, however, forces were at work that would make indigenous survival in Seattle virtually impossible. During those years, the city saw its most explosive period of urban growth, which spelled disaster for Native people trying to live in traditional ways and places. By the 1920s, in fact, indigenous Seattle—the geographies and communities that predated the founding of the city—would come to an end, even if Indian Seattle would not. The wholesale transformation of the urban landscape dramatically altered indigenous subsistence practices and created a new place-story in which the "vanishing race" and the ghostly Indian haunting the city were self-fulfilling prophecies. The Indian people who remained in Seattle, meanwhile, became almost invisible as they adapted to life in a new metropolis.

According to oral tradition, Seeathl had seen this change coming. During treaty negotiations in 1855, he had warned his people to pay special attention to the Americans and their government. "You folks observe the changers who have come to this land," he told those gathered. "You folks observe them well." In calling the Americans "changers," Seeathl invoked the figure of Dookweebathl, the Changer, who had organized the chaotic landscape of deep time and made the world habitable for the human people. It was a particularly apt choice of terms. As powerful forces reshaped Seattle in the decades around the turn of the century, indigenous people found themselves caught up in a transformation of their world nearly as dramatic as those described in the ancient stories. By 1920, Seattle had become the city of a new kind of Changers.[2]

AT FIRST GLANCE, SEATTLE'S TWO most important fires seem unrelated. The first, in 1889, utterly destroyed the city's commercial district; the second, four years later, obliterated several Native longhouses along the West Seattle shoreline. In Seattle's urban mythology, the earlier conflagration is one of the city's great turning points, the phoenixlike moment from which the city rose up to become the Northwest's premier metropolis. The other is a mere historical footnote, forgotten by nearly all of Seattle's chroniclers even though it made headlines at the time. But the two stories they represent—Seattle's urban triumph and the dispossession of local indigenous people—are in fact one story. The path between a boiling pot of glue in 1889 and an arsonist's torch in 1893 represents not just the trajectory of those four years but a broader pattern: in the last two decades of the nineteenth century and the first two decades of the twentieth, indigenous people in Seattle found themselves on the losing side of urban development. Although many of the specifics of this "dispossession by degrees" are lost to the historical record, the shared context of these two fires offers insights into the seemingly inexorable, yet often invisible, marginalization of the Duwamish, Shilshole, and Lake peoples.[3]

Rudyard Kipling, imperial apologist and rhetorical bearer of the white man's burden, is an unlikely figure to appear in a history of Seattle, but he offers a graphic (if typically acerbic) description of the city just after the Great Fire of 1889. Arriving in late July as part of a transcontinental tour, he described the near-apocalyptic aftermath. "The wharves had all burned down, and we tied up where we could, crashing into the rotten foundations of a boathouse as a pig roots in high grass," he wrote. "In the heart of the business quarters there was a horrible black smudge, as though a Hand had come down and rubbed the place smooth. I know now what being wiped out means." Kipling also noted the scores of canvas tents set up among the ruins, full of men carrying on with "the lath and string arrangements out of which a western town is made."[4]

Seattle had nearly been *un*made by the terrible events of a few weeks earlier, when early in the afternoon of 6 June, a pot of glue boiled over and started a fire at Victor Clairmont's basement cabinet shop at the corner of Front and Madison. The flames rapidly spread upward and outward to surrounding wooden buildings. Thanks to brisk late-spring winds and a laughably insufficient water system, by nightfall sixty acres (thirty-three blocks), including virtually the entire business district, had burned to the ground and to the waterline. Yesler's wharf, the Lava Beds, and other Seattle institutions all disappeared into Kipling's black smudge. The fire could be seen miles away; one Snohomish Indian woman recalled seeing her older relatives cover their faces with their hands, rocking and wailing as the southern horizon glowed redly throughout the night.[5]

Seattleites moved quickly to repair the damage. As soon as the ashes cooled, business owners resumed their affairs in the canvas tents, but they expended little effort on their less seemly neighbors, many of whom had lost everything to the flames. Orange Jacobs recalled that "the fallen angels and the upper class of gamblers could take care of themselves," while other, less fortunate citizens required "careful and necessary scrutiny" to prevent the handing out of "free lunches."[6] The long-standing enmity between the people of the Lava Beds and their more strait-laced neighbors shaped responses to the disaster, but as before, the two elements of Seattle society had always existed in a symbiotic relationship. Before long, the Lava Beds had resumed activity. In fact, within months, they were more active than ever, as the Great Fire spurred a riot of urban development in the old commercial district. Wooden structures lost to the fire were replaced by ones of brick and stone, and as capital poured in to rebuild the city, so did new immigrants. For the next year, more than two thousand new immigrants arrived in Seattle every month, nearly doubling the city's population to over forty thousand people by the Great Fire's first anniversary. In terms of the built landscape, population growth, and civic self-identity, the Great Fire was a critical juncture in Seattle's urban story.

But, in fact, the Great Fire had only accelerated growth already under way. It was not the flames of a boiling glue pot but rather those inside a Northern Pacific Railroad engine that had truly sparked Seattle's great lurch toward metropolis. In 1883, the city held its Railroad Jubilee, which included a massive salmon barbecue hosted by local Indians. The Jubilee proved premature, however; the first Northern Pacific train would not arrive until June 1884, over tracks laid by some 1,400 Chinese laborers and heralded by a twenty-one-gun salute using cannon from the 1856 Battle of Seattle. Even then, service was poor, uncomfortable, and inconsistent, leading to complaints from locals and the eventual abandonment of the line by the Northern Pacific. It took yet another year for the "Orphan Road" to become a functioning railway, but when it finally did, in late 1885, it began a new wave of immigration to Seattle that had yet to peak when the city burned.[7]

Eight years later, the 7 March edition of the *Seattle Times* noted a sharp increase in the number of "red denizens" on Ballast Island on the rebuilt Seattle waterfront. Ballast Island was exactly what its name implied: a massive pile of rock, brick, and other debris dropped by ships near the foot of Washington Street. It was one of the few places in town where large groups of Indians were tolerated. On this day in 1893, ten large dugout canoes and several smaller ones, some loaded down to the waterline with furniture, tools, and trunks of clothing, had, along with their owners, attracted a "large and curious crowd of spectators." Dispatched to Ballast Island by his editors, the reporter soon learned that the canoes' occupants had been burned out of their homes on the West Seattle shoreline. According to the Indians, eight houses had been destroyed, their owners and inhabitants "turned out indiscriminately, without reference to the disposition of the Indians, who, however, took the matter without resistance." Some of the now-homeless Native people were quite elderly and had lived in West Seattle for many years, carrying monikers like West Seattle Jack, West Seattle Jim, and West Seattle Charlie to prove it. Indeed, these were the people of Herring's House, the old indigenous town, which had survived the early phases of urban development. But the Saturday before, a man named Watson, with the help of several other West Seattle residents, had started the fire that brought centuries of Herring's House's history to an end.[8]

At first glance, the Gilded Age razing of this small Native neighborhood in West Seattle seems an anomaly. The deliberate destruction of Herring's House seems more in keeping with the spasmodic violence of Seattle's early years than with the nascent progressivism of the 1890s. But the events of March 1893 were part of a larger urban process of indigenous dispossession that had begun decades before, although that process accelerated in the late nineteenth century with Seattle's metropolitan ascent.

Not long before the fire of 1893, West Seattle had still been an isolated community, separated from Seattle by Elliott Bay and the wide, muddy Duwamish estuary. By the late 1880s, its residents were clamoring for regular connections with Seattle, while Seattleites became increasingly interested in excursions to (and suburban homes on) the West Seattle peninsula, with its beaches, fresh air, and views of the waterfront and Olympic Mountains. And so on Christmas Eve 1888, the ferry *City of Seattle*, equipped to carry wagons, buggies, and cattle, began regular eight-minute passages between the two cities, subsidized by the West Seattle Land Improvement Company, itself bankrolled by San Francisco capitalists. With the new maritime connection, the company began buying and clearing land, building roads and sidewalks, and establishing a cable car line from the ferry landing to a new business district. As one observer recalled, "it was quite the thing for newcomers to ride back and forth just for the pleasure of the fresh salt air. Even retired deep-sea captains enjoyed the trip." Wharves and grain elevators near the ferry terminal soon followed, and by 1893 West Seattle was in the midst of a development boom, in no small part thanks to the population explosion after the Great Fire of 1889. Muckleshoot tribal member Gilbert King George described his mother's stories of what that had meant for the people of Herring's House:

My mother told me of the days when this area was being claimed, and play-mates' homes were destroyed for relocation purposes. I always remember because she was so puzzled by what happened to her friends' home. She got up the next day, there was a pile of ashes there. Whole families were removed. Relocated. So you have to wonder, you know, what are the mental impacts on a mother and a father, grandparents, who have to literally pick up their family and have to move.

The Great Fire of 1889 had spurred growth in West Seattle, which in turn encouraged the fiery ouster of indigenous people living in places slated for "improvement."[9]

The fire of March 1893 is unusual only in that it merited the attention of the press. Other fires, ignored in newspapers and other historical documents, continued to smolder in the memories of indigenous people who had witnessed them. Occasionally, these memories found their way into the written record. During a landmark 1920s land claims case, for example, older Duwamish Indians recalled what had happened to their villages as Seattle grew around them in the second half of the nineteenth century. Major Hamilton described how, "when the settlers came, they drove us away and then they destroy the house and even set fires to get us away from these villages." Similarly, Jennie Davis, a Lake Indian (and the daughter of Chesheeahud, the indigenous home-steader on Lake Union's Portage Bay), portrayed the transition from Native to settler residences: "Some of [the Indian houses] was gone and I see where the construction of some of the buildings." West Seattle itself was the scene of more than one fire; Sam Tecumseh, the son of one of Arthur Denny's close Indian allies, recalled the large "potlatch house" that had once stood at Herring's House along with the smaller longhouses. The result of two summers' worth of labor by nearly a score of skilled builders, the big house alone was valued in 1920s currency at around $5,000. "When the white settlers came," he told the courtroom through an interpreter, "then they took possession of [the Indians'] cleared land and also destroyed the house." These indigenous place-stories link the fire of March 1893 to a longer history in which urban development and Indian dispossession went hand in hand.[10]

Seattle's growth also caused a major shift in the urban labor pool. Gone were the days when settlers needed the work of Native people to conduct everyday town life, when Henry Yesler needed Indian men for his sawmill or white women needed Indian women to do their laundry. As more and more newcomers arrived, many indigenous people were pushed aside, their services no longer necessary. For the Duwamish man Dzakwoos, who had kept a homestead on Lake Union, the loss of work forced him to abandon his homestead and relocate to the east, where he would become part of a Native community living at Monohan on Lake Sammamish, where mill jobs remained. This community would come to be part of the modern-day Snoqualmie Tribe, and present-day tribal members understand the changing demographics and economy in and around Seattle as a key reason for the development of this new community. Snoqualmie elder Ed Davis recalled, for example, that the people at Monohan, including Dzakwoos and his extended family, "all come together when they run out of jobs."[11]

And so the refugees from Herring's House, characterized as indignant but "philosophical" by the reporter, had some decisions to make as they gathered on Ballast Island in 1893. They could move to the "lighthouse colony," a windblown squatters' encampment at West Point north of town, and some apparently did. Or they could move upriver: the area around the confluence of the Black and Duwamish rivers had been the eponymous Duwamish "inside" for centuries, and in the 1890s several Indian families still lived there, in a narrow stretch of the river valley that settlers simply called Duwamish. (The descendants of many of those people would become the modern-day Duwamish Tribe.) The refugees' third option was to go further afield and apply for an allotment of land on one of Puget Sound's reservations, such as Port Madison (later known as Suquamish), Muckleshoot, or Tulalip. For many, this last option seemed to be the safest. At a time when Indian people enjoyed few legal rights, faced discrimination and hostility from many of their non-Native neighbors, and were often forced to live at the peripheries of the new economy, land, even when held in trust, could offer security that life in and immediately around Seattle could not.[12]

Ironically, the rapid urban expansion that had fueled the fire in West Seattle, with its ferries and beach cabins, slowed soon after the community of Herring's House was razed and its members dispersed. Just a few weeks after Watson's arson, the stock market collapsed and banks began to fail across the nation. The Panic of 1893 was on. In West Seattle, the Panic led to what one observer called a "nervous breakdown": the ferries and cable car stopped running, real-estate ventures crumbled, and growth came to a standstill. The depression that followed dampened Seattle's spirits for four long years, and we might ask whether West Seattle Charlie and his neighbors might have still had homes on the shore there if only the timing had been a little different.[13]

Meanwhile, other Native people continued to live in Seattle, albeit in diminishing numbers, after the burning of Herring's House. In fact, it was those diminishing numbers that would lead to a change in the way indigenous people were portrayed in Seattle—indeed, the fact that they were portrayed at all. Whereas the workings of indigenous dispossession in the late nineteenth century rarely appear in the historical record, by the dawn of the twentieth century, Indians in Seattle—especially ones that seemed to be vanishing—were front-page news.

ON THE LAST EVENING of May 1896, Kikisebloo, the daughter of Seeathl, died of tuberculosis in her home on the Seattle waterfront. Her passing was big news in the city, where shops sold postcards of her image and where a chance encounter with the "Indian princess" was one of the highlights of the urban experience. Children sneaked into the city morgue to see her body, while undertakers argued over who had the right to bury it. When the funeral finally took place on 6 June, thousands of Seattleites lined downtown streets to watch the procession make its way to a full requiem mass at Our Lady of Good Hope. Afterward, Kikisebloo was laid to rest in Lakeview Cemetery in a canoe-shaped coffin, next to her old friend and ally Henry Yesler. Her grandson Joe Foster, whose terrorized mother had committed suicide so many years before during Seattle's "village period," was the sole Indian present.[14]

[handwritten marginal note: Consumed by white people]

Kikisebloo's life had been like Seattle's Indian history writ small. Present with her father at the Denny Party's settlement at Alki, she was closely allied with Seattle's founding families, many of whom employed her as a washerwoman. Simultaneously noblewoman and drudge, Kikisebloo elicited a wide range of reactions from her white neighbors: some revered her as a touchstone to the indigenous past (case in point her much-ballyhooed introduction to visiting U.S. president Benjamin Harrison in 1891), while others, especially young people, were more likely to throw rocks at her as she passed in the street. For her part, Kikisebloo was famous both for her loyalty to pioneer families and for throwing stones of her own (or clams or potatoes, depending on what was handy) at her tormentors. In the last years of her life, she lived in poverty on the Seattle waterfront, simultaneously watched over by solicitous society women and lampooned in the press. By the time of her death, Kikisebloo had come to represent both the "noble savage" (expressed best by the urban legend that she had brought warning of the 1856 Indian uprising to Seattle residents) and the stubborn, backward "Siwash" doomed to extinction.[15]

In the nineteenth century, Kikisebloo's life had reflected many of the contradictions inherent in Seattle's Indian story. On the eve of the twentieth century, however, her death heralded a new pattern. The presence of indigenous people in Seattle was used by white observers to craft a powerful new narrative about the inevitable disappearance of Indians from Seattle and the modern world. Native people had always been symbols in Seattle—witness the debates about vice, fire, and disease in the village period—but in earlier decades, they had also been a force to be reckoned with. As their numbers dwindled in the early twentieth century, local Indians were recast as stock characters in melodramatic stories about urban progress, representing both the inevitability of indigenous decline and the inexorable ascent of metropolitan Seattle. Here was a new place-story.

While she was by far the most celebrated of Seattle's "last" Indians, Kikisebloo was by no means the last of the last. Other Duwamish, Lake, and Shilshole people continued to live in Seattle well into the twentieth century. Some displayed a remarkable commitment to particular places. On Salmon Bay, for example, the small cedar-plank home of Hwelchteed and his wife, Cheethluleetsa, also known as Madeline, was a distinctive landmark on the shore opposite a settlement now known as Ballard. Cheethluleetsa and her husband harvested clams, salmon, and berries to sell in Ballard, using the income to purchase items from area merchants or for ceremonies held with visiting relatives. Like another Salmon Bay Indian, nicknamed Crab John, whose shouts of "salmon, ten cents" were a fond memory of many Ballard residents, Hwelchteed and Cheethluleetsa were living links between the indigenous town of Tucked Away Inside and the modern town of Ballard. Indeed, Hwelchteed portrayed himself as the hereditary headman of the Shilsholes and, as such, garnered much attention from residents and tourists alike, particularly after the death of Kikisebloo.[16]

Meanwhile, on Portage Bay at the eastern end of Lake Union, Chesheeahud and his wife, Tleebuleetsa (confusingly, also called Madeline), regularly entertained visitors from area reservations at their homestead. When Tleebuleetsa lay dying in the spring of 1906, relatives came from area reservations and elsewhere to keep vigil, and a *Seattle Post-Intelligencer* photographer captured the image of family members as they arrived at the small house on the flats of Portage Bay. In the background of the photo, the new University of Washington campus and streetcar suburbs reach to the horizon. Two supposedly separate worlds—the urban and the indigenous—were in fact the same place. (Nowhere is this clearer than at Chesheeahud and Tleebuleetsa's graves, which lie in the old section of Seattle's Evergreen-Washelli Cemetery immediately next to that of Hiram Gill, a controversial Seattle mayor who made his career playing off the bad blood between Lava Beds society and the "law and order crowd.")[17]

Hwelchteed, Chesheeahud, and their wives were relatively successful at surviving in Seattle, but other indigenous people had a harder time of it. Living among the marshy suburbs on Portage Bay was one thing; trying to eke out a living on the industrial downtown waterfront was another. In 1910, a Duwamish couple named Billy and Ellen Phillips made the headlines after a winter storm destroyed Billy's crabbing boat, their primary source of income. Identified as a nephew of Seeathl, Billy (whose Whulshootseed name was Sbeebayoo) and his wife quickly became a minor cause célèbre. The *Post-Intelligencer* printed graphic descriptions of the couple's living conditions in their cabin at the foot of Stacy Street: both were malnourished, Billy was nearly blind, and Ellen was suffering from chest pains. For some time, they had been surviving on neighbors' stale bread and on fish donated by a nearby cannery. The *Post-Intelligencer* coverage inspired a broader charity campaign aimed at not just keeping them alive but also paying for their relocation. As reporters milked the story for all it was worth, they also chronicled the process by which a skilled fisherman and his wife had been reduced to such dire circumstances. His camping places along the Puget Sound shoreline had become private property, and the new owners resented Indian trespassers. Both game and fish were harder to come by, as habitat loss, pollution, and commercial fishing took their toll. Even Billy's canoe had been lost. These factors, combined with age and ill health, had nearly spelled the end for Ellen and Billy.[18]

The struggle of the Phillips was not unique to Seattle. Throughout Puget Sound, indigenous people were finding fewer and fewer places to call their own. While the treaties of 1855 had allowed Indians to leave the reservation to hunt and fish and work, *living* off-reservation was another matter, especially as the non-Indian population continued to burgeon. Bureau of Indian Affairs agent S. A. Eliot described the situation in the 1910s:

The most serious situation among the Sound Indians is occasioned by the large number of homeless vagrants. . . . The reservations on the Sound are now all allotted and there remains a remnant variously estimated at from one to three thousand Indians who are landless and homeless. These people wander up and down the Sound, living on the beaches and constantly evicted or ordered to move on by their white neighbors. In one or two places they have established considerable villages, but they have nothing there but squatter's rights.

In the 1920s, Suquamish tribal member Charles Alexis reported seeing other Indians living in impoverished conditions on sandspits and in other marginal locations around Puget Sound in earlier years. The "lighthouse colony" at West Point, to which some of the refugees of the Herring's House arson had briefly removed, was one such place. While Alexis and Eliot had very different perspectives on these landless Native people—one as a tribal witness in a land claims case, the other as a government advocate of Indian "industrial and moral development"—they both saw Indian landlessness in urban Puget Sound as a dilemma.[19]

For many Native families still living in and around Seattle in the 1910s, allotment at Muckleshoot, Suquamish, and other reservations remained the most realistic solution to this dilemma. In their applications for allotment, Indian men and women both outlined their long connections to Tucked Away Inside and other indigenous communities, as well as to Seattle itself, and exchanged those connections for a new kind of security on the reservations. Even "Lake Union John," the man named for his place, left the city: soon after his wife's death in 1906, Chesheeahud sold his property on Portage Bay (making him one of the richest Indians in Puget Sound) and removed to the Port Madison Reservation, where he died four years later. The only reminder of his presence on the bay was the name of the plat set up on his former homestead; even today, legal descriptions of lots in the neighborhood designate them as part of "John's Addition."[20]

Billy and Ellen Phillips did not initially relocate to a reservation. Instead, with the help of cousins from Suquamish and donations from non-Indian Seattleites, the couple moved into a new cabin on Salmon Bay, next to that of Hwelchteed and Cheethluleetsa, who may have been relatives. The little enclave near old Tucked Away Inside would not exist much longer, though. Sometime in 1914 or 1915, during construction of locks for a ship canal connecting Puget Sound to Lake Washington, Cheethluleetsa died. Three months later, Indian agents from Port Madison came to take Hwelchteed to the reservation. Soon after that, Billy Phillips burned their home in keeping with Native strictures against moving into a house where someone had died. Neighbor Andrew Jacobsen recalled that the Phillips place caught fire as well: "He let that burn too; he was clearing the land." When the locks were completed in 1916, none of the old indigenous people remained near the site of old Tucked Away Inside; the only Indian people living on Salmon Bay were the mixed-race inhabitants of Ballard and surrounding neighborhoods.[21]

Although they offer glimpses into the concrete workings of indigenous marginalization, contemporary accounts of Seattle's "last" Indians also reflect deep-seated assumptions about the racial destiny of Native people in general. Not unlike tales of Indian ghosts, these are place-stories inhabited by the "vanishing Indian" and a cast of characters drawn from the broader national imagination. Princess Angeline was "the Pocahontas of the West," the Phillips were members of the "fast falling band of Siwashes," and Lake Union John and Madeline represented a final chapter in the "romantic history of early Seattle." As elsewhere in the country, indigenous people who survived in Seattle seemed like temporal anomalies, holdouts from an earlier age. Of Native women selling wares on the city's streets, for example, one writer claimed that "nothing has ever happened to any of them in the city, but they remain what Darwin calls a persistent type, and stuck like a porous plaster." White writers described other Native Seattleites in similar ways. Mandy Seattle lived "in the past . . . when she herself was young and straight as the shoots of the alder in springtime," while her kinswoman Mary Sam Seattle, who had once helped clear land for the first settlers, had been "left by the side, jetsam thrown up by the ebb and flow of human activities, as exemplified in the upbuilding of this city." Simultaneously stuck in the past and vanishing into it, indigenous people in Seattle were characterized by local newspapers as "Our Citizens of Yesterday" and a "wretched remnant."[22]

Accounts of people like Salmon Bay Charlie, then, were often clouded by powerful ideas about the inevitable decline and disappearance of Indians as a race. They also reflected a major shift in the place of Indian people in urban affairs. As combatants and laborers, alleged vectors of contagion and supposed purveyors of vice, Indians had played a central, and material, role in civic politics in the nineteenth century. By the early twentieth century, however, Indians were no longer a threat. No one was worried about Hwelchteed and his wife bringing smallpox to town or about Tleebuleetsa and her husband burning down the city. And aside from the few who ponied up cash for the Phillips' move, neither did white Seattleites seem all that concerned about their long-term welfare. Instead, the presence of people like Mandy Seattle simply served as an allegory about both the fate of the vanishing race and the city's urban success. Seen as having little material use, indigenous people could still serve a rhetorical purpose. They could still be used to tell place-stories.

Like indigenous people, indigenous places also served important symbolic roles in twentieth-century Seattle. There was a growing interest in Seattle, and around the country, in "Indian" place-names. Both University of Washington anthropologist T. T. Waterman and his history department colleague Edmond S. Meany, for example, received regular requests for "picturesque" and "quaint" Indian names for estates, beach cabins, boats, and parks. Elsewhere, such names could be used to market urban development itself. In the spring of 1909, for example, the real-estate firm of Calhoun, Denny, and Ewing held a promotional event for their new residential plat, just in time for the Alaska-Yukon-Pacific Exposition. Called Licton Springs, the neighborhood-to-be just beyond Seattle's northern city limit drew its name from the red pigment that Native people had collected there for use in ceremonies. In fact, it was this connection to the indigenous past that made Licton Springs desirable. "The opening of a plat with these natural features in the East would create a riot," crowed one advertisement. "They have learned to appreciate such treasures. Apparently Seattle is arriving at such a stage." Using "legends of our Indian tribes now extinct" to sell suburban homesites made perfect sense in Seattle, where actual indigenous people seemed to be on their way out, save for "here or there a relic."[23]

As "great throngs" rode new trolleys to Licton Springs, they took the waters, visited the nearby shake cabin that had once belonged to David Denny, and entered contests to win free lots. However, should one of those Indian "relics" deign to "worship the God of Health" at the springs—or, more tellingly, should one of their ghosts choose to haunt the place—one writer warned what would happen:

And it may come to pass that if the spirit of Chief Seattle or Leschi, or what-soever Hyas Tyee was wont to come to mix his war paint at Licton Springs in the centuries that are passed, should chance again this way on a similar mission bent, he would come plum against a blue-coated, brass-buttoned caretaker, who would take him by the lapel of his war bonnet and, leading him down the cement walk, among the electric lights to the confines of Licton Park should tell him to move on. For this is the 20th Century, and to "move on" is the edict for all of us.

Taken alongside the experiences of Sbeebayoo and other Native men and women, this Licton Springs place-story suggested that there was very little room for indigenous people—alive or undead—in modern Seattle. Their legends and place-names, on the other hand, made great copy. Even the symbolic landscape now seemed to belong to the new Changers.[24]

S EATTLE IS A BAD PLACE to build a city. Steep hills of crumbly sand atop slippery clay, a winding river with a wide estuary and expansive tidal flats, ice age kettle lakes and bogs, and plunging ravines and creeks are all sandwiched between Puget Sound and vast, deep Lake Washington. But it was built anyway, despite all this, and today Seattle's watersheds in particular are among its most transformed landscapes: where four rivers once joined to become the Duwamish, now only one flows; Lake Washington empties to the west instead of the south and is shallower; other lakes, creeks, and beaches have been filled, dredged, culverted, and bulkheaded. In the last decade of the nineteenth century and the first two decades of the twentieth— roughly the same years that the "last" Indians populated Seattle headlines—the city undertook a series of massive engineering projects that turned hills into islands, straightened one river and obliterated another, and reshaped entire watersheds, driven by what one urban scholar has called the "leveling impulse."[25]

Seattle civic leaders had long held ambitious visions for improving what they called the "natural advantages" of their city. The deepwater port backed by two significant bodies of freshwater had spelled opportunity since the Fourth of July, 1854, when Thomas Mercer gave the name Lake Union to a body of water he hoped would someday link Lake Washington with Puget Sound. Despite various attempts at linking the lakes with flumes and ditches, large-scale efforts were beyond the reach of the young city. Other problems—most notably the steep hills that ringed downtown and the untidy margin between land and sea— remained unsolved throughout much of Seattle's early history. By the end of the nineteenth century, however, the technology and capital were available to begin serious attempts at terraforming. In 1895, former governor Eugene Semple proposed cutting a canal through Beacon Hill to connect Lake Washington with the Duwamish River, which until that point had only connected via the shallow, sluggish, and snag-filled Black River. Authorized by the state legislature, construction began in 1901, with soil and clay from Beacon Hill being used to fill the tidelands at the mouth of the Duwamish. While the South Canal project never reached completion—cave-ins and spiraling costs proved its death knell—Semple's passion for reshaping the Seattle landscape continued in the works of other men. The managers of the Seattle General Construction Company, for example, carried on with the filling of the tidelands, using sediments dredged from the Duwamish. Eight years and 24 million cubic yards of silt later, the company had replaced the river delta with the world's largest man-made island, flat, dry, and ready for industrial tenants. That same year, the flood-prone, meandering Duwamish, long a source of frustration, became the focus of engineers' efforts with the creation of the Duwamish Waterway Commission. Dredging began in the fall of 1913, and by 1920, only one original bend of the river remained within the city limits; the rest was a more-or-less straight, fifty-foot-deep channel ideal for large seagoing vessels.

The most dramatic project, however, took Semple's idea of a canal and moved it north. Under the leadership of Hiram M. Chittenden, of the Army Corps of Engineers, and Seattle City Engineer Reginald H. Thomson, the Lake Washington Ship Canal linked Puget Sound, Lake Union, and Lake Washington through state-of-the-art locks at Salmon Bay, opening the lakes to maritime traffic beginning in 1917. Denny Hill was mostly gone by then, too, its earth used to fill tidelands that now fronted a wide, straight, and deep Duwamish Waterway. The Lake Washington watershed had been reoriented entirely; instead of flowing south out of the Black River, it now moved north and west through the Hiram M. Chittenden Locks in Ballard, and the lake itself was ten to twenty feet lower. Together, all of these changes would have profound impacts on indigenous people and places.[26]

For the men who envisioned and then enacted these changes, Indians were irrelevant. Except as emblems of a vanishing past, Native people virtually never appear in the writings and plans of Thomson, Chittenden, and the other modern Changers. Instead, the creators of Seattle's new urban ecology thought they were improving nature. Thomson, for example, called the Duwamish's natural curves "ugly" and "unsightly," preferring a channelized and useful river to one that was messy and unpredictable. Meanwhile, ship canal visionary Chittenden argued that the transformation of Lake Washington and Lake Union was "distinctly a case where utilitarian ends can be accomplished without any sacrifice of sentimental interests." Each of these men downplayed the social costs of reengineering Seattle's landscape; relocating undesirable people, when mentioned at all, was simply one of the benefits of efficient urban planning.[27]

That none of them mentioned Indians should not come as a surprise. For one thing, adherents to the modern urban-planning tradition paid little attention to local knowledge or history; instead, they looked to abstract, positivist models in which attachments to place and past bore little relevance. In other words, indigeneity and modernity were mutually exclusive in the minds of urban planners. At the same time, urban Indians were disappearing into a diverse category of people and communities known as Seattle's underclass, a grouping that would serve as the bogeyman in planning schemes for decades to come. The presence of Indian people, when noticed at all, could in fact mark areas in "need" of urban renewal. In 1892, for example, one observer described the "Shantytown" neighborhood around Kikisebloo's house on the waterfront in language similar to that used to malign the Duwamish and the places where a canal needed to be built:

What a blemish on this fair and growing city is that particular locality, where scores of shanties, lean-tos, and sheds, holding a heterogeneous mass of humanity, are huddled together—little children with old faces, unkempt men and women, dirty dogs, stray cats, the sewage from unclean sewers pouring down contagion and filth, moral and physical ill-being—all down that hillside, where the tumble-down dwellings are piled in many cases one over the other.

In a pattern that had begun with the old Lava Beds and that would continue into the late twentieth century, Indianness became a marker of urban disorder. In the case of Thomson, Chittenden, and their fellow Changers, though, those in charge of landscape change were more likely to ignore indigenous people altogether.[28]

Not that there wasn't evidence of Native people all around Thomson and the others; beyond the front-page stories of Billy Phillips and other beleaguered "last" Indians, large-scale civic-engineering projects could themselves reveal evidence of the indigenous inhabitants of Seattle. This was particularly true in the case of the Lake Washington Ship Canal. In 1913, workers exposed a deep shell midden that had once been part of Tucked Away Inside. And when Lake Washington dropped several feet in 1916 as the last barrier between it and Lake Union was dynamited, even older relics were revealed. At a marshy cove on Union Bay, rows of wooden posts—the remains of the fishing weir at the indigenous town of Little Canoe Channel—stood exposed, and ancient stone hearths resurfaced along the new, lower shoreline. But even these discoveries could serve as arguments for the "improvements" to Lake Washington. In the *Seattle Town Crier*, M. J. Carter wrote that the hearths, created by a "dusky race of primitive men," proved that the canal was a "natural" improvement. "Nature moves slowly and on many feet," he wrote, "but man, harnessing the pent forces of the earth to his needs, strikes with irreverent hand, and the entombed secrets of the past stand revealed." Rather than evoke the importance of such places to indigenous people, these unearthings only confirmed the naturalness of the engineering marvels that revealed and then obliterated them. These men thought they were restoring nature.²⁹

But for Native people trying to maintain connections to traditional places within Seattle, the changes to the landscape in the first two decades of the twentieth century were far from irrelevant—they were devastating. Simply finding traditional foods, for example, had become close to impossible. The Duwamish estuary's eelgrass beds, which had sheltered young salmon and armies of herring, were gone, buried under the fill of Harbor Island and bisected by the new Duwamish Waterway. The great middens around Smith's Cove—proof of the spot's wealth of clams and other shellfish—were now covered by a landfill. The oxbows and bends of the Duwamish, once home to clouds of waterfowl, had become avenues for global shipping. And when Lake Washington dropped with the opening of the ship canal, its outlet, the Black River, ceased to exist. Duwamish descendant Joseph Moses recalled that it "was quite a day for the white people at least. The waters just went down, down," he told a local historian, "until our landing and canoes stood dry and there was no Black River at all. There were pools, of course, and the struggling fish trapped in them. People came from miles around, laughing and hollering and stuffing fish into gunny sacks." And on Lake Union, business and residential development wiped out the trout population. "Too much house now—all gone," Chesheeahud told one observer, not long before he finally just sold up and left for the reservation. In reordering the landscape for urban utility, Seattle's Changers had dramatically reduced the utility—and habitability—of that landscape for indigenous people.³⁰

There was an element of truth, then, in the "lastness" of Indians in Seattle. In the 1910s, anthropologist Thomas Talbot Waterman noted that Seetoowathl, Ollie Wilbur's relative with the crazy wife, was one of the only indigenous people left in Seattle. In many ways, men and women like Seetoowathl and Mandy Seattle *were* the last indigenous generation. Certainly, there were people of indigenous ancestry who continued to live in the city. Across Salmon Bay from Hwelchteed and Cheethluleetsa, for example, several families of Shilshole heritage lived in Ballard, and people with roots in communities such as Herring's House and Place of the Fish Spear could be found in other parts of the city. In them, the so-called vanishing race carried on. But in terms of indigeneity—which we might define by subsistence patterns, use of traditional places, ceremonial practices, firsthand experience with the pre-urban landscape, and, not insignificantly, the perceptions of observers—the deaths and departures of Tleebuleetsa, Chesheeahud, and the others did in fact mark a discontinuity in Seattle's Native history. The first decades of the twentieth century did not spell the end of Indian Seattle by any means, but they were the end of *indigenous* Seattle.[31]

During those same decades, indigenous knowledge of Seattle often came to be located outside the city, on reservations like Muckleshoot and Suquamish or in small enclaves like the Duwamish community at Black River. When academics and amateur ethnographers went in search of Native knowledge of the places that had become Seattle, they rarely went to the city. Their lists of collaborators, in fact, read like shorthand for the slow erosion of indigenous presence in Seattle. Waterman's informants Anne Seattle and Lucy Eells, living at Muckleshoot, both had fathers who were born at Little Crossing-Over Place, the settlement now buried under downtown's King Street railway station. Julie Jacob, born African American and abandoned as an infant on Ballast Island before being adopted by Jacob Wahalchoo and his wife, shared her cultural knowledge in her home on the reservation at Suquamish. So did Jennie John Davis, the daughter of Chesheeahud. Local knowledge was no longer local; understanding of indigenous Seattle could best be obtained by getting out of the city.[32]

Meanwhile, for people whose indigenous ancestors had left Seattle decades earlier, places in Seattle remained important: clam beds, fishing sites, campgrounds. But just as urban landscape change brought Billy Phillips and his wife to the brink of starvation, it would also erode connections between outlying Native communities and indigenous places within the urban fabric. In a 1994 interview, for example, Muckleshoot community member (but enrolled Puyallup) Art Williams, born in 1913, described traveling to Alki Point during the summers of his childhood. There, his parents would build a small timber and buckskin shelter, and for two or three weeks, they and other families would harvest clams, mussels, geoduck, octopus, and salmon from Elliott Bay and the Duwamish estuary. "All along, you'd see bonfires," he told the interviewer, "all along the beaches, where they cooked clams and do everything." Accompanied by drumming, songs, and stories, the annual trip to Alki was a continuation of older seasonal rounds. Fishing and clamming were only part of the action; the main event took place across Elliott Bay, at the foot of James Street on the Seattle waterfront. There, Native people would trade "whatever you got," in Williams's words: woolen blankets and dried clams, camas bulbs and buckskins. For two or three weeks, they would "have a big potlatch . . . everybody come there and say goodbye to one another . . . 'til next year comes, and then have it over again."[33]

That was about to end. As Art Williams got older, the trips to Alki Point and the Seattle waterfront became more difficult. As white Seattleites began to build beach houses with names like Dewdrop Inn and Bide-a-wee facing the beach at Alki, Indian encampments were less welcome. "No, no, no camping no more," Williams recalled. "They said no, no more camps. They wouldn't let us." Incorporated into Seattle in 1907, West Seattle had changed from an outlying community to an urban neighborhood, leaving less and less room for Native encampments. Urban growth and its attendant environmental impacts, meanwhile, led to new conservation law. Indigenous people would bear the brunt of these changes as well. State records pertaining to the arrest of Native people for fishing in the Duwamish and on Elliott Bay no longer exist, but Jennie Davis testified some years later that the Duwamish and other local Indians had to stop fishing "or they will be arrested." Indian agent Charles M. Buchanan was particularly strident in his opinions about the criminalization of indigenous fisheries on Puget Sound, especially in urban places. "The Indians of this agency have donated to the white man all of the great townsites of Puget Sound," he argued in 1916. "No

Indian has given more—no Indian has received less!" He placed the blame on "the stringent and harsh application to Indians of the State game and fish laws . . . done under color of law." Enforcement of these unjust laws, moreover, led to real criminality, reducing Indians to "beggary and theft." By 1922, when Art Williams returned from the Chemawa boarding school in Oregon, he and his family had to "sneak around different places" to harvest fish and clams. They found, however, that shellfish harvests at Alki Point had dwindled, and Williams attributed this not just to urban development and scapegoating laws but to the fact that Indian people were no longer allowed to go there simply to pray for the clams' continued abundance. Indigenous stewardship of the environment, with all its religious components, had been sundered.[34]

And much more than clams had disappeared; urban growth had also destroyed the numinous forces that had given many local places their meaning. The story of Ballard's early political history, for example, is the story of residents struggling to keep each other's cattle from fouling the creek that was the town's main water supply. To the Shilsholes, that creek had once been known as Spirit Canoe after the power that resided there, but by the early twentieth century the power was said to have fled, likely offended by the feces and urine of the Bostons' beasts. By the early twentieth century, there were fewer out-of-the-way places for spirit powers and the practices that accessed them to carry on unmolested. Meanwhile, a Duwamish elder described to ethnographer John Peabody Harrington the effects of urban development on a supernatural horned serpent known to inhabit the Lake Washington shoreline and once employed by some of the most powerful and feared shamans. Harrington's notes simply say that by the 1910s it was "gone, not there now." Around that same time, a boulder inscribed with shamanic power figures on the West Seattle shoreline was buried under fill and concrete foundations. In the late twentieth century, some Indian people would return to sacred sites in Seattle, but during the years of the city's most rapid growth, at least some local indigenous people felt that urban change had destroyed, dispersed, or submerged many of the landscape's spiritual, and thus most fundamental, qualities.[35]

In fact, the primary place-story local indigenous people told about Seattle in the early twentieth century was one of alienation and erasure. Other informants recounted for Harrington what had happened elsewhere in the city, contrasting indigenous places with their current conditions. Of the firs at Little-Bit-Straight Point, where a settlement and stockade had once guarded the mouth of the Duwamish River, settlers had "cut them long ago," and in their place stood the Rainier Brewery. The nearby town of Place of the Fish Spear, meanwhile, now lay beneath the Seattle Electric Company machine shops. And new calamities always seemed possible; when construction of the Alki Playground in West Seattle uncovered the remains of several smallpox victims in 1911, some local Indians were concerned that a new epidemic would be visited upon the area. Together, these stories made up an indigenous accounting of urban transformation, in which a new kind of changer, men like R. H. Thomson and Watson the arsonist, had reworked the creations of the original Changer. For people like Hwelchteed, who resisted leaving Salmon Bay until the very end of his life, and for Art Williams, who had never called Seattle home but who came there every year, connections to Seattle's indigenous landscape had been almost severed.[36]

This is not to say that people from reservations and tribal communities stopped coming to the city. As it did for most people living in outlying areas, Indian or otherwise, the city offered services and amenities and jobs that were unavailable elsewhere. Parents brought children from Suquamish to visit doctors in Seattle; Muckleshoot men and women came to the city to shop. A Skagit shaman could get cataract surgery in the city; Tulalip allottees could go to the courthouse to demand land payments. And in a city still fueled by sawmills, canneries, and shipyards, there was always the possibility of paid work. The new urban landscape—the glitter of the department stores, the seediness of Skid Road, the bustle of the waterfront—might have destroyed the indigenous landscape of horned serpents and herring runs, but it still attracted Indian people, who engaged the city on Indian (if not always indigenous) terms.[37]

For all their differences, Seattle's indigenous and urban landscapes were often closer together than they seemed. While one had appeared to give way to the other in a dramatically short period of time, in reality both existed simultaneously in the minds of many Native people. Muckleshoot elder Florence "Dosie" Starr Wynn, for example, told an interviewer about trips made to the city in the 1930s and about the persistence of Seattle's indigenous landscape in her grandmother's memory:

We went to the waterfront, and we went up to the public market, and we used to go up there. And when we'd take her shopping, we'd go through that road through Duwamish, that way. And she named all the rocks. The hills—well, they're gone now, because of blasting and new homes going in, and businesses. But they had names for every one of them rocks down there. . . . Stories about those hills. All along that valley, there.

The place-stories Dosie's grandmother told her were those of North Wind and South Wind, of the dwarves that helped Spirit Canoe travelers, and of lookouts posted on hills to warn of slavers from the north. The landscape might have been changed almost beyond recognition—the sacred horned snake "gone, not there now"—but the memory of these things remained vital for the descendants of Seattle's indigenous people. In 1931 Suquamish elder Mary Thompson said it best, telling a *Seattle Times* reporter that although she seldom visited the city named after her great-grandfather, she remained connected to the place. "I always feel that I own it somehow," she said. Meanwhile, a small community of Duwamish people continued to live within the city, blending in as far as outsiders could tell but maintaining their own sense of themselves as a people. Decades later, their story would resurface, and the transition between indigenous and urban ecologies, represented by changes like the Lake Washington Ship Canal, would be central to that story.[38]

And then there is the indigenous name for the city itself. When ethnographers like Harrington and Waterman in the 1910s and Marian Wesley Smith in the 1940s interviewed elders throughout Puget Sound, they found that most did not refer to the city by the name chosen by Arthur Denny and his pioneer compatriots. Instead, they used the name of the indigenous settlement buried long ago under the sawdust from Yesler's mill. On the eve of the Second World War, almost a century after the founding of Seattle, Little Crossing-Over Place continued to exist in the hearts and minds of Indian people.[39]

T HE FLOAT HOUSE at Tideflats where Seetoowathl lived with his unpleasant wife at the turn of the century did not escape the Changers. The couple had struggled in the first years of the twentieth century, as the dogfish oil industry collapsed with the introduction of petroleum products. Some of their Indian neighbors moved on to the reservations, while others passed away. Meanwhile, the Duwamish River on which their home rose and fell with the tides had changed dramatically. After all the dredging and filling and straightening, they now lived on the last remaining natural bend of the lower river. Relatives came less frequently; Ollie Wilbur and her parents had stopped coming because they "didn't care to go there anymore." It might have been that isolation, together with infirmity and the industrial landscape that surrounded them, that spelled the end. In the 1910s, Thomas Talbot Waterman described Seetoowathl as "hale-appearing," but that would change very quickly. In the winter of 1920, Seetoowathl and his wife starved to death. "He died, you know," recalled his great-grandniece Ollie, "and they just cremated his body, you know."[40]

The crazy woman and the old man who refused to speak English had chosen to stay on the river, and that choice had cost them their lives. The fact that two old people, Indian or otherwise, could starve to death in Seattle in 1920 is an indictment of the failings of the Progressive Era. The city now had over 300,000 residents and had achieved remarkable successes. Most notably, the tallest building west of the Mississippi—the Smith Tower, completed in 1914—stood within sight of the Duwamish, a testament to wealth, competence, and confidence. From its upper floors, one might have been able to see the curve of the river at Tideflats, but the Progressive ethos of reform, charity, and order, for all its successes, could not make the cognitive leap from skyscraper to float house. Then again, the Progressive Era, which saw great leaps forward in medicine, social work, conservation, and suffrage, was also the era of Jim Crow, the Alien Land Law, the first Red Scare, and the disaster of Indian allotment. Why should Seattle have been any different?

During construction of the Lake Washington Ship Canal, engineer Hiram Chittenden had once written that critics of the canal disliked such projects "simply because they destroy old associations . . . those who have been familiar all their lives with certain conditions are naturally loth [sic] to see them changed." For many Indian people, the "old associations" had been destroyed almost completely. In the decades between the coming of the railroad and the Great Depression, Indian agency in Seattle is hard to find. It is there, though: in the applications for allotment, in the death vigil held near the university grounds, in the "sneak fishing" on the Duwamish. These small acts would provide tenuous links between the indigenous past and future reclaimings of urban space by Indian people. Meanwhile, during the same decades that indigenous Seattle was reaching its nadir, another kind of Indian history was on the rise. In describing her kinsman's house on the river, Ollie Wilbur recalled that a number of the Indians living at Tideflats were not kin of hers or of anyone she knew. They were what those who still spoke Whulshootseed called by a name that meant something like "from the surf's mouth." They were from far, far away, and they had come to make Seattle theirs.[41]

6 / The Woven Coast

A VISITOR TO SEATTLE in the summer of 1900 would have been impressed. Where a town of fewer than four thousand people had existed only twenty years earlier, a city of eighty thousand now crowded the shores of Elliott Bay. A newly commissioned army fort guarded the bluffs above West Point, a massive railroad and shipping terminal was under construction at Smith's Cove, and electric lights illuminated much of downtown, powered by distant dams. More than forty labor unions represented workers in the city, including the longshoremen who shepherded millions of dollars in international commerce into and out of Elliott Bay. The Duwamish River still curved chaotically toward the Sound, but its meandering days were numbered; plans were already under way to transform it into an organized channel of commerce. Even Ballast Island, where the refugees from Herring's House had come to protest seven years before, seemed to reflect Seattle's urban fortunes, growing each year as bricks, rocks, and other detritus were added by ships from Manila, Honolulu, Valparaiso, San Francisco, and Sydney. Metropolis had arrived.[1]

But in 1900, it was not the people of Herring's House who now camped on Ballast Island. Instead, it was people from the Strait of Juan de Fuca. These were S'Klallam people, thirteen dozen men, women, and children who had come to the city from their homeland on the northern shore of the Olympic Peninsula. Their canoes, and those of other Native people from even more distant Native places, had inspired some observers to dub Seattle's waterfront the "Venice of the Pacific." S'Klallam people camped safely in the territory of the Duwamish: clearly, the city's Indian terrain had shifted.[2]

Meanwhile, several blocks away, on the site of Henry Yesler's old mill, a second kind of new Indian terrain existed. On a triangle of greensward known as Pioneer Place Park, wedged in among the banks and hotels, a massive Tlingit carving rose over flowerbeds and a neatly clipped lawn. At its base, mythic ancestor Raven-at-the-Head-of-Nass anchored a series of striking figures: a whale with a seal in its mouth, a smaller raven, a mink, a woman holding her frog-child, and yet another raven carrying a crescent moon in its beak. This was the Chief-of-All-Women pole, carved to memorialize a woman who had lived and died a thousand miles from Seattle. It was an unlikely candidate for the city's first piece of public art, but there it stood. According to one observer, it even made Seattle unique, "the only city in the world which possesses a monument of this character to a fast departing race."[3]

The story of how canoes from the Strait of Juan de Fuca and a totem pole from Alaska got to Seattle is the story of the city's arrival as a regional metropolis, of the linking of distant places to each other and to that metropolis, and of the creation of a new urban story. Just as Ballast Island was a physical manifestation of Seattle's connections to distant ports, Indian people and images in Seattle reflected the city's new economic and cultural boundaries, which by the twentieth century reached as far north as Alaska. Indian canoes arriving on Seattle's waterfront from far-flung places heralded the creation of an urban Indian hinterland of which Seattle was one nexus. Meanwhile, Seattle's experience of regional empire, spurred in part by the discovery of gold in the Klondike in 1897, led to a new urban vocabulary that used Native imagery such as totem poles to highlight the city's new position as gateway to the North. Seattle's Indian hinterland stretched along a coast woven together by new urban and indigenous connections, and through that new weaving, both Native people and the city would be changed.

I N AUGUST 1878, the *Seattle Daily Intelligencer* reported that scores of Native men and women were camped at the foot of Washington Street on their way to the hop fields of rural Puget Sound country. Perhaps they were the people immortalized in Mr. Glover's bird's-eye panorama of the city. If not, they were people like them. Above the tide line, temporary shelters and dozens of canoes filled with personal belongings turned the waterfront into a sudden and unmistakable Indian neighborhood. The paper predicted that after three or four weeks earning "considerable money" from labor in the fields, the Indians "will then return, on their way stopping at Seattle to spend the larger part of their earnings." The movement of working Indian people—and, not insignificantly, their money—in and out of Seattle was becoming part of the city's urban calendar and a central facet of life in Native communities far beyond Puget Sound. Canoes from Washington's Pacific coast, the islands and inlets of British Columbia, and as far north as Alaska were more than just modes of conveyance toward economic opportunity: they were vehicles in which Indian people traveled toward a new identity crafted through their encounters with the urban.[4]

Long before hops and cities reoriented Native lives on the Northwest Coast, indigenous people had come from great distances to visit Puget Sound. In the 1990s, archaeologists working on the site of a new sewage treatment plant at West Point in Seattle found two remarkable pieces of carved stone, one worked from dark green nephrite and the other hollowed out of light gray stone. These were labrets, ornaments that had once pierced the lower lips of elite Native people; the green one even bore scratches where it had rubbed against the teeth of its wearer. They were at least three thousand years old, and their origins lay far to the north; no societies south of the central British Columbian coast had ever worn them. While the labrets are a mystery (were they worn by men or women, slaves or invaders, spouses or traders?), they attest to ancient voyages along the vast edge of a continent.[5]

Stories of such journeys come from shallower time as well. During the same decades that Vancouver and Wilkes explored the Northwest Coast for their empires, indigenous people with their own ambitions were making thousand-mile journeys in forty-foot canoes to the places that would become Seattle. Shilshole elders, for example, told one local historian of raids by Stikine Tlingit from southeast Alaska; those unable to escape into the backcountry around Tucked Away Inside were either taken as slaves or killed, their heads thrown into Salmon Bay. The Lekwiltok Kwakwaka'wakw of the northern Strait of Georgia had earned a similar a reputation in Puget Sound by the 1820s, their raids appearing in the oral traditions of both peoples. Even after non-Indian settlement in Puget Sound, these northern Indians (described by settlers as "northern British Indians" or even "British-Russia red-skins" to distinguish them from local indigenous people) continued to make forays into the inland waterways near Seattle, sometimes turning their attentions to white schooners and farms.[6]

But in the late nineteenth century, the nature and frequency of Native visits to Puget Sound and Seattle changed. Drawn by seasonal work in the region's burgeoning economy, Indian men, women, and children began traveling huge distances, often every year, to Seattle and its outlying areas. As Puget Sound's first large-scale agricultural commodity, hops played the largest role in these migrations, but over time other kinds of crops—berries, vegetables, herbs, flowers—demanded Native labor. For tribal communities all along the coast, occasional forays into Puget Sound became regular peregrinations. By the early twentieth century, the city was a well-established stopover for Indian laborers whose home communities ranged up and down the Northwest Coast.[7]

Canoes going to and from Seattle changed both their home communities and the city. The most obvious effects were monetary: Indians fresh from the hop fields and other jobs injected large sums of money into Seattle's economy. One Seattle newspaper noted in 1879, for example, that Native visitors brought "great trade" to the city's merchants, and that "between their calls going and returning they will leave several thousand dollars in Seattle." Native shoppers in Seattle quickly established a reputation for shrewdness, with one paper referring to them as "sharp, close traders [who] look upon the Bostons with a suspicious eye." According to some observers, Indians' spending made them preferable to other minorities in the city. One paper reported that they were better than Chinese immigrants "as they spend the money they receive . . . and keep it in the country, instead of hoarding it and shipping it to a foreign land, from whence no dollar returns." While not on a par with tourist dollars or large-scale capital investments—particularly in later decades, as the urban economy reached metropolitan proportions—Indian cash nonetheless helped to fill urban coffers.[8]

Things bought in Seattle could be used to maintain Native traditions in the hinterland, as the purchase of material goods in Seattle and other urban centers meshed with indigenous notions of prestige. One observer, for example, noted that "it was a common thing to see several sewing machines in one Indian house or half a dozen phonographs, and beds and tables by the dozen but never used. . . . If by chance the owner of the house should die, to ease his condition in the next world all these household goods were piled upon his grave, often including the very doors and window sashes of his house." Goods procured in urban places—phonographs and bedsteads as well as more mundane resources like flour and coffee—helped maintain and even augment indigenous institutions like the potlatch. Sometimes the potlatches, important ceremonies in which Natives displayed their wealth, reaffirmed their status, and cemented kinship and community ties, were even held *in* Seattle. Orange Jacobs recalled one such event in the 1880s, when a Canadian Indian named Jim gave away hundreds of dollars' worth of blankets, calico, suits of clothing, and "Indian trinkets" to dozens of participants on the tidelands south of town. Even the journey itself could be a display of status; Pacheenaht chief Charles Jones once boasted that he had paddled from Vancouver Island to Seattle in a single day. The urban experience did not necessarily erode indigenous traditions; it could in fact strengthen them. This was perhaps especially true for Native people whose homes were in British Columbia, where the potlatch was outlawed beginning in 1885.[9]

Casting one's lot with the vagaries of the American agricultural economy, however, brought risks for travelers and those they left behind. One Canadian Indian agent noted in 1891, for example, that Seattle-bound Tsimshians had "failed to obtain much labour, and realized but little profit." Likewise, Kweeha Kwakwaka'wakw Charles Nowell recalled one season when he, his brother, and some in-laws stayed in Seattle for only two or three days after learning that hops were "all burnt," and returned home virtually broke. Labor gluts and disasters like the hop louse infestations of the 1890s could wreak havoc with Native fortunes. In 1906, some unlucky Sheshahts from Vancouver Island were forced to spend the winter digging clams and selling them in Seattle for meager returns because of losses earlier in the season. Meanwhile, migrants' absences could leave their kin vulnerable on remote reserves: an agent on eastern Vancouver Island reported in the late 1880s that Cowichan elders faced hardship as younger relatives spurned local subsistence activities to pursue wealth elsewhere.[10]

But perhaps the greatest challenge posed by annual migrations came from disease. Economic vectors between Seattle and its Native hinterland were mirrored by biological vectors, pathways where contagion traveled with the phonographs and cash. Those vectors had helped fuel Seattle city leaders' racist paranoia in the 1870s, but if the paranoia had mostly ended by the last years of the nineteenth century, the continuing effects of such diseases had not. In fact, the prevalence of measles, tuberculosis, and other illnesses among Native travelers allows us to locate them in the urban landscape. Death records for King County during the late nineteenth and early twentieth centuries show clusters of Indian mortality among the tidelands and shanties near the old Lava Beds. Canoes lay at the foot of Weller Street, for example, while their owners and passengers died just blocks away. The diseases went home with the survivors. Indian agents on Vancouver Island were especially aware of the illnesses that struck communities whose members had gone to town. In 1888, Agent Harry Guillod reported that many Kyuquot and Chickleset children had died of measles on the way back to Vancouver Island from the Sound while the Hesquiaht, who had stayed home, had been spared. Two months later, the province's Indian superintendent reported that the same outbreak was now raging everywhere on the British Columbia coast. Hundreds of miles from urban centers, Native cemeteries bore the marks of diseases that blossomed in crowded cities.[11]

Migration to and from Seattle had its more subtle costs as well, eroding connections to indigenous places in the hinterland. Among the Tlingit, for example, the central element of social life, the *kwáan*, or clan, was a map of sorts, a linkage between a group of people and a place expressed through subsistence activities and oral tradition. Through relationships with urban places, however, these intimate connections between people and place were shifting. Charlie Jim Sr., or Tóok', a Hutsnuwu Tlingit Raven who often came to the city, told a biographer that in the early twentieth century he sometimes felt "like a man without a country" because of his regular movements between southeast Alaska and Seattle. For someone who defined himself in large part by his *kwáan*, and thus his place, this was a telling statement. His story, likely not unique, suggests that, while the coast was being woven together in some ways, it was being sundered in others.[12]

For all its risks, though, migration to Seattle and Puget Sound gave Native people a chance at independence and presented challenges to federal Indian policies in both the American and the Canadian parts of the Northwest Coast. Treaties with Washington State and the rules of the reserve system in British Columbia allowed for the movement of Native people off of reservations and reserves, but it often seemed to agents that such travel undermined efforts to "civilize" Native people. From the Makah Reservation, for instance, whole families headed to the hop fields, leaving agency schools empty, Bibles unread, and lessons unlearned. Makah Daniel Quedessa wrote to a white friend in the 1880s that he would soon leave with his parents to go to pick hops, adding that "I guess every one of the School childrens will go up to pick hops." Meanwhile, Canadian missionaries across the Strait of Juan de Fuca found it "very up-hill work" persuading families to stay on the reserve during the school year when work and wages beckoned from the south. Native travel to Seattle thwarted the larger goals of national policies, much as it had in earlier periods of Seattle's history. As before, efforts to define who belonged where rarely worked out as planned.[13]

For all the agents' complaints, though, canoe trips to Seattle actually helped Native people integrate themselves into settler society. Few extant sources indicate how Native people perceived places like Seattle, but it appears that, for some, encounters with urban life inspired new, cosmopolitan ambitions. It is likely that many found the material abundance, social opportunities, and general spectacle of Seattle an exciting change of pace. Many Native men and women may have agreed with Tsimshian Arthur Wellington Clah, who simply called Seattle a "great city" in his 1899 diary. Others seem to have aspired to an urbanity of their own; on Vancouver Island's west coast, one sign of prestige at the turn of the century was a home sporting bay windows and Victorian fretwork, emulating houses seen in Seattle and elsewhere. The urban experience left subtle marks on communities hundreds of miles from the city itself, both augmenting traditions like the potlatch and inspiring a new, cosmopolitan Indianness.[14]

Over time, the attractions of the city even inspired some Native people to become longer-term residents, spending more than the summer months in Seattle. In 1886, for example, a group of Kyuquot families chose to winter over and dig clams to sell in the city. Meanwhile, an Indian couple from an unidentified Northwest Coast community worked as "fiery Baptist missionaries" in Seattle in the first years of the twentieth century, attracted by the souls that needed saving on what was left of the old Lava Beds. Among the Makah, living in Seattle for varying lengths of time became a normal part of life in the 1910s. Neah Bay was "almost deserted" in the summers as people went to the city and the hop fields, and some did not come back at all. In fact, Seattle had become so central to Makah economic life that Daniel Quedessa lamented in 1915 that "I can not even go to Seattle for a trip. I can't go some place for week so I stay here [in Neah Bay on the Makah Reservation] all the time. That's why I dont make money. I always wishing if I could go away and make little money." For many of the Makah, Seattle had become an indispensable part of getting by, and for some, it was becoming a home in its own right.[15]

Coming to Seattle meant that Native people from the city's hinterland sometimes came into contact with local indigenous people. Suquamish elder Amelia Sneatlum, for example, recalled the time in the early twentieth century when her family was camping on the beach at Seattle and a Yakama man stabbed and nearly killed her father. At the other end of the spectrum, Muckleshoot elder Art Williams described friendly encounters with Native migrants on Elliott Bay, which were facilitated by the use of Chinook Jargon and, in later years, English. At the same time, the erosion of indigenous communities in and immediately around Seattle also provided openings for migrants from the hinterland. The Sheshahts who stayed in town to dig clams, for example, could do so because many indigenous Duwamish families with traditional rights to those beds had moved to area reservations or given up clamming. The growth of one kind of Native presence in Seattle, then, existed in a sort of inverse relationship with another kind of Native presence— at least until the clam beds were destroyed altogether by urban change.[16]

Meanwhile, a new kind of urban Indian history was on the rise. As Native people arrived in Seattle in canoes (and, more commonly in the twentieth century, on steamers), they entered a city with a new vocabulary. Throughout the city, totem poles and other Native symbols, drawn from the very same hinterland places whence the travelers had come, marked shop fronts and street corners. If the movement of Indian people to and from the city had changed both the Native hinterland and its urban center, the movement of Indian things had also changed both places as well, providing a new iconography of urban empire.

SOMETIME NEAR THE CLOSE of the eighteenth century, a Tlingit noblewoman of the Ganaxádi Raven clan, Chief-of-All-Women, drowned in the Nass River while on her way to comfort an ill relative. After lengthy and heartfelt mourning rituals, clan members in her community of On the Cottonwood on Tongass Island in southeast Alaska hired a carver to commemorate her life and her heritage. Drawing on ancient stories of Raven-at-the-Head-of-Nass and other figures associated with her lineage, the carver produced a fifty-foot cedar pole that was erected next to the clan's longhouse. For more than nine decades, the Chief-of-All-Women pole, with the dead woman's cremated remains inside it, reminded the Tongass Tlingit of Ganaxádi origins and social standing.[17]

Then, in 1899, a group of men from Seattle—among them clergymen, land developers, and bankers—arrived at On the Cottonwood on a ship chartered by the *Seattle Post-Intelligencer*. Coming ashore to see the "totem poles" and longhouses of the Tlingit community up close, they were particularly taken by the Chief-of-All-Women pole. Thinking it would make a fine souvenir of their journey to Alaska—and later claiming that the village was deserted—the men sawed through the pole at its base, discarded Chief-of-All-Women's remains, and floated the pole out to their ship, breaking off the beak of Raven-at-the-Head-of-Nass in the process.[18]

Several weeks later, on 18 October 1899, the Chief-of All-Women pole was erected in Pioneer Place Park, a spot of sod at the heart of Seattle's first plats. "All day long people paused and gazed; went away, returned and gazed again," crowed the triumphant *Post-Intelligencer*, "and said it was a great and wonderful thing and a grand acquisition to the city." In a fit of Victorian flourish, another observer gave voice to the pole itself:

I am the only Civilized totem pole on earth,
And civilization suits me well

. . . .
While all the others of my kind
Are slowly settling on their stems
Among the salmon scented Silences,
Sequestered from the sight of man,
Here in Seattle's surging scenes
I stand, incomparable

. . . .
So here's farewell to all my past
And welcome to the things that are;
With you henceforth my die is cast,
I've hitched my wagon to a star.
And by the Sacred Frog that hops, And by the Bird that flies,
And by the Whale and the Bear, I sunder all the ties
That bound me to the ancient creed which holds my people flat,
And I will be a Totem pole
That knows where it is at.

Abandoning its backward creators, the Chief-of-All-Women pole now served a higher purpose: advertising Seattle. Where it was "at," among the city's "surging scenes" and far from the "salmon scented Silences," seemed not only preferable but natural. Seattle knew where it was "at" as well; at the dawn of the twentieth century, it was the gateway to a new empire that stretched from its railroad stations and wharves, along the rainy northwestern edge of North America, and into the high Arctic. Just as Native people moved up and down the coast, Native objects and images began to move as well, and both Seattle and its hinterland were changed. Here was a city that highlighted its urban modernity by telling stories about places far from the bustle, about silent places in the distant wilderness over which it held sway.[19]

As early as 1870 the *Alaska Times* was being published in Seattle, but it was the arrival of the steamer *Portland* in 1897 that truly hitched Seattle's wagon to the North's star. Soon after the *Portland* hove to on the waterfront with half a ton of Yukon gold on board, Seattle established itself as a fulcrum in the economy and ecology of gold, a crucible that turned raw yellow metal into cash, food, clothing, real estate, patronage, and more. While other developments helped spur the eight-fold expansion of the Seattle economy between 1895 and 1900 (steamship trade with Asia and South America, as well as increases in commercial rail shipping to markets back East), the gold rush became the dominant explanation for Seattle's new international prominence.[20]

As the launching point for voyages to Alaska, Seattle became an entrepôt not just for yellow metal but for encounters with the Native peoples of the North. Anthropologists had been working the coast for years, but the massive migration of non-Indian people, diseases, technologies, and goods into Seattle's northern hinterland quickened the "scramble" for Northwest Coast materials and gave rise to a salvage mentality among scholars. Anthropologists came to document cultures that seemed on the verge of extinction; tourists came in search of exotic Others who called the northern wilderness home. Most of them came from Seattle, particularly after its status as the commercial center of the gold rush was clinched, and were encouraged along their way by guidebooks printed by railroads, steamship companies, and Seattle's own Chamber of Commerce. Native people and things, along with the spectacular scenery of the Inside Passage, were the chief attractions of trips from Seattle to Alaska. As early as 1890, naturalist John Muir described mobs of totem-seeking tourists on the waterfront at Wrangell, Alaska. "There was a grand rush on shore to buy curiosities and see totem poles," he wrote. "The shops were jammed and mobbed, high prices being paid for shabby stuff manufactured expressly for the tourist trade." And once

Seattle had established itself as the gateway city, tourists need not go as far as Wrangell to purchase a piece of the North. Ye Olde Curiosity Shop, opened in 1899 by J. E. "Daddy" Standless among the steamer wharves of the waterfront and still in business today, became a nexus of the trade in Native material culture and the greatest of dozens of such emporia in Seattle. In addition to outfitting "Indian corners" in private homes, the Curiosity Shop and its competitors helped fill the American Museum of Natural History and the Field Museum; curio shops were places where popular imagination, ethnographic impulses, and urban ambitions joined. But the movement of Native things—such as the miniature argillite totem poles, ivory shaman's tools, and cedar canoe models at the Curiosity Shop—from Seattle's hinterland was made possible by Native people. Just as Indian men and women met the throngs at Wrangell's wharves, they also worked at the heart of the trade in Seattle. One such man was Sam Williams, a Ditidaht carver from Vancouver Island. First coming to Seattle around the turn of the century, Williams settled on the tideflats like so many other migrants, and in 1901, his skills came to the attention of Daddy Standless. Over the next four decades, Williams carved hundreds of miniature and full-size totem poles for the Curiosity Shop. Several of Williams's children and grandchildren also carved for Standless, and a handful of his poles can still be found at the Curiosity Shop.[21]

The Chief-of-All-Women pole, erected in Pioneer Place Park at the height of the gold rush, was the most famous example of this migration of Native objects and imagery. It instantly became an icon of Seattle's promise and one of the "must-see" attractions of excursions to the Northwest. In the April 1905 *Journal of American Folklore*, anthropologist John Swanton wrote, "Every visitor to Seattle, Washington, has been attracted and more or less interested by the great totem pole that adorns its main square." As its image circulated around the globe on *cartes des visites*, "Seattle's Totem Pole" provided a frontierish frisson that set the city apart from its competitors. Indeed, the Chief-of-All-Women pole was all the more exceptional because of its urban backdrop. "This totem pole is such a curious object!" wrote one observer to her Massachusetts kin in 1901, "especially when seen right in the business part of the city as ours is." In 1907, temperance writer Agnes Lockhart Hughes cast the pole as a zero-datum marker for the city's growth:

For less than a decade of years this heraldic monument has gazed upon the many changes in its vicinity, and shortly, on all sides it will be overshadowed by the immense business structures now in [the] course of construction. Relentlessly the hands of a nearby clock mark the speed of fleeting time . . . seemingly unmindful of the grotesque Totem Pole. . . . Its lips tell nothing of its past, its ears are deaf to the roar of traffic around it, but its eyes gaze down on the rapid progress of Seattle, the wonderful Queen City of the West.

For observers like Hughes, the pole in Pioneer Place linked the banks, law firms, and other businesses of the city's commercial district—many of which fronted the park where the pole stood—with the goldfields and other resources of the new Alaskan frontier. The fact that the pole faced northwest was deliberate: a trophy of the gold rush boom, the Chief-of-All-Women pole became a symbol of Seattle's metropolitan reach, and thus its modernity. Other imperial cities had created visual languages to reflect their ambitions and the nature of their holdings; Seattle had looked North and found a totem pole.[22]

Like Indian migration to and from Seattle, represented by canoes on the waterfront, the hinterland represented by the Chief-of-All-Women pole was manifested in comings and goings. A canoe capsized in the Nass River, inspiring the carving of a pole. A chartered ship dropped anchor at Tongass Island, its passengers hungry for a trophy, while steamboats spilled tourists onto wharves in search of Alaskan souvenirs. Railcars emptied at Seattle stations, to be filled again with masks and rattles on their way to eastern museums. Lines on tourist brochures linked Seattle with Alaskan places like Wrangell and Sitka. Urbanites took the trolley downtown to see a pole erected, and postcards traveled the world, naming Seattle Gateway to the North and City of Totems. Through routes of travel and commerce that linked places like On the Cottonwood to places like Pioneer Place Park, Indian images came unmoored and could serve new masters.

This was a powerful new place-story, literally: the creation of Seattle's new urban vocabulary carried with it new power relations. Within months after the Chief-of-All-Women pole was taken in 1899, for example, the Tlingit people of On the Cottonwood accused eight of the *Post-Intelligencer* expedition members of theft. Seeing little cause for concern, the "Committee of Eight" filed a mock suit against themselves, bringing Lake Indian Chesheeahud from his home on Lake Union to play the role of plaintiff. That ploy was dropped when a federal grand jury indicted the committee, but the presiding judge soon dismissed the indictment after a dinner held in his honor by committee members. Drafting a retroactive bill of sale, the committee paid $500 to the people of Tongass Island and then sat back to bask in their newfound notoriety. The Ganaxádi Ravens and the Seattleites had been connected to each other in new and unexpected ways, in an urban warp and indigenous weft that bound up a continent's vast edge.[23]

THE KLONDIKE GOLD RUSH symbolized Seattle's imperial education; the Alaska-Yukon-Pacific Exposition was its coming-out party. Held in 1909 on the shores of Lake Washington, the AYPE trumpeted Seattle's status as "Queen City of the Pacific," and its massive Beaux Arts–style buildings, made mostly of plaster, stood as symbols of "the awakening of the Pacific, and transforming of the backyard of the world into the front." The neoclassical White City confections impressed visitors, but so did the presence of "Jap-Alaskan" architecture and other Indian-inspired spectacles, especially on the amusement strip known as the Pay Streak. "The red man of the Pacific Coast is present everywhere," announced the *Seattle Times:* "His crude art, always symbolical and sometimes hideous, glares and grins at the visitor from the red and dun-colored totem poles marking the way to the Pay Streak; the carved tribal history of Alaskan tribes upholds the beautiful 'Tori' arch of the South Gate, and figures in many of the postcards sold by dealers in such wares." Beyond the Pay Streak, Indian things filled the displays of the fair: Seattle photographer Edward S. Curtis's photogravures, S'Klallam ceremonial objects, even human scalps recalling the "red man of J. Fenimore Cooper" in the Government Building's Dead Letter Department. Virtually every exhibit included some sort of ethnographic display, and the message was clear: these Indians were our people—not in the sense of being *us*, of course, but in the sense of being *ours*. Like other world's fairs, the AYPE was intensely didactic, brazenly ambitious, and thoroughly racist.[24]

For all the power of Curtis's photos and the titillation of scalps and "grotesques," it was the display of actual Native *people* that most captivated the attention of Seattle fairgoers. The most popular attraction of the entire exposition was the Eskimo Village on the Pay Streak, where "expert reindeer men, skin-boat builders, ivory carvers and the best looking women," most of them from Siberia, served as living examples of primitivism as they undertook everyday activities in their plaster "frozen north." Meanwhile, Indian schoolchildren from Tulalip were put on display to show "what the bureau of Indian affairs has accomplished for the Indian people during the last few years." And just outside the fairgrounds at the White City Amusement Park, Cheyenne, Arapaho, and Lakota men attacked stagecoaches day after day as part of a Wild West Show, only to be rebuffed every time by white gunslingers. Whether as harmless primitives, emblems of assimilation, or violent barbarians, Native people, like Native things, were used by fair organizers to articulate a clear message: witness our realm, see our burdens.[25]

It is all too easy to see Native people at the AYPE as mere captives to Seattle's imperial fantasies. To some extent, they were. But at the same time, Native people had their own reasons to go to the fair. Two days after arriving in Seattle to tend reindeer at the Eskimo Village, for example, Iñupiat Oliver Angolook decided to return to his community near Nome. When the agent who had procured his services confronted him at the wharf, Angolook was reported to respond, "Got money. Pay my own fare." Indeed, Angolook's salary was reportedly enough to "keep an entire family in affluence through several seasons"—and ironically, it provided the means for him to leave Seattle altogether. Similarly, many Indian Wild West Show participants saw such performances as a way to visit faraway places while earning money for displays of traditional skills like horsemanship. Still another performer, the "Eskimo belle" known as Columbia, reaped a more unique reward; after winning the

AYPE beauty contest (trouncing several white competitors), the young Labrador Inuit woman received a lot in one of Seattle's new suburbs. Like hop fields or curio shops, the AYPE was an opportunity. Meanwhile, Skhandoo, a Chilkoot Tlingit shaman, wowed audiences with dances and ceremonies at the Eskimo Village alongside other Tlingits of the Chilkat, Hoonah, and Taku bands. He had once earned great wealth thanks to the Otter spirit that gave him power to heal, harm, and see far-off events, but after two prison terms for deaths caused by his ministrations, he found himself destitute until landing the job at the world's fair. For Skhandoo, the AYPE served two purposes: it allowed him to continue performing the work for which he had received prestige from both Tlingit and white observers, and it provided him with a living. For a man in Skhandoo's tenuous position, participation in the AYPE may have been the best of few options. For all these Native people, coming to the fair, like coming to the city more generally, often simply made good economic sense.[26]

Seattle's fair was also a place to play out long-standing rivalries between indigenous communities. In early 1909, for instance, fair organizers received a telegram from Harry Hobucket, a Quileute from Washington's outer coast, noting that the rival Makah were having trouble acquiring a gray whale to bring to the fair and offering to bring one on behalf of the Quileute. While exposition organizers appear to have declined the offer, the proposal suggests that some Native people saw the fair as an opportunity to shame old enemies in a new setting with a huge audience. Several weeks later, a challenge came from Chief Taholah of the Quinault and his sub-chief Pe-ka-nim of the Hoh to Indians everywhere, "and especially to their old enemies," to join in a canoe race at the fair. But such competitions, like the canoe races on 6 September, "Seattle Day," could also facilitate new alliances among tribal communities. As teams from Washington's Skokomish and Tulalip reservations and British Columbia's Lyacksun and Penelekuts reserves attracted thousands of spectators to the shores of Lake Union, they both drew white approval and helped craft a shared Native identity.[27]

At least one Native group came to Seattle explicitly to resist white authority. These were the Tsimshian of Metlakatla, a Christian settlement founded in 1862 by the missionary William Duncan, who sought to isolate the Tsimshian from outside influences. Many Tsimshian people saw this isolation as a barrier to opportunity and began to rebel against Duncan's authority, and by 1909, various American governmental bodies had gotten involved as Tsimshians and others complained to the Department of Interior and the Alaskan educational authorities. While the Metlakatlan contributions to the fair—a brass band and a ladies' auxiliary known for its needlepoint—were portrayed as the products of civilizing efforts, several Tsimshian fairgoers were in fact trying to oust the man seeking to civilize them. The auxiliary president, for example, was Mrs. Bertrand Mitchell, whose husband was in the midst of a campaign against Duncan, writing to Alaska school commissioners, "We are slaves here. We are getting poorer all the time and Mr. Duncan is getting richer. What is the matter with the government?" Meanwhile, William Pollard, assistant leader of the brass band, had also vocally opposed Duncan's rule. Needlepoint and rousing marches, then, were a way for Tsimshian people to join the outside world. Coming to the AYPE was an act of resistance.[28]

Finally, Native people also came to the fair as full-fledged spectators, taking in the urban spectacle like everyone else. The *Post-Intelligencer* reported that Indian observers at the canoe races, for example, "put the organized yells of some rah, rah boys completely to shame." Meanwhile, several Lakota Wild West Show performers and their families, "decked out in all the picturesque attire of the cow country—sombreros, chaps and all the rest of it," went to the Pay Streak one afternoon for fun and encountered a group of Flathead Indians. "To the uninitiated it looked as if a real war whoop was the next thing to be expected," winked the *Times*, but "then the chief of the Rosebuds gave a guttural command and his braves lined up in single file and slowly approached a similar file which formed on the instant among the Flatheads. For fifteen minutes the warriors of the two tribes shook hands silently. Not a word was passed between them and there was never a smile until the ceremony was over and then they fraternized as if they had come from the same reservation." The two groups then went to visit the Eskimo Village, where they showed the Siberians, the Tlingit shaman Skhandoo, the "Eskimo belle" Columbia, and the gawking crowds "what a war dance is like when danced among friends." Then the Lakotas and Flatheads finished the day with a ride on the Ferris wheel.[29]

We cannot know what the Indians on the Ferris wheel thought of the Eskimo Village, the Baby Incubators, the Upside Down House, or the Temple of Palmistry. Native people probably found the AYPE awe inspiring, offensive, hilarious, and perhaps even boring. But they may also have seen deeper meanings for themselves—a Wild West Show as a mark of prestige, an invitation to the Pay Streak as a gesture of friendship, a "war dance among friends" as a step toward a shared Native identity. As the center of a vast regional empire, Seattle had become an important venue in which to pursue old and new Native ambitions. Not only did canoes represent Indian migration to and from the city, but when paddled in AYPE races, they also signified the development of a shared Native identity. Totem poles represented not only Seattle's imperial claims on the North but also the people who traveled to the city in pursuit of economic independence, social status, or a good show. While on its surface a spectacle of urban dominance and white racial superiority, the Alaska-Yukon-Pacific Exposition also reflected the ambitions of its Native participants, who came from the far ends of Seattle's hinterland on their own terms.

ONE OF THE MOST STRIKING PHOTOS in any of Seattle's archives dates from the first years of the twentieth century. Taken by an unnamed photographer in front of the Frederick and Nelson Department Store at the corner of Second and Madison, it captures a Native woman, likely Makah or Nuu-chah-nulth, sitting against the building's stone façade and selling baskets, blankets, and other handicrafts. She looks ahead and slightly down, avoiding the gaze of a well-dressed white woman who leans over her with an I-assume-you-can't-speak-English-so-I'll-talk-louder expression. A third woman of indeterminate race, possibly Indian, watches the exchange as busy urbanites rush by, among them a particularly dowdy older woman who seems to observe the scene with disdain. It is a moment of encounter, where women of different races and classes came together for a moment on the streets of the city to haggle over a basket.

Weaving was not just a metaphor for what happened on this coast. Like canoes and totem poles, baskets were both product and symbol of Seattle's Indian hinterland. Throughout the late nineteenth and the early twentieth century, sidewalk encounters between Indian vendors and white customers were a part of everyday life in Seattle. One 1905 newspaper article might have been describing this very photo: "Uptown, on First and Second avenues, many an important corner was given a touch of nature by the presence of a wrinkled old squaw, leaning her toil-bent back against the supporting columns, while around are arrayed canoes and baskets and mats, in reckless profusion, all ready to be traded for the money of whites." Travel correspondent Nina Alberta Arndt described the ubiquity of similar "touches of nature" in the *Overland Monthly* three years later, noting that Indian women and their wares could be found "upon the steps of the principal banks, on the sidewalks of the business thoroughfares, or again . . . in the aisles of some department store." Local newspapers identified Indians "squatting in characteristic attitudes with 'hiyu iktas' [many things] spread around them" as "one of the most common sights along the pavements of Seattle . . . intrud[ing] itself on the vision of every pedestrian." Meanwhile, "more eager seekers" of curios could visit Native encampments on filled land south of the city. No need to go to Neah Bay, Prince Rupert, or Sitka; the hinterland came to Seattle, bringing touches of distant nature to the heart of urban America. And, in fact, most of the basket vendors on Seattle streets at the turn of the century were not from Puget Sound. According to the *Post-Intelligencer*, many were Makah or Nuu-chah-nulth from Vancouver Island (and her baskets' designs suggest that the woman in the Frederick and Nelson's photo was as well). An agent among the Sheshahts at Port Alberni on Vancouver Island confirmed that many Seattle vendors were his charges: "during the winter months the women often engage in the manufacture of baskets . . . which, being . . . a distinct novelty, are readily disposed of in the larger towns in the state of Washington." Like canoes and totem poles, baskets connected Seattle street corners to Native communities hundreds of miles from the city.[30]

Eastern tourists to Seattle often saw a basket or other Indian "curio" as the requisite souvenir of a trip to the city, meaning that a Sheshaht basket could easily end up in Boston or London or St. Louis. Indeed, for some Native vendors, eastern customers were preferable. According to one Seattle paper, "an Indian curio-shop manager at the corner of a Seattle block can tell an Easterner from a Western product. He knows the 'cheechaco.' A sale with an Eastern tourist is easily landed, and probably a hundred percent on the real value is assessed at that." The sale of baskets, then, drew attention to the boundaries not just between white and Indian but between westerner and easterner, captured best in the Chinook Jargon word *cheechako*, literally meaning "newly arrived" but also glossed as both "easterner" and "greenhorn." Baskets linked places to each other but also differentiated places as well, distinguishing Seattle and its people from their eastern counterparts. Here was a city where Native nature could be acquired without venturing into actual wilderness, and where urban America had an Indian edge.[31]

Gullible easterners were not the only collectors of baskets, however. Throughout Seattle, in places socially, if not physically, distant from the tideflat encampments and street corners, white women added baskets and other items to "curio corners." A *Post-Intelligencer* article describing the best collections in town reads like a clipping from the society page: the wives of mill owners and other civic elites all had extensive collections. Carrie Burke, married to a judge, even had a new wing added to her house specifically for her Indian collection. In fine homes on the hills of Seattle such as the Frye mansion at Ninth and Columbia, upper-class white women used the collection of Indian things to mark their own social status. Just as totem poles spoke of Seattle's metropolitan status, cedar bark and maidenhair fern from Vancouver Island could help a banker's wife in Seattle tell stories about privilege and power and showed how tightly the urban center and indigenous periphery were woven together along the coast that Seattle dominated.[32]

This was a new kind of imbrication, different from the landscape Mr. Glover had hinted at with his 1878 bird's-eye sketch of Seattle. The treaties had been signed for fifty years, the indigenous towns had long been burned, Kikisebloo had died a decade earlier—and yet Indian people remained a highly visible part of Seattle's urban landscape. But instead of the Whulshootseed word *yiq*, these people might have used other words to describe the process of imbricating themselves into Seattle's landscape, taken from their own languages: words for "weaving" like the Quileute *tsikbay*, the S'Klallam *ekwel*, and the Kwakwala *yepá*, or words for "worrying into tight places" like the Tlingit *dik'eek'* or the Nuu-chah-nulth *pithlqa*. And as the indigenous languages spoken in Seattle had changed, so had the city's civic vocabulary. Croaking amid the urban din of Pioneer Square, Raven-at-the-Head-of-Nass told a place-story of transformation, but he was not alone. Like Mrs. Burke displaying her baskets, Seattle's civic leaders had found new ways to talk about the city and its past. Inspired by the memory of urban conquest and the creation of a regional hinterland, the city's leaders set about crafting a new set of place-stories that cut to the very heart of what it meant to be white, American, and of this place.[33]

7 / The Changers, Changed

I N 1866, SEEATHL, SEATTLE'S NAMESAKE, died at Place of Clear Water, the community from which Jacob Wahalchoo had once gone out in search of power below the waters of Puget Sound. He was buried on the Port Madison Reservation across Puget Sound from Seattle, not far from the enormous main longhouse at Place of Clear Water that settlers called Oleman House or Old Man House, meaning "worn-out house" or "venerable house" in Chinook Jargon. The death of Chief Seattle garnered little official attention in the city that bore his name; no Puget Sound newspapers announced his passing, and while settlers who knew him surely noted his death—perhaps some even mourned—Seeathl seemed to fade quickly from prominence in Seattle's civic consciousness. A few years later, government agents burned Oleman House, seeing it as a hindrance to their civilizing mission. Meanwhile, the descendants of Seeathl and their fellow Suquamish tribal members tended his grave; occasionally a white visitor from off the reservation would place American flags there in memory of the indigenous leader's contributions to the birth of Seattle. But more often, the madrone-ringed cliff-top cemetery, facing Seattle across Puget Sound, remained a quiet place.[1]

In 1911, the scene at Seeathl's grave could not have been more different. Hundreds of visitors from Seattle were on hand, enjoying the late August weather and the U.S.S. *Pennsylvania*'s brass band following a welcome from the local Indian agent. Seattle mayor George W. Dilling, jurist Thomas Burke, and University of Washington history professor Edmond S. Meany each gave an address describing Seeathl's hospitality toward the first settlers, and patriotic songs were sung in English and Chinook Jargon. As souvenirs, each guest was given a photograph of the grave courtesy of printer (and future mayor) Ole Hanson. This was Chief Seattle Day. "The sentiment of a Chief Seattle Day, in commemoration of the Indian chief who befriended the white man in the early days of the Puget Sound country," wrote one participant, "has appealed strongly to many of Seattle's prominent citizens." Those citizens made good on their sentiment; by the 1930s, Chief Seattle Day included special Black Ball Line excursions, picnicking, and saltwater swimming, while plans were under way to construct a baseball diamond and tennis courts next to the cemetery. Place of Clear Water, once a fusty impediment to civilization, had become a pilgrimage site for those wishing to commune with their urban indigenous past.[2]

Arthur Denny might have been Seattle's founding father, but Seeathl—generous toward the settlers at Alki, powerfully articulate during treaty negotiations, and unswervingly loyal during the "Indian War"—was its patron saint. Nowhere was this more obvious than in the bad poetry inspired by visits to his grave. One particularly florid example, penned by Professor Meany himself and using the old Whulshootseed name for Puget Sound, was read at the 1911 pilgrimage to Suquamish and later to the University of Washington's graduating class of 1912:

Peace be with thee in thy honored grave,
O, Chieftain, as pilgrims we lovingly come,
Drawn to a shrine by Whulge's cool wave;—
Suquamish, sad fragment, in fir-girdled home.

. . . .

Slowly the smoke from the log cabin curled,
From hearth of white stranger near wilderness shore,
Hearth and a home at the edge of the world,
With bold Saxon faith in a hut's open door.

. . . .

Raging with anger, demons of hate,
The howling foes fought through the battle's long day.
Chieftain, O, Chieftain, blest was our fate!
Thou stoodst like a rock in our tempest strewn way.
Sweet be the flower, O, child, that you bring,

And pure be the prayer that you Heavenward send,
Soft be the song as wild robins sing,—
A shrine in the grass by the grave of our friend.

Seemingly the noblest of savages, Seeathl was the Indian benefactor to a Saxon city; the place-story of the man and the city that bore his name relied on two premises: a notion of a vanishing race and a belief in inevitable Anglo-American racial supremacy.[3]

Other would-be poets made the connection between Seeathl and Seattle even more explicit, often apostrophizing the person and the place in the same stanza as California resident Florence Reynolds did in the 1920s:

Oh! City so marvelously fair of face,
You were born of a noble Indian race,
And to honor their chieftain you were given his name.
Oh! Seattle, great warrior of deathless fame—
You have a monument that ever will stand,
A tribute of Love to your character grand;
A city of beauty that is fast growing great—
A "Wonder Spot" in a wonderful State.

For Reynolds, a grave paled in comparison to a city itself as a marker of Seeathl's life. Similarly, white Suquamish resident T. M. Crepar, a contemporary of Reynolds, suggested an even closer connection between man and metropolis:

There's a people that's proud of the story,
There's a city that's proud of its name,
Like the Chief he was in his glory,
For Sealth and Seattle's the same.
. . . .
'Neath a whitened cross and mound of sod,
The bones of Chief Seattle lies [sic];
While across the bay, where once he trod,
Seattle towers to the skies.

Included in a brochure sold to gravesite visitors by Princess Angeline Souvenirs, the poem's claim that "Sealth and Seattle's the same" reflected popular linkages between the man and the city. Talking about Seeathl and Seattle in the same breath—using an Indian to explain the city—seemed only natural. And, in fact, nature was at the core of this particular place-story, which expressed longing for the lost world of the "first Americans."[4]

Stories about Chief Seattle had little to do with the real man named Seeathl. In a pattern that would come to dominate urban discourse over the twentieth century, the city's namesake was often little more than a character from central casting, and the circumstances in which his image appeared rarely had much to do with actual Indians, typically revealing far more about the portrayers than about Seeathl. And, in fact, the symbolic resuscitation of Seeathl in the early twentieth century was but one example of the ways in which white Seattle residents used Indians and Indian imagery to tell urban place-stories. More than appropriations of Indian symbols—a time-honored American tradition—these stories were also ways to work out concerns about a changing city, and as such, they reflected the conflicting ambitions and anxieties of Seattleites. They were stories about place: about what had happened here, about who belonged here. As white Seattle turned to Indians to tell urban place-stories, it was clear that the "Changers" had also been changed by the experience of urban conquest and the transformation of this place called Seattle.

O N 17 JULY 1912, a new kind of Indian arrived in Seattle. Like so many who had come before on their way to the hop yards or the tideflats, he came from the north. But there was something different about this Indian. Perhaps it was that he arrived aboard the *Portland*, the same auspicious ship that first brought Alaskan gold to Seattle. Perhaps it was his dress: rather than the plain pants and shirts that most Native men wore, he sported a Chilkat blanket and the tall headpiece of a Tlingit noble, abalone and copper and yellow cedar announcing an ancient lineage. Perhaps it was the presence of the *Fox* and the *Davis*, twin U.S. Navy destroyers that flanked the *Portland* as it entered Elliott Bay, or the thousands of Seattleites gathered on wharves and rooftops, blowing whistles to greet him and cheering as calliope music filled the air. What made this "Indian" most different from his predecessors, though, was that he was not an Indian at all and no newcomer. Underneath the mountain-goat wool and cedar headdress were the business suit and balding pate of George Allen, Pacific Northwest manager of the National Surety Company of New York. On this day, however, Allen was no run-of-the-mill insurance executive: he was Hyas Tyee Kopa Konoway—"Great Chief of Everything" in Chinook Jargon—and he had come to Seattle to potlatch.[5]

Between 1911 and 1914 and again in the 1930s, Seattle's premier urban festival was the Potlatch. Like the Alaska-Yukon-Pacific Exposition (AYPE), the Potlatch drew on symbols of the city's northern hinterland and trumpeted the unique virtues that assured a great future for Seattle, its residents, and its investors. More than just another example of public relations, though, Seattle's Potlatch festival was also a way for a certain class of Seattleites—specifically, the city's new commercial elite—to tell stories about the city and its history. Called a "triumph of symbolism" by one observer, the Potlatch appropriated Native imagery to create a regional vision of civic development. In telling stories about the places that had been linked to Seattle through its imperial networks, Seattle's Potlatchers crafted a new narrative about what it meant to be not just in this place but in this place that dominated other places: in the premier city of the Northwest Coast.[6]

Seattle's Potlatches, like the AYPE before them, were indicative of the heated competition among Western cities in the early twentieth century. While Seattle's regional dominance was largely a fait accompli by the first Potlatch in 1911, the urban West remained a volatile place, where the fortunes of cities could still be won or lost. Potlatch organizers sought to cement Seattle's position by creating a signature event, "all that the Mardi Gras is to New Orleans; all that La Fiesta is to Los Angeles; all that the Rose Festival is to Portland." But why call it Potlatch? To highlight the city's modernity, why did festival promoters choose a Native tradition as their leitmotif? The answer centers on the question of wealth and on the idea of a civic generosity that offered the promise of prosperity to all those who lived in Seattle and its hinterland. That an Indian ritual could best articulate this vision made perfect sense to Potlatch promoters:

To the Indian of the Northwestern water reaches [Potlatch] means a feast to which all of the tribe are bidden and whence they return to their tepees laden with gifts.

Seattle has adopted the Indian name and applies literally the Indian definition. It spends $200,000 or more upon its annual festival, and offers it, as free as its Northwestern air, to whomsoever may fare this way.

No feature of the whole delightful celebration is offered at a price, for The Potlatch is not established for profit. Rather it is an annual thank-offering for a prosperity that seems perennial; for such beauties of climate and nature as have nowhere on earth their parallel.

Potlatch promoters, then, cast themselves as humble "chiefs" generously bestowing the fruit of civic and ecological wealth upon the people of Seattle and their guests.[7]

Their choice not only served the message of the festivals but also expressed a long-standing fascination with the potlatch among non-Indians. Identified by outsiders as a trademark cultural element of the Northwest Coast, "potlatch" was in fact a constellation of diverse practices used by indigenous people all along the northwestern edge of the continent as a way to manage social, economic, and spiritual relationships. In Puget Sound, for example, the practice of *sgweegwee*, from the Whulshootseed word for "invite," linked elite families, their resources, and their spirit powers over great distances through the public performance of a spiritually sanctioned sharing ethic, often on occasions such as funerals. As one elder said in the 1910s, *sgweegwee* both made a wealthy person's name "high" and made it "go all over the place." This notoriety brought responsibility; Tulalip elder Gram Ruth Sehome Shelton (Seeastenoo) pointed out that the primary purpose of the practice was to "keep up the poor," to maintain social cohesion through sharing.[8]

Puget Sound potlatches, however, were overshadowed in the public eye by those held further north. Marked by more lavish ritual per-

formances, the public destruction of wealth, and the pageantry of dancing societies, the potlatches of the Kwakwaka'wakw and other northern Northwest Coast peoples fascinated academics and the public alike
and inspired a vast scholarly and popular literature. Fascination, however, was tempered by colonial revulsion at the seeming profligacy of
Indian society, expressed in the de jure repression north of the U.S.-
Canada border and in de facto repression south of it. In Seattle, though,
potlatch became the inspiration for appropriation. To borrow Gram Shelton's words, Seattle's urban Potlatchers would use Native symbolism to
make the city's name high and to make it go all over the place. Here,
then, was an event that represented yet another weft of the woven coast,
showing how completely Seattle's urban identity had been transformed
by encounters with its indigenous hinterland.[9]

It did not start out this way. The first Potlatch, in 1911, used Klondike
imagery: the presiding figure was King D'Oro, the avatar of golden
wealth, who arrived on the *Portland*—always the *Portland*—with a retinue of hoary prospectors and rambunctious dancing girls. The following
year, though, D'Oro was succeeded by Hyas Tyee Kopa Konoway. The
brochure for the 1912 festivities described this new incarnation:

Seattle's Potlatch is unique, for it is based upon and is true to the rich tradition and history of Puget Sound and the Alaskan coast. Every pageant, every
spectacle, is colored with the original pigments. Its principal pageant is a line
of a thousand totem poles; its emblem is an Alaskan grotesque; its "patron
saints" the Whale, the Crow, the Seal, the Bear and other quaint and startling
crests of the native of the Northland.

This was, in effect, the AYPE's appropriation of "Indian" images metas-
tasized citywide. The "Alaskan grotesque," inspired by the totem poles
of both Seattle and Alaska, was the Potlatch's mascot, known as the Big
Bug. Simultaneously an emblem of the festival and an object of racist
derision, the Big Bug was a regional cousin to Sambo, drawn not from
the imagined plantations of the South but from the Northwest Coast
of popular imagination. The Big Bug's nearer kin were everywhere in
Seattle during Potlatch: the Chanty Tyees quartet ("the singing chiefs

of the Seattle Press Club") sang "Chinook choruses" for Hyas Tyee Kopa Konoway Allen during his official tour of the city, which including making "good medicine" over the new liner *Potlatch* at the Seattle Construction and Dry Dock. Across town, three dozen young men performing the "Totem Pole Dance" as part of the play *The Alaskan*, written by Joe Blethen, son of the owner of the *Seattle Times*, proved a far greater success than the sourdoughs and sad old King D'Oro. Upon Hyas Tyee Allen's ritual departure, the *Times* observed that "ever after Seattle will look to the Potlatch for an Indian chief and not for a king or queen as high ruler."[10]

The *Times*'s rejection of royalty suggests that the Potlatches were democratic, or even populist, in their conception. Indeed, they were—designed as participatory spectacles, the events brought Brahmin and lowbrow together in a unified civic identity. But for all the nods to generosity and philanthropy, it was Potlatch organizers who gained the most from civic potlatching, and they did so through an organization that stood at the core of urban power: the Tilikums of Elttaes. Making their official debut at the unveiling of a newly painted Chief-of-All-Women pole in the fall of 1911, the Tilikums ("friends" in Chinook Jargon; Elttaes is Seattle spelled backward) included the most powerful men in Seattle. During the 1912 Potlatch parade, for example, one of the highlights was "Chief Skowl's War Canoe," crewed by some thirty Tilikums. Among them were Hyas Tyee Allen's insurance industry colleagues, as well as bankers, attorneys, a Presbyterian pastor, the Seattle postmaster, and staff from both the *Times* and the *Post-Intelligencer*. The canoe also carried J. C. Marmaduke, general manager of the New Washington Hotel and the Alaska Building; Colonel William T. Perkins, an executive with the Northern Exploration and Development Company, the Alaska Midland Railroad, and the Northern Securities Company; Clyde Morris, president of Nome-based General Contractors and the Arctic Club; and Joshua Green, president of the International Steamship Company. Called "the livest of the live wires" in Seattle, these Tilikums had made fortunes from the city's hinterland, whose images their friends at the papers now used to sell the city. So perhaps civic potlatching was not about generosity after all.[11]

Soon after their appearance, the Tilikums became one of the largest civic organizations in Seattle. A competition among their three component "tribes" in 1913, for example, brought in 1,547 new members, bringing the total to 2,588 Tilikums, a significant portion of the city's white, middle- and upper-class men. Their induction ceremony involved the climbing of a totem pole, and tongue-in-cheek gossip of human sacrifice circulated through town, a reminder of the fascination with rumored cannibalistic rites among Northwest Coast peoples. "Playing Indian" was a well-established American pastime and had always expressed a wide range of political and cultural notions, but if the Tilikums tried to look like Indians, they behaved more like their white counterparts in fraternal organizations throughout the country. Concerned—at least on the surface—with more than simply making money, the Tilikums also sought to create a new moral climate in the city. During their inaugural year, for example, they erected a totem pole downtown that literally spelled out the values of the Tilikums. A far cry from the Chief-of-All-Women pole at the other end of the downtown, this one stood atop seven steps, each engraved with a virtue: Energy, Loyalty, Tradition, Truth, Ability, Equality, and Success—all spelling Elttaes. For all its gaiety, the work of the Tilikums was also a moral project, its apparent confidence belying deep-rooted concerns about modern urban life and the reforming impulses of the Progressive Era.[12]

The work of the Tilikums was also a historical project. The 1912 Potlatch parade, for instance, was a wheeled chronology of Seattle's imperial past, its place-story cast in crepe and cardboard. First came a float belonging to a "shaman," who used rattles to clear "evil spirits" from the parade route, followed by the Hyas Tyee's own float of walruses, ravens, and golden cornucopias representing the North's abundance. Then came the Tilikums themselves, some wearing papier-mâché bear, eagle, and whale masks and others dressed as totem poles, with horns braying and drums pounding in "the way in which the Indians of the North called together the chieftains." Next came a Native potlatch scene complete with slaves and giant feast dishes, followed by Russian Alaska: a miniature replica of the Orthodox church at Sitka and

"Russian priests, Cossacks and Indian slaves." Last, but certainly not least, came the American period, represented by a huge eagle perched on a map of Seward's purchase, a re-creation of Chilkoot Pass with a regiment of sourdoughs, and lastly the Home Government float, "a patriotic conception of what the future holds for Alaska." Looking north to articulate Seattle's urban future, Potlatch organizers expended little energy on the local past: Chief Seattle, the pioneers at Alki, and other figures and events from Seattle's pre-imperial history rarely appeared at Potlatch. This was a story about place, and the place in question was the salmon-scented silences, gold-strewn Arctic creek beds, and totem-poled villages of Seattle's hinterland—not the lands and waters upon which Seattle had been built.[13]

The kind of place-story the Tilikums told had everything to do with the kind of men they were, and with the kinds of experiences they had had with both cities and Indians. Most members of the Tilikums of Elttaes were *cheechakos,* people who had arrived during Seattle's period of rapid population growth that began in the 1890s. Few of them had experienced Seattle Illahee. For them, the city had always been a place of banks and steamships and railroads and tall stone buildings, all connected to Alaska and the North Pacific. To be fair, Potlatch—which, after all, began as Alaska Day—was never really about Seattle's history in the first place. A glorified street party and public-relations campaign, Potlatch was an escape from the past, created by men with little interest in reliving a history few of them had known firsthand. At the same time, convincing residents, visitors, and investors of Seattle's current and future greatness required the creation of a historical trajectory— a story for the city. And, in a sense, the Tilikums' version of Seattle's history *was* a local story; in the crowded world of twentieth-century urban competition, Potlatches and totem poles and tribes could provide the city with a unique urban identity among its rivals. But their definition of place was a new one: as the Northwest Coast's greatest metropolis, the hinterland had for the Tilikums become part of Seattle's local terrain.

The Tilikums might have escaped the local past, but they could not escape the global present. The 1913 and 1914 Potlatches resembled that of 1912 in all the important ways—totem poles lining the streets,

Tilikums in their war canoes, and the Big Bug leering at the throngs—but Seattle's biggest festival became increasingly entangled in events in the broader world. The 1913 Potlatch was marred by running battles between enlisted men and the Industrial Workers of the World, and as the world embarked upon the Great War in 1914, Potlatch was scaled back to only four days and received only subdued press coverage. In fact, the 1914 Potlatch would be the last for two decades. The festival was revived again in 1934 to bolster the spirits of a suffering city, thanks to a new generation of Tilikums with their own Hyas Tyee Kopa Konoway, tribal chieftains, and shamans. By the Aviation Potlatch of 1941—the last Seattle Potlatch, as celebration gave way once again to war—images borrowed from Seattle's experience with empire, and versions of history that emphasized the regional over the local, had come to seem like natural expressions of Seattle's past. Although the Tilikums had been responsible for creating this new sense of the local, based in their own lived experiences in a regional metropolis, they did occasionally venerate local history. Even in the years when Potlatch was not held, the Tilikums participated in other urban ceremonies, throwing their weight behind both Chief Seattle Day and commemorations of the landing of the Denny Party at Alki Point. And when the men who dressed as totem poles, who shook Tlingit rattles and spread cannibal rumors about themselves, came together to remember these turning points in the local past, they came into contact with another group of Seattleites who told a very different place-story but who also used Indians to do it.[14]

THE TILIKUMS OF ELTTAES told one kind of urban story in the early twentieth century; pioneers told another. As the "live wires" that powered the dynamo of urban growth, the Tilikums used Indian imagery to sell the city, but pioneers and their descendants used Indian imagery to express ambivalence about the losses attendant to that growth. Potlatches were optimistic festivals of promotion, while pioneer stories were sentimental markings of the passage of time. The two had different purposes: one to drum up attention in the noisy marketplace of civic public relations, the other to preserve local heritage and revisit fading memories. The Tilikums looked to the future, while the pioneers gazed longingly into the past. What they had in common, though, was that both told stories about Indians to give shape to the history of the city. To craft their place-story, pioneers used accounts of local indigenous people to commemorate their own lives in the city's lost landscapes and, in doing so, cast themselves as a "vanishing race" in their own right. The Tilikums were not the only white people playing Indian in Seattle.

In 1938, the same year that the Tilikums dragged the Big Bug through the city for a "Potlatch of Progress," Seattle pioneers and their families gathered at the Stockade Hotel at Alki Point. While Potlatches were about extravagance, hyperbole, and celebration, the gathering at Alki was something quite different. "The blazing logs crackling in the fireplace," noted a *Seattle Post-Intelligencer* observer, "imparted an air of authenticity and quiet corroboration to the ceremonies which were simple but heartfelt." The guest of honor that day was Rolland Denny—an infant when his parents and their cohort landed on 13 November 1851, the last living member of the Denny Party, and, as such, the only surviving link to those hallowed events. Denny's presence also made Seattle unique; in his address to the group, Mayor Arthur Langlie pointed out that Seattle was one of the few cities where one of the original founders still lived—a backward-looking kind of boosterism. (Seattle's uniqueness in this regard was to last only a few more months: Rolland Denny was dead by the following year's gathering.)[15]

This was not the first such gathering. For nearly half a century, early Seattle settlers, like their counterparts in other Western places, had been coming together to commemorate and commiserate. The Society of Washington Territory Pioneers—"pioneer" defined as someone who had arrived prior to the indigenous uprising of 1856—was incorporated in Seattle in 1872, with Arthur Denny, Henry Yesler, William Bell, and Henry Van Asselt among the founding members. It merged with the larger Washington Pioneer Association in 1886. From the outside, the group's annual meetings, usually held in Seattle, seemed almost funereal. Except for quaint anecdotes of settler life—a litany of hapless Indians, runaway horses, and jokes about mud—the reunions seemed like a deathwatch. A Seattle newspaper described one such proceeding in the 1890s:

Charles Prosch . . . read his annual report as secretary, which was interesting and of pathetic interest, especially when we have the names of those recently dead. The pathos of this was heighted [*sic*] when, in response to the reading of the roll call, the answer several times given from those present was, "He is dead," these being the names of those who had gone, but of whose death Mr. Prosch was not aware.

The paper then enumerated the dead by name: thirty-seven for that year, including Henry Yesler. Press accounts of pioneer reunions, which typically included page after verbatim page of members' reminiscences, highlighted the fact that the generation that had settled Seattle, along with the way of life they represented, was fast disappearing before the onslaught of modern urban life. Pioneer stories were a way to talk about urban change and offered a counterpoint to the enthusiastic promotion of boosters like the Tilikums of Elttaes.[16]

Arthur Armstrong Denny set the precedent; if he is the "father of Seattle," then he should also be known as the father of Seattle pioneer malaise. In the first published history of the city—*Pioneer Days on Puget Sound*, printed in 1888—Denny was the first to express anxiety about the urban transformations taking place around him:

It is now thirty-six years since I came to Puget Sound, and I am more and more impressed with the fact as each succeeding year rolls by that the early settlers of the country will very shortly all have crossed over the river and be soon forgotten, for we may all concede the fact that we shall be missed but little when we are gone, and that little but a short time; but when we have met the last trial and our last camp fire has died out some may desire a knowledge of such facts as we alone can give.

Here was another kind of crossing in the crossing-over place of Seattle: between two kinds of Bostons, to use the old Chinook Jargon term for the Americans. In one particularly petulant passage, Denny penned that it is a common occurrence for parties who have reached here by the easy method of steamer or railway in a palace car, to be most blindly unreasonable in their fault finding, and they are often not content with abusing the country and climate, but they heap curses and abuse on those who came before them by the good old method of ninety or a hundred days crossing the plains.

Denny made a clear distinction between his generation and the burgeoning tide of *cheechakos,* many of whom would go on to become members of the Tilikums of Elttaes. He became increasingly dejected in his public musings about the passing of his generation and the ascendancy of Seattle's new civic society; in an 1890 interview with historian Hubert Howe Bancroft, for example, Denny lamented his own obsolescence and seemed to look forward to what he called "crossing over." Even the physical evidence of his role as founder of the city had disappeared; in 1892, the remains of that first log cabin at Alki were razed, despite Denny's efforts to save it. Denny might have been the father of Seattle, but he seemed surprisingly lost in the city's modern incarnation.[17]

Denny may have been the first—and the most pessimistic—Seattle pioneer to articulate this anxiety over modern urban life, but he was by no means the last. Major J. Thomas Turner, who had first come to Seattle in the 1850s, noted in his 1914 reminiscences that "times have changed," not unlike the North American landscape. "There are no more Rocky Mountains," he wrote, "no more Indians, no more buffalo, and the Great Plains have disappeared. Come to think of it, were there ever any, or were [sic] their existence only an iridescent dream?" Meanwhile, Charles Kinnear, after describing scenes of 1870s Seattle in his own memoirs, ended with the acknowledgment that "this was in those long haired Siwash Indian days on what is now the city's main waterfront, and the like of it cannot be seen here any more." Similarly, Edith Sanderson Redfield mourned the passing of Seattle's "wilderness," its "virgin shore," and the race of "Redmen" who lived there in a 1930 poem:

All, all are gone, the men, tepees
E'en gone the trickling streams, the trees.

Seattle now in pride surveys
Its ports—its buildings—railroads—ways,
Where money comes and money goes;
Whose right supreme? Who cares? Who knows?

Turner, Kinnear, and Redfield each linked their history to specific places lost to urban development, and filled those places with remembered Indians.[18]

As pioneers told stories about Indians and nature to measure what had been lost, they produced a place-story that challenged the one told by the Tilikums, and they knew it. Pioneer poet Francis Henry, for instance, had written in 1874 about the "pleasant condition" of the early settler who was no longer the "slave of ambition" and who found a new life in the Northwest surrounded by "acres of clams." Some years later, Henry felt compelled to pen a bitter sequel:

Some say this country's improving,
And boast of its commerce and trade,
But measured by social enjoyment
I find it has sadly decayed.
In the pioneer days on the Sound,
When the people had little to wear,
And subsisted on clams the year round,
We'd hearty good fellowship here.
. . . .
Not only our friendly relations
Are dropped for the worship of gold,
But the solid backbone of the country
Is recklessly bartered and sold.

The poem continues with complaints about logging, the commercial harvest of those sacred clams, and other emblems of industrial Puget Sound. That Henry used gold as a metaphor for the lack of "friendly relations" in the new, metropolitan Seattle was no accident. He and his pioneer compatriots were crafting an urban story that directly challenged the one promoted by the Tilikums in the Potlatch festivals. Instead of a story in which the city's northern hinterland—and the wealth that had sprung from it—was the driving force, pioneers crafted a story in which Seattle's origins lay in a close-knit community set in a nigh-Edenic landscape.[19]

The local press also became involved in this clash of urban histories. In 1913, just before the start of the third Potlatch festival, a writer for the *Patriarch* complained that "publicity has developed into a system in the present day. That which is not unworthy of publicity is considered, by the public, to be not worth notice." The writer then listed all the civic holidays in Seattle—including Tilikums' Day and Boosters' Day—before pointing out that the "Hegira" of the pioneers had nothing to do with gold and that "theirs was no feather-bed Pullman car luxury, such as is now enjoyed by those insolent 'chee charcos' who presume to treat them with patronizing condescension." The tension between Potlatch parades and pioneer reunions, then, reflected a much deeper conflict between the *cheechako* and the pioneer generations and the social orders they each represented. Some pioneers had benefited from Seattle's metropolitan status; in fact, many of the founding families had become important members of the civic and commercial elite. But in the new cities of the West, as historian David Wrobel has shown, pioneers' political and economic power was usually slight—even if their cultural and moral status was not—and their accounts of the past contrasted sharply with the efforts of boosters to imagine places like modern Seattle into existence.[20]

As more and more of Seattle's first settlers died, it fell to their children and grandchildren to keep the pioneers' place-story alive. Not surprisingly, the Denny clan was at the heart of things. In a series of enormously popular books, Emily Inez Denny (the daughter of David and Louisa Boren Denny) and her second cousins Sophie Frye Bass and Roberta Frye Watt (the granddaughters of Arthur Armstrong Denny himself) equated Indians, nature, and the pioneer way of life more explicitly than their predecessors ever had. Denny's 1909 family memoir *Blazing the Way; or, True Stories, Songs, and Sketches of Puget Sound and Other Pioneers* is filled with passages in which the first white woman born in Seattle grieves for a time when "our play-grounds were the brown beaches [and] the hillsides covered with plumy young fir trees." The playground was made all the more wonderful by the "friendly advances" of Native children, who "in their primitive state . . . seemed perfectly healthy and happy little creatures." All this would be swept away by the inexorable tide of progress:

To the few of our pioneers who are left and who were once the barefooted boys and girls who played the roads that are now First and Second Avenues the past seems like a beautiful dream, wherein people of another world dwelt; the red man with his picturesque garb of blankets and beads; the pioneer in his buckskin hunting blouse and coon skin cap; the sailors from white winged ships, and the jolly Jack tars from the old man-o-war.

Denny's "beautiful dream" contrasted starkly with the urban landscape she now saw around her.[21]

Denny's kinswomen Sophie Frye Bass and Roberta Frye Watt were brought up with tales of Seattle's village period and, like Denny, told stories about Indians to talk about Seattle's metropolitan transformation. Bass in particular used changes in the urban landscape to distinguish between the Indian past and the urban present: "Third Street with its neighborly homes, beds of pansies and mignonette, shade trees, picket fences, along with the lum-me-i (old woman) and her micka tickey clams (Do you want to buy some clams) is of yesterday, while Third Avenue with its hurrying throng, its roar of traffic and brilliant lights— is of today!" She described the deaths of indigenous people like Kikisebloo and the city's massive engineering projects in the same sentence; she mourned the time before conservation laws, when local settlers could come home with bags full of game. To talk about urban change, it seemed, required talking about Indians. Watt followed a similar path; in writing of her uncle Rolland, for example, she cast the Indian and urban as antonyms:

His life has spanned the years from the Indian cayuse to the automobile, from the Indian canoe to the airplane. He has seen Seattle grow and change from one roofless cabin in the wilderness to a city of towering buildings; he has seen the winding Indian trails give way to straight and paved streets; his ears have heard the cry of the cougar, the chanting of the medicine man—and the voice of the radio.

In fact, in lamenting the loss of the pioneer way of life, with its romantic scenery and encounters with Indians, the Denny women and other pioneers created a framework in which Indians and cities seemed as though they were mutually exclusive. Just as "pioneerness" seemed impossible in twentieth-century Seattle, so too did "Indianness." Some even went so far as to equate themselves with the Indians who peopled their stories. In describing the passing of the settler generation, Bass described the factors that had led to the dispossession of many *real* local Indians—in particular, large-scale urban engineering—as if she and her ancestors were a vanishing race as well. And when her family home burned in the 1870s, she recalled feeling as though "I could say with the Indians when they were driven from their homes, 'chad-quid-del-el' ('Where is my home?'),' using a Whulshootseed phrase to express the terror of homelessness. In Bass's urban story, pioneers practically *were* Indians.[22]

The Denny family writers mourned the effects of urbanization—in particular, the perceived loss of community, freedom, and closeness to nature—and used stories about Indians to do it, but they rarely spoke of the processes by which indigenous land had become Seattle. For example, none of the women mentioned the 1866 petition that had prevented the creation of a Duwamish reservation near Seattle—a petition their fathers, uncles, and grandfathers had all signed. Instead, they emphasized the "incalculable injury, outrages, indignities, and villainies practiced upon the native inhabitants by evil white men." Like their ancestors, Watt, Bass, and Denny saw Indian-white hostilities as the fault of the "wrong" kind of settlers, whitewashing both their own past and Seattle's urban history. Avoiding the connections between urban founding, Native dispossession, and metropolitan dominance, the creators of pioneer place-stories absolved themselves of responsibility for both the indigenous past and the urban present. *It wasn't us*, they seem to protest. *It was somebody else, the squaw men or those damned* cheechakos.[23]

DESPITE THE CONTRASTING PLACE-STORIES they told, and the real differences those stories represented, the Tilikums and the pioneers had many things in common. One of those things was Edmond S. Meany. A University of Washington historian, Meany played a critical role in documenting the local past, often in collaboration with pioneer societies, but also participated actively in the civic boosterism and cultural borrowing of the Tilikums. Meany consulted with Broadway High School students on a historical pageant that stretched from Vancouver's voyage to the creation of the Ship Canal and the Smith Tower, and he was one of the lead organizers of the AYPE, ensuring that the University of Washington would benefit from the development of the fairgrounds. He advised Tilikums on the "proper" meaning and use of the term "potlatch" and regularly answered letters inquiring about "Indian names" for young-businessmen's clubs, high school yearbooks, real-estate developments, and vacation homes. Meany's life and work blurred the distinctions between Potlatcher and pioneer, academic and booster, archivist and appropriator.[24]

Beyond the tireless Professor Meany, the Tilikums and the pioneers had something else in common. Together, they crafted Seattle's most powerful place-story, in which something called the Seattle Spirit, born in the founding at Alki Point, triumphed over both nature and Native people. This story was transmitted most explicitly on the anniversary of the Alki landing, known as Founders Day. While Founders Days in the nineteenth century had been reserved observances, by the twentieth century they had become urban spectacles, second only to the Potlatches, joining memories of Indian "depredations" to calls for a renewed civic consciousness and grafting local stories onto national narratives. In reenactments and other rituals, Seattle's "Pilgrims" were not just founders of one northwestern city but players in a triumphant drama of civilization-versus-savagery that had begun at Plymouth Rock. Every November, Seattleites made their city's place-story and their nation's place-story one and the same.

One of the first large public observances of Founders Day came in 1905. Hundreds gathered at the corner of First and Cherry, the site of the blockhouse where settlers had cowered during the indigenous attack on the town in 1856, to witness the installation of a plaque commemorating survivors of the "Battle of Seattle." Pioneer attorney Cornelius Hanford gave the keynote address, describing in vivid detail the "sanguinary struggle." While noting that only a few settlers had been killed in the uprising, Hanford pointed out that "it was an earnest war, and waged for the purpose of expelling or exterminating all of the white people." But the pioneers had persevered, eventually allowing landscapes locked in Native possession to achieve their full potential:

Necessity, which is natural law, justifies the exercise of power of dominant races to occupy and use the land for the purposes for which it is adapted. . . . The Caucasian race acquired North America, partly by purchase and partly by conquest of the native inhabitants, who, as occupiers of the land failed to use it as God intended that it should be used, so as to yield its fruits in abundance for the comfort of millions of inhabitants.

For Hanford, and likely for many in the audience that day, the connection between indigenous resistance and urban development was clear: the former had almost ended but ultimately justified the latter, and it was the land, *this place*, that joined those two stories. In later years, Hanford would hone this logic. In his 1924 subscription history *Seattle and Environs*—along with books by the Denny clan, part of Seattle's historical canon—he wrote that the attack stemmed from Indian resentment of a "stronger and more enlightened people." In the end, Native envy had faltered before the Seattle Spirit, which had existed "from the time when the founders landed . . . intangible as the souls of men and yet a real force, giving community identity distinct as the individualities of persons." The birthplace of Seattle, then, was located both at Alki Point and in race war.[25]

Some observances of Seattle's birthday were held in public places like the corner of First and Cherry; others were held in private homes where old friends gathered to share their memories. One such gathering took place in 1914 "in a proud old house on the top of First Hill, where the ceilings are high, and the roof is mossy, and the stairs are square, and the light comes through the windows in rainbow patches." This was the home of Vivian Carkeek, one of the éminences grises of Seattle society. He was a pioneer; in fact, he had been born in a waterfront house built on the place where, back in 1862, David Kellogg had watched Bunty Charley's initiation into a Duwamish secret society. As founders of the Seattle Historical Society and with links to Seattle's village period, Carkeek and his peers crafted a genteel vision of the past. But there was also a darker side to that history: among the teacakes and crinoline at his party could be found "an Indian costume or two for grim reminder." For all their gentility—or, rather, because of it—pioneers saw themselves as noble survivors of the violent tensions that had dominated Seattle's first years. One of Carkeek's friends wrote, for example, that "as ever the case from Massachusetts Bay to Puget Sound the white and red man go to war." Linking Seattle's creation to that of the nation, pioneers saw their city's foundations laid in the inevitability of racial conflict and in the moral fiber that had ensured American victory. From Pawtuxent to the Little Crossing-Over Place, the story seemed the same.[26]

This vision of civic and national origins was not limited to the pioneers. Pioneers and Potlatchers alike told stories about interracial violence as a way to remind modern Seattleites of the travails of their forebears. Abbie Denny-Lindsley, one of Arthur and Mary Denny's daughters, cautioned in 1906 that if modern urban residents could "awaken from their uneasy slumbers some night and find Seattle as she was forty-five years ago, they would think it a pipe dream and feel for their scalp locks." That same year, attorney and civic busybody W. T. Dovell—a candidate for future Tilikum membership if ever there was one—echoed Denny-Lindsley's sentiment, contrasting the softness of twentieth-century city life with the grim realities of the frontier. "Where in those days the stranger, who struggled to these shores, found no warmer welcome than that accorded by the lurking savage who coveted his scalp," Dovell said in an address later printed in the *Washington His-*

torical Quarterly, "he is now received into the abiding place of luxury and wealth." And at a 1938 pioneer reunion, Mayor John Dore warned the younger people present that "the race is getting soft [but the] pioneers lived hard. It would be well if you children could understand the hardships these people went through." Certainly, there were other Seattle Spirit stories: the lost railroad-terminus battle with Tacoma in the 1870s, the imposition of law and order during anti-Chinese violence in the 1880s, and the struggle for Alaska gateway status in the 1890s. But it was the Indian challenges of those first years that had the most power and that would continue to reverberate for much of the twentieth century.[27]

That power sprang from the resonance between local place-stories and the national narrative. American thinking about the frontier, best articulated by historian Frederick Jackson Turner at the 1893 world's fair in Chicago, linked the belief in a national character shaped by the frontier experience to concerns about the fate of a nation whose frontier had just "closed." Just as Mayor Dore worried about the loss of the Seattle Spirit, Americans in general wondered who they were without the twin threats of Indians and wilderness. Meanwhile, the Indians in Seattle's stories also looked familiar: Seeathl was the noble savage par excellence, assuaging the guilt of conquest through hospitality and prophecy; the Big Bug and other icons of Potlatch reflected fascination with the exotic and, ultimately, the laughable and primitive; and the Seattle Spirit drew on the long history of American fear in which the ignoble savage, with his tomahawk and shrill war cry, skulked in the dim forests of the imagination. The creation of stories like these had become a national pastime. Like countless new local historical societies, Grand Army of the Republic reunions, and reenactments at Plymouth Rock, Seattle's Potlatches, pioneer gatherings, and Founders Days were part of what historian Michael Kammen has called a new civil religion of historical observance. Stories about Indians created meaning in modern America. They established pioneers' social status in a wealthy new metropolis, they voiced dissent regarding environmental and cultural change, and ultimately, they justified urban conquest. And in the years leading up to the Second World War, Seattle's place-stories went largely unchallenged, even by Native people themselves.[28]

D
URING THE YEARS THAT the "Changers" transformed Seattle's indigenous and urban landscapes and crafted civic place-stories using Indian images, few Native people resisted either development in explicit ways: the 1893 protest by refugees from Herring's House on Ballast Island was a rare exception. Certainly, indigenous people had their own place-stories of the city's growth—Chesheeahud's comment about "too many houses now," for example—but those stories were almost never told in public. Instead, Native men and women often participated in the events through which white place-stories were transmitted. They were there at the 1911 Potlatch, paddling a canoe against the University of Washington's crew team. (The Indians lost, proving yet again, according to the *Post-Intelligencer*, that "the red man and his handiwork could be no match for the white man and his skill.") They sometimes came to pioneer gatherings; Suquamish elder Jennie Harper, for example, was brought across Puget Sound to sit at the head table during Rolland Denny's final reunion at the Stockade Hotel. And in 1936 Snohomish elder Harriet Shelton Williams unveiled the new official city seal—a suspiciously Roman-looking profile of Chief Seattle—on Founders Day, while her father, Tulalip chief William Shelton, told stories about Seeathl in Whulshootseed, Chinook Jargon, and English. At events like these, indigenous people's participation seemed only to confirm the civic story. Meanwhile, Native people from Seattle's hinterland, lacking the authority that being local bestowed, had even less of a voice.[29]

Even at Chief Seattle Day celebrations, held on a reservation, Native people were active participants in observances that told stories serving white urban interests. Beginning with the first Chief Seattle Day in 1911 and continuing through the 1940s, the Suquamish were gracious hosts to hundreds of visitors from the city, decorating Seeathl's grave, coordinating massive clambakes, playing the bone game, and entertaining with "quaint old Indians [*sic*] songs." In formal speeches, hereditary chiefs and other tribal leaders spoke of Seeathl's generosity, called

for peace between whites and Indians, and conducted graveside ceremonies. In doing so, they asserted their own ceremonial and political
presence, but if there was resistance to the Seattle place-story embed-
ded in Native participation in Chief Seattle Days, no one outside the
indigenous community seemed to notice. Native people surely had their
own Seattle place-stories; as historians of other places have shown, private stories shared among communities with limited access to public
discourse can be the basis for a vibrant alternative historical consciousness. Around kitchen tables, at winter dances, and in tribal council meetings, tribal people surely told their own stories about what Seattle—the
man and the city—meant from their own perspectives, keeping alive
their own memories of urban conquest. It would be years, however,
before those place-stories reached white audiences.[30]

Stories have a past; they come from somewhere. Stories also perform
work; when they are told, they enact power. Seattle's place-stories both
reflected and reinforced the city's patterns of power, as illustrated by two
final Potlatch stories. Leon Metcalf, who spent many years recording the
stories of Puget Sound Indian people, saw firsthand the power of Seattle's urban narrative. Late in his life, he recalled attending the Golden
Potlatch of 1912, where the Big Bug and the Tilikums commanded the
thoroughfares, where totem poles decorated downtown, and where
indigenous people were among the throngs. "My father and I were walking across a street after the parade had gone past," he told an interviewer,

but there was still lot of racket, it was very loud. There were two Indian women,
probably Duwamish Indians, that were there selling clams and baskets, probably. One turned to the other and I listened to hear what she was going to say.
What she said was [we are making noise] . . . it was kind of a pun, a play on
words, on her part.

From our perspective almost a century later, it is hard not to see the
Duwamish woman's Whulshootseed wordplay as a sardonic reference
to the extravagant chaos that the Tilikums had orchestrated, or perhaps
even as a protest against the public silence of local indigenous people
in civic discourse. In a city that used Indian images and stories to make

sense of itself, real Native people, and especially those not affiliated with totem poles, were pushed to the margins of urban society. They now had little impact on the shape of Seattle's urban narrative—except maybe as metaphors.[31]

More than two decades later, in 1939, Snohomish elder Harriet Williams fondly recalled the Potlatches and expressed hope that more would be held in the future:

> I have a jumbled, but happy memory of Seattle's Potlatch—walking along avenues full of many shops—many people and the hum of many voices—the thrill of watching various drill teams and bands march with perfect precision— so many beautiful floats, the result of thought and work . . . yes, I had a most enjoyable time.

Like Skagit shamans visiting the optometrist, Plains warriors on the AYPE Ferris wheel, or Haida assembly-line workers, Williams's memories of Potlatch reminded readers that Native people, so often relegated to Seattle's urban past, were also part of Seattle's urban present. But as she continued, Williams also drew attention to all that had been lost:

> But I somehow still long for those past days—I can see the approach of count- less canoes, the sounds of drums and the rhythms of different chants—my own language, which I hear so seldom now. But such is progress—and so the Indian of today brings his dollars and cents to Potlatch and receives various pleasures in return—and hopes Seattle will keep on having Potlatch.

By the 1930s, this kind of image—the sweeping away of the city's complicated past (and most of its Indians) before a crushing wave of metaphors, marketing, and metropolis—had become received wisdom and common knowledge. But just as tides come in, they rush out again, and Williams's words were spoken on the eve of a new era in Seattle's complicated Native histories in which the place-stories told in Seattle, and the people doing the telling, would change yet again.[32]

8 / On the Cusp of Past and Future

MARIAN WESLEY SMITH, an anthropologist at Columbia University, spent much of the 1930s conducting research among the Native peoples of Puget Sound. Her travels brought her into contact with the descendants of the indigenous people of Seattle, and the urbanized landscape of the pre–Second World War maritime Northwest shaped much of what she had to say about the state of Indians in the region. Native people on Puget Sound, Smith argued, had "come through remarkably well" considering the "rigorous mushroom development" of places like Seattle. "No other Indians of the whole continent have been similarly engulfed by the sudden growth of city populations [or] have been exposed to the full impact of twentieth-century urban society," she wrote in the 1940s. To Smith, the successful adaptation of Puget Sound's Native peoples was "certainly better than that of many Indians classified as less primitive." In fact, she wrote, "it is this sort of dilemma that throws doubt upon classification schemes." Despite the near-total dispossession of indigenous people from Seattle's urban landscape, surviving Native peoples' accommodation to urban change in Puget Sound seemed to challenge her discipline's very foundations.[1]

The conditions of Indian people in urban Puget Sound also threw doubt upon another kind of classification scheme: the boundaries between past, present, and future. Smith saw this just as clearly. "If today Salish life is mingled with, and sometimes indistinguishable from, modern American and Canadian life," she wrote, "so much the better. If the past and the present converge, and the future may be expected to partake of both, so much closer to reality is our picture of the Northwest." And for Indians in Seattle in the 1930s, the past, present, and future did seem to converge. Like the years surrounding 1880, the 1930s were a transition between two periods in the city's urban and Indian histories, a hinge between one era and another. The years around 1880 had represented a transition between a strong indigenous presence in Seattle and indigenous dispossession, as well as the beginnings of a regional Indian hinterland. By the 1930s, Seattle had developed a complex interweaving of multiple Native histories: Duwamish descendants of the area's indigenous communities and Native people from far away shared a city studded with totem poles and explained by stories about Indians. Mr. Glover's bird's-eye panorama, the 1880 census, and other sources had offered glimpses of Native Seattle on the eve of a massive urban transformation. Sources from the 1930s show the results of that transformation and offer their own glimpses into a city that, unbeknownst to its residents (Indian or otherwise), was on the eve of yet another great change.[2]

In 1930, Seattle was a bona fide metropolis, a city of 350,000 people. Few vestiges of the indigenous landscape remained—the Duwamish River had been straightened, the waters of Lake Washington now flowed through the Hiram M. Chittenden Locks rather than the extinct Black River, and new neighborhoods of bungalows and apartments blanketed hills that had once been barriers to urban growth. It seemed that Seattle had made good on its urban promises. But instead of optimism, there was anxiety. Seattle was experiencing the first throes of the Great Depression and, as it had during the Panic of 1893, Seattle's boom-and-bust economy was suffering greatly. The crash of 1929 also changed the lives of Indian people in Seattle. Many of the small firms that had fueled annual migrations of Native men and women to Seattle—farms, sawmills, canneries—laid off their Indian workers first, then closed as banks failed. Layoffs and business failures slowed the widespread movements of Native people up and down the coast and from reservations in Puget Sound, where many of the descendants of Seattle's indigenous people now lived. The Depression also wreaked havoc on Indian attempts to establish a permanent presence in Seattle. For example, Ralph Young (or Looshkát), a Hoonah Raven Tlingit and founding member of the Alaska Native Brotherhood, found his fortunes changing in the 1930s. After helping discover the wildly successful Chichagof Mine in Alaska, Young and his uncle had traded their shares in the mine for property along the industrializing Duwamish. Soon after the market collapse, however, the men were forced to forfeit the profitable land (which would eventually be occupied by the Boeing Company) because of unpaid taxes and return to Alaska.[3]

Despite the dislocations of the Depression, however, Indian people had found ways to call Seattle home. The manuscript of the 1930 census offers insight into the lives of the city's Native men, women, and children. Their numbers were not great—less than 1 percent of the urban population—but their circumstances speak to the roots that Indian people from other places were putting down in Seattle's urban soil. Those roots, like the city itself, were often thoroughly working class. Across the city, Indian men and women could be found in Seattle's bungalow neighborhoods of modest income. On Beacon Hill, Choctaw pipe fitter Franklin Turner came home from long days at the oil plant to a neighborhood of mechanics and construction workers where his white wife, Ellen, kept house. On Capitol Hill, mixed-blood, Canadian-born Lily Lee lived with her white husband, Lorn, who helped build and maintain the city's bridges. Like that of the Turners, the Lees' neighborhood was mostly white and thoroughly working class, with neighbors working as bakers and seamstresses, cashiers and electricians. So was the Admiral neighborhood on Duwamish Head, where truck driver Robert Lee (no relation to Lorn) and his full-blood "Washington Indian" wife, Minnie, provided for their eight-year-old son, Eugene. And Admiral was much like South Park along the Duwamish, where the white-Inuit Ryner family lived off the money husband Homer earned as a stone polisher in a local factory. There was also a cluster of mixed-race families around Salmon Bay. Swedish immigrant Paul Peterson, a deckhand on a tug, lived with his Skagit wife, Clara, and their teenage sons, Bernard and Chester, on the flats near the western stretch of the Ship Canal. Nellie Wooley, an Alaskan Haida, kept house for her boatbuilder husband, John, in the industrial area that had sprung up on the now-filled estuary between Salmon Bay and Smith's Cove. On the south side of Salmon Bay, not far from the site of Hwelchteed's old place, the Scottish and

Stoney Indian Darling family got by on John Darling's earnings as a construction worker.[4]

Although the experiences of most of these families are lost to history, two mixed-race families living near Salmon Bay left some records behind, giving us a sense of their lives beyond the census enumerator's rows and columns and offering insights into what it meant to be Indian in Seattle. One family, the Youngbloods, lived in the Crown Hill area north of Salmon Bay. Bowhertta Ladder, the matriarch of the family, had been born among the Nuu-chah-nulth but raised by the Makah, and now made baskets and sold them downtown for up to ten dollars each. Her daughter Minnie worked as a domestic servant, and son-in-law John Youngblood ran a gas station. For all their seeming success, the family faced challenges. Barry Hawley, whose father married into the family, recalled that "Indians . . . were discriminated against in many bad ways. It was very hard for those young people." Meanwhile, Karl Peterson, a Swedish-born longshoreman, mourned the recent death of his Makah wife, Ann, and struggled to raise their daughter, Helen. Helen Peterson Schmitt described a city where "No Indians Allowed" signs hung in shop windows, leading her to hide her Makah ancestry. For Schmitt, the lutefisk, glögg, and hambos of her father's people were the ethnic traditions with which she identified, and only decades later would she reconnect with her Makah relatives. On the other hand, one of the few things Schmitt knew for sure about her mother was her visibility as an Indian. "When the police had a little lost Indian person who didn't speak English," she told an interviewer decades later, "they brought her to my mother, so she'd help with them." Despite the pressures to hide one's Native ancestry, then, the story of Ann Peterson suggests that Indians were recognized, and recognized each other, in the city.[5]

In the 1930s, Indianness could also shape white identities in Seattle. Poet and novelist Richard Hugo, for example, once described the death of an Indian first-grade classmate, who drowned after becoming trapped under a log boom on the Duwamish. ("His mother flipped and for years called him to dinner every evening in prolonged fits of scream," Hugo recalled.) But despite their role as friends and neighbors, Native people in Hugo's neighborhood were also markers of the lower class. To kids like Hugo who grew up in poor Duwamish River neighborhoods like Youngstown and Riverside, middle-class West Seattle "towered over the sources of felt debasement, the filthy, loud belching steel mill, the oily slow river, the immigrants hanging on to their odd ways, Indians getting drunk in the unswept taverns, the commercial fishermen, tugboat workers, and mill workers with their coarse manners." For Hugo, Indian people were simultaneously neighbors and metaphors, members of the urban lower classes as well as symbols of urban poverty. He was not alone. In a 1935 master's thesis examining the social dynamics of Hooverville, the homeless encampment on the old Duwamish tideflats, sociologist Donald Roy described the residents as "natives," noted that their homes resembled those of "the Siberian Chuckchee," and described prostitutes who sometimes visited Hooverille as "squaws." Although only 4 out of Hooverville's 639 residents were Native according to Roy's count, he nonetheless used Native imagery to highlight the poverty of Seattle's homeless. We might wonder whether the "natives" on the tideflats were called that thanks to memories of Native migrants camped in those same places only a few years earlier.[6]

There was some truth to the connections made by Hugo and Roy between poverty and Indian identity. Beyond the working-class neighborhoods where some mixed-race families lived, Native people in 1930s Seattle were most likely to be found in places inhabited by the city's poorest people. One such place was the district of single-resident occupancy (SRO) hotels that made up much of downtown's landscape, including Pioneer Square and Chinatown, two dense neighborhoods that had grown up on the site of the old Lava Beds. There, Indian men and women found shelter among the flophouses and apartment buildings. Frank Griffey, an Indian railroad worker from Indiana, lived at the Interurban Hotel on Occidental Avenue, while Tlingit radio musician Jimmie Thomas rented a room in the Grant Hotel on Seventh Avenue South. Other Native people found slightly more reputable accommodations in apartment hotels further uptown: Estelle Hovland, a Métis waitress from North Dakota, lived in the "Newly Decorated and Refurbished" Hotel Rehan on Seventh and Union, while Greek immigrant track layer George Ramos and his Blackfoot wife, Hazel, lived with their newborn son in the Yale Apartments at Sixth and Columbia. Hotels and apartments like the Yale and the Interurban often had their own reputations among Native people. Makah people told one anthropologist, for example, that some SRO hotels were quite notorious among their people:

Those who make short trips to the cities stay in hotels patronized by whites, though the hotels most generally frequented would be regarded as third or fourth rate. One hotel popular with the Makah is over a noisy dance hall where incoming sailors gather. One of the hotel chambermaids swore that she would not stay in the place overnight, that it was bad enough to have to work there during the day. However, both white men and white women stay in the hotel which was once one of the good hotels in the city. Others from Neah Bay patronize hotels in quieter locations, which are said to have better reputations.

Just as the presence of Indians could be a marker of poor neighborhoods in the eyes of white observers, whiteness, as well as class distinctions, played a factor in Makah people's understandings of the city.[7]

Life in Seattle in the 1930s brought Native people into contact with more than just the city's white residents. Both the Interurban and Grant hotels—as well as the Hotel Marion, where Joseph Carrasco, a Chilean–Alaskan Indian steelworker, lived, and the Kenney Apartments on James Street, where widowed Tlingit domestic worker Mary Bezonoff roomed—were run by Japanese immigrants and their American-born children. Meanwhile, life in the SRO districts also meant that many Indian people had everyday encounters with Filipino sailors, agricultural workers, and laborers, who made up a significant—if often transient—part of Seattle's downtown population. Some of these men would also become the fathers of a generation of mixed-ancestry people. Diane Vendiola was one of these; her Swinomish mother met her Filipino father, a laborer and boxer, in Seattle in the 1930s. According to Vendiola, "it was natural for them to come together." Similar Indian-Filipino relationships resulted in the birth of a generation that would go on to shape Seattle's politics in the decades to come: both Bernie Reyes Whitebear, founder of the United Indians of All Tribes, and Bob Santos, a leader in the city's Asian–Pacific Islander community, were what Santos called "Indipinos." In the working world of Depression-era Seattle, new kinds of Indian identities were being formed and the stage was being set for a new political landscape in the city.[8]

Finally, the 1930 census includes the institutionalized Indians of Seattle: the men, women, and children of the city's asylums. At the Sacred Heart Orphanage, four young children from Washington tribes, including the Makah and S'Klallam—James Henry, Angeline La Belle, and the siblings Bernice and Carl Kavanaugh—appear in the rosters among their majority white compatriots. At the King County Hospital, where full-blood Yakama Ernest Spencer worked as a truck driver, the list of Native patients and their tribes is like a directory to Seattle's Indian hinterland: Tlingit, Haida, Snohomish, Tsimshian, Canadian Métis. These were also perhaps some of Seattle's poorest Native people; ranging in age from twenty to nearly sixty, all but one of the hospital's Indian patients were listed as unemployed. This was also the case for Cherokee Harry Marshall and "Siwash" Dorothy Martin, the two Indian residents of the city jail. These were men and women for whom life in the city had not been easy, particularly in the lean years of the 1930s.

Census tables for the hospital and jail suggest that there were other Native people in Seattle in 1930, people the enumerators would have missed: the homeless, the transient, and the seasonally migrant. Surely, many of these harder-to-find (or easier-to-ignore) Indians existed, invisible to the census takers. And except for people like Ann Peterson, the Makah woman who opened her Ballard home to needy Indians, and the Native neighbors whose presence shaped Richard Hugo's class consciousness, Indian people were largely invisible in Seattle's urban landscape. Unlike the Seattle of the 1880s, where well-known Indian enclaves existed on the Lava Beds and the waterfront, in 1930 Native people were integrated into the city's poor and working-class districts but had little public presence. And unlike in 1878, when real Indians and their canoes appeared matter-of-factly in Mr. Glover's drawing of the city, living Indian people were largely absent from the city's self-image. Indian images, however, were not. The urban landscape in which these Indian people lived had changed dramatically in only a few short decades. Through stories of Chief Seattle and doomed "last" Indians, and through the city's encounter with its Indian hinterland, Seattle had developed not only a new set of place-stories but also a new landscape that was marked by Indian symbols. By the late 1930s, Seattle had become a city of totems.

Indian images guarded most approaches to the city. On the west, a totem pole stood on an overlook offering views of the city from Duwamish Head, while others graced the ship canal locks and the downtown waterfront. On the north, tourist establishments—the Thunderbird Hotel, the Totem Pole Motel, and the Twin Teepees Lounge—used Indian images to attract travelers motoring on the new Pacific Highway. On the east, visitors plying the state-of-the-art floating bridge across Lake Washington entered a tunnel under the city's hills by passing through a portal surrounded by Northwest Coast–style designs and text that read "Seattle: Portal to the Pacific." Along with the Potlatches, Founders Day events, busts and seals and statues of Chief Seattle, and other urban place-stories, the urban landscape itself spoke to the importance of Indians as defining elements of Seattle's civic self-image.[9]

In Pioneer Place Park, at the heart of the city's oldest neighborhood, the Chief-of-All-Women pole that had been stolen from On the Cottonwood in 1899 remained the grandest and eldest of Seattle's Indian icons. But then, just after 10 P.M. on 22 October 1938, an unidentified man placed gasoline-soaked rags against the base of the pole, set the rags on fire, and disappeared into the darkness. To this day, no one knows why. But as Seattleites decided how best to replace the irreparably damaged artifact, a clear distinction was made between Indian imagery in the city and urban Indians themselves. At first, two local Suquamish men, accomplished lumbermen employed by the Works Progress Administration (WPA), were asked to carve the new pole. However, many observers feared that Richard Temple and Lawrence Webster (the grandson of Wahalchoo, who had once dived for power off Alki Point) might introduce "some goofy innovations," and one reporter who visited their homes across Puget Sound was disturbed to find that they spoke English fluently and even drove trucks. Ethnographer Melville Jacobs, for his part, argued that only his white colleague Viola Garfield could do the job right. Meanwhile, the *Times* solicited opinions from Native people at a baseball game in North Seattle, only to find that these Indians hardly seemed Indian at all: they were playing an "American" sport, one of the men was carving a pole with Teddy Roosevelt on it, and another suggested painting the pole with store-bought paint instead of traditional pigments. This was the standard kind of urban-versus-Indian history at work: Indians in the city were in fact no longer Indians, and Native truck-drivers and ballplayers were ignorant and undeserving of the Indianness the Chief-of-All-Women pole represented. In the end the job was given to carvers at Saxman in Alaska, some of whose ancestors had once lived in On the Cottonwood, in exchange for the remains of the original pole. Never mind that the carving of the replacement pole was sponsored by a federal agency, the Civilian Conservation Corps; these were real Indians, not only because they came from a "totem pole culture" but because of their perceived distance from urban life. Far-off Indians, exotic and abstract, were preferable to familiar ones who called Seattle home, and were the only ones deemed fit to hew "sixty feet of freshly-carved monsters ferocious enough to set a lady tourist tittupy with horror."[10]

Despite this tension between Seattle's Native imagery and its Indian residents, Native people were sometimes active participants in the creation of the city's Indian iconography. Enumerators of the 1930 census, for example, found a family from Ucluelet on Vancouver Island living along the Duwamish River, not far from where Seetoowathl and his wife had starved to death in 1920. Like many other Nuu-chah-nulth people, Simon Peter, his wife, Annie, their grown son, Solomon, and their younger children, Evelyn, Arthur, and Elsie, had come to Seattle in search of opportunity. For Solomon, that meant hard work as a general laborer on the docks and in the industrial areas of town. But for Simon, work in the city meant carving totem poles, which were then sold to places like Ye Olde Curiosity Shop. For Simon Peter, being urban and being Indian were not necessarily in conflict—in fact, one facilitated the other. This was also the case for Jimmy John, another Nuu-chah-nulth. From the community of Mowachat on the west coast of Vancouver Island, John had traveled regularly to Seattle with his family and often sold items he carved from wood and silver to Ye Olde Curiosity Shop and other tourist outlets. One of his most lucrative opportunities, however, came in 1936, when he was hired by a curio-shop owner to carve a series of totem poles that would be incorporated into the design of a new building. By 1937, the misnamed Haida House was doing a brisk business in baskets, masks, model canoes, and miniature totem poles out of a building adorned with Thunderbirds, bears, and eagles carved by John in return for room and board. The Haida House—now the Totem House Fish and Chips shop—was part of a new 1930s vernacular that used totem poles, tipis, and other Indian images to capture the attention of tourists, but behind the seeming kitsch lay the labor and expertise of a Native artisan. For John, who lived in Seattle for ten years before returning to British Columbia to become a leader in the renaissance of Northwest Coast art, urban life provided not just economic opportunity but a chance to establish himself as a Native artist. And in doing so, he helped craft Seattle's Indian iconography.[11]

In the late 1930s, though, the shape of the city, and of urban history itself, was about to change. The lean years in the city of totems were about to end, as mobilization for global conflict dramatically transformed the city, its population, and its economy. In later decades, many of Seattle's older residents, as well as some of its historians, would come to see the 1930s as the last years of "old Seattle." In a series of interviews conducted at the beginning of the twenty-first century, for example, Seattle residents who remembered Depression-era Seattle—wealthy and poor, black and white, radical and conservative—described the traits that made Seattle of the 1930s so different from the city of later decades. For WPA artist Bill Cumming, broadcasting heiress Patsy Collins, unrepentant Wobbly Jesse Petrich, African American dietician Marian Valley-Lightner, and Puget Power technician Tom Sandry, seemingly intractable racial and social divisions, radical politics, and an economy still driven by extractive industries distinguished the 1930s. Their descriptions of "Old Seattle" are exercises in nostalgia, but they also reflect the very real transformations that took place during and after the Second World War. As the lean years came to an end for many of Seattle's residents, so too did one era of the city's history.[12]

This was true for Seattle's Indian history as well. In the years surrounding 1880, Seattle had been on the cusp of an urban and Indian revolution. Back then, "Seattle Illahee"—a mixed-race town on the urban indigenous frontier—was about to give way to a modern city of the Changers that used Native imagery to explain itself to the world, that dispossessed local indigenous people, and that spawned an Indian hinterland. In the 1930s, that imagery, dispossession, and hinterland remained largely in place, but the beginnings of a new kind of urban Indian history were visible as well. Stoney and Choctaw women and men arriving from beyond the city's regional hinterland, a Makah woman helping lost Indian children, and a Hesquiaht carver using a job in the city to launch a Native renaissance each helped lay the foundations for a new chapter in Seattle's Indian and urban histories. But in the 1930s, on the cusp between past and present, Indian people were often overshadowed by Indian imagery. When Mac and Ike, the heroes of John Dos Passos's working-class epic *The 42nd Parallel,* arrived in Seattle, for example, their experiences there reflected not only the fears and aspirations of the Great Depression but the landscape of urban conquest:

The next day was sunny; the Seattle waterfront was sparkling, smelt of lumberyards, was noisy with the rattle of carts and yells of drivers when they got off the boat. They went to the Y.M.C.A. for a room. They were through with being laborers and hobos. They were going to get clean jobs, live decently and go to school nights. They walked round the city all day, and in the evening met Olive and Gladys in front of the totempole [*sic*] on Pioneer Square.[13]

Of course they did.

9 / Urban Renewal in Indian Territory

N THE CITY OF TOTEM POLES and Native ghosts, real live Indians seemed to reappear suddenly in 1970. On the morning of 8 March, more than a hundred Native men, women, and children gathered at Fort Lawton, a decommissioned army base on high bluffs in northwest Seattle. Spreading out, they quickly entered the fort from all sides, scaling the fences while a diversionary force raised a ruckus at the main gate. As military police descended, Puyallup activist Bob Satiacum read a statement addressed to the "Great White Father and All His People" claiming Fort Lawton "in the name of all American Indians by the right of discovery." Invoking treaties supposedly promising surplus government land to tribes, the activists demanded the fort. Most of the proclamation went unheard in the ensuing chaos of scuffles and handcuffs, but news of the invasion quickly spread around the world. According to the *Seattle Times*, an Italian News Agency correspondent had asked, "You can't imagine how fascinating this story is in Europe. Indians attacking a fort in the West of the United States. Tell me, do you have an Indian problem out there?" Meanwhile, front-page photos of uniformed white men carting Native women and children off to jail ensured that Seattle's "Indian problem" joined student protests and carpet bombings as early-1970s hot political topics.[1]

This was political theater at its best. The Native invaders of Fort Lawton had no legal authority on which to claim land in Seattle. Even if their proclamation did riff on the legal frameworks established by treaties, these were urban Indians, most with no connections to the Duwamish, Lake, and Shilshole peoples whose territories had become the city of Seattle. But by 1970, what it meant to be Indian in America—and what it meant to be American on Indian land—was changing, and as a result, the place-story Native activists were telling in Seattle was a new one. This city and this land are ours, they shouted—and for the first time, Seattle, and the world, seemed to be listening.

But this was only one of several place-stories being told by urban Indians in postwar Seattle. As Native people from many tribes and nations worked to make the city home, they told stories as diverse as their communities of origin. Some actively participated in the city's romantic narrative of the Denny Party, while others wove Seattle's urban history into a broader story of genocide and dispossession. Still other urban Indians, including the city's most destitute, struggled simply to assert their basic humanity in a civic story that cast them as little more than symbols of racial decay. In each case, the stories Native people told about their place in Seattle had everything to do with the changes in the city and in what it meant to be Indian and American. As cultural, political, and even environmental landscapes shifted in the decades after the Second World War, so would Seattle's Indian place-stories, and those stories would be as complicated and diverse as urban Indians them-selves. Urban renewal would have many conflicting meanings as Native people worked to make Seattle home.

T O SAY THAT SEATTLE'S URBAN Indian activism began with the invasion of Fort Lawton in 1970 is a bit like saying that Seattle's urban history origins lie only at Alki Point. If the "Indian attack" of the Vietnam era took most of Seattle by surprise, it was only the latest and most visible of a series of efforts by urban Native people to claim space in Seattle. To understand the origins of Indian struggles to find home in Seattle, we must go back to an earlier war. Epidemics and railroads had been the great forces that shaped Seattle's urban history in the nineteenth century, but the pivot on which the city's twentieth-century history turned was war. The Great War had helped complete Seattle's arrival on the world stage, but it was the Second World War that would truly transform Seattle into a city of global significance. More than perhaps any other American city, Seattle would be changed by the necessities of prosecuting war in Europe, Africa, and the Pacific. The changes were most obvious in the kinds of work people did in the city. Where in the 1930s lumber mills and canneries were the main industry in the region, by the 1950s the shipyards and hangars and foundries that supplied the Allies with machines of war had changed the city's economy in profound ways. Between 1939 and 1941, for example, Seattle's manufacturing base doubled; the number of people employed in manufacturing went from 35,000 in 1940 to 115,000 in 1943. Across the American West, cities were being transformed by wartime industry. The battleships and warplanes from Seattle—including one called *Chief Seattle*—helped turn the course of global conflict, just as they cemented Seattle's new role in the global economy. Seattle was now Boeing's town.[2]

The Second World War had begun a new chapter in Seattle's urban story, and it also marked a turning point in Indian history, as Indians moved to the city to work on behalf of the war effort. Adeline Skultka, a young Kaigani Haida from Craig, Alaska, was one of these. After graduating from high school, she came to Seattle with her sister and a cousin and immediately found work on a Boeing assembly line and as a welder in a local shipyard; soon after, she met her Filipino husband, Genaro "Gerry" Garcia. Despite the long history of Indian migration to Seattle, for people like Skultka, moving to the wartime city involved a steep learning curve—but as before, the city beckoned with opportunity, especially compared to the grim prospects back home. "A lot of them had never been off the reservation before," remembered Lillian Chapelle (Cowlitz-Yakama), "and yet there were jobs here in Seattle." Like service on the battlefield, work on the home front proved that Native people could be both Indian and American.[3]

The enthusiasm and opportunity of the war would soon fade, though. When, at war's end, cancellation of government contracts at the shipyards and factories led to layoffs and as returning soldiers clamored for jobs, women and people of color were the first to go. Meanwhile, Native veterans struggled to reintegrate into civilian society, and Indians who depended on the waning extractive industries of Old Seattle found themselves increasingly adrift. Although the economy regained its footing in the 1950s, the benefits of the boom rarely trickled down to urban Indians, who experienced discrimination in virtually every aspect of life: Chinese restaurants that refused to hire nonwhite waitresses, vacant apartments mysteriously rented, hospitals that refused to serve Native people, murders of homeless Indians that went uninvestigated. During a period when federal Indian policy enthusiastically encouraged assimilation into mainstream society and few, if any, resources existed for the Native community, the economic and social realities of 1950s Seattle afforded urban Indians little security and even less hope.[4]

The result was that many Indian men and women who came to Seattle ended up on Skid Road, the area that included Pioneer Square and much of First Avenue, stretching all the way north to Belltown. In his much-beloved 1951 history *Skid Road*, Murray Morgan described "men sitting on curbs and sleeping in doorways . . . , condemned buildings . . . , missions and taverns and wine shops and stores where you can buy a suit for $3.75." For Morgan and many other Seattleites, downtown—particularly Belltown, First Avenue, and Pioneer Square—had become "the place of dead dreams," populated by the aging workforce of Old Seattle, which one 1950 memoir called "the discards from the maelstrom of industrial activity." The streets and run-down hotels of Skid Road were also home to hundreds of Indians. Colville architect Lawney Reyes, for example, recalled that during those years "if you wanted to see an Indian in Seattle you'd jump in the car and go down to Skid Row." In the 1960 census, 30 percent of Pioneer Square's inhabitants were either "Indian or Oriental," and the district included the largest, most concentrated population of Native people in the city. Out in the hinterland, many Indian reservation residents described skid roads as places where people disappeared, almost as if they had died—and, sometimes, the deaths were real: cirrhosis, a fall under a passing train, tuberculosis, a knife in the ribs. After the brief window of wartime opportunity, life in Seattle was almost as bleak as ever for its Indian population—if not worse.[5]

The seven women who came together in the 1950s to address this problem were unlikely activists. Most had come to Seattle during the Second World War to work in the defense industries and, unlike most Native people, now enjoyed the relative security of working- and middle-class life, focusing their energies on volunteering at churches and their children's schools. On the surface, they were paragons of assimilation— Christian, married with mixed-race children, and productive members of postwar society. At the same time, it was these seven women who would lay the foundations for the radical action at Fort Lawton more than twenty years later. They first met in 1958 under the leadership of Pearl Warren, a Makah who had come to the city after the war. Pearl's daughter Mary Jo Butterfield had recently brought home a desperate Indian couple, left on the streets after the wife was discharged from the hospital. Like Ann Peterson's home in 1930s Ballard, this postwar Makah household was a refuge for urban Indians. Inspired in part by that experience, Warren, Butterfield, Adeline Skultka Garcia, and their friends decided that if resources for Native people in Seattle were going to exist, Native people needed to create them. They began visiting apartment buildings, downtown hotels, and the Greyhound station—anywhere they might find other Indian women. By the fall of 1958, they had more than fifty members, whose tribal communities ranged from Washington and Alaska to Canada and the Plains. With the help of Erna Gunther, a University of Washington anthropologist, the group incorporated that year as the American Indian Women's Service League.[6]

For almost two decades, the Service League would be Seattle's leading urban Indian organization. Pearl Warren, Adeline Garcia, and the other founders described the role they hoped to play in the inaugural issue of the Service League's newsletter:

The newcomer to the city will find [the Service League] a good place to meet other Indian women and make new friends; and those who want to learn more about conditions and developments that may eventually affect their own lives—Indian legislation, medical care, employment, etc.—will hear new and vital information at each meeting. And to those who can see a way of picking up and straightening out the threads from the tangle of Indian affairs, there is the opportunity of doing a real service to the Indian community— locally, statewide, or even nationally.

And always, the leaders of the Service League connected everyday life both to tribal traditions and to Indian politics, on scales ranging from the local to the national. "Where else but in an Indian paper," asked one writer in the newsletter, "would you find such unique receipts [sic] such as 'Sturgeon Spinal Cord' and 'Buckskin Bread,' legends written as told by the old people, the 'Lord's Prayer' in Chinook?" She then continued by pointing out that the newsletter would also cover "land and claim decisions, inter-tribal meetings, fishing and hunting, House and Senate Bills pending on local and national levels" and other key issues in Indian political life.[7]

But creating community in the city also meant finding a place. With that in mind, the Service League opened Seattle's first Indian Center in 1960 in a rented storefront at First and Vine at the northern end of Skid Road. Two years later, they moved into a larger space across from the Greyhound Bus depot. Where totem poles and statues of Chief Seattle greeted non-Indian visitors to Seattle, here real Indians greeted real Indians as Service League members kept an eye on the bus station, looking for new arrivals.[8] Fond memories of the Indian Center highlight the sense of community created by the women who ran it. In 1970, for example, Choctaw Seattleite Harvey Davis and his wife, Nellie, recalled the many things the center had provided over the years:

Food if he was hungry. A friend if he was friendless. Shoes if he was barefoot. Sympathy and advice if he was troubled. Thrown out if he was drunk. Returned to his people if he was lost. A quiet place to sit and read or contemplate. Free clothing on Thursdays. An opportunity to help our less fortunate tribesmen.

Most important for the Davises, the center provided "a feeling of warmth and friendship which can be found in few, if any, other places in Seattle." In a city where most Indian people were at worst ostracized or at best neglected, the center was a kind of home, where even the poorest of Seattle's Indian community could contribute. Adeline Garcia recalled how "those bums on [First] Avenue, they'd come in and clean up the place," bringing produce and fish from the Public Market when they could afford it and offering skills such as carpentry in return for a hot meal and a place to "stretch out and rest." Mary

Jo Butterfield, meanwhile, described the struggles of one Blackfoot Indian Center volunteer:

Sitting in a house out at High Point [public housing] with five hungry kids and you're an alcoholic and you're trying to dry out and take care of your kids and you can't feed them and you don't have any money—you don't have bus fare to get to the Indian Center to get groceries. And you don't have a phone. Those kind of people were the ones that worked the hardest and got the most out of it.

Here was self-help, here were grass roots, here were Indian people of many nations, creating a place in the city.[9]

But despite the efforts of the Service League, not everyone felt comfortable being Native in Seattle, where those "No Indians Allowed" signs still hung in windows and, according to Puyallup activist Ramona Bennett, "a lot of Indians were still trying to pass as Italian." In response, the Service League saw public relations as a critical element of its mission, equal to providing services to Native people. The 1961 North American Indian Benefit Ball at the Masonic Temple, for example, showcased crafts and dances and used television and radio spots to encourage non-Indians to attend. Similarly, well-attended picnics at Seward Park on Lake Washington involved Lummi dancers, speeches and stories in the Makah language, and door prizes of baskets and handmade sweaters. But the group's signature event was the salmon bake at Alki Point, which by 1967 was feeding more than two thousand people and had become a highlight of the annual Seafair festivities, often as part of reenactments of the Denny Party's landing at Alki. League members, then, did not work to overturn the city's place-story in the 1960s. Instead, they lobbied to become part of it—as living Indian people.[10]

Participating in celebrations of urban founding did not preclude outspoken advocacy on Native political issues. In particular, Service League members worked to increase non-Indians' awareness of the shortcomings of federal Indian policy: most notably the relocation and termination policies of the postwar years, one of which sent Native people to cities only to abandon them, and the other of which sought to negate treaties by dissolving reservations and annulling the federal-tribal relationship altogether. Pearl Warren, for example, represented the Service League in particular and urban Indians in general before a U.S. Senate subcommittee on Indian affairs in 1968, and that same year, the Service League helped organize an international urban Indian conference in Seattle that welcomed activists and community organizers from the United States and Canada to share stories and strategies. But funding for their efforts was hard to come by, even as the city's political landscape shifted toward a multicultural civic politics and as the federal government began to fund programs in other minority communities. "So much money was coming into Seattle," recalled Lakota Service League member Letoy Eike, "and Indians were not getting anything." For two years, Service League members tried to convince city officials to earmark money for an Indian Center in a vacant site at the south end of Lake Union, but as one observer commented, the city "passed the buck" while "millions of dollars poured into the [predominantly African American] Central District." One Model Cities project even paid for Central District youth to carve a totem pole portraying the nation's black history, which must have underscored the disparities between the city's black and Indian communities.[11]

Urban Indian strategies in Seattle were about to change, however. For some younger urban Indians, including an Indian Center volunteer named Bernie Whitebear, the frustration was building. Whitebear, born Bernie Reyes and a Colville from eastern Washington, was one of many who had come to Seattle to work at Boeing. In that sense, he was like Adeline Garcia, but Whitebear's activism represented a new style of Indian leadership in Seattle. Although concerned by the dominance of African American concerns in Seattle racial politics, he was also inspired by the work of Seattle's black, Latino, and Asian American communities. Whitebear and his allies began to formulate a more multicultural—and more radical—approach to claiming space in the city. And so when the city, the army, and the Bureau of Indian Affairs dragged their feet on a proposal for a new Indian Center at the recently decommissioned Fort Lawton and Indian activists took over Alcatraz Island, the stage was set for a new chapter in Seattle's urban Indian history.[12]

The occupation of Alcatraz by American Indian Movement activists and others in 1969 had garnered international attention, and by capitalizing both on the successes of other movements' radical strategies and on a growing popular interest in (and sympathy toward) indigenous peoples, the occupation of Alcatraz was a turning point for Native activism, focusing international attention on the everyday lives of Indian people in the United States. While the takeover of Alcatraz was a failure in the sense that Indian people and institutions never achieved permanent tenure on the Rock, it was a phenomenal success in that it inspired similar tactics among "Red Power" activists throughout the nation and brought public attention to Native issues. And so on that brisk March morning in 1970, more than a hundred Indians "took" Fort Lawton.[13]

The invasion was a radical departure from the more diplomatic traditions of the Service League activists. Nothing made this more obvious than the allies the takeover attracted: Alcatraz veteran Leonard Peltier, radical black comedian Dick Gregory, and antiwar feminist Jane Fonda all came to offer their support. (So did the radical Seattle Liberation Front, which had recently held a protest naming part of the University of Washington campus "The People's Republic of Leschi" after the man who led the 1856 attack on the city.) The tactics of the takeover were a far cry from the salmon bakes and mayoral meetings of the Service League: protestors were more than willing to be arrested, and they even hired a skywriter to pen "A New Day . . . Fort, Give Up . . . Fort, Surrender" over the city. There were, however, connections between the Fort Lawton activists and the Service League. League founder Ella Aquino, for example, was among those who scaled the fences at Fort Lawton, and she and other League members, "armed with sandwiches and coffee," supported the occupation from behind the scenes and reprinted the Fort Lawton proclamation in *Indian Center News*. And in a broader sense, the Fort Lawton leadership carried the same hopes as the Service League. In their proclamation, protestors described their vision for Fort Lawton:

We feel that this land of Ft. Lawton is more suitable to pursue an Indian way of life, as determined by our own standards. By this we mean—this place does not resemble most Indian reservations. It has potential for modern facilities, adequate sanitation facilities, health care facilities, fresh running water, educational facilities, and transportation facilities.

Point for point, this was the same vision that Pearl Warren had pursued for years; she had always wanted to move beyond a crisis-driven Indian Center and create lasting, proactive Indian institutions in the city. Despite their more radical and visible tactics, the "invaders" of Fort Lawton were the political descendants of those first seven women who had come together back in 1958.[14]

Many non-Indian Seattleites dismissed the invasion of Fort Lawton as mere silliness; one Native woman, for example, quit her job after her boss told her that the takeover "was pretty stupid, and that the Indians were dumb for doing it and had no reason for doing it." But despite negative reactions from some non-Indians (eggs and insults thrown, death threats made, and neighborhood petitions calling for an end to the "noise and stupid acts"), by the end of the invasion, more than forty non-Indian organizations in the city had come to support the occupation, including the Seattle Human Rights Commission, whose bias toward African American concerns had frustrated Indian leaders in the past. And within two years of the invasion, United Indians of All Tribes, as the activists came to be known, had negotiated an agreement with the city with the help of Senator Henry "Scoop" Jackson. Sixteen acres of Fort Lawton, soon to be renamed Discovery Park, would be leased for an Indian cultural and social-services center. When the Daybreak Star Cultural Center finally opened in 1976, the *Post-Intelligencer* called it a "proud day," not just for Indians but for the city that had found ways to compromise with activists. As Service League member Arlene Red Elk put it, "They got their spot."[15]

The spot they had gotten was a distinctively Indian one. Designed by architect Lawney Reyes, Bernie Whitebear's brother, the Daybreak Star Cultural Center was inspired by Lakota spiritual leader Black Elk's vision of a star that had come down to earth and taken root to form a sheltering tree, and the building's four wings, built of timber donated by Northwest tribes, represented the four directions. Meanwhile, the public spaces of Daybreak Star were filled with art made by Indian people of many tribes: Creek, Tlingit, Chiricahua Apache, Caddo, Cowlitz, and Aleut, among others. Just as Seattle's connections to the world had widened in the years since the Second World War, so had its Indian hinterland. No more was that hinterland just a woven coast; it was now a woven continent.[16]

But the outward successes of the urban Indian community, symbolized by the opening of Daybreak Star, masked new rifts that were starting to open within that community. One rift came from the leftist, multiracial mode of organizing that Whitebear and his supporters had pursued. According to Diane Vendiola, whose Filipino father and Swinomish mother had met in Seattle back in the 1930s, these activists had pursued what she called "the city mode." Its confrontational strategies and connections to other minority communities—especially African Americans and antiwar radicals—alienated some older activists. This same tension would also arise on reservations as Indian men and women, energized by leftist tactics honed primarily in urban places, brought those visions of revolution back to their home communities. Other rifts were widened by success itself; as urban Indian programs began to finally receive public funding, they seemed to become less Indian to many community members. As Marilyn Bentz explained it, "once money came into the picture, things changed, and it got a lot more political . . . that turned off a lot of people." Harvey and Nellie Davis felt the same way, recalling the early Indian Center as a place "without a lot of gobbledy-gook, double talk, social service workers lingo," unlike the new post–Fort Lawton institutions. For many members of the urban Indian community, the institutional success of the Indian Center made it less of a Native place and more like any other social-service agency.[17]

At the same time, the successes of Seattle's Indian community had profound impacts far beyond the city, as volunteers, activists, and service professionals earned their stripes in the urban milieu and then took their skills and experience back out into Indian country. Women who had been involved in the American Indian Women's Service League (which carried on with its work even as United Indians of All Tribes grabbed most of the public attention) were among the best examples of this new generation of Native leadership that had been forged in Seattle. Adeline Garcia went on to become a board member of the innovative Seattle Indian Heritage High School and served as a liaison among reservations, the Seattle Public Schools, and colleges. Ramona Bennett became chair of her Puyallup Tribe, while Joyce Reyes, wife of Lawney and president of the Service League after Pearl Warren, became a Bureau of Indian Affairs administrator. These and other women would play crucial roles in the ascent of self-determination—Indian control over Indian lives—in the 1970s.[18]

But back in Seattle, where the Daybreak Star Cultural Center, with its origins in the work of the Service League, told a new place-story by claiming that the city could indeed be Indian land, there was another new urban Indian place-story taking form. This one told a very different tale from that of United Indians of All Tribes and the American Indian Women's Service League. As it would turn out, the postwar successes experienced both by the Indian community and by Seattle itself were a double-edged sword. As public dollars poured into the city to support programs like Model Cities, Daybreak Star, and the new Indian Center, other forces of urban renewal were at work. During the same years that Indians and other activists claimed spaces in a newly multicultural city and demanded public investment in communities of color, other civic leaders began to invest in the city's historical heritage. For Native Americans on Skid Road, life was about to get more difficult, as the same forces of urban affluence that helped to create new Indian spaces in the city forced the city's poorest Indians, quite literally, onto the streets.

I N 1991, THE SEATTLE ARTS COMMISSION launched an ambitious program called In Public, a citywide set of installations designed to inspire dialogue about the role of art in everyday urban life. From the enormous proletarian *Hammering Man* in front of the Seattle Art Museum to huge banners hung from light poles demanding "DO YOU PREFER BEING ON WELFARE?" In Public was edgy and controversial. One of the most confrontational pieces, by Cheyenne-Arapaho artist

Hachivi Edgar Heap of Birds, was installed in Pioneer Place Park along-side the Chief-of-All-Women pole and the bronze bust of Chief Seat-tle. Called *Day/Night*, it consisted of two ceramic panels inscribed with dollar signs, crosses, and text in Whulshootseed and English that read "Chief Seattle now the streets are your home. Far away brothers and sisters we still remember you." Dedicated to the city's homeless Indi-ans, *Day/Night* challenged Seattle's other place-stories. "In the city of Seattle there are countless references to our indigenous people," wrote Heap of Birds, "from professional football helmets [of the Seahawks, Seattle's NFL team], to towering totem poles . . . to the name of the city itself [but] we do not find institutionalized evidence of the living indige-nous people."[19]

Day/Night also drew attention to the fact that the city's new Indian institutions did not necessarily benefit all Indian people. "Daybreak Star . . . is beautiful," Heap of Birds told one reporter, "but Pioneer Square and Occidental Square are also Indian centers." In fact, by the 1970s, Skid Road had become "Indian territory," as one observer called the area around Pioneer Square. It was an urban neighborhood with its own traditions, institutions, and ways of operating. But as urban renewal, historic preservation, and heritage tourism—all supported by the same kinds of public reinvestment that had helped fund the Indian Center and Daybreak Star—became dominant themes in the 1970s and beyond, Native Skid Road would disappear, to be replaced by historic districts catering to tourists. And as downtown was transformed from historical Skid Road to historic Seattle, it would be filled with art like *Day/Night*. Here was the ironic history behind Heap of Birds' instal-lation: at the same time that it told a radical new place-story, confronting the inequalities of postwar urban Native life, it was also made possible by those inequalities and by the destruction of an Indian neighborhood.[20]

And a neighborhood it was: for all its dysfunction, for all the poverty and discrimination and cheap booze, Indian Skid Road was a commu-nity with its own rules and its own distinctive identity. To begin with, the Native population on Skid Road tended to be fairly stable. Accord-ing to one source, they accounted for half the city's "home guards"— residents whose home base was in Seattle, as opposed to the rootless "bindle stiffs," many of them increasingly elderly white men, who migrated from place to place. And unlike the general population of Skid Road, the downtown Indian community included many women, who often held down jobs as barmaids and cooks. One former Skid Road resident said it seemed as if every tavern had a Native woman in the kitchen. Like their Service League counterparts, the women of Skid Road were problem solvers; they could be depended on, for example, to know about openings in berry picking, dock work, carpentry, and other jobs. Among the black jazz clubs, gay cabarets, Chinese restaurants, and Filipino night cafés that had also sprung up in the area, Native Skid Road had by the 1960s developed into a functioning, if troubled, community with three key institutions: the Indian bar, the single-resident occupancy (SRO) hotel, and the streets themselves.[21]

At the end of the Second World War, it remained illegal to sell liquor to Indians in Seattle, and most downtown taverns refused entry to Indian men and women, relegating them to the streets. But in the late 1950s, a general relaxing of state liquor laws allowed the formation of what the local bartender's union called "bow and arrow joints"—Indian taverns like the Lotus, the Anchor, and El Coco—scattered along First Avenue from Pioneer Square to Belltown. Each had its own niche: one attracted Native Alaskans, who left the bar virtually empty during the summer fishing and logging season; another served a younger crowd, with more expensive drinks and Indian go-go girls; while a third, frequented by both Indians and Mexicans, had the roughest reputation. The best documented of the Skid Road Indian bars, the Britannia Tavern, catered to veterans, loggers, railroad men, and migrant laborers, most with tribal origins in Canada, Washington, Alaska, and the northern-tier states. At the Britannia, Indians could catch up on gossip from the reservations, drop the guards required by urban life, and simply be Indian. As at the Service League's Indian Center, there was a sense of family at the Brittania; patrons often referred to the bar's co-owner, a Puget Sound Indian woman, as "Ma," "Mom," and "Little Cousin." Even Native people who did not live on Skid Road found the Britannia to be "home territory"; one veteran who lived in a middle-class neighborhood often came to the tavern on weekends because "his people" were there.[22]

If the "bow and arrow joints" of Skid Road were homes away from home, it was another downtown institution, the SRO hotel, which often provided actual shelter. In more than two dozen hotels, some 1,700 single-occupancy rooms provided cheap accommodations for Native people and other Skid Road residents. Even the most run-down SRO hotel could be home. Despite the "long, dingy, and bitter-smelling corridors" of the Morrison Hotel, for example, one young Indian woman said, "I loved it here," and having one's own hotel room was a sign of status among the Indian Skid Roaders. For those who were not so fortunate, the Romanesque terra-cotta portico of the Pioneer Building, the benches under the totem pole, and the alleys off the main streets were often the only option. These public spaces were also Native meeting grounds, where answers could be found to questions like "What's happening?" "Who's around?" "Is Joe at the Anchor?" "Will he lend me five dollars?" Skid Road, then, was truly Indian territory.[23]

But time was not on the side of Skid Road, Indian or otherwise. Since the 1950s, civic leaders had been entertaining proposals for the revitalization of downtown, and especially of Pioneer Square. Most proposals included historic preservation (after all, this was the city's birthplace), but the plan that became the favorite of business leaders, John Graham and Company's 1966 design, proposed razing all but four blocks around Pioneer Place Park. The Chief-of-All-Women pole and the bronze bust of Chief Seattle would stay as part of a historic plaza—those place-stories merited preservation—but skyscrapers, parking lots, and a new highway would replace the rest of Skid Road. In the late 1960s and early 1970s, however, historic preservation and heritage tourism, like multiculturalism, had become part of Seattle's new civic language. Citizen activists quickly decried the Graham proposal, lobbying instead for the preservation of the entire neighborhood as a National Historic District. Not unlike the pioneers several generations before, who had looked to their Indian past as metropolis was born in their midst, now many of the city's residents had begun to look to the city's historic places as a balm against rapacious urban development in the postwar era.[24]

And so the Pioneer Square Historic District, among the first in the nation, was established in 1970 to much self-congratulation on the part of historically minded Seattleites. But a nagging question remained: what to do with the people who actually called the ground of history home? The answers ranged from the derisively violent to the sympathetically exploitative. One downtown businessman simply called Skid Road residents "scum of the earth" who should be run out of town, while one Native Skid Roader remembered a policeman saying to him, "They didn't play cowboys and Indians long enough . . . they should have killed all you bastards off." As for Graham and Company, the foiled levelers of Pioneer Square, they argued that the people of Skid Road added "little, if anything, to the economy of downtown" and suggested relocating those who could not be institutionalized in prisons or asylums. Some supporters of preservation, however, saw the "denizens" of Skid Road as having value—not as urban citizens but as part of the historic urban landscape. Mayor Wes Uhlman, for example, delighted in welcoming visitors to the city with a tour of Skid Road. "I was the only mayor in America who could do that," he mused, proud of the combination of historic buildings and seedy characters that Pioneer Square provided. Bill Speidel, who led wildly popular historical tours of Pioneer Square's underground network of streets and storefronts, agreed, pointing out that "if we didn't have the bums around, we've have to hire them from central casting." For Uhlman and Speidel, the people of Skid Road had a role to play—literally—in the district's place-story. This would be especially true for Indians, who for so long had been used to represent so much.[25]

Armed with new preservation and safety ordinances, city officials shut dozens of SRO hotels, and by the mid-1970s, three quarters of the city's downtown housing stock had been lost and nearly 60 percent of Pioneer Square's countable population had disappeared. The Morrison Hotel, for example, closed in 1976. It eventually reopened, but by 1981, more than 15,000 units of SRO housing had been lost in downtown Seattle. Meanwhile, the Britannia had shut its doors many years before—in 1970, the same year that the first historic preservation ordinance was passed—and many of Seattle's downtown "bow and arrow joints" followed suit soon after.[26]

For people who remained on Skid Road, downtown's "renaissance" was a disaster. "A large portion of the city's heritage and architecture has been saved, business has been improved, tax revenues are up," noted one critic in 1972. "Everything is fine except for the people who used to live here. Their condition has not been improved, but has been made worse." And as the hotels closed, the people who remained downtown tended to be poorer, sicker, more often homeless and unemployed, and less likely to be white. Skid Road residents who could move on did so, while those left behind depended upon the few missions and social services that remained downtown. In just a few short years of urban renewal and historic preservation, the Skid Road Native community and many of its diverse neighbors had been almost entirely erased by a district of art galleries, bookshops, restaurants, and taverns catering to tourists and the young and middle class. Indian people, meanwhile, remained the most visible minority on what was left of Skid Road, struggling to survive alongside more new totem poles. One writer noted that "victims of the white man's scorn can still be seen in doorways and around Seattle's taverns near Pioneer Square, or lolling on the area's few park benches," as though the Britannia, the Morrison, and the other institutions of Native Skid Road had never existed. Seattle's third Indian place-story, of the homeless Native person as an urban allegory, had been literally built into the landscape.[27]

Indian people on Skid Road were more than aware of their own visibility. As early as the 1970s, a handful of voices from Skid Road expressed defiance toward the role Indians had been told to play in Seattle's urban narrative. Mexican Indian J. A. Correa, for example, wrote in 1972 about the visibility of Indian people in the district:

Pawn shops / and / broken people / who drink and sing / and beg for wine / they provide amusement/ for the tourists / who believe in / historical sites / and little kids / from school / are taken there by / devoted bored teachers / to see the heart of their / grandparents' city.

Correa's poem is a dramatic alternative to the story of downtown's "renaissance," illustrating the human costs of urban renewal and what it meant to try to live in what was now the ground of Official Urban

History. Meanwhile, architect Laurie Olin described meeting some of the remaining Skid Road Indians while sketching Pioneer Square streetscapes in the 1970s:

One morning under the pergola an Indian sat down next to me and said: "How are you at drawing scars?" and grinned. . . . These people whose identity has been so brutally denied wanted to see that they were still there. My drawings seemed to reaffirm their existence. "Draw me, man, draw me; draw me next, I'll hold still right here," said one.

A quarter century later, Earle Thompson, a Yakama writer who had spent years on Skid Road, highlighted the ongoing visibility of homeless Indian people downtown:

In a mission / doorway / a in-num [Indian] / puts / a green bottle / up to his lips. / He begins / to sing: / "Gimme 5 / minutes / only five minutes more; / let me stay / ah-yah-aye . . ." / He pounds his fist / on the wall. / A couple passes / and he smiles / at them.

Like the Service League members holding their public events and the Fort Lawton activists reading their proclamation, here at last, twelve decades after the founding of Seattle, were Indian voices telling a new place-story. Or more to the point, here at last, twelve decades after the founding, someone was listening and writing it down.[28]

It was against this backdrop of historic preservation and the erasure of Skid Road's Indian history that Edgar Heap of Birds' *Day/Night* was installed to wide acclaim. Columnist and cartoonist David Horsey wrote, for example, "Amid the human wreckage congregating around the Pioneer Square pergola, it seemed that it would be redundant to point out the tragic circumstances of some of Chief Seattle's tribal descendants. But, instead, the panels stand like exclamation points among the living proof of their indictment." The irony of *Day/Night*, though, is that it too is part of the gentrification of the neighborhood, created to speak to those who visit Pioneer Place Park and Pioneer Square in search of stories about the city. When asked in 1997 what she thought of

Day/Night, Margaret, a homeless Aleut woman, referred to it simply as "fucking white man bullshit." To some extent, she was right. Without the crowds who frequent historic Pioneer Square, *Day/Night* would have little meaning and even less of an audience. And perhaps most importantly, it says what many expected all along: that Indians and cities cannot coexist. After all, Heap of Birds took his piece's title from one version of the Chief Seattle Speech: "Day and night cannot dwell together. The red man has ever fled the approach of the white man, as the changing mist on the mountainside flees before the blazing sun." In both English and the first language of this place called Seattle, here again is what we mistake for history: a place-story telling us what we already thought we knew.[29]

DAYBREAK STAR, *DAY/NIGHT*: two astronomical metaphors, speaking radically different place-stories. One tells us: *This city is Indian land.* The other: *This city is no place for Indians.* Their conflicting tales of the connections between Native people and the city capture the conflicts inherent in urban Indian history: What does it mean to be Native in the city? Can people even *be* Native in the city? And what about the fact that, throughout Seattle's history, whether during the creation of the ship canal or the ouster of Native Skid Road, civic leaders seemed determined to make the city into a place that was no place for Indians? The story of Indian activism in the city and the destruction of Indian Skid Road can be understood only in the context of the changing nature of Seattle itself. Before the Second World War, Seattle was a city of lumber mills, racial segregation, and Skid Road. Fifty years later, it was city of white-collar industry, multicultural politics, and urban renaissance, in which reinvestment in city-hood meant both the creation of institutions like the Indian Center and Daybreak Star and the destruction of an Indian neighborhood in the name of historic preservation. As in earlier periods in Seattle's past, changes in the city led to new possibilities and challenges for the Native American community, just as changes in Seattle's Native community led to new urban stories. For all their complexity, these stories together attest to a single, clear fact: that Indian history can, and does, happen in urban places.

More than thirty years after the invasion of Fort Lawton, new stories are still being written. In 1970, there were some four thousand Indians in the city; by the end of the century, there were nearly three times that number. Despite the rise in Native population, though, voluntary groups like the Service League had begun to fade soon after the successes of the 1970s. "Indian people were more able to get jobs and education and so forth," recalled Marilyn Bentz, with the result that "the volunteers weren't as necessary." Meanwhile, the radical activism that had helped reconfigure civic politics faded as well, as life in the city got better and ethnic institutions became more bureaucratic.[30]

But challenges remained, and at the beginning of the twenty-first century, the range of Native organizations in Seattle attests both to the ongoing pressure to reconcile what it means to be Indian with what it means to be urban, and to the amazing capacity of the Indian community to respond to its members' needs. At Daybreak Star, United Indians of All Tribes offers Head Start classes, foster-care advocacy, culturally appropriate therapy, outpatient treatment for substance abuse, GED (general equivalency diploma) courses, and housing referrals, in addition to its annual powwow and an ongoing art market. The Seattle Indian Health Board—housed in a building named after Leschi—offers medical and dental services and coordinates access to traditional healers. A group called Queer Oyate supports Native people with HIV and AIDS, while the Chief Seattle Club, founded without permission by a Jesuit priest in the 1960s to serve homeless Indians in Pioneer Square, still manages to operate among the galleries and nightclubs. There are even a couple of Indian bars in town. Meanwhile, the Service League is undergoing a renaissance of its own, with members involved in virtually every aspect of the community, and the I-Wa-Sil youth group has recently formed the nation's first urban Indian Boys and Girls Club. All speak to the enormous creativity and strength of Native people in Seattle, according to Lawney Reyes, the architect of Daybreak Star:

I'm very proud of the survival of urban people. The government, they're still scratching their head. . . . We're supposed to be extinct by the help of our own government. And somehow we have managed to survive even when

Native people have been placed in environments that are unlivable. We still find a place to create home.

All that was unlivable—the benches in Occidental Park, the dingy rooms in the Morrison Hotel, the projects at High Point—is being transformed.[31]

Perhaps the most ironic result of that transformation, and of Seattle's urban Indian story, comes from this place itself: from ideas about the connections between Indians and nature and from the simple fact that the city's Native community, made up of families and individuals from scores of tribes, has grown up on territory that once belonged to other Native people. Back in 1970, Bernie Whitebear had played the nature card: "If we're allowed to take over this land we would leave it in its natural state," he told the press at Fort Lawton. "We wouldn't destroy the natural areas there. We would preserve the land, the way the Indians have always done." Later, when Daybreak Star finally opened, the progressive *Seattle Weekly* saw the new facility as part of an "Indian Renaissance" that would lead to preservation of the earth. But twenty years later, the idea of Indians as inherent environmentalists would come back to haunt Daybreak Star when United Indians of All Tribes proposed building conference and museum facilities—a People's Lodge—in Discovery Park. Concerned over aesthetics, parking, and open-space preservation, local non-Indian residents highlighted the plans' seeming betrayal of "Indian environmental values." Having played the ecology card in their claims to Fort Lawton, the founders of Daybreak Star were now held accountable to the stereotype of the ecological Indian.[32]

In responding to the complaints just before his death in 2000, Whitebear unwittingly highlighted the deepest irony about an urban Indian community built on indigenous land. "From the window of my office," he wrote in the *Seattle Times*, "I look north from Magnolia Bluff and imagine the warriors of the Haida Nation who once paddled their great canoes into Puget Sound and beached them on the shores below in what is now called Shilshole Bay." Thinking of those ancestors, he recalled the words attributed to Seeathl that claimed that the white man would never be alone in the city. But Whitebear neglected to mention that those ancient Haida warriors had been raiders, come to enslave and kill the Shilsholes. And so the place-story of one urban Indian activist came into conflict with another kind of place-story that had been rising during the same years. For while Seattle's urban Indian community had been making a place for themselves in the city, other Indian voices—the descendants of the indigenous people of Seattle—were also laying claim to the city.[33]

10 / The Returning Hosts

THE SEATTLE SPIRIT, the story of a city's birth in pioneer stalwartness, could take its adherents in strange new directions. On the centennial of the landing at Alki, it could lead them into the Cold War. The Founders Day celebrations of 1951 were like those in the past, full of pomp and pageantry. Some celebrants attended performances of "The Landing of the Calico Pioneers" followed by baton twirling and a "God Bless America" sing-along at the Alki Field House, while more studious participants visited City Hall to view the city's original charter and various other "musty old files." And like other Founders Days, the centerpiece of the centennial was a reenactment of the Denny Party's landing, where junior high school boys in badly dyed wigs played Indian, awaiting the arrival of grown-ups playing pioneer. As the founders strode ashore, Mayor William Devin smashed a bottle containing the commingled waters of Seattle's lakes and rivers against the Alki Monument, the Hiawatha Sparklers did an "Indian dance," and serial salute bombs closed the program.[1]

The reenactment of the landing at Alki was the heart of the centennial program, but its headliner was General Douglas MacArthur. Thousands of Seattleites went to the University of Washington the next day to hear him extol the lessons of Alki Point. He told his audience that Seattle had been the "full beneficiary of what the pioneering spirit has wrought upon this continent" but warned that said spirit was still very much needed. "Should the pioneering spirit cease to dominate the American character," MacArthur continued, "our national progress would end. For a nation's life is never static. It must advance or it will recede." Invoking long-standing anxieties about the loss of the frontier, the man who so famously strode ashore in the Philippines proposed an agenda for the nation: "To the early pioneer the Pacific Coast marked the end of his courageous westerly advance—to us it should mark but the beginning. To him it delimited our western frontier—to us that frontier has been moved beyond the Pacific horizon." Broadcast on national television— one of Seattle's first appearances in the medium—MacArthur's speech linked the Seattle Spirit to the nation's interests in the Pacific. The story of Seattle's birth in a wilderness with its own "red menace" could now resonate for a new generation, and the Seattle Spirit, always linked to the nation's own place-story, helped lead the nation, for better or mostly for worse, into new places around the world.[2]

For all its historical rhetoric, MacArthur's speech had little to do with the past and much more to do with the future. It was much like another centennial event: the burying of a time capsule on Alki Beach. The capsule's contents were not listed in the *Post-Intelligencer* story announcing its burial, but the author's vision of the future was richly detailed. Seattleites might, for example, "shoot over" to Alki Point in their "personal atomic cruisers" to watch the opening of the time capsule on 13 November 2051. "We'll probably be wearing a spun air afternoon dress with radium buttons," imagined journalist Dorothy Hart, "and nary a qualm about the weather! Before the days of atmospheric control, we understand, Seattle women carried umbrellas!" Here was Seattle's space age future, full of technocratic optimism and personal affluence despite threats abroad. Here was a Seattle that had escaped its past (not to mention its ecology).[3]

Although surely tongue in cheek, Hart's vision of twenty-first-century Seattle reflected its time, that period in the 1950s when consensus politics, consumer confidence, and scientific progress augured a bright future for Americans. In the years to come, however, history would intervene. The consensus would crack as social unrest transformed public discourses on race, inspired in part by the unjust ways in which postwar affluence had been distributed. The American Indian Women's Service League and United Indians of All Tribes made that point beautifully. Meanwhile, Hart's atomic cruisers and radium dress buttons would come to seem like naïve paeans to a nuclear industry that, only a few short decades after its inception, was seen by many to be an ecological nightmare. Instead of a nuclear-powered, climate-controlled, deracinated futuropolis, Seattle became a place where both multicultural politics and environmental anxieties dominated much of postwar civic life.

Most important to our story, the legacy of Seattle's urban and Native histories would come back to haunt the city in the postwar era. As in the apocryphal Chief Seattle Speech, the white man—and all the other new people here, including urban Indians from other places—would "never be alone." But it was not the ghosts of Seattle's indigenous people that returned to the city: it was their living descendants. Fueled by both the new activism shared by other urban Indians and growing unease about the legacies of urban conquest, the grandchildren and great-grandchildren of the Duwamish and Shilsholes and Lakes began to exert new influences over both urban environmental affairs and the civic story. By the late twentieth century, even if Seattle continued to use Indian imagery to market itself on the global stage, it could no longer easily do so without taking into account the city's real Native past. It appeared that Seeathl's "returning hosts" had indeed come back to town, in ways that MacArthur and the Hiawatha Sparklers never could have imagined.

FROM ELVIS PRESLEY MOVIES to reruns of the popular television series *Frasier*, the Space Needle has replaced Princess Angeline (and perhaps even her father) as the symbol of Seattle. Rising hundreds of feet over where Denny Hill once stood before it was washed away by the regrades, it symbolizes the squeaky-clean, nervous optimism of the Camelot-and-Apollo 1960s expressed at Seattle's second world's fair, the Century 21 Exposition, for which the Space Needle was built. The fair's logo was a circle topped by an arrow pointing skyward (the symbol for masculinity, as the city's budding feminists pointed out), and along with the Space Needle, Century 21's exhibits reflected Americans' unswerving faith in the future. At the World of Tomorrow, the Bubbleator carried fairgoers to showcases of personal gyrocopters, interoffice "micro-mail," and kitchens that washed themselves. At the World of Science extravaganza, visitors were taken on a ten-minute expedition into outer space, while in the adult-entertainment area of the exposition men could snap photos of nude "Girls of the Galaxy." When the fair received its second *Life* magazine cover in May 1962, showing the futuristic Monorail streaking along with the Space Needle rising in the background, it was described as being "OUT OF THIS WORLD," and there was some truth to this. For six months and ten million guests, the fair had captured the ethos of the era, in which ecological and technological constraints—even gravity itself—seemed a thing of the past.[4]

But less than a decade later, something had shifted: Seattle had become ecotopian. In truth, well before the 1975 publication of Ernest Callenbach's mediocre but wildly popular utopian novel *Ecotopia*, in which Seattle, Portland, and San Francisco became the centers of a secessionist nation organized around environmentalist principles, Seattle's culture of nature was undergoing a radical transformation.[5] Confronted by the pollution attendant to rapid urban and suburban growth, and fueled by a growing emphasis on health, aesthetics, and an outdoor lifestyle, Seattleites began in the late 1950s to undertake massive campaigns to undo environmental damage in and around the city. Cleaning up Lake Washington, protecting green spaces, and enhancing salmon runs became major civic projects, while Seattle became a haven for environmentalist organizations that hoped to change policy throughout the region and beyond. By the 1970s, these efforts had helped to shape an environmentalist ethic in Seattle that, if by no means monolithic, dramatically reoriented the city's self-image. Gone was the Seattle that prided itself on lumber mills and regrades and rail connections; in its place was one of the few cities in the world that one moved *to* in order to get closer to nature. Now, the Space Needle simply offered the best view of Sound and mountains.[6]

Few things reflected this cultural shift more, or had more implications for Native people, than the symbolic resuscitation of Chief Seattle. Just as Seattle the city was born again as an environmentally friendly metropolis in the 1970s, Seeathl the symbolic Indian was reborn as well. More than the city's patron saint, he now became the city's first environmentalist. This was not just a local phenomenon. Following the publication of an augmented version of the speech in which Seeathl anachronistically mourned the coming of the railroad and the passing of the buffalo, the words attributed to the Native leader became famous around the world, particularly among European environmentalists, progressive Christians concerned with human rights, and some Native rights activists. Soon, the city's public image became closely linked to the ostensible environmental message of its namesake, as well as to a growing concern for the predicament of Indian peoples.[7]

But the question remained: who was Seeathl now being asked to serve? While many Native peoples, and in particular Puget Sound area tribes, used the Chief Seattle Speech as evidence of their claim to the lands in and around Seattle, for many non-Indians, the words of the long-dead indigenous leader had a different purpose. Theologian and ecophilosopher Thomas Berry, for example, found the speech to be a "profound insight into the enduring trauma being shaped in the psychic depths of the white man," referring particularly to the prophecy that settler society would never be alone and would be haunted by Indian ghosts. "These voices are there in the wind, in the unconscious depths of our minds," Berry continued. "These voices are there not primarily to indict us for our cruelties, but to identify our distortions in our relations to the land and its inhabitants, and also to guide us toward a mutually enhancing human-earth relationship."[8] For all their sympathy toward indigenous people, Berry's words were statements about history and about power. The words attributed to Seeathl were not about conflict but about healing, and at their core, they were most valuable, not in how they could serve Seeathl's own people or in how they might bring to light the injustices of the past, but in how they might assuage the environmental ills of modern American society. As has so often been the case in Seattle's history, stories that non-Indians told about Native people were in fact not about Native people but about non-Indians.

But beginning in the late 1960s, something new was happening. Whereas, in the past, whites and others had often been able to tell stories about Indians and the city without taking into account actual Native American people and their concerns, new political, legal, and cultural developments brought Indian people back into the center of urban life. Seattle's ecotopian turn was accompanied by a parallel resurgence in

Native American activism—not just among the urban Indians of the Service League and United Indians of All Tribes but among local tribes as well. These developments allowed the very real descendants of Seeathl and their tribal compatriots to assert a new kind of influence over the city. As new ideas about nature and progress came to dominate Seattle's civic consciousness, local tribes achieved a new degree of control over their ancient territories as ecological stewards and protectors of cultural patrimony, even if those territories had been changed irrevocably.

That local tribes would come to be seen as urban environmental stewards seemed unlikely in the 1960s, when members of the Muckleshoot Tribe, whose reservation was upstream from Seattle (and whose population included some descendants of the Duwamish), became scapegoats for the depletion of salmon runs. Criminalization of indigenous subsistence practices, begun decades earlier, continued well into the postwar period. In 1963, for example, Harold E. Miller, director of the new regional environmental and planning entity known as METRO, characterized the gillnetting practiced by Muckleshoots upstream from the city as anathema to urban environmental restoration. Miller claimed in the *Seattle Times* that "all we have done in the Duwamish is being offset by this [fishing] activity." Never mind urban development and the wholesale transformation of local rivers; the disappearance of the fish was clearly the Indians' fault.[9]

Beginning in the late 1960s, however, Native people became increasingly defiant about the state-sponsored repression of treaty fishing rights and staged fish-ins throughout Puget Sound and even in and around Seattle, bringing salmon conservation and human rights to center stage in local, national, and international media. One morning in the early 1970s, for example, Muckleshoot fishermen convened on the shore of Lake Washington with members of the American Indian Movement and with other Northwest tribes. "Makahs were prepared to die for our cause," recalled Gilbert King George, and until the drums and songs of the protestors convinced the well-armed fish and game wardens to back down, violence seemed imminent. The presence of the American Indian Movement, the National Indian Youth Council, and other allies also spurred fish-ins on the tidal Duwamish. "By then, our group was growing and growing, and we outnumbered the state agents," King George remembered. "What's one or two guys mean when they come down the river banks, and we are about 12, 18 ornery old Indian people, standing up for what they firmly believed in?" The fish-ins brought together many strands of Seattle's Native community: one Muckleshoot activist recalled that she already knew most of the American Indian Movement people from her days on Skid Road, and the American Indian Women's Service League got involved as well, publishing articles about fishing rights in *Indian Center News*. So while urban Indians and local tribes had very different histories in this place, this place also brought them together in defense of Native rights as a shared principle.[10]

Meanwhile, many non-Indian Seattleites had come to support treaty fishing rights, thanks in part to the savvy media techniques of Indian activists. By 1974, when George Boldt, U.S. District Court judge, finally ruled in favor of the tribes in *United States v. Washington*, ordering the state to allocate half the harvestable salmon to treaty tribes, many Seattle residents (with the noticeable exception of the city's large commercial fishing industry) had in fact already become outspoken advocates of both tribal sovereignty and a new, socially informed approach to conservation. Throughout the "fish fights," progressive churches, civil-rights organizations, and other groups decried the arrests and intimidation faced by tribal members and played critical roles in garnering support for fishing rights. By the 1980s, Seattle had become a center of pro-Indian and pro-environment sentiment, perhaps best symbolized in the formal apology for cultural genocide and religious oppression that was issued by Seattle-area churches in 1987.[11]

These new urban attitudes toward nature and Native peoples were often linked to each other through the increasingly iconic image of the salmon, a connection that had lasting implications for tribal authority in the city in the years to come. The Muckleshoots and Suquamish, federally recognized tribes whose membership included many descendants of the indigenous people of Seattle, began to assert themselves as stewards of Seattle's environment. They focused their attentions in particular on fisheries, empowered both by Boldt's ruling and by Seattle's growing urban environmental ethos. In 1982, for example, the tribes intervened against the proposed Seacrest Marina, a $13 million project that would have occupied 1,600 feet of shoreline between Duwamish Head and the mouth of the Duwamish. Tribal concerns over the impact on fisheries, along with opposition from urban environmentalists, led to the scrapping of the Seacrest proposal. Despite opposition from developers, right-wing ideologues, and many commercial fishermen, tribal efforts to manage urban nature earned positive reviews from environmental organizations and the mainstream press. When the Muckleshoots created a tribal fishing reserve in Elliott Bay in 1988, for instance, the *Seattle Times* referred to the tribe as a "fine conservation example," a total reversal of the scapegoating so common only twenty years earlier. In the fourteen years since the Boldt decision, tribes had exerted their authority over environmental issues just as those issues were coming to dominate civic consciousness. In the city named for an indigenous man now thought of as its "first environmentalist," Native authority had returned.[12]

But, like other developments in Seattle's postwar Indian history, the path to tribal control over urban places had its ironies. For example, the Treaty of Point Elliott was the legal basis for tribal fishing in the waters in and around Seattle. The treaty assured Indians access to the "usual and accustomed" places and resources that their ancestors had managed for millennia. But those places had often been transformed beyond recognition by urban development. As Muckleshoot fishing nets tangled with pleasure boats in the Lake Washington Ship Canal in the 1980s, for instance, they did so in a waterway that did not exist at the time of the treaty. The same engineering marvels that had destroyed indigenous subsistence in and around Seattle had also created a new and spectacular fishery that was neither usual nor accustomed. Similarly, tribes and their environmentalist allies won major concessions in a sixty-five-acre marina development on the north shore of Elliott Bay— concessions that included tribe-operated pens for up to one million farmed coho salmon. If tribal concerns sprang out of historic connections with the indigenous landscape, their modern manifestation sometimes bore little relation to the indigenous geography of salmon. Finally, despite tribal claims on the city's environment and a strong environmentalist ethic among many Seattleites, by the end of the twentieth century, the salmon were almost gone; indeed, some of them had been placed on the Endangered Species List. For all the power local tribes had gained over urban nature, the city's environmental history had not been reversed. And resentments over the new tribal authority continued to simmer: when the Muckleshoots legally killed two sea lions that had been devastating salmon runs at the ship canal locks, the tribe received threats, including one warning that an Indian would be killed for every dead sea lion. The hunt also brought the tribe into conflict with environmentalists; the Progressive Animal Welfare Society and the Humane Society were among the hunt's most outspoken critics. Indians as symbols of nature were one thing; Indians as real-life hunters in the city were quite another.[13]

The Muckleshoots and Suquamish emerged from the fish-ins and other wranglings of the 1960s and 1970s as legally enfranchised stakeholders in the urban environment. As federally recognized tribes, they asserted their treaty rights and sought, in many cases successfully, to become comanagers of significant elements of the urban environment. By the end of the twentieth century, the two tribes had become stewards of Seattle's waterways and shorelines, even if those places had been transformed almost beyond recognition. While their ascendancy was related to a broader national—even international—movement toward tribal self-determination beginning in the 1970s, local forces, including urban ones, had also helped to set the stage for this new development. Their activism, while rooted in their own reservation experiences, was also influenced and supported by Indian allies whose traditions of protest had grown out of the more radical, multicultural, urban work of groups like United Indians of All Tribes. Meanwhile, their successes, in the public eye if not necessarily the courtroom, hinged to no small degree on the fact that the non-Indian Seattleites, questioning the social and environmental legacies of their city's growth, seemed readier than ever before to acknowledge tribal peoples as having a stake in environmental management. But the Suquamish and Muckleshoots were not the only local Indians to place new claims on Seattle in the late twentieth century.

T HE BOLDT DECISION, as *United States v. Washington* soon came to be known, was a stunning victory for the people whose ancestors had settled the shores of Salt Water millennia earlier. It was also a victory for indigenous peoples around the world: its basic premise—that indigenous peoples, by definition, have unique claims on their territories—has become the basis for successful legal arguments throughout the United States as well as in Canada, Australia, and New Zealand. At the same time, it also set local tribes against each other, creating legal conflicts over shared or overlapping traditional territories. The Duwamish Tribe, including descendants of the Lakes and Shilsholes, had been involved in land claims cases throughout the twentieth century, its members giving testimony alongside relatives and allies from reservations at Muckleshoot, Tulalip, Suquamish, and elsewhere. But in many ways, the Duwamish had always been different, for one simple reason: their territory included the Pacific Northwest's largest city and the region's most valuable real estate. Arbiters of Indian law rarely recognized that value; after decades waiting for settlement of their claims, Duwamish tribal members each received $64 in 1971 for lands in what was now Seattle.

But for the Duwamish, a greater offense was yet to come. In 1979, five years after his decision in *United States v. Washington,* Judge Boldt determined that the Duwamish and four other Puget Sound Native communities no longer met all of the seven criteria required for inclusion on the list of tribes eligible for treaty fishing rights. In the case of the Duwamish, the disqualifier was an apparent ten-year break in the tribe's political leadership (one of the seven criteria required showing continuous tribal organization from the signing of a treaty to the present). The decade in question stretched from 1916 to 1925, the years immediately after the completion of the Lake Washington Ship Canal and the destruction of the Black River, where many Duwamish people had still been living. The chaos of those years now had its consequences some six decades later. The modern-day Duwamish officially ceased to exist in the eyes of the federal government and thus were considered to have no legal claim over the city named for their ancestral leader. (Never mind that government agents had included the Duwamish during discussions of proposed tribal termination policies of the 1950s.)[14]

Bureaucratic extinction is one thing; actual disappearance is quite another. So while the decision to extinguish Duwamish treaty status might have been a massive blow to the tribe's claims, it also opened new doors in terms of public sentiment. During the same years that the Muckleshoots and Suquamish were angling—literally—for control over the city's environment, the Duwamish, even without federal recognition, laid their own claims on Seattle. Stripped of legal authority, the Duwamish capitalized on changes in what it meant to be urban—most notably, the ascent of environmentalism and multiculturalism in civic politics and new ideas about history—to assert a kind of cultural authority. In doing so, they would not only challenge their own alleged extinction but capsize the city's very story of itself.

The Duwamish River was a place utterly transformed by 1975, the year after *United States v. Washington*. Only a single curve of the indigenous estuary still existed, near the place where Seetoowathl and his wife had starved half a century earlier. This backwater bend sheltered by a sliver of scrubby island was all that remained of the once-fecund interface between river and Salt Water. For some, though, even that was too much "unproductive" nature: in 1975, the Port of Seattle proposed to dredge and fill it to make way for a new container ship terminal. During initial surveying, an Army Corps of Engineers archaeologist identified the riverbank—then sporting five dilapidated houses—as a site of significance; historical documents and shell middens suggested that the site had once been an indigenous town. It appeared that the Duwamish village of Basketry Hat had been rediscovered. But in early 1976, the Port made a mistake. While demolishing the old houses, a bulldozer operator obliterated most of the archaeological layers at the site. Almost immediately, the local press blasted the Port for destroying a crucial piece of Seattle's heritage. (Business and maritime editors were less outraged; one longed rather confusingly for the days "when there were many more acres of clams here and digging for those clams was the only dig that man worried about.") In its own defense, the Port contended that it did not know the houses were on top of the archaeological site, and since public corporations could not be sued, it could not be held accountable anyway. These excuses did little to satisfy those who saw the Port's actions as the wanton destruction of civic patrimony.[15]

Then Cecile Maxwell stepped into the fray. As the young chairwoman of the Duwamish Tribe, Maxwell was, like many Indian leaders in her generation, including Bernie Whitebear, unafraid of controversy and extremely media savvy. Her own activism, however, was also shaped by her family's connections to local places and by watching, for example, her brother being arrested for fishing on the Duwamish. Soon after the bulldozer had done its work in 1975, Maxwell used her anger and expertise to begin telling a new kind of place-story. With the help of other Duwamish tribal members and allies in the local press, Maxwell connected what had happened at Basketry Hat to broader urban and Native narratives. In one interview, for example, she lamented that "we have no culture left, no history left. That's because we have no land base," linking the Port's blunder to a longer history of dispossession. Meanwhile, activist and journalist Terry Tafoya pointed out in the *Post-Intelligencer* that Europeans "were in the dark ages" when the longhouses of Basketry Hat were built and that "perhaps a thousand years from now, Indians will discover the decaying remains of the Space Needle." For their part, the *Post-Intelligencer*'s editorial staff noted that the pioneers who arrived at Alki Point were "Johnny and Janie-come-latelies," going on to ask, "Who says that Seattle was founded in 1851?" And when the dig went public in 1978 with free tours, the site was interpreted as "a boon, not only to the public, but also to the Duwamish people" and presented a chance "to learn about the way of life of the Duwamish people, whose past has almost been completely wiped out by a growing city."[16]

Here, then, was the overturning of Seattle's narrative. Like the "treaty" read at Fort Lawton or the fish-ins on Lake Washington, these were new kinds of public place-stories about Seattle and about urban meaning and often seemed to arise directly out of the ground itself. In 1994, for example, construction crews disturbed cultural deposits while building a new sewage treatment plant at West Point. Builders immediately halted construction and allowed excavation to take place under tribal oversight and at a cost of one month and $3.5 million. *Post-Intelligencer* arts writer Solveig Torvik noted that Seattle residents and the tribes would be "inestimably poorer" if sites like West Point were destroyed; as at the lauded opening of Daybreak Star, civic and Indian goals appeared to merge. But tensions remained. In early 1998, while digging footings for the new Seattle World Trade Center, a Port worker discovered a woman's skull attached to a piling. Having learned from past mistakes, the Port stopped work and contacted the Suquamish and Muckleshoots, but they neglected to notify the Duwamish, who learned of the discovery only through the media. Under the leadership of Cecile Maxwell—actually, now known as Cecile Hansen—the Duwamish picketed the dig. "Seattle promotes itself as a place of great cultural sensitivity," Hansen told a *Seattle Times* reporter. "I am here to tell you this cultural sensitivity has not been measurably extended to Seattle's indigenous Duwamish Tribe and its people." Even though the nature of Seattle's relationship to its indigenous past had changed, for some that change had not gone nearly far enough.[17]

Still, the fact that the Duwamish, with no legal standing as a tribe, were able to garner significant media attention and public sympathy spoke to the cultural authority they had acquired in Seattle's urban imagination. That attention and sympathy increased in the new millennium as the Duwamish worked to have their federal recognition reinstated. Working with local archivists and historians, they sutured together the alleged ten-year break in tribal organization using oral histories, Catholic Church records, and genealogical research. Recognizing the disruptions caused by environmental transformation, the Duwamish argued that what seemed like a break in organization was in fact simply a change from one generation of tribal leadership to another within a single, identifiable Duwamish community. Their argument must have been convincing: on the last day of the Clinton administration, Cecile Hansen received a phone call from the Bureau of Indian Affairs, telling her that the Duwamish had been recognized. The victory was short-lived, however; only a few days later, the new Bureau of Indian Affairs administrator appointed by George W. Bush informed Hansen that the decision had been reversed. Stunned, Hansen, other members of the Duwamish Tribe, and their allies vented their anger in the local press. But the greatest opportunity to express their outrage was yet to come: fifty years after MacArthur's speech, Seattle was about to celebrate its 150th birthday.[18]

The coverage of the Duwamish recognition fracas, which included front-page stories in local papers as well as some international coverage, dovetailed with the run-up to the sesquicentennial of Seattle's founding. By November 2001, it was clear that it would no longer be possible to tell Seattle's story without the participation of Native people and in particular without the Duwamish. And so when actors playing the Denny Party came ashore in a drenching rain at Alki that 13 November, they were welcomed not only by hundreds of spectators as in past reenactments but by Cecile Hansen and other representatives from the Duwamish Tribe. After a series of speeches, many of which noted the tribe's recognition struggle, city leaders unveiled two new plaques at the Alki Monument: one commemorating the women of the group, the other honoring the Duwamish who had made survival at New York–Alki possible. Meanwhile, at a luncheon attended by members of the Denny, Bell, Boren, Terry, and Low families, Ruth Moore, the great-granddaughter of John and Lydia Low, told those gathered that "we need to let the federal government know that those Indians made the city possible—and I love them for it."[19]

Sesquicentennial events often emphasized either the positive interactions between pioneers and Native people in the first months of settlement or the multicultural sentiments of the late twentieth and early twenty-first centuries. They left out much of what had happened in between: the burning of the longhouses, the attempts to keep Indians out of town, the fish fights. In crafting a new, multicultural place-story, anniversary organizers had perhaps stilled the Manichean heart of the Seattle Spirit, but they had also whitewashed much of Seattle's real history. On a handful of occasions, however, a more confrontational version of Seattle's urban story rose to the surface. As part of a local museum exhibit, Anne Overacker Rasmussen described the shame she had once felt at being Duwamish, even in a city named for one of her Duwamish ancestors: at long last, memories of "No Dogs or Indians Allowed" were creeping into the mainstream urban narrative. Meanwhile, at the pioneer family reunion, historian David Buerge, who had helped craft the Duwamish petition for recognition, pointed out that "if the Duwamish had a nickel for everyone who said something should be done for them, they could afford to buy back a considerable chunk of [Seattle]." He thus highlighted the difference between honoring the city's Indian past and addressing its Indian present. And at a sesquicentennial Rotary luncheon, Duwamish tribal member James Rasmussen balked at reciting the speech attributed to Seeathl. "The Duwamish are staring down the maw of extinction while you talk of progress. I won't do this," he told them before abruptly walking off the stage. And as the final event of the year-long sesquicentennial, Duwamish tribal members welcomed canoes full of Indian people from many tribes ashore at a new city park at the site of Basketry Hat, asserting their status as guardians of their traditional homeland.[20]

The sesquicentennial might have ended, but the efforts of the Duwamish to obtain federal recognition did not. After a series of inquiries into criminal wrongdoing in the Bureau of Indian Affairs during both the Clinton and the Bush administrations, the issue came to down to technicalities: when a particular set of papers was signed and whether those papers were drafts or final copies. Finally, in the spring of 2002, Interior Secretary Gale Norton reaffirmed the government's position against recognition despite a concerted campaign on the part of Seattle-area religious organizations and other Duwamish allies. These included more than six dozen descendants of Seattle pioneers, who signed a petition calling for the creation of the Duwamish reservation that their ancestors had petitioned *against* more than a century earlier. Meanwhile, federally recognized tribes in the area had staked out a wide range of positions on Duwamish recognition. The Suquamish across Puget Sound supported it; the Tulalip Tribes to the north said they would not fight it, having lost a similar battle with the Snoqualmie Tribe in the 1990s; and the Muckleshoots announced plans to fight Duwamish recognition should it ever be granted through an act of Congress, the only option left. This would be the great irony of *United States v. Washington:* in settling old disputes, it had opened new legal, political, and cultural rifts in the city and beyond. Meanwhile, the forces of urban dispossession that had rendered the Duwamish invisible in the early twentieth century continued to have powerful effects in the twenty-first.[21]

The Duwamish have continued their efforts to carve out a place in the city. With the financial support of individual donors, companies, and local governments, Cecile Hansen and her group purchased land on West Marginal Way, just across the street from Basketry Hat, with plans to build a longhouse and cultural center. "This longhouse won't just be for us," Hansen told a reporter the summer before the sesquicentennial. "It will be for everyone who lives in and visits Seattle." As with Bernie Whitebear's People's Lodge and Edgar Heap of Birds' *Day/Night*, a large part of being Indian in modern Seattle involved showing yourself to non-Indians on your own terms. The Duwamish longhouse, once built, would be a way for one Indian community to tell its place-stories to a larger community that finally appeared to be listening. Recognition and a reservation, however, seem farther away than ever.[22]

BACK IN 1925, BOOSTERS ruled the day. Only aging pioneers and a few Indian people saw fit to question Seattle's rise to metropolitan primacy, and their accounts of vanquished spirit powers and bucolic village life were not often heard among the shouts and bellows of the advocates of metropolis. One of those *cheechakos,* his name now lost to history, scripted one of the thousands of promotional brochures that beckoned visitors to look around, settle down, and buy in. He began with his own encounter with the city: "First impression! As I found her so will I always think of Seattle. As young and eager. Life still the great unexplored; living still the great adventure. With no old past to stop and worship; no dead men's bones to reckon with; no traditions chained to her ankles." Here, then, was the prevailing place-story of the modern era (and not just in Seattle): that the past was irrelevant (although it had been a great adventure), that only the future lay ahead of the city and nation, that all negative consequences of modern urban life would be outweighed by the benefits. No old bones.[23]

Not so; just ask Jan Deeds and Ron Mandt. Three quarters of a century after that anonymous promoter crowed about Seattle's freedom from the past, laborers unearthed old bones—two adults and a child, to be exact—while repairing the foundation of Deeds and Mandt's home near Alki Point. As work came to a halt and the coroner was called, the homeowners soon learned that this was not the first time Indian graves had been disturbed here. Half a century before, an earlier resident had experienced "a little excitement" when he found bones under the house. In those days, aside from meriting a bemused article in the *Seattle Times*, such a discovery carried no consequences. But for Deeds and Mandt, who lived in a very different Seattle at the beginning of the twenty-first century and were trying to sell their house, there were definite consequences, which they bore with great decency: calls to the Suquamish and Muckleshoot tribes (but not to the Duwamish), thousands of dollars paid to privately hired archaeologists, and buyers who withdrew their offer. Finally reburied in accordance with tribal wishes and the state's Indian Graves and Records Act, the family first laid to rest here long ago showed that there are, in fact, old bones to reckon with in Seattle. Boosters may still run the show, but at least now they have to share the stage. Word has gotten around: the past has consequences.[24]

The central challenge of Seattle's Native histories, however, has been to acknowledge those consequences. The struggles of the Duwamish Tribe in the last quarter of the twentieth century typify the tensions inherent in Seattle's Native pasts. On the one hand, they show the lasting social and environmental consequences of the city's urban development. On the other hand, the attention the Duwamish received at the end of the century, and especially around the time of the sesquicentennial, shows the metaphorical place some Native people have come to occupy in the urban imagination: as environmental stewards, as indictments of injustice, and as indigenous hosts of civic history. And so we return to the central problem of Seattle's Native pasts: the distance between the imagined Indian in the city and the real experiences of Indian people and the tensions between fantasy and reality, symbolism and history, ghosts and humanity. All too often, the tendency remains to talk about Seattle's Indian imagery and Seattle's Indian people as though they have little to do with each other. During the sesquicentennial, for example, the vocal presence of the Duwamish Tribe was at times overshadowed by Seattle's symbolic Indians, especially in discussions of one of the thorniest urban concerns of recent years: transportation.

Seattle has some of the worst traffic in the nation, and efforts to build mass transit systems have been hampered both by citizen-sponsored tax revolts and by infighting among transit organizations. What is fascinating about the transportation debates, however, is how often metaphorical Indians have been part of them. The winner of a *Seattle Weekly* poetry contest, for example, had Seeathl cursing Seattle with Tim Eyman, the notorious spokesperson for several antitax initiatives:

Arrrrrgh! Nixoney chu-ga roalhop Eyman non-shaman Hooog in facto. We Chinnok cho killa firebo an der baa baa Healtee err an errer!

(Arrrrrgh! Cursed, treaty-breaching fiends, may a smiling White Devil [Eyman] eviscerate your roads, your emergency and health services, and your quality of life and community for ever and ever!)

Meanwhile, Indian author Sherman Alexie penned a sarcastic column in the city's other alternative weekly, *The Stranger*, about the ancient monorail of the Kickakickamish people, which had been destroyed along with most of its builders by vengeful neighbors. "It was genocide," Alexie wrote, noting that the current monorail was still haunted by the ghosts of the Kickakickamish, who would tear to pieces any expansion of the space-age sky-train's route. Then, for a story a few months later about sports utility vehicles, the *Weekly*'s front cover showed the statue of Chief Seattle sticking out of an electric car's sunroof over the tagline, "What Would Chief Seattle Drive?" Like other Indian images in Seattle's past, these stories were not really about Native people at all. That is exactly the point: even today, Indians in Seattle are often more visible as metaphors than as people. When, for example, an emcee quipped at the Rotary's sesquicentennial luncheon that "Native canoes are moving smoothly through the Black River S-Curves" in a mock nineteenth-century traffic bulletin, he linked one of the Seattle area's worst highway interchanges with the empty riverbed nearby—as a joke. No wonder James Rasmussen, whose Duwamish ancestors had once lived on the Black River, had walked out.[25]

Debates over traffic and mass transit are closely related to the urban malaise experienced by many Seattleites during the 1990s, when the phenomenal wealth and growth of the dot-com boom seemed to threaten the city's identity. Among the most vocal of those concerned was writer Fred Moody, who had spent years chronicling the high-tech industry's effects on the region. He lamented the loss of a more working-class, slower-paced Seattle, a place his intellectual forebear, the irascible newspaperman Emmett Watson, had dubbed "Lesser Seattle" back in the 1970s. Moody's lament drew from the Native past:

The better the city's material prospects, the worse its psychological prospects. I sat up late one night and regarded the history of Seattle as a history of diminishment, boom by boom. I remembered reading . . . how the tribes finally were forcibly put on a boat and sent out into the sound. . . . Now I saw their expulsion as equal parts exile and deliverance. They were our first lesser Seattleites. Fully aware that a material boom would bring a spiritual bust to their homeland, they served by their very existence to mock the pretensions of newcomers intent on bringing civilization and wealth to the Northwest's paradise.

In Moody's estimation, the Seattle of Microsoft, Starbucks, and Amazon.com had gone overboard: "New-York-Pretty-Soon had grown into More-Than-New-York-Right-Now," he complained, continuing that Seattleites like him and his downwardly mobile friends were "practically the next best thing to Native Americans." Arguing that the defining characteristic of a "lesser Seattleite"—and of lesser Seattle itself—was the forswearing of ambition, Moody realized that the question "What kind of city is Seattle becoming?" was also "What the hell am I turning into?" The interesting thing was how crucial Indians were to the answer.[26]

On the other side of the debate over Seattle's soul, Robert Ferrigno, a contributor to Microsoft's online *Slate* magazine, pointed out that Seattle's problems in fact stemmed from the "sloth and poor economic policies of its other tenants: Indians, Scandinavians, and hippies." The indigenous tradition of the potlatch, Ferrigno claimed, had prevented "research and development," and the potlatch's supposed values ("No investments. No competition. No ego. No progress.") had prevented Northwest Indians and their slow-growth descendants from reaping the rewards of urban achievement. A similar story about the so-called Seattle Freeze, the idea that people in the city are superficially friendly but distant and hard to get to know, meanwhile, referred back to Emmett Watson's tongue-in-cheek claim that "Seattle" was "Indian for 'stay away from here.'" According to these observers of local culture, both the best and worst things about Seattle—its disappearing authenticity, on the one hand, and its stubborn resistance to progress and chilly social climate, on the other—could be explained by telling stories about Indians.[27]

These place-stories from millennium's end and new millennium's beginning, for all their postindustrial irony and anomie, sounded remarkably like those told generations earlier. Aging pioneers were replaced by aging lefties and upstart *cheechakos* shape-shifted into venture capitalists from California, but otherwise, the anxieties and conflicts were the same: between native and newcomer, between competing visions of urbanity, between the past and the future. Again, the debate centered on what kind of place Seattle was and who belonged there, and again, imagined Indians gave that debate its rhetorical heft. This is perhaps the most powerful historical impulse in Seattle: to try to understand the urban present through the Native past. Often, it is a noble compulsion, inspired by the need to question economic avarice, environmental degradation, or social disintegration. But only when it is grounded—in the specifics of local history and in the context of present-day Indian realities—does the impulse become something more than blurry-eyed nostalgia or insensitive mockery.

Occasionally, however, there are moments when Seattle's Native pasts have been connected in meaningful ways to its urban and Indian present. Near the boundary between Seattle and its southern neighbor Tukwila ("hazelnut" in Chinook Jargon), three hills guard the Duwamish River and its valley. These were the hills that Dosie Wynn's grandmother told her about on trips to Seattle from the Muckleshoot Reservation back in the 1930s, sharing stories of battles between North Wind and Storm Wind and how the world came to be as it is. Members of the Duwamish Tribe, for their part, understood the landscape around the hills as the place where the world began. But urban history had not been kind to the hills: one had been quarried down to less than half its original size, another had been bisected by a freeway exit, and at the end of the twentieth century, the third—known locally as Poverty Hill—was put up for sale and was most likely going to be leveled. Then in 2000, a group of neighbors contacted local tribes and began to organize on behalf of Poverty Hill. In the end, the Friends of Duwamish Riverbend Hill raised over a million dollars to purchase and preserve the site through the auspices of the Cascade Land Conservancy. On the summer solstice in 2004, the Friends' coalition came together to celebrate the hill's preservation and unveiled plans for restoring the hill's native ecosystems and for building trails with signs interpreting the Duwamish Valley's history. Local and state officials, representatives of environmental organizations, and, most notably, members of both the Muckleshoot and Duwamish tribes (as well as Indian people from other places), all spoke of the importance of Poverty Hill: as a symbol of racial reconciliation and faith in good government, as much-needed open space in an underserved industrial neighborhood, and as tribal cultural patrimony. At Poverty Hill, ecotopian impulses for restoration, preservation, and the ever-elusive "sense of place" intersected with tribal interests in protecting sacred sites and traditional cultural properties. The key was that the parties involved moved beyond the metaphors. Indian people at Poverty Hill were not just symbols of an endangered landscape but active partners in, and beneficiaries of, its preservation.[28]

But the desire to protect and restore urban nature using the Native past can also make for bad history. Not far away from Poverty Hill, for instance, more than a thousand tons of contaminated soil has been removed to create a new estuarine refuge for salmon on the polluted and channelized Duwamish River. Named Herring's House Park after the indigenous town razed in 1893, the site aims to link restoration to local history. The problem, however, is that the park is in the wrong place: it is not on the site of Herring's House, which is downstream; it is on the site of Basketry Hat. Herring's House was a more "ecological" name, though, and so marketing trumped history. Meanwhile, ironically, native-plant restoration on the site obliterated some of the last visible evidence of Seattle's indigenous geography: broken shells that were part of Basketry Hat's middens. In this case, restoring (and repackaging) the landscape for ecotopian Seattle has only further muddled this place's history. Meanwhile, across the street, a large sign proclaims that someday, if the funding (far less than the cost of restoring the park) can ever be found, the Duwamish Tribe will have a longhouse here again.[29]

In repairing Seattle's landscape, restorationists were also re-*storying* that landscape. Like city leaders warning of Indian-borne apocalypse in Seattle Illahee of the 1870s, Tilikums using totem poles to sell the city in the 1910s, and pioneer descendants playing Indian to lament urban growth in the 1930s, restorationists were using the Native past to understand, and in some ways to mitigate, the urban present. But restoration of indigenous places is deeply problematic: there is no guarantee that the salmon or anything else can be brought back or that such efforts will actually improve the material conditions of modern Indian lives. The question remains, then: good intentions aside, whom do these place-stories of "restoration" truly benefit? To *when*, and to *whom*, is *what* being restored, exactly?

OBSERVERS OF U.S. HISTORY have often written that one of the central American cultural projects has been to find a way to belong here on this continent, to craft an identity from Old World origins and New World circumstances. Very often, that project has involved using Indian imagery to tell American stories: Boston Tea Party activists dressed as Indians, James Fenimore Cooper's *Leatherstocking Tales*, the YMCA's Indian Guides, Chief Seattle's fifth Gospel. But this need to become Native in order to be American runs counter to the real history of our nation's engagements with indigenous societies. For every buckskin-clad frontier hero of American folklore, there was a Sand Creek or Trail of Tears; for every literary Noble Savage, there was a smallpox blanket or a boarding school; for every New Age eco-shaman there was a missionary's insult or a game warden's handcuffs. If the chief American cultural project has been to bury Indian facts under American fictions, then perhaps the new project in Seattle's case, means moving beyond the recycled place-stories—beyond the seeming inability of Indian and urban histories to coexist—and understanding the work our stories have done in this place: what they have ignored, what they have allowed, whom they have benefited.

One way to begin is through knowing, and sharing, the history that has woven lives together in the city and its hinterland, and imagining what might have been different. In *Facing East from Indian Country*, his provocative account of early American history from the vantage point of the continent's indigenous peoples, historian Daniel Richter has argued that the chaos and violence of that history were never inevitable. Indians and whites had to *learn* to hate each other. This is also true on Puget Sound, where the future was never preordained and where the idea that Indian history and urban history were somehow separate had to be created in town ordinances and racial theories, transmitted through pioneer memoirs and Potlatch parades, and literally built into the environment through ship canals and historic districts. Comprehending Native pasts entails connecting urban and Indian histories and understanding the processes through which indigenous places have been dispossessed, expropriated, and transformed. It means knowing the history of the indigenous peoples on whose homelands Seattle was built, the Shilsholes and Lakes and Duwamish and Suquamish and Muckleshoots, as well as the history of the Native peoples and territories who have been drawn into the city's urban orbit, the S'Klallams and Tlingits and Coeur d'Alenes and Aleuts and Blackfeet. Unearthing Seattle's Native pasts requires us also to look critically at which stories we tell about our shared past and why we tell them. Lastly, it demands that we see the ways in which Native people have actively contributed to, shaped, or resisted those stories.[30]

Stories matter. Throughout Seattle's history, actions have sprung out of stories, just as actions—tidelands filled, basket weavers paid, "bow and arrow joints" shut down—have in turn resulted in new narratives about this place and who belongs here. At the beginning of the twenty-first century, Seattle's urban palimpsest surely has room for new stories. It is possible, as some of the elders once said, that the horned serpents are gone, banished by "too many houses" and too much change. There are so many moments where Seattle's history might have gone in other directions: a longhouse unburned, a mortuary pole left where it stood, a lake not lowered. We may look back, but we cannot go back. The past will not be undone. "For better or worse, this native history belongs to us all," Daniel Richter writes, continuing by saying that understanding that past might allow us to "find ways to focus more productively on our future."[31]

Perhaps in the revival of indigenous place-names and in powwows at Daybreak Star, in the growing respect for the treaties and in every college diploma earned by an Indian, in the restoration of urban nature and in the willingness to challenge narratives of progress, there is hope that Seattle's Native past—or, more accurately, its many Native pasts—can be unearthed. These place-stories, linked to urban and Indian presents and futures, will not simply be cautionary tales, smug jokes, or nostalgic fantasies but will be dialogues about the transformations of landscape and power in the city and about strategies for living together humanely in this place. Bringing new stories to light and considering how those stories can inform new kinds of action should be our agenda for the future, and it is crafted in the moments when we simply ask each other, *What happened here?*

An Atlas of Indigenous Seattle

Coll Thrush and Nile Thompson
Maps by Amir Sheikh

Historical Introduction by Coll Thrush

ANSWERING THE QUESTION *What happened here?* requires asking
another: *What was here before?* In Seattle, as in most cities, the pre-urban
landscape has been transformed almost beyond recognition. Tracing
the course of the Duwamish River as it was in 1851, for example, can
be a daunting task. Understanding the ways in which Indigenous people
inhabited that landscape, meanwhile, can be even more difficult. In
short, there is virtually nothing left to see—earlier generations of Seattleites made sure of that—and so comprehending the city's indigenous
geography involves peeling back decades of development and imagining the possibilities. Even then, the risk remains that we will imagine only what we expected to see all along—noble savages, empty
wilderness, totem poles—rather than what might have actually once been
there. Seattle's Native pasts have been full of such imaginings. Luckily,
through the work of two men and the Indian people who collaborated
with them, we have a rare opportunity to envision in specific, concrete
ways the places that would eventually become Seattle. In the 1910s, both
men collected information about traditional Indigenous geographies of
the Seattle area, working both with Duwamish men and women living
in and around the city and with Muckleshoot and Suquamish informants from area reservations.

The first of these researchers was Thomas Talbot Waterman
(1885–1936). A student of Franz Boas, Waterman taught anthropology
and sociology at the University of Washington in the early twentieth
century. Although he lived in Seattle for only a handful of years, the
city held a special fascination for him. "The actual topography is very

interesting," he noted, "and the spot is doubly interesting because of the great city which has grown up there." Even better, though, the urban landscape that had grown up on central Puget Sound was still populated by Indian people. Some of them, like Seetoowathl in his float house, shared their knowledge with him from within the city limits. Others, like Jennie Davis and Amelia Sneatlum from Suquamish and Betsy Whatcom from Muckleshoot, educated him in their reservation homes. The resulting manuscript, entitled "Puget Sound Geography," includes the names of hundreds of places, from the Cascade Mountains in the east to the western shores of Puget Sound and from Whidbey Island in the north to the many-armed southern reach of the Sound. The names speak about the everyday practices of life here: places where fish were caught, places where canoes could be portaged, places where games were played. They tell of the landscape's intellectual elements: the connections between bodies, houses, and the earth; ways of measuring the land and moving on the waters; spirit forces that gave life meaning. Most importantly, they are proof of the profound "inhabitedness" of this first country: the towns, the trails, the stories from deep time.[1]

Waterman's work did have its problems. He often misunderstood the elders and sometimes failed to obtain the meanings of the place-names he was offered, and his maps are consistently bad. His greatest error, though, was in the attitude he brought to his research. Noting, for example, that indigenous people on Puget Sound might have twenty names for places along a river but no name for the river as a whole, Waterman commented that "from our own standpoint, the Indian's conception of the size of the world is startlingly inadequate." Waterman saw Indigenous people as his intellectual inferiors, inhabiting a lower rung on the ladder between Savagery and Civilization. To strengthen this point, Waterman compared, for example, place-naming practices among the peoples of the Pacific: some Polynesian societies had names only for small places, while others, like the Samoans, had achieved a "national and archipelagic designation." It was clear which societies Waterman found to be more civilized. While his work is a testament to the richness of indigenous inhabitance in Seattle and Puget Sound, it is also an example of the kind of thinking that placed

Indians in the category of "primitive"—and that justified their dispossession.[2]

For all its biases, the biggest problem with "Puget Sound Geography" has been its inaccessibility. Available for decades only in the Bancroft Library, Berkeley, a photocopy of the unfinished manuscript was obtained by the University of Washington in the 1980s. Despite its poor quality, outdated and inconsistent orthography, and chaotic strikethroughs and marginalia, the University of Washington copy has been a boon both to archaeologists and to historians but has remained inaccessible and unusable to all but the most intrepid or formally educated researchers. In the 1990s, Upper Skagit tribal member Vi Hilbert, anthropologist Jay Miller, and amateur linguist Zalmai Zahir edited the manuscript, putting the elders' words into modern orthography, translating a number of place-names that Waterman had not, and, most importantly, linking the work to present-day efforts to reawaken the indigenous language of the region. Even though their edition was published in 2001, the information remained relatively inaccessible because the limited printing run of this latest incarnation of Waterman's research meant that it was expensive and difficult to find.[3] The present atlas builds on the work of Hilbert and her colleagues but also returns to the original Waterman manuscript in an effort to expand the number of translations and to correct past mistranslations.

In addition to the material gathered by Waterman, this atlas makes use of certain field notes of John Peabody Harrington (1884–1961). Heavily influenced while at Stanford University by the work of the renowned anthropologist A. L. Kroeber, Harrington began graduate studies in Germany but soon dropped out to become a high school teacher in California, using his summers off to conduct fieldwork. In 1910, he came to Seattle to teach summer courses in linguistics and Northwest Coast ethnology at the University of Washington, as well as to conduct a series of public lectures entitled "The Siberian Origin of the American Indian." During the summer of 1910, he conducted fieldwork with Duwamish people, including hereditary Duwamish chief William Rogers, on the Suquamish Reservation. Rogers, an Indian man named Moore, and the informant and interpreter Edward Percival joined Harrington on visits to the Seattle and Renton area, contributing the place-names included in this atlas. This research, along with his more extensive work on the last speakers of several California languages, brought Harrington to the attention of the Bureau of American Ethnology, which hired him as an ethnographer in 1915.

Over the next four decades, Harrington went on to collect materials on more than a hundred additional Indigenous languages of North America and became a pioneer of linguistic recordings. Reclusive and eccentric, Harrington received little academic recognition during his life, but after his death, his colleagues discovered enormous amounts of field notes, squirreled away in garages and storage units up and down the West Coast. These field notes have supplied subsequent generations of scholars with remarkable insights into languages and cultural practices that are now lost. (Also, unlike Waterman, Harrington rarely made explicit written judgments about Native societies but appears to have had a deep appreciation for the sophistication of Indian languages, technologies, and cultures.)[4]

Except where noted, the information in this atlas comes from the original Waterman and Harrington materials, the field notes and plat maps of the General Land Office's cadastral survey conducted in the 1850s, a list of villages and longhouses that was an exhibit in a 1920s land claims case, and Erna Gunther's classic *Ethnobotany of Western Washington*. Unless noted otherwise, archaeological data come from the database held and maintained by the University of Washington's Burke Museum of Natural History and Culture. In many cases, additional information about the history of specific sites can be found within the main text of the book.[5] We have chosen somewhat arbitrarily to limit the scope of the atlas to Seattle's current boundaries, with a handful of exceptions in which a site immediately outside the city limits was important to understanding places within Seattle (e.g., entries 82–89) or where a site spoke directly to the broader themes of this book (e.g., entry 127).

The concerns of present-day tribal peoples dictate how this atlas should be used. Despite the tumult of regrades and ship canals, artifacts of Seattle's indigenous past surely remain undisturbed throughout the city. With that in mind, the maps have been created at a scale that prevents the specific location of individual sites. We have also with-held mention of ancestral burial sites or of Indigenous remains that have been found in the city. But should a reader inadvertently unearth something (or someone) while digging a basement or clearing brush, a call to the tribes or to the Burke Museum should be the first response—not just because it is the right thing to do but because it is in keeping with any number of state and federal laws. Finally, although many elders once said that sacred sites in Seattle had lost their power due to urban development, some are being used again today and should be treated with respect. Just as this is not a pot hunter's or grave robber's guide to Seattle, it is also not a primer for playing Indian in the city.

Maps are risky things. Publishing this information lays bare traditional knowledge, and in doing so, risks intrusion upon the intellectual and cultural rights of modern tribal people. But there is also another kind of risk: getting the history wrong. The tighter the geographical focus, the less clear the information tends to be; the result is an atlas that includes conjecture, speculation, and goings-out on various limbs in the interest of imagining the possibilities. Of course, the simple fact that in many cases this geography is speculative—the untranslatable words, the mysterious meanings, the unclear uses of places—is a result of the history described in this book; it is part of the historical silence created by epidemics, dispossession, and forced assimilation.

Waterman himself fretted about how much had already been lost when he was collecting the place-names nearly a century ago: "On Puget Sound alone, there seem to have been in the neighborhood of ten thousand proper names. I have secured about half this number, the remainder having passed out of memory. I am continually warned by Indians that they give me for my maps only a small part of the total number which *once* was used. The rest they have either forgotten or never heard. 'The old people could have told you all' is the remark most commonly heard."[6] The math is off—Waterman and his students collected less than 10 percent of the names he claimed must have existed—but the point stands. So much was lost prior to the 1910s that we are bereft: the view offered by Waterman's informants looks out on only a tiny fraction of the richness that was once here. Considering the power of what we do have, the reality must have been staggering. Instead of just over ten dozen names for Seattle, we might have had a thousand if only history had worked out differently. That said, the maps that follow are not intended as a complete or comprehensive survey of Seattle's Indigenous geography; rather, they are mere glimpses of what was here before.

The final risk of maps such as these is that they might give the impression that such geographies were static and unchanging. This was surely not the case, especially in a geologically, ecologically, and culturally dynamic place such as Puget Sound. Even before the arrival of the Denny Party and others, the Indigenous maps of this place surely changed over time as sites and their uses changed. Instead of a stable "zero datum" on which the rest of Seattle's history takes place, it is perhaps more accurate to think of this atlas as merely a partial snapshot of the Indigenous world just prior to white settlement. It is also useful to consider the other maps that could be made to represent Seattle's diverse Native pasts: the locations of mixed-race and Indian families in Seattle's neighborhoods, the installations of totem poles in the city, and the geographies of Skid Road. Each of these landscapes could—and perhaps should—be mapped as well and interleaved with the maps presented here for an even fuller accounting of the erasures, ironies, and persistences that make up the palimpsest that is Seattle's history. I hope these maps are a step in that direction.

Introduction to the Revised Atlas
Coll Thrush

Much of the work reflected in the following atlas is that of linguist Nile Thompson, who worked closely with me on the first edition of *Native Seattle*. Drawing on the earlier research of ethnographers like Thomas Talbot Waterman and John Peabody Harrington, and on the scholars who collaborated with Upper Skagit elder and linguist Vi taqšəblu Hilbert, Nile produced new translations for many of the place names in Seattle whose meanings had largely been lost. The result captures the richness of the landscape, the creativity of the people who lived there, and in some cases the persistence of place names across the decades since the arrival of colonists.

As Nile wrote in his introduction to the first edition's atlas,

The place names of Puget Sound Salish peoples have a wide range of reference, from myth to human activity, from spirit power to animal species, and from natural resource to natural landmark. A site could be named in isolation or it could be contrasted with other like features. The place-names themselves can refer to broad expanses or areas or to specific sandspits or rocks. Along the coastline, places were generally named from the perspective of looking toward the shore from Puget Sound.

Nile also made note of the deep connections between bodies, landscapes, and material cultural belongings in Coast Salish society. Whulshootseed is known for using something called lexical suffixes that link place names to living bodies and to the things of everyday life. For example, the suffix –us could refer both to a face or a bluff; –aqs could refer to a nose, a point, or a pointed object; and the –ootseed of Whulshootseed refers to the human or animal mouth, the mouths of waterways, and language itself. Each of these suffixes, so central to many of the place names included herein, speak to the integrated world of Duwamish and other Coast Salish peoples.

Thankful as always for the profound insights of Nile's translation work, I have chosen to make one significant change to the atlas. While working on the original edition in 2005 and 2006, Nile developed a spelling system intended to make the reading and pronunciation of Whulshootseed words easier for readers and speakers of English. In the years since, however, none of the local tribes have chosen to take up that spelling system, and so I have transliterated Nile's system into that used by most tribes in the region today, which is based on the International Phonetic Alphabet. While some of the characters are perhaps a bit intimidating to non-speakers, they are designed to accurately represent the sounds of Whulshootseed. Use the following pronunciation key, based on 1994's *Lushootseed Dictionary* by Dawn Bates, Thom Hess, and Vi Hilbert, to guide your learning along with the approximate pronunciations following each place name. Remember, too, that the English translations are powerful windows into historical Seattle landscapes, even as it is critical that Whulshootseed, which is today experiencing a resurgence, continues to be spoken in a city that, after all, carries a Coast Salish name.

ʔ	glottal stop; like the break in the middle of 'uh-oh'
a	as in 'ma'
b	as in English
c	the –ts sound at the end of 'cats'
c̓	this is a glottalized c; as with other letters augmented with an apostrophe, a 'popping' noise is created by building up air behind the tongue or lips and releasing it suddenly
č	like ch in 'church'
č̓	glottalized version of the above
d	as in English
dᶻ	like the ds in 'kids'
ə	the schwa, pronounced like the u in 'but'
g	always hard, as in 'give'
gʷ	a g pronounced with rounded lips, as in 'Gwen'
h	as in English
i	most commonly pronounced like the ea in 'clean' but can also sound like the ai in 'bait'
k	as in English
k̓	glottal k, pronounced with a popping sound
kʷ	k pronounced with rounded lips, as at the beginning of 'queen'
k̓ʷ	the above sound glottalized
l	as in English
ł	a whispered l, similar to the double-l in Welsh – put your tongue against the back of your teeth and breathe out the sides
λ̓	one of the trickiest sounds, a loud clicking sound that also sounds something like a t and an l pronounced together
m	as in English
p	as in English
p̓	glottalized version of the above

q	like a k, but pronounced at the back of the throat
q̇	glottalized q; a popping noise at the back of the throat
qʷ	back-of-the-throat k made with rounded lips
q̇ʷ	a glottalized q made with rounded lips
s	as in English
š	like the sh in 'ship'
t	as in English
t'	t made "explosive"
u	usually pronounced like the oo in 'boot'
w	as in English
xʷ	breathe through rounded lips, as if blowing out a candle
x̌	similar to the ch in the Scottish word loch
x̌ʷ	the above sound made with rounded lips
y	as in English

The best work is always collaborative, and the genealogy of this atlas stretches from Nile and me back to our teachers, to the others living and dead who have worked on creating a formal written form for the language, to earlier scholars like Harrington and Waterman, and most importantly to those Duwamish and other Indigenous men and women who chose to share the names of their world with newcomers. I respectfully thank all of them.

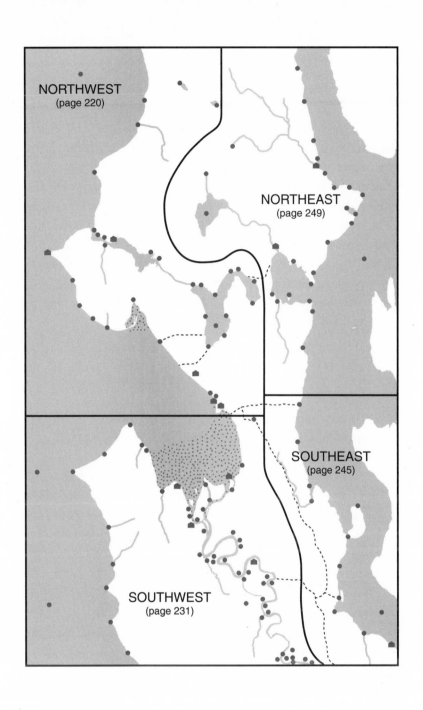

NORTHWEST
(page 220)

NORTHEAST
(page 249)

SOUTHEAST
(page 245)

SOUTHWEST
(page 231)

Map 1: Northwest

The four European compass points were not necessarily the most important directions in Puget Sound indigenous life. While Indigenous people recognized east and west as the places the sun rose and set, and north and south as places that sent different kinds of weather, orientations such as landward, seaward, downriver, and upriver were just as important, if not more so. Similarly, early settlers on Puget Sound had a sense of direction quite different from that of modern residents. Like Indigenous people, the first generation of settlers experienced this region from the water, and so, for them, traveling south to Olympia meant going *up* the Sound, while returning to the north meant going *down*-Sound. Imagine, then, that we are on a landward journey up the Sound, visiting first the territory of the Shilshole people and then moving into the outlying lands and waters of the Duwamish proper.

Place Names with Pronunciation

1   *Salt Water*   x̌ʷəlč   hwultch
   Theodore Winthrop's 1862 travel narrative *The Canoe and the Saddle* used the anglicized form of this word to denote both "Indian Whulgeamish and Yankee Whulgers" who lived along the Sound. In the century and a half since, this word for Puget Sound, spelled in various ways, has occasionally resurfaced, most notably in the well-known series of guidebooks profiling hikes and other excursions around the Sound published by The Mountaineers.[7]

2   *Blackcaps on the Sides*   čálqʷadi   CHAL-qua-dee
   This place-name refers to the blackcap (*Rubus leucodermis*), a native fruit whose berries and shoots were harvested around the shores of this small lake. Now known as Bitter Lake, Blackcaps on the Sides was also a refuge for the Shilshole people during raids by northern slavers.

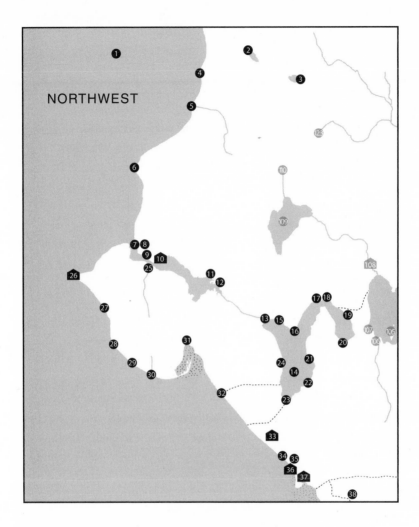

NORTHWEST

3   *Calmed Down a Little*   sisáłtəb   see-SATHL-tub
    Haller Lake's original name likely refers to its role as another refuge dur-
    ing slave raids. Projectile points have been found nearby, suggesting that
    the lake was also a hunting site. Trails likely connected Calmed Down
    a Little to other upland sites like 110 and 123 below.

4   *Sharp Rocks*   x̌ʷíx̌ʷəcíls   HWEE-hwut-seels
    Like many Whulshootseed place-names, this name for the sharp bluffs
    just south of Spring Beach is straightforward and descriptive, aiding

travelers on the Sound in identifying the landmark. Like many other rocks along the coastline, these may have been blasted away.

5   *Dropped Down*   qʷátəb   QUAH-tub
Piper's Creek runs through a deep canyon here in an otherwise gently sloping landscape, which may explain the name. Once the site of large salmon runs, the creek has been restored after decades of neglect.

6   *Canoe*   qílbid   QEEL-beed
Most likely, Meadow Point (today's Golden Gardens Park) was used as a storage area for saltwater canoes since at low tide there was not enough water for the people of the nearby Shilshole (today's Salmon Bay) to have access to or from their village.[8]

7   *Lying Curled Up*   čə́tqidəd   CHUT-kay-dud (lit. 'tip brought up to the head')
Waterman's informant described this small sandspit at the site of the Shilshole Marina as "lying curled like a pillow" and noted that it was well known as a place for gathering fine clams.

8   *Hanging on the Shoulder*   kiłalabəd   keethl-al-a-bud
Like many of the place-names around Seattle and throughout Puget Sound, this one, for the knoll at the north end of the railroad crossing of Salmon Bay, uses language of the body to describe the land.

9   *Mouth of Shilshole*   šəlšúlucid   shul-SHOOL-oot-seed
The narrow mouth of Salmon Bay takes its name from the Indigenous community at entry 10. One of Waterman's informants described the passage through here as "like shoving a thread through a bead." This statement probably reflects the lack of navigable water; longtime Ballard families report that prior to the building of the locks, one could wade through the water at the mouth of Salmon Bay at low tide.[9]

10   *Tucked Away Inside*   šəlšúl   shul-SHOOL
This large village was the home of the Shilshoolabsh, or Shilshole people,

who had two large longhouses here, each 60 by 120 feet, and an even greater "potlatch house." Devastating raids by North Coast tribes in the early nineteenth century may explain both the name (which Harrington described as "going way inland") and the village's location inside Salmon Bay. Despite settlement by non-Indians, some Shilshole people remained here until the construction of the Hiram M. Chittenden Locks in the early twentieth century, while others became part of the community of Ballard or moved to area reservations. Relatively little is known about this settlement, as construction of the locks destroyed most of it in the 1910s. In the 1920s, however, archaeologist A. G. Colley conducted an excavation of the western part of the site, where the wakes of canal-bound boats had been wearing away several feet of shoreline every year. He found tools made of antler, stone, bone, and even iron.

11   *Spirit Canoe Power*   bətədáqt   buh-tuh-DAHQT
The power that resided in this creek allowed indigenous doctors to reach the world of the dead to recover the souls of ailing or troubled people. Doctor Jim, who hung himself on Salmon Bay in 1880, likely was connected with the creek, which by then had been befouled by cattle belonging to Ballard's farmers.

12   *Serviceberry*   q̓ʷəlástab   qwuh-LAH-stahb
Waterman's "small bush with white flowers and black berries" is a clear reference to serviceberry (*Amelanchier alnifolia*), whose wood was used for gaming pieces and whose berries were eaten either fresh or dried.

13   *Outlet*   gʷáx̌ʷap   GWAH-hwahp (lit. 'leak [at] bottom end')
This was the outlet of a stream, known to settlers as Ross Creek, that emptied Lake Union into Salmon Bay and was the passageway of several runs of salmon (chum, pink, chinook, and coho).

14   *Small Lake*   x̌áx̌ə?ču   HA-huh-choo (lit. 'small great-amount-of-water') This is the diminutive form of the word used to denote Lake Washington (see entry 90), in keeping with the lakes' relative sizes.

15 *Thrashed Water*   sčaxʷʔálqu   s-tchahw-AHL-qoo
or
Covered Water   sčuxʷʔálqu   s-tchoohw-AHL-qoo
People drove fish into this narrow, brushy stream by thrashing the water
with sticks. The stream now flows in a pipe somewhere under the streets
of the Fremont neighborhood.

16 *Extended from the Ridge*   stáčič   STAH-cheech
Now the site of Gas Works Park, this point was described by Waterman's informants as leaning against the slope of the Wallingford neighborhood like a prop used to hold up part of a house.

17 *Prairie*   báqʷab   BAH-quahb
This was one of several small prairies maintained in what is now Seattle; as such, it was likely an important site for cultivating and gathering
roots and other foods that Indigenous people propagated through burning and transplanting. The right to dig and burn on prairies typically
passed down through women; the rights to this prairie likely belonged
to women from entry 10 above and/or entry 108 below. Ancient tools
made from obsidian have been found here; the raw material for the
tools likely came from central Washington or perhaps as far away as
central Oregon.

18 *Croaking*   waqíqab   wah-KAY-qahb (lit. 'doing like a frog')
Perhaps this small creek on the north side of Portage Bay was known
for its amphibious inhabitants, or perhaps it burbled in a way that
reminded local people of frogs. The site might also have had religious
significance; Frog was a minor spirit power that helped even the most
common folk sing during winter ceremonies. A man named Dzakwoos, or "Indian Jim Zackuse," whose descendants include many
members of the modern Snoqualmie Tribe, had a homestead here
until the 1880s.[10]

19 *Lowered Promontory*   sk̓ʷíćaqs   SKWEE-tsahqs
The "top" of Lake Union seems an odd place for a "low" name, but the

word for this place most likely refers to the point's relationship to the surrounding, and much higher, landscape. Long before white settlers envisioned a canal linking Lake Washington and Lake Union, Indigenous people used this corridor to travel between the backcountry and the Sound.

20 *Marsh* spálax̌ad SPATHL-ah-hahd
The wetlands on the south shore of Portage Bay must have been a fine place for hunting waterfowl. Chesheeahud, or "Lake Union John," owned several acres here from at least 1880 until 1906, a fact commemorated in a "pocket park" at the foot of Shelby Street by a plaque and depictions of salmon by an artist of the Puyallup Tribe.

21 *Jumping over Driftwood* saxʷabábac sah-hwab-AHB-ahts (lit. 'jump over tree trunk')
The Lake Union shoreline was thick with logs here. A similar place-name, Jumping Down (*saxʷsaxʷáp*), was used for a Suquamish gaming site on Sinclair Inlet across Puget Sound; that name refers to a contest in which participants vied to see who could jump the farthest off a five-foot-high rock.[11]

22 *Deep* sƛ́ə́p s-tluhp
This is a typically no-nonsense description of the place where the steep slope of Capitol Hill descends into the waters of Lake Union.

23 *Trail to the Beach* sčákʷšəd s-CHAHKW-shud (lit. 'the foot end of the beach')
A trail from Little (or Large) Prairie (entry 33) ended here. An elderly Indigenous man named Tsetseguis, a close acquaintance of the David Denny family, lived here with his family in Seattle's early years, when the south end of Lake Union was dominated by Denny's sawmill.[12]

24 *Deep for Canoes* x̌əpíl?wił tluh-PEEL-weethl
Although this name is similar to Deep (entry 22), the difference mat-

ters. Such distinctions were critical to correct navigation and the sharing of information. According to the maps created by the General Land Office in the 1850s, there was a trail near here that skirted the southern slope of Queen Anne Hill on its way to Elliott Bay.

25 *Lots of Water*   hiwáyqʷ   hee-WHY-qw
This creek in the Lawtonwood neighborhood, now known as Kiwanis Creek and the site of a large heron rookery, was a reliable source of freshwater in all seasons.

26 *Brush Spread on the Water*   paq̓ácałču   paq-AHTS-athl-choo
Excavations for the West Point sewage treatment plant in the 1990s uncovered a history of settlement here that stretched back more than four millennia. Even as landslides, earthquakes, and rising sea levels transformed the point, Indigenous people continued to use it to process fish and shellfish. Of particular importance are the trade items found here: petrified wood from the Columbia River, obsidian from the arid interior, and carved stone jewelry from British Columbia, all attesting to far-reaching networks of commerce. Although this deep-time settlement seems to have been forgotten by Waterman's twentieth-century informants, during the nineteenth century the site served as home to dispossessed Duwamish Indians. Waterman was told that the name described the act of pushing or thrusting one's way through brush, or the opening of leaf buds—apt similes for the way the point emerges from the thickly wooded bluffs that overhang it.[13]

27 *Spring*   búlac   BOO-lahts
Harrington collected this name for waters that emerged from the Magnolia Bluffs. Springs like these, arising where water sinks through sand and soil and then reaches nearly impermeable clay, help lubricate the landslides that have destroyed a number of homes near here.

28 *Cold Creek*   ƛ̓uxʷálqu   tloo-HWAHL-qoo   (lit. 'cold freshwater')
This is a small creek flowing off the Magnolia Bluffs that may have

been a reliable source of freshwater for travelers on the Sound. There is some disagreement between Waterman and Harrington regarding this site and that of entry 30 below; Waterman seems to have confused meanings and words, transposing this name to the other site but giving it that site's meaning. Such discrepancies attest to the imperfect nature of the process by which the two ethnographers gathered their data.

29 *Covered by Covering* líplipałax^w LEEP-leep-athl-ahw
and
Rock čə́λ̌a TCHUH-tlah
Now known as Four Mile Rock, this massive glacial erratic sits at the foot of Magnolia Bluffs. The meaning of one of its names appears to refer to a story about the boulder. According to oral tradition, a hero named Stakoob once took a huge net woven of cedar and hazel and cast it over this rock from the far side of the Sound. The other name is purely descriptive, like the use of the word for 'spring' for various sites.

30 *River Otter Creek* q̓aλ̌ałqu qahtl-ATHL-qoo
The intermittent stream in today's Magnolia Park was probably once inhabited by *Lutra canadensis*; it now is mostly covered by a road descending into the park.

31 *Mouth along the Side* siláq^{w}ucid see-LAH-qwoot-seed
When Dr. Henry A. Smith, the man who would eventually pen the first written version of Seeathl's famous speech, moved here in the 1850s, several Indigenous families still lived in this place. The slopes above the salt marshes between Smith Cove and Salmon Bay were refuges during slave raids, but a large shell midden excavated nearby in 1913 suggests their importance during times of peace and prosperity as well.

32 *Aerial Duck Net* túqap TOO-qahp (lit. 'blocked at bottom')
This is a common place-name in Puget Sound, referring to nets that were strung between tall poles and used to catch waterfowl. This unique technology mystified British explorer George Vancouver, who

wrote that it was "undoubtedly, intended to answer some particular purpose; but whether of a religious, civil, or military nature, must be left to some future investigation."[14] Waterman was told that the ducks would be "started up" at Lake Union, then caught in the net here. One of Harrington's informants, Percival, had camped here regularly before the site was urbanized and recalled that a small creek ran year-round at the site. This place-name can also describe someone who is constipated.

33 *Little Prairie*   babáqʷab   bah-BAH-qwahb
    or
    Large Prairie   báqʷbaqʷab   BAHQW-bahqw-ahb
    Indian witnesses in a land claims case in the 1920s identified this place as the site of two longhouses, each 48 by 96 feet. The residents of these houses would have made good use of the large patches of salal (*Gaultheria shallon*) that could be found here, either eating the fruit fresh or drying it into cakes for the winter. Middens found along the shoreline here attest to the area's importance as a shellfish-processing site as well. Settler William Bell staked his claim here, and until the early twentieth century, the Belltown shoreline was an important camping place for Native people, including migrants from Alaska, British Columbia, and Washington's outer coast.

34 *Sour Water*   sčapaqʷ   s-chah-pah-qw
    Harrington collected this name for a hole in the sand that could be seen at low tide, about two blocks north of the foot of Pike Street. His informants told him that the hole was believed to connect via an underground channel to Lake Union. Young whales were said to have swum through the tunnel to the lake. A similar story is told about entry 116, and in fact, stories of such subterranean waterways abound throughout the region.[15]

35 *Spring*   búlac   BOO-lahts
    This spring, located on what would become Arthur Denny's homestead, was likely a less important source of freshwater for indigenous people, since it had the same unadorned designation as entry 27. Had it been

more significant, it likely would have had a name like those for 58 and 99. This spring and others inspired the names of Spring Street and the Spring Hill Water Company, Seattle's first municipal water supply, which was organized in 1881.[16]

36 *Grounds of the Leader's Camp* q̓əlx̌áqabixʷ   quhl-HAH-qah-bee-hw
This place-name is said by Harrington to be the 'chief place' and another name for 'Seattle'. Most likely this was the name for a camp of a man known as either Kelly or Seattle Curley (Soowalt), who was the head-man of the Duwamish village in what is now downtown Seattle. He was a brother of Seeathl. His camp was located between Columbia and Cherry streets and First and Second avenues by one source but closer to Seneca or Spring by others. This camp also appears in the Phelps map of the Battle of Seattle, reproduced elsewhere in this book.[17]

37 *Little Crossing-Over Place* sdᶻídᶻəlʔalič   s-dzee-dzuhl-ahl-eetch
(lit. 'little crossing of the back')
The name refers to a small portage. Up to eight longhouses once existed here; only the ruins of one remained when Seattle was founded in 1852. Waterman penned his informant's description of the site as fol-lows: "In the vicinity of the present King Street Station in the city of Seattle, there was formerly a little promontory with a lagoon behind it. On the promontory were a few trees. Behind this clump of trees a trail led from the beach over to the lagoon, which gave rise to the name. There was an Indian village on each side of this promontory. Flounders were plentiful in the lagoon. This [the tidal marsh] is exactly where the King Street Station now stands."[18] According to other informants who worked with amateur ethnographer Arthur Ballard, this village was located at the foot of Yesler Way. If that were the case, the name would refer to the trail that crossed over the hill to Lake Washington in what is now the Leschi neighborhood.

Pioneer daughter Sophie Frye Bass described a second trail that came down to the Sound here: from the Renton area, it "straggled on to Rainier Valley and approximately along Rainier Avenue, then zig-zagged across Jackson, Main, and King Streets to salt chuck (water)."[19]

Until at least the Second World War, Whulshootseed speakers used this name when referring to the modern city of Seattle.

38 *Greenish-Yellow Spine*   qʷátsič   QWAH-tseech
This name for Beacon Hill may refer to the color of the hillsides; General Land Office survey field notes from the 1850s show that many maples, alders, and other deciduous trees grew here.

Map 2: Southwest

This time we arrive from the south (from up the Sound), following the West Seattle coastline and curving around into the estuary of the Duwamish River. These waters connected the Duwamish people with not only other Puget Sound Salish tribes such as the Suquamish and Snohomish but also more distant Coast Salish groups like the Twana of Hood Canal. Then we enter the lower valley of the Duwamish River, where the intensity of environmental transformation is matched by the intensity and density of Indigenous inhabitance. The farther upriver we go, the closer we get to the core territories of the Duwamish proper. Beyond them lay the lands of the Stkamish, a group that became part of the present-day Muckleshoot Tribe.

39   *Place of Scorched Bluff*   dxʷḵʷásus   duhw-KWAH-soos
     The bluffs here had black markings, hence the name. Such descriptive terms were critical for travelers on the Sound, who typically described and conducted long voyages in terms of the number of points that were passed during the journey rather than time or a consistent unit of measurement.[20]

40   *It Has Changes-Its-Face*   basʔayáhus   bahs-eye-AH-hoos
     Brace Point is one of two places in Seattle that was inhabited by a horned snake, one of the most powerful spirits used by Indigenous healers. (The other site is 100.) The large red boulder on the shoreline here was also associated with the spirit power; some people believed the boulder could change its shape and that anyone who looked at it would be twisted into a knot.

41   *Tight Bluff*   čəx̌áydus   tchuh-HIGH-doos
     This former name of Point Williams describes the dense plant growth on this headland and helped distinguish it from other points in the promontory-based system of measurement described at entry 39. It is now the site of Lincoln Park.

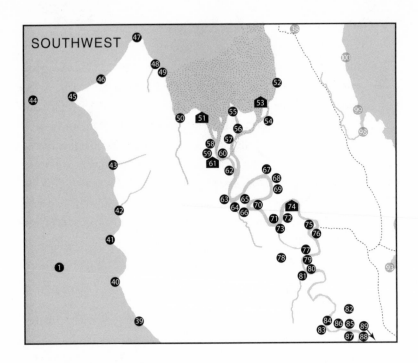

42 *Capsized*   gʷəl   gwuhl

This inauspiciously named creek enters Puget Sound at the north end of Lincoln Park. The old name might be a warning about the offshore potential for the tipping of a canoe.

43 *Rids the Cold*   təsbəd   TUSS-buhd (lit. 'implement for ridding cold')

While the name of this site may be a reference to the battle of the winds described at entries 82–88, since the fleeing North Wind was known to have alighted briefly at other places along the Sound, it is more likely a reference to the bricks that were made out of clay here by settlers very early in Seattle's development. Native people would certainly have been aware of the insulating properties of brick, even if they could rarely afford to build their houses out of the new material.

44 *Wealth Spirit*   tiyúɬbax̌   tee-YOOTHL-bakh

Jacob Wahalchoo, a signatory of the Treaty of Point Elliott, dove beneath the waters of Puget Sound here in search of a spirit power that lived in a huge underwater longhouse. This power brought wealth and generosity to those who held it. It could cause neighboring families to offer their daughters in marriage without asking a bride-price or could make game drop dead at its holder's door during winter dances.[21]

45   *Prairie Point*   sbaqʷábaqs   sbah-QWAH-bahqs
An island connected to the mainland by two sandspits—a double tombolo—this windswept place remains the birthplace of Seattle in popular memory but was an Indigenous place and point of colonial reconnaissance well before 1851. Prairies here were almost certainly maintained through seasonal burning by indigenous cultivators. Pressings of plants from this prairie, most now extirpated from Seattle, can be found in the University of Washington's botanical collections.

46   *Place That Became Wet*   dxʷqʷútub   duhw-QWOO-tub
or
Place for Reeds   dxʷkútʔi   duhw-KOOT-ee
Waterman and Harrington collected two different versions of the name for this place. Luckily, they seem to corroborate each other in terms of what kind of place it was: a wetland rich with resources such as highbush cranberries (*Vaccinium oxycoccus*), which were eaten fresh and dried, and cattails (*Typha latifolia*), which were used in fabricating mats. Many of Seattle's upland areas, especially the West Seattle peninsula and the Greenwood neighborhood, were filled with wetlands and bogs. One such bog is currently being restored near this site, at Roxbury Park at the headwaters of Longfellow Creek.

47   *Low Point*   sgʷədaqs   sgwuh-dahqs
This ancient name for Duwamish Head can also mean 'base of the point'. This beach was an important fishing site; it was here that Captain Robert Fay tried to establish a commercial fishery employing men recruited by Seeathl. According to Duwamish elder Alice Cross, there was once a large boulder covered with petroglyphs on the beach near here, each carving symbolizing a spirit power employed by local shamans.[22]

48   *Place of Waterfalls*   dxʷcə́tx̌ud   duh-TSUHT-hood (lit. 'where water falls over a bank')
Shell middens have been found all along the shoreline near this steep gully.

49   *Caved-In*   aslíq̓ʷ   ahss-leeqw
As in many places around Seattle, the bluffs here are very unstable. In fact, this part of the West Seattle landscape continues to live up to its indigenous name, with elaborate restraints only partially able to keep the land from moving during small earthquakes or periods of heavy rain.

50   *Smelt*   t̓ʔáwi   t-AH-wee
This is a local form of the word for smelt, *Hypomesus pretiosus*. The indigenous name for Longfellow Creek suggests a traditional fishery. Carbon dating of the remains of an old shellfish gathering and fishing campsite here shows it was in use as far back as the fourteenth century. Today, local residents are struggling to restore the creek and its salmon runs; despite their efforts in the upper watershed, the old estuary is still straddled by industrial development, most notably a busy foundry. Smelt, meanwhile, have largely disappeared from Elliott Bay: the shallow-sloped gravel beaches with freshwater seepage, upon which they depend for spawning, have almost all been destroyed by development.

51   *Herring's House*   túʔulʔaltxʷ   TOO-ool-ahlt-hw
This was an important town; it included at least four longhouses and an enormous potlatch house, and middens have been found throughout this area. Important figures residing here included a headman named Tsootsalptud and a shaman called Bookelatqw. Two sisters-in-law of Big John, an important informant and early fishing-rights advocate among the Skwupabsh (Green River People, who lived upriver from Auburn), came from this village as well. The burning of Herring's House in 1893 is one of the few times when the destruction of Indigenous Puget Sound settlements by Americans appeared in the official historical record. Its

name has since been applied to a city park along the Duwamish River, located at the site of entry 61.

52   *Burned-Off Place*   dxʷpáštəb   duhw-PAHSH-tub
This small spit at the foot of Beacon Hill was likely an ideal place for camping, and its name suggests there may have been a small cultivated prairie here as well. Billy and Ellen Phillips, a Duwamish Indian couple, managed to eke out a living at the foot of nearby Stacy Street until 1910.

53   *Little-Bit-Straight Point*   tutúłaqs   too-TOO-thlahqs
Waterman recorded this small promontory on an island as the location of a small stockade and lookout, used to defend settlements farther upriver. During a land claims case in the 1920s, however, Duwamish and Muckleshoot elder Major Hamilton testified that three longhouses had also once been located here. Long buried under fill, the site is near the old Rainier Brewery along Interstate 5.[23]

54   *Canoe Opening*   slúwił   SLOO-weethl
This word, like its diminutive form (108), has two meanings. It can refer to the tiny holes made in canoes during carving to help measure hull thickness. Informants told Waterman with respect to this site that the name refers to channels, or 'canoe-passes', in the grassy marsh through which canoes can be pushed to effect a shortcut.

55   *A Cut*   x̌ʷəq̓   hwuhq
This was the widest of the several mouths of the Duwamish River, which once carried the commingled flows of the White, Green, Black, Cedar, and Sammamish rivers. Today, only the waters of the Green enter Elliott Bay.

56   *Uprooted Trees*   qəlqəládi   quhl-quhl-AH-dee
      or
      Bad Bank   qəlqəlíqad   quhl-quhl-EE-qahd
Waterman and Harrington recorded differing versions of the name for

this site along the shore of x̌ʷəq̓ (55). Both of them agreed, however, that the name referred to the limited access to the site. The similarity in their pronunciation suggests that one of them, after being misheard or misremembered, could have easily shifted to the other. Together, however, they paint a vivid picture of this place, now somewhere in the middle of Seattle's industrial harbor.

57   *Tideflats*   cə́qas   TSUH-qahss (lit. 'rotten or fermented flats')
This is where Seetoowathl and his wife starved to death in their float house. Kellogg Island, a wildlife preserve on the lower Duwamish, is a remnant of an original, larger island.

58   *Crying Face*   x̌ax̌abus   ha-ha-boos
A small creek, likely fed by springs "weeping" from the face of the hillside, flowed across a small flat here. Tribal elders testified in the 1920s that three longhouses once stood here; the many middens found in the area are reminders of that lost settlement.

59   *Cottonwood Trees*   q̓ʷadq̓ʷad?íq̓ʷac   qwahd-qwahd-EE-qwats
Black cottonwoods (*Populus trichocarpa*) were, and still are, relatively common in the Duwamish estuary. While cottonwood leaves and bark had some medicinal uses, this name has the suffix *-ac*, which actually refers to the whole, growing tree as opposed to its component parts.

60   *Backwater*   sqabqabap   sqah-qah-bahp (lit. 'very still bottom')
This quiet place in the river, on the south side of Kellogg Island, exists today as the last remaining bend of the Duwamish River's original course.

61   *Basketry Hat*   yəlíqʷad   yull-EE-qwahd
Around a millennium ago, the Seattle Fault violently and suddenly slipped several meters, dramatically altering the nature of this place. Despite such catastrophes, excavations done here in the 1970s and 1980s show that indigenous people used this site for several centuries both before and after the earthquake. As early as the first century BCE,

when the site was an open, wet terrace above the river, people camped here during the spring to harvest fish and roots. By the time of the earthquake the site was being used far more intensively: faunal remains from that period were overwhelmingly those of salmon but also included dogfish, cod, grebes, deer, seals, mussels, clams, octopuses, elderberry, and wild onions. After the earthquake, the site was higher and drier and became a permanent settlement surrounded by forest.

Muckleshoot informants in the 1920s recalled hearing of three houses located here on the west bank of the river, each 60 feet wide by 120 feet long, although the site appears to have been abandoned during the epidemics of the 1770s. The name refers to a type of woven hat worn by Yakama women, suggesting trade networks across the Cascades, while a clay-pot fragment found here may have come from the Columbia River. When the Port of Seattle uncovered the settlement in the 1970s, the resulting excavation provided the unrecognized Duwamish Tribe with a highly visible venue for their claims. This site is now Herring's House Park, a name that has "migrated" upstream from the site of entry 51.[24]

62   *Giant Horsetail Place*   x̌əbx̌əbáli   hub-hub-AHL-ee
This grassy, level, and very wet place was rich with giant horsetails (*Equisetum telmateia*), whose little black roots were peeled and eaten raw. As one of the first green plants to appear in the spring, these were an important source of food and nutrients after a long winter of preserved foods.

63   *Aerial Duck Net Place*   təqbáli   tuhq-BAL-ee
As at the site of entry 32, a large trap stood here along a river bend at the foot of the bluffs. Enormous flocks of waterfowl would have populated the rich estuary of the Duwamish, particularly during spring and autumn migrations, making nets like these hugely successful. By the early twentieth century, though, most of the birds were gone, and the imposing net structures were a largely forgotten technology.

64   *Fish Drying Rack*   ťálič   TAHL-eech (lit. 'covering for sliced [fish]')
Wooden frames for drying fish were set up along the bank at what is
now known as Puget Creek. One of the salmon runs that would have
been harvested here, the Duwamish chinook (*Oncorhynchus
tshawytscha*), is now listed under the Endangered Species Act.

65   *Head of the Shortcut*   taX̌qíd   tah-tl-QEED (lit. 'head of extension
between two points')
The river curled back on itself here, creating a convenient detour at
high tide.

66   *Little Bends at the Tail End*   pupiʔálap   poo-pee-AHL-ahp
The name of this small creek which flows into the Duwamish River is
actually a diminutive form of the name of the Puyallup River, which
flows into Puget Sound at Tacoma. Both names describe the curves of
a watercourse's lower reaches.

67   *Lots of Douglas Fir Bark*   čłčáčabid   ch-thl-CHAHCH-ah-beed
(lit. 'made [fire] increaser')
Unlike entry 59, which refers to an entire tree, this name lacks the
-ac suffix and thus refers only to the useful parts of the Douglas fir
tree. Indigenous people used Douglas fir (*Pseudotsuga menziesii*) primarily for firewood because of its easily collected bark, hence its name
of 'fire increaser'. Preferring drier soils, this species is uncommon in
estuaries, but here along the base of Beacon Hill, ancient lahars (catastrophic mudflows) from Mount Rainier built up a higher, drier terrace
with ideal growing conditions for the huge conifer. Tiny pieces of fir
found by archaeologists at the site of entry 61 quite possibly came from
this very place, which is now part of the Georgetown neighborhood.

68   *Missing in the Middle*   subʔídgʷas   soob-EED-gwahss
The name refers to the middle section of the bank having caved in.
It seems possible that this name and the following one in fact refer to
the same place. This one was collected by Harrington; entry 69 was
collected by Waterman.

69 *Eroded Bank* biʔabtəb bee-ahb-tub (lit. 'bank has been acted upon by usual means')

At this place, sand and other debris constantly fell into the water as the river ate away at the lahar terrace on its eastern bank. When the King County Poor Farm was built here in the nineteenth century, its gardens benefited from the shell-enriched soil of ancient middens.

70 *House Post* cq̓ʷálad ts-QWAH-lahd

According to Waterman's informants, the river curved here in a way reminiscent of the forked cedar posts used to hold up longhouse roofs.

71 *House Beams* t̓ált̓ałusad tahthl-tahthl-oos-ahd

This site's name refers to a house's crossbeams. One of Harrington's informants said that at one time there had been a village here, but that there was "nothing but sticks left" by the early twentieth century. The name may be a description of those ruins.

72 *Hand Causing Ill Will* həčsáči huhch-SAH-chee

The original course of the river still exists here, in the form of a channel dead-ending among industrial buildings on East Marginal Way just south of Ellis Street. Indian people who worked with Waterman called this a "bad place" because of its resident spirits. In deep time, the Changer came upon two men fighting here. He transformed one into a cottonwood on the west bank and the other into a white fir (*Abies grandis*) on the east bank, and bright sparks were said to fly between the two ancient enemies even in Waterman's informants' time.

   The name of the site refers to a third spirit, which lived in the river itself, occasionally rising above the water in the form of a hand missing its fingers. Such a hand was known to other Coast Salish groups as well. There was a "bad hand" in Maggie Lake in Duhlelap Twana territory on Hood Canal. In Steilacoom territory south of Tacoma, a "large human hand, opened flat with the fingers close together," was a feature of American Lake. Native people believed that if "the hand slowly disappeared again into the water the beholder was sure of a near death."[25]

73   *Abandoned*   łəwáłb   thluh-WATHL-uhb

This place-name refers to a former river channel that, having become an oxbow lake, was no longer used by travelers. The oxbow saw a renaissance of sorts in the early twentieth century when it was dredged to create the Duwamish Waterway.

74   *Place of the Fish Spear*   dxʷqʷíƛ̓əd   duhw-QWEE-tluhd

This site was situated on a large flat in a bend of the Duwamish River. Waterman mistook his informant's description of this town's site ("a large open space; a plain") for the meaning of its name. Sam Tecumseh, whose ancestors once lived here, said in the 1920s that the town included two large longhouses and several acres of potatoes. The villagers are said to have been described as "proud or confident people." Once the site of the Georgetown race track, it now lies under the north end of Boeing Field. The author of a 1949 *Seattle Business* article offered a powerful description of this place's history, writing that the area was once "just reed-grown duck marsh" but was now inhabited by "mechanical birds for test and flight."[26]

75   *Rafter Support Post*   təč̓was   tutch-wahss (lit. 'sticks into the rib')

An old trail, likely from the vicinity of entry 94, came down to the river here. A landslide had buried the trail, and Waterman posited that some of the trees that had slipped with the earth might have looked like braces used to support a house's rafters, thus inspiring the name.

76   *High on the Neck*   cəqálapsəb   tsuh-QAHL-ahp-sub

This narrow, necklike isthmus was the site of a small prairie where the nutritious bulbs of the camas lily (*Camassia quamash*), and surely other plant resources, were cultivated and gathered.

77   *Lift It Over*   xʷápičad   HWAH-pee-chahd

This was a wide flat at the southern end of the abandoned river channel. While Waterman did not understand the name's meaning, it likely refers to the portaging of canoes.

78 *Beach Worm's Throat*   q̓iyawálapsəb   qee-yah-WAHL-ahp-sub
The creature after which this site—an expansive flat containing three
hills in the present-day South Park neighborhood—is named was identified by local informants in two ways: as an eel or as a long, green
beach worm that inhabits driftwood and can be used as bait. The con-
fusion may stem either from the superficial resemblance between the
two animals or from an informant's not knowing the precise English
term for an organism he of course knew well. The solution is found
in a Suquamish place-name, *sq̓əyáwəb*, which is based on *q̓əyáw*
'long green grubs' that are found in old logs. Candidate species include
blennies of various genera and nereid worms (*Nereis* spp.).[27]

79 *Much Paddle-Wood*   x̌ubx̌ubtay   hoob-hoob-tie
According to General Land Office surveys of the 1850s (as well as tribal
informants), a grove of Oregon ash (*Fraxinus latifolia*) grew on this flat
in a bend of the river. It was the favored wood for paddles among
many of the Northwest's Indigenous peoples.

80 *Hollers after Eating*   c̓ic̓q̓dib   tseets-q-deeb
"Hollers after eating' is the name of a small, active shorebird that bobs
up and down and has a loud cry, possibly the lesser yellowlegs (*Tringa
melanoleuca*) or the spotted sandpiper (*Actitus macularia*).

81 *Sweat House*   gʷə́x̌ʷʔaltxʷ   GWUHW-ahlt-hw
This is the name of a small creek entering the Duwamish River. The
Southern Puget Sound Salish, including the Duwamish, used sweat
bathing for bodily cleanliness and to aid physical well-being, but not as
a cure to any serious ailment. This contrasts with the Northern Puget
Sound Salish, who used it in preparation for spirit questing.[28]

82 *Meanie*   sx̌ayákʷ   s-high-AHKW
Three hills (82, 85, and 87) sit near each other in this part of the Duwamish Valley. Once islands in an arm of Puget Sound, they remained largely
unchanged as catastrophic lahars created the valley floor around them
in the millennia since the last ice age. Not surprisingly, they are land-

marks in Indigenous tradition, being the site of an epic battle between great forces of nature. Although this hill's name was translated by Waterman as 'beaver', the name he recorded is actually the diminutive form of the word for a mean person, a fitting description given the story recounted below.

In addition to their cultural significance, the hills here served a more practical purpose as places to keep watch for friends and enemies. Muckleshoot elder Dosie Wynn recalled that her grandmother had told her "they climbed up on them rocks. And they had scouts, Indian scouts, and they could look out [from] there." Today, the Boeing Access Road exit from Interstate 5 crosses over part of this hill, and Airport Way cuts deep through its core in what must have been a very expensive off-ramp.[29]

83   *North Wind*   stúbəlʔu   STOO-buhl-oo

There are many versions of the epic associated with this part of the Duwamish Valley. Most, however, focus on a great battle between North Wind, a force of cold and betrayal (and the 'meanie' of entry 82), and Storm Wind, who ultimately vanquished North Wind and helped establish the present-day climate. This place, located on the hillside to the west of the river, was the site of North Wind's ancient village. The epic suggests the persistence of deeply held memories stretching back to the retreat of the great ice sheets.[30]

84   *Barrier*   qəláx̌ad   quh-LAH-hahd

A ridge of stone in the riverbed, visible at low tide from the footbridge at South 112th Street, is all that remains of North Wind's ice weir, which had once kept salmon from swimming upstream to Storm Wind's people. According to one version of the story, the Barrier also served as a demarcation of territory during deep time, when trespassers were hanged. After North Wind fled the area, the portion of his fish weir that was not washed away in a flood was turned to stone. In the post-contact period, the same word by which this site was known was used for 'fence' or 'stockade'.[31]

85 *Beaver*   stəqáxʷ   stuh-QAH-hw (lit. 'dammer')

This second hill is associated both with the story of the winds, described above, and a story about beavers, given below. Local Indian people have maintained the memory of these hills and their stories despite dramatic changes to the landscape. Also known locally as Poverty Hill, the site has recently been preserved; eventually, interpretive signs and restored native plantings will highlight the valley's rich history and ecology.

86 *Little North Wind*   stútublə   STOO-too-bluh

This was a small rock on the west side of the river above 84 and down-hill from 85. It was usually submerged, but during low tide it was out of the water. This tidal fluctuation mimics that portion of the story in which North Wind kept setting his daughter by the river. Every time he did so, the water would rise because her icy earrings would melt.[32]

87 *Caused to Be Burnt or Blackened*   sq̓ʷəlʔads   sqwuhl-ahds

The name of this place refers to dark striations on the hill. In the epic story associated with this region, Raven, the slave of North Wind, perched above South Wind's grandmother, whose house was on this stone mountain, and defecated down on her. The paintlike marks on the hillside represented her face covered with the filth of Raven and her own frozen tears.

This hill and Beaver (85) also feature in a story about a battle between Beaver and five brothers, one of them imbued with Thunder power, which split a single eminence into these two hills. Indigenous people also claimed that splashing a canoe paddle in the river here or pouring water against the hillside would bring rain.

Today, the north end of the hill has been quarried away and replaced with an office park, while a new housing development covers its southern slope and Highway 599 separates the hill from the river. Muckleshoot elder Bena Williams told an interviewer that "when they started having a quarry there, then I don't think anybody goes there anymore."[33]

88   *Unclean Rock*   sqəlíls   squh-LEELS

Described as 'unclean' in the sense of impure or bad rather than simply unwashed, this location just a hundred yards upstream from Beaver (85) is almost certainly connected to the story of the winds and most likely refers to the befouling that South Wind's grandmother was forced to endure at the hands of the 'meanie' North Wind and his birds.

89   *Inside Place*   dxʷdəw   d-hw-doo

The region farther upstream, away from the open saltwater, was known as "inside" for its location inland off Puget Sound. This word is the base of the term "Duwamish." The valley where the Black, Cedar, and White-Green rivers came together to form the Duwamish was a center of Indigenous settlement. There were towns here named Meeting of the Rivers, Crags, Little Cedar River, and Confluence, and the area also became an important refuge for local Native people during Seattle's urban development. Today, only the Green River flows through this area, becoming the Duwamish below the former confluence with the Black, which disappeared with the lowering of Lake Washington in 1916. (The Cedar was rerouted north to Lake Washington, and the White was sent south to Tacoma.)

Map 3: Southeast

Leaving the Inside Place, we enter the homelands of the Lake People. The richness of the place-names along the Seattle side of Lake Washington is mirrored by that on its eastern shores and around the edges of Mercer Island.

90   *Lake*   xačʔu   hahtch-oo (lit. 'great amount of water')
A generic term for large bodies of freshwater, *xačʔu* gave its name to the Hachooabsh, or Lake Indians, a branch of the Duwamish proper who lived around the shores of Lake Washington. On some early maps of the area, this lake appears as "Lake Duwamish."

91   *Swimming Hole*   sxʷtʼičib   s-hw-TEE-tseeb (lit. 'usual place to swim or wade')
This town, located in what is now the Bryn Mawr neighborhood, was reputedly the birthplace of Chesheeahud. It is unclear how many houses were located here.

92   *Ducklings*   cípcip   TSEEP-tseep
This onomatopoetic place-name has been replaced by the name "Taylor Creek," which flows through Dead Horse Canyon on Seattle's southeastern boundary. It may in fact be the name of a particular unidentified species of small duck.

93   *Loon Place*   dxʷúqʷib   d-HWOO-qʷeeb
Loons would have found the Lake Washington shoreline an ideal habitat, and this marshy area would have been a particularly good spot. Prominent in Puget Sound tradition, Loon was a powerful spirit for warriors, hunters, and the owners of slaves. This place-name is a little puzzling in that the ending is *-ib* instead of the expected *-ad*.[34]

94   *Small Island*   ƛə́ƛacas   TLUH-tlah-tsahss
This is perhaps one of the best places to see the results of the lowering of Lake Washington. Prior to the completion of the ship canal, there

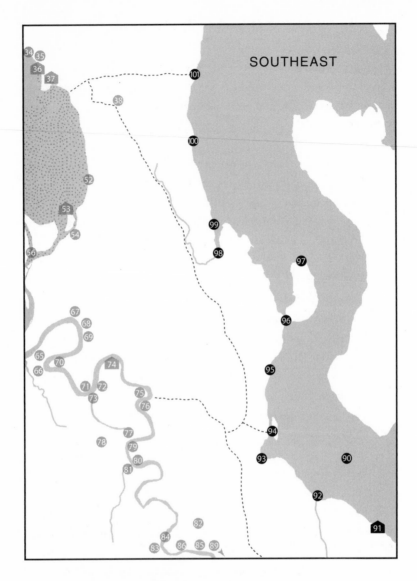

had been a small island here, parallel to the shoreline and separated by a marsh where, according to Harrington's informant, one "could pull canoes through except for [the] reeds." Today, "Pritchard's Island" is now firmly attached to the mainland, although the former marsh is still a relatively wet area and is undergoing ecological restoration. A trail beginning near here went west over the hills to the Duwamish River.

95   *Taboo Container*   x̌ax̌aʔúlč   ha-ha-OOLCH
Some kind of malevolent power or spirit being resided at this place,
now the site of Martha Washington Park. A Suquamish site near
Manette with a name based on the same root was called x̌ax̌a 'to be
taboo' and signified the location of canoe burials in trees. (There is
no evidence, however, of such a use for this location.) The term x̌ax̌a
has a wide range of meanings, from 'taboo' and 'forbidden' to 'holy'
and 'sacred' and also 'ritually impure'.

96   *High on the Neck*   cǝqálapsǝb   tsuh-QAHL-ahp-sub
Indigenous people were most likely responsible for burning the open,
oak-dotted prairie slopes found near this isthmus by General Land
Office surveyors in the 1850s.

97   *Noses*   sqǝbáqst   squh-BAHQST
Jutting out into Lake Washington, the Bailey Peninsula is home to
Seward Park and some of Seattle's oldest trees. The name likely
refers to the fact that the peninsula, which would have almost been
an island before the lowering of the lake, has points at both its north
and south ends.

98   *Cooking Fish on a Stick*   scak̓ácid   s-tsahk-AHT-seed
Low-lying Genesee Park was once Wetmore Slough, which reached
nearly to Columbia City's business district. It mouth was blocked up
by logs and other debris that provided shelter for a large run of silver
(coho) salmon (*Oncorhynchus kisutch*). The name of the place refers to
one traditional method of cooking fish, still practiced today: the whole
fish is opened lengthwise, splayed on sticks, and leaned over an open
fire. A hop yard stood here in the nineteenth century, gathering in the
fruit of Native labor from the fields of Puget Sound country.

99   *Breast, Nipple, Breast Milk*   sqǝ́bʔu   SQUHB-oo
The reason behind this name for a spring near Wetmore Slough has
been forgotten; it may be a reference to milky, mineral-laden waters
or simply to its nourishing qualities.

100   *Changes-Its-Face*   sʔayáʔus   s-eye-AH-oos

Leschi Park, named after the Nisqually warrior who led the assault on Seattle in 1856, was once the home of a supernatural horned snake, similar to the one at the site of entry 40. One of the most powerful spirits available to Puget Sound shamans, Changes-Its-Face was enormous, had retractable horns that resembled an elk's antlers, could also live in the sky, and could see in all directions. Young people were warned to reject this spirit if at all possible, perhaps because of the heavy punishments meted out against healers who failed to cure their patients, but also because it could cause its holder to do malevolent things. One of Harrington's informants told him that the serpent that resided here departed during the early years of urban expansion.[35]

101   *Saw-Grass Point*   xʷqʷíyaqʷayaqs   hw-QWEE-yahqw-eye-ahqs

This site was a place for gathering tules, or bulrushes (*Scirpus acutus*), which were woven into everyday household mats and screens. It was also the eastern end of a trail from Little Crossing-Over Place (37); as such, it served as the departure point for Leschi's attack on Seattle. Settlers used the trail as well, and the beach here became a popular "wilderness" destination during the city's early years and eventually part of the city's string of public spaces along the Lake Washington shoreline.

Map 4: Northeast

Besides being home to the Lake People, Lake Washington was also a transition to the Duwamish backcountry. The people living near the headwaters of the Sammamish watershed (the Sammamish River enters Lake Washington from the northeast) were often regarded as lower class by their neighbors, in part because they had direct access neither to the riches of Puget Sound nor to trade routes across the Cascades. Nothing captures this sense of "backwoodsness" more than the phrase used by coastal people to admonish an ill-bred child or an adult with bad taste by referring to a poor town in the remote hinterland: "dił čəx̌ʷ ə ti?ił tul?ál sq̓ʷax̌" (This person is like someone from Issaquah).[36]

102   *It Has Wolves*   bastiqíyu   bah-stee-QEE-yoo
      Wolves once hunted throughout what is now Seattle but had been extirpated by the time white settlement reached the shores of Lake Washington.

103   *Chopped*   x̌iƛ̓   heetl
      or
      Gnawed   x̌iƛ̌il   heetl-EEL
      Two slightly different names were collected for the shoreline south of Madison Park. Waterman's name, Chopped, probably refers to dense forest that would have provided fine timber for canoes and house posts. Harrington's version, however, refers to things that have been gnawed, and his informant figured that there must have been beavers here. Prior to the excesses of the fur trade, beavers shaped the landscape nearly as much as their Indigenous human neighbors by creating ponds and wetlands.

104   *It Has Skate Fish*   baskʷíkʷi?ł   bah-SKWEE-kwee-thl
      Skates, as a saltwater species, did not live in Lake Washington; this name more likely refers to the low, flat shape of the land here at what is now Madison Park.

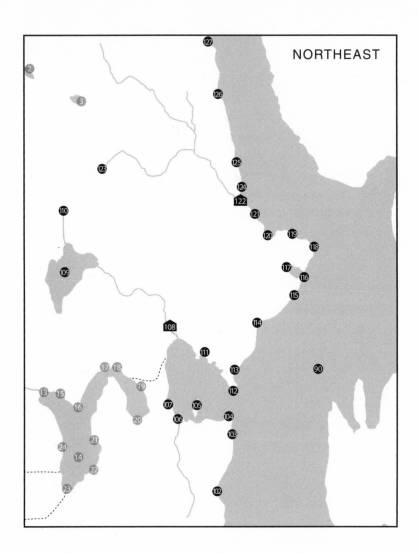

105   *Little Island*   stítči   steet-chee

Now the southern half of Foster Island in the Washington Park Arboretum, this was a cultural site associated with entry 108.

106   *Baby Fathom*   stálał   stahthl-ah-thl

The fathom, or more correctly the width of an adult's outstretched arms, was a common unit of measurement in Puget Sound Indigenous life. This diminutive version of 'fathom' could also mean 'niece' or 'nephew'.

107   *Carry a Canoe*   sxʷácadwiɬ   s-HWAH-tsahd-weethl

In 1854, pioneer leader Thomas Mercer visited Lake Union and envisioned a canal that would someday link the lake to Puget Sound and Lake Washington. In the 1860s, a settler named John Pike began digging a canal here by hand, and for a time there was a small log flume that connected the two lakes. Indigenous people had been crossing this isthmus for centuries, either carrying their canoes or shoving them along an intermittent creek that appeared when Lake Washington overflowed. General Land Office surveys from the 1850s show a well-worn "Indian trail" just north of here, approximately where the Burke-Gilman Trail is now, and oral tradition cites another trail to the south. With all this traffic, then, one wonders if the idea of the "union" of lakes and Sound was really Thomas Mercer's after all.

108   *Little Canoe Channel*   sɬuwíɬ   s-thloo-weethl (lit. 'little canoe hole')

Bearing the diminutive form of the name of entry 54, this was an important town with at least five longhouses and a large fishing weir on Ravenna Creek. The remains of that weir were exposed when Lake Washington was lowered in 1916; any evidence of the town itself has long been obscured by development around today's University Village shopping mall.

109   *[Unknown]*   dxʷƛ̕ə̓š   duhw-tluhsh

Green Lake must have been a fine fishing spot, surrounded by deep woods and close to the town at Little Canoe Channel (108). In addition to the salmon run in the lake's outlet, which we now call Ravenna Creek, the lake was known for suckers (*Catostomus* sp.) and perch (*Perca* sp.), the latter, interestingly enough, an introduced species, suggesting that Native fishermen visited this place well after resettlement by non-Indians.

110   *Red Paint*   líqtəd   LEEQ-tud

Licton Springs bears one of Seattle's few modern place-names derived directly from Whulshootseed. People came here to gather clay, which was baked and mixed with tallow to create a red paint.[37] The area was one of David Denny's properties, then a health spa, and finally a street-car suburb. The rust-red springs are still visible today in Licton Springs Park.

111   *Dear Me!*   ádid   AH-deed
This small cove was an important place to gather to play *sləhal*, the bone game; its name is an exclamation that must have echoed out over the water during many a session. Waterman's informant said that this place was "set aside" as a camping spot for Indians. This was most likely during the 1870s, when Henry Yesler operated a sawmill on the cove and would have needed all the workers he could get. The bone game sessions surely continued after a hard day's work in the mill.

112   *Drying House*   šab?altxʷ   shahb-ahlt-hw
Exposed to the sun and to winds off the lake, this point would have been an ideal place for drying salmon in open frame structures. Waterman noted that his Indian informants also referred to this place as Whiskey Point, perhaps a reference to the liquor obtained via the cash and contacts made at Yesler's mill.[38]

113   *Place of Whitened Clay*   dxʷčáxʷəb   duhw-TSAH-hwub
White clay was found here at the base of steep, forested cliffs. Mixed with grease, earth pigments like those from here and Licton Springs (110) are still used in important ceremonies.

114   *Minnows, or Shiners*   ƛils   tleels
Lake Washington was home to many kinds of fish, from the huge sturgeon (*Acipenser transmontanus*) and the prolific sockeye salmon (*Oncorhynchus nerka*) to smaller species like those caught at what is now the private Windermere Park.

115   *Small Prairie Point*   babqʷábaqs   bahb-QWAH-bahqs
To Indigenous foragers, the similar, but slightly different, prairie names around Seattle likely each signaled a different suite of plant resources.

Some might have had particularly good camas, while others were better for salal or rice-root lily. In other words, the subtle diversity of names for similar kinds of places likely mirrored subtle forms of ecological diversity.

116 *Digging in the Water* čaʔáɬqu chah-ATHL-qoo
Lakes throughout the region were thought to be connected to Puget Sound. In this case, a hunter was dragged into Lake Washington by an elk he had wounded, and the bodies of both were found a month later on the shore of Puget Sound at Richmond Beach, north of Seattle. (Compare entry 34.) The name of this outlet to a small pond at today's Sand Point, however, is almost certainly a reference to the gathering of wapato (*Sagittaria latifolia*), a starch-rich aquatic tuber that once grew prolifically in the 4,000 acres or so of wetlands around the shores of Lake Washington.[39]

117 *Sand People* wistalbabš wee-stahl-bahbsh
Before it was filled by the navy, this pond at Sand Point was known for a short time as Mud Lake. Efforts are under way to restore some of the marshes here.

118 *Fog* sqʷsəb s-qw-sub
This is the name for Sand Point, an extensive, flat promontory. Fog is a feature of the lakefront here during certain times of the year.

119 *Snowberry* t̓udáxʷdi too-DAHW-dee
Snowberry (*Symphoricarpos albus*) was used to disinfect festering sores, and its inedible fruit was used as an indicator of the size of a given year's run of dog salmon (*Oncorhynchus keta*): the more plentiful the berries, which were referred to as the salmon's eye, the more plentiful the run. Snowberry thickets have been replaced here by the massive buildings of the former naval air station.

120 *Much Inner Cedar Bark* slagʷlagʷac s-lahgw-lahgw-ahts
Pontiac Bay, once a stop on the Seattle, Lakeshore, and Eastern Rail-

way, was before that a place for gathering the bark used in everything from baskets to diapers.

121 *Hunt by Looking at the Water*   xʷixʷíyaqʷayas   hwee-HWEE-yahqw-eye-ahs
The fact that this name refers to hunting, rather than fishing, suggests that hunters would seek deer or other animals that came down to the shore here.

122 *Silenced (or Quieted) Place*   dxʷx̌úbəd   duhw-HOO-bud
There was at least one longhouse here at the mouth of Thornton Creek. Stone tools and an adze have been found in the watershed between here and site 123. Farther up the watershed, on the 7200 block of Twenty-eighth Avenue Northeast, is a huge boulder that according to local lore was an Indigenous gathering place located at a junction of the upland trail system.[40]

123 *Bald (or Peeled) Head*   łuqʷqid   thlooqw-qeed
Remnants of this upland marsh can still be seen at North Seattle Community College, but a sense of the larger sweep of Bald Head can be gained by driving on Interstate 5 and noticing the "bowl" in which the college and Northgate Mall now sit. One of the sources of Thornton Creek, these wetlands would have been an ideal place for gathering highbush cranberries, marsh tea (*Ledum groenlandicum*), and other resources.

124 *Osprey's House*   čix̌čix̌ʔaltxʷ   tseekh-tseekh-ahlt-hw
Waterman incorrectly identified the large nest here as belonging to an eagle. Ospreys (*Pandion haliaetus*) continue to nest around the shores of Lake Washington.

125 *Thunderbird's House*   x̌ʷiqʷádiʔaltxʷ   hwee-QWAH-dee-ahlt-hw
In Puget Sound Salish religion, Thunderbird is one of the most powerful spirits, offering skills of oratory, wealth, bravery, and health to those, including Seeathl, who have held it. Thunderbird's child is

Thrush (*Catharus* spp.), who brought languages to the various human peoples. According to some elders, Thunderbird was a small, pure-white bird, about the size of a gull. But for most, it was a giant bird (probably the condor, *Gymnogyps californianus*). In either case, it threw off pieces of flint, or lightning, from its open mouth as it flew, while the sound of thunder came from the beating of its wings. Thunderbird was thought to live here on the lakeshore at the edge of this tall bluff. At least some of the Puget Sound Salish believed that the Thunderbird made its home in a rock (note nearby boulders at 122 and 127).[41]

126   *Deep Point*   sƛ̓ɔ́paqs   STLUHP-ahqs

According to Waterman's informants, people who swam here on the edge of the lake were often taken away by "something."

127   *It Has a Rock*   basčíƛ̓a   bahs-TCHEE-tlah

This tiny stream, which runs in a deep ravine just north of the Seattle city line, is now officially known as Bsche'tla Creek thanks to a group of neighbors who asked the Lake Forest Park City Council to restore its original name. A large glacial erratic sits near the creek's mouth.

NOTES

1 / The Haunted City

1. Only a handful of North American places use Native imagery to market themselves as explicitly as Seattle does. The American Southwest, and especially Santa Fe, have a long history of using local (and other) Indian motifs. Vancouver, Victoria, and many other British Columbian places have used Northwest Coast imagery for a long time. For studies of these two regions and their employment of Native iconography, see Leah Dilworth, *Imagining Indians in the Southwest: Persistent Visions of a Primitive Past* (Washington: Smithsonian Institution, 1996); and Michael Dawson, *Selling British Columbia: Tourism and Consumer Culture, 1890–1970* (Vancouver: University of British Columbia Press, 2004).

2. William Kittredge, *The Nature of Generosity* (New York: Alfred A. Knopf, 2000), 8. While the term "place-stories" is mine, the concept is inspired by the work of others. E.g., see Keith H. Basso, *Wisdom Sits in Places: Landscape and Language among the Western Apache* (Albuquerque: University of New Mexico Press, 1996); Crisca Bierwert, *Brushed by Cedar, Living by the River: Coast Salish Figures of Power* (Tucson: University of Arizona Press, 1999), esp. 36–71; and Dolores Hayden, *The Power of Place: Urban Landscapes as Public History* (Cambridge, MA: MIT Press, 1995).

3. Carol Lind, *Western Gothic* (Seattle: Lind, 1983), 2; Babs Babylon, "In the Dark: Casper Central," *Seattle Weekly*, 26 October 1994, 59; Jessica Amanda Salmonson, *The Mysterious Doom and Other Ghostly Tales of the Pacific Northwest* (Seattle: Sasquatch Books, 1992), 3–12, 91–102, 137–42; and personal communications with Jay Miller and with Dana Cox, Seattle Underground Tours.

4. For the original printing of the speech attributed to Seeathl, see the 29 October 1887 edition of the *Seattle Star*. For reprintings and embellishments of the speech in local histories, see Frederick James Grant, *History of Seattle, Washington* (New York: American, 1891); Clarence B. Bagley, *History of King County, Washington* (Chicago: S. J. Clarke, 1929); and Roberta Frye Watt, *Four Wagons West: The Story of Seattle* (Portland, OR: Metropolitan Press, 1931). See also Eric

Scigliano, "Shaping the City: A New Book Looks Over a Changing Urban Space," *Seattle Times Pacific Northwest Magazine*, 10 November 2002.

5. For discussion of the Chief Seattle Speech and its various interpretations and uses, see Rudolf Kaiser, "Chief Seattle's Speech(es): American Origins and European Reception," in *Recovering the Word: Essays on Native American Literature*, ed. Brian Swann and Arnold Krupat (Berkeley and Los Angeles: University of California Press, 1987), 497–536; Vi Hilbert, "When Chief Seattle Spoke," in *A Time of Gathering: Native Heritage in Washington* State, ed. Robin K. Wright (Seattle: University of Washington Press, 1991), 259–66; Denise Low, "Contemporary Reinventions of Chief Seattle: Variant Texts of Chief Seattle's 1854 Speech," *American Indian Quarterly* 19, no. 3 (1995): 407–22; Albert Furtwangler, *Answering Chief Seattle* (Seattle: University of Washington Press, 1997); and Crisca Bierwert, "Remembering Chief Seattle: Reversing Cultural Studies of a Vanishing American," *American Indian Quarterly* 22, no. 3 (1998): 280–307.

6. Jean-Claude Schmitt, *Ghosts in the Middle Ages: The Living and the Dead in Medieval Society*, trans. Teresa Lavender Fagan (Chicago: University of Chicago Press, 1998), 1; Judith Richardson, *Possessions: The History and Uses of Haunting in the Hudson Valley* (Cambridge, MA: Harvard University Press, 2003), 3–6; Renée Bergland, *The National Uncanny: Indian Ghosts and American Subjects* (Hanover, NH: University Press of New England, 2000), 3; and Marian W. Smith, *The Puyallup-Nisqually* (New York: Columbia University Press, 1940), 97.

7. Timothy Egan, *The Good Rain: Across Time and Terrain in the Pacific Northwest* (New York: Vintage Books, 1990), 90.

8. Jack Cady, *Street: A Novel* (New York: St. Martin's Press, 1994), 13, 25; Tom Robbins, *Still Life with Woodpecker* (New York: Bantam Books, 1980), 69, 132; Jonathan Raban, *Hunting Mr. Heartbreak: A Discovery of America* (New York: Edward Burlingame Books, 1991), 261–62.

9. Cady, *Street*, 34–36; Sherman Alexie, *Indian Killer* (New York: Atlantic Monthly Press, 1996), 195, 409.

10. Grant Cogswell and Rick Levin, "Screw the Space Needle: Seattle's True Landmarks," *Seattle Stranger*, 21 September 2000, 38–39; Emily Baillargeon, "Seattle Now: A Letter," *New England Review* 20, no. 2 (1999): 148; and Brian Goedde, "Visions of the Ave: Despite Fears of Failure, the U-District's Heart Is Still Beating," *Seattle Real Change*, 20 September 2001, 8–9.

11. For examples of urban pictorials, see John W. Reps, *Panoramas of Promise: Pacific Northwest Towns and Cities in Nineteenth-Century Lithographs* (Pullman: Washington State University Press, 1984). For images of Indians in the American imagination, the classic work remains Robert F. Berkhofer Jr., *The White Man's Indian: Images of the American Indian from Columbus to the Present* (New York: Knopf, 1978). Images of Gast's *American Progress* can be found easily on the Internet; one example is the Central Pacific Railroad Museum website, at cprr

.org/Museum/Ephemera/American_Progress.html. For the 1906 real-estate brochure, see C. B. Bussell, *Tide Lands: Their Story* (Seattle: n.p., 1906).

12. For discussion of Western cities and their hinterlands, see Richard C. Wade, *The Urban Frontier: The Rise of Western Cities, 1790–1830* (Cambridge, MA: Harvard University Press, 1959); William Cronon, *Nature's Metropolis: Chicago and the Great West* (New York: W. W. Norton, 1991); and Gray Brechin, *Imperial San Francisco: Urban Power, Earthly Ruin* (Berkeley and Los Angeles: University of California Press, 1999). For three of the handful of works linking indigenous history to urbanization in the American West, see Lisbeth Haas, *Conquests and Historical Identities in California, 1769–1936* (Berkeley and Los Angeles: University of California Press, 1995); Kate Brown, "Gridded Lives: Why Kazakhstan and Montana Are Nearly the Same Place," *American Historical Review* 106, no. 1 (2001): 17–48; and Eugene P. Moehring, *Urbanism and Empire in the Far West, 1840–1890* (Reno: University of Nevada Press, 2004). For the frontier's place in American thinking about the West, see John Mack Faragher, ed., *Rereading Frederick Jackson Turner: The Significance of the Frontier in American History and Other Essays* (New York: H. Holt, 1994); Henry Nash Smith, *Virgin Land: The American West as Symbol and Myth* (New York: Vintage Books, 1957); and Kerwin Lee Klein, *Frontiers of Historical Imagination: Narrating the European Conquest of Native America, 1890–1990* (Berkeley and Los Angeles: University of California Press, 1997).

13. A complete list of works on Native history in the West would be too long to include here. For a beginning overview of the literature, see Clyde A. Milner II, Carol A. O'Connor, and Martha Sandweiss, eds., *The Oxford History of the American West* (New York: Oxford University Press, 1996).

14. General studies of urban Indians include W. T. Stanbury, *Success and Failure: Indians in Urban Society* (Vancouver: University of British Columbia Press, 1975); Alan L. Sorkin, *The Urban American Indian* (Lexington, MA: Lexington Books, 1978); Russell Thornton, Gary D. Sandefur, and Harold G. Grasmick, *The Urbanization of American Indians: A Critical Bibliography* (Bloomington: Indiana University Press, 1982); and Donald L. Fixico, *The Urban Indian Experience in America* (Albuquerque: University of New Mexico Press, 2000). For published studies of postwar urban Indian institutions and identities, see S. A. Krouse, "Kinship and Identity: Mixed Bloods in Urban Indian Communities," *American Indian Culture and Research Journal* 23, no. 2 (1999): 73–89; Edmund Danziger, *Survival and Regeneration: Detroit's American Indian Community* (Detroit: Wayne State University, 1991); Joan Weibel-Orlando, *Indian Country, L.A.: Maintaining Ethnic Community in Complex Society* (Urbana: University of Illinois Press, 1991); Deborah Davis Jackson, *Our Elders Lived It: American Indian Identity in the City* (DeKalb: Northern Illinois University Press, 2002); Nicholas Rosenthal, "Repositioning Indianness: Native American Organizations in Portland, Oregon, 1959–1975," *Pacific Historical Review* 71, no. 3 (2002): 415–38; Nancy Shoemaker, "Urban Indi-

ans and Ethnic Choices: American Indian Organizations in Minneapolis, 1920–1950," *Western Historical Quarterly* 19, no. 4 (1988): 431–47; and especially *American Indian Culture and Research Journal* 22, no. 4 (1998), a special issue devoted to urban Indian identity and literature. For Seattle-based studies, see Howard M. Bahr, Bruce A. Chadwick, and Joseph H. Stauss, "Discrimination against Urban Indians in Seattle," *Indian Historian* 5, no. 4 (1972): 4–11; Bruce A. Chadwick and Joseph H. Stauss, "The Assimilation of American Indians into Urban Society: The Seattle Case," *Human Organization* 34, no. 4 (1975): 359–69; Bruce A. Chadwick, Joseph Stauss, Howard M. Bahr, and Lowell K. Halverson, "Confrontation with the Law: The Case of the American Indians in Seattle," *Phylon* 37, no. 2 (1976): 163–71; Larry E. Williams, Bruce A. Chadwick, and Howard M. Bahr, "Antecedents of Self-Reported Arrest for Indian Americans in Seattle," *Phylon* 40, no. 3 (1979): 243–52; Jonathan R. Sugarman and David C. Grossman, "Trauma among American Indians in an Urban Community," *Public Health Reports* 111, no. 4 (1996): 321–28; Maria Aurora Holloway, "Illness Perception and Knowledge among Seattle Urban Indians" (M.Nur. thesis, University of Washington, 1974); and John Zoltan Bolyai, "The Seattle Diphtheria Epidemic of 1972–1973 and Its Relationship to Diphtheria among North American Native Americans" (M.P.H. thesis, University of Washington, 1974).

15. James P. Ronda, "Coboway's Tale: A Story of Power and Places along the Columbia," in *Power and Place in the North American West*, ed. John M. Findlay and Richard White (Seattle: University of Washington Press, 1999), 3.

16. R. Cole Harris, "How Did Colonialism Dispossess? Comments from an Edge of Empire," *Annals of the Association of American Geographers* 94, no. 1 (2004): 165–82.

17. Edwin G. Burrows and Mike Wallace, *Gotham: A History of New York City to 1898* (New York: Oxford University Press, 1999), xiv–xvi.

18. Greg Dening, *Islands and Beaches: Discourse on a Silent Land, Marquesas, 1774–1880* (Honolulu: University of Hawaii Press, 1980), 3; Colleen J. McElroy, "To the Crow Perched on Chief Sealth's Fingertips," in *Traveling Music: Poems* (Ashland, OR: Story Line Press, 1998), 56.

2 / *Terra Miscognita*

1. Sophie Frye Bass, *Pigtail Days in Old Seattle* (Portland, OR: Metropolitan Press, 1937), 13; Murray Morgan, *Skid Road: An Informal Portrait of Seattle* (New York: Viking Press, 1951), 24.

2. Stephen Jay Gould, "The Creation Myths of Cooperstown," in *Bully for*

Brontosaurus: Reflections in Natural History, by Stephen Jay Gould (New York: W. W. Norton, 1991), 48.

3. For further analysis of the diorama, see Coll-Peter Thrush, "Creation Stories: Rethinking the Founding of Seattle," in *More Voices, New Stories: King County, Washington's First 150 Years,* ed. Mary C. Wright (Seattle: Pacific Northwest Historians Guild, 2002), 34–49.

4. Welford Beaton, *The City That Made Itself: A Literary and Pictorial Record of the Building of Seattle* (Seattle: Terminal Publishing Co., 1914), 19; George F. Cotterill, *Climax of a World Quest: The Story of Puget Sound, the Modern Mediterranean of the Pacific* (Seattle: Olympic Publishing Co., 1928). For one of the best examinations of the "vanishing Indian" narrative in American culture and history (and for its role in shaping federal Indian policy), see Brian W. Dippie, *The Vanishing American: White Attitudes and U.S. Indian Policy* (Lawrence: University Press of Kansas, 1982).

5. Jacob Wahalchoo's story is recounted in Jay Miller, *Lushootseed Culture and the Shamanic Odyssey: An Anchored Radiance* (Lincoln: University of Nebraska Press, 1999), 11–12.

6. Paul Carter, *The Road to Botany Bay: An Exploration of Landscape and History* (Chicago: University of Chicago Press, 1987), xxiv. Carter draws upon the formulation crafted by geographer Yi-Fu Tuan in *Space and Place: The Perspective of Experience* (Minneapolis: University of Minnesota Press, 1977), in which Tuan distinguishes space—undifferentiated, abstract, untrammeled by experience—from place, which is specific, local, and shaped by lived experience. See also Daniel W. Clayton, *Islands of Truth: The Imperial Fashioning of Vancouver Island* (Vancouver: University of British Columbia Press, 2000).

7. For information on Clear Water, see Clarence B. Bagley, "Chief Seattle and Angeline," *Washington Historical Quarterly* 22, no. 4 (1931): 243–75. For discussions of indigenous towns in Puget Sound, see Jay Miller, *Lushootseed Culture,* 10.

8. Marian Smith, *Puyallup-Nisqually,* 17; and Wayne M. Suttles, "Persistence of Intervillage Ties among the Coast Salish," in *Coast Salish Essays,* by Wayne M. Suttles (Seattle: University of Washington Press; Vancouver: Talonbooks, 1987), 209–30.

9. Edmond S. Meany, ed., *Vancouver's Discovery of Puget Sound* (New York: Macmillan, 1907), 105, 108, 124. For analysis of the notion of "people without history," see Eric R. Wolf, *Europe and People without History* (Berkeley and Los Angeles: University of California Press, 1982). For the most comprehensive study of epidemics on the Northwest Coast, see Robert Boyd, *The Coming of the Spirit of Pestilence: Introduced Infectious Diseases and Population Decline among Northwest Coast Indians, 1774–1874* (Seattle: University of Washington Press, 1999).

10. For a summary of archaeological information for the region, including material drawn from at least one site in Seattle, see Charles M. Nelson, "Prehis-

tory of the Puget Sound Region," in *Handbook of North American Indians,* ed. William C. Sturtevant, vol. 7, *Northwest Coast,* ed. Wayne Suttles (Washington: Smithsonian Institution, 1990), 481–84. For linguistic evidence, see Wayne M. Suttles, "Northwest Coast Linguistic History—a View from the Coast," in *Coast Salish Essays,* 265–81. For stories of the Changer, see Arthur C. Ballard's collections *Some Tales of the Southern Puget Sound Salish* (Seattle: University of Washington Press, 1927) and *Mythology of Southern Puget Sound* (Seattle: University of Washington Press, 1929). For prehistoric natural disasters, see Arthur Kruckeberg, *A Natural History of Puget Sound Country* (Seattle: University of Washington Press, 1991); and Lynn L. Larson and Dennis E. Lewarch, eds., *The Archaeology of West Point, Seattle, Washington: 4,000 Years of Hunter-Fisher-Gatherer Land Use in Southern Puget Sound* (Seattle: Larson Anthropological/Archaeological Services, 1995). For the words arising from *dookw,* see Dawn Bates, Thom Hess, and Vi Hilbert, *Lushootseed Dictionary* (Seattle: University of Washington Press, 1994), 84–85.

11. Charles Wilkes, *Narrative of the United States Exploring Expedition during the Years 1838, 1839, 1840, 1841, and 1842* (New York: G. P. Putnam, 1844), vol. 4, 483; and Edmond S. Meany, ed., "Diary of Wilkes in the Northwest," *Washington Historical Quarterly* 17 (1926): 139.

12. Meany, "Diary of Wilkes in the Northwest," 137–40. For accounts of epidemics in the 1830s and 1840s, see Boyd, *Coming of the Spirit of Pestilence,* 155, 267. For discussion of the Ex. Ex., see Nathaniel Philbrick, *Sea of Glory: America's Voyage of Discovery, the U.S. Exploring Expedition, 1838–1842* (New York: Viking, 2003). For Fort Nisqually, see Cecelia Svinth Carpenter, *Fort Nisqually: A Documented History of Indian and British Interaction* (Tacoma, WA: Tahoma Research Services, 1986), and William Fraser Tolmie, *The Journals of William Fraser Tolmie: Physician and Fur Trader* (Vancouver: Mitchell Press, 1963), 216.

13. Samuel Hancock, *The Narrative of Samuel Hancock, 1845–1860* (New York: R. M. McBride and Co., 1927), 94–95.

14. Arthur Armstrong Denny, *Pioneer Days on Puget Sound* (Seattle: C. B. Bagley, Printer, 1888), 9–10; and undated George Brock obituary, Scrapbook 21, p. 7, Oregon Historical Society, Portland.

15. Arthur Denny, *Pioneer Days on Puget Sound,* 10–12; Andrew Jackson Chambers, *Recollections* (n.p., 1947), 28–29; Thomas W. Prosch, *Chronological History of Seattle from 1850 to 1897* (Seattle: n.p., 1900), 24; Watt, *Four Wagons West,* 28–29; Frank Carlson, "Chief Sealth" (M.A. thesis, University of Washington, 1903), 26; and Emily Inez Denny, *Blazing the Way; or, True Stories, Songs, and Sketches of Puget Sound and Other Pioneers* (Seattle: Rainier Printing Co., 1909), 43.

16. Marian W. Smith, "Petroglyph Complexes in the History of the Columbia-Fraser Region," *Southwest Journal of Anthropology* 2, no. 3 (1946): 315; Roger Sale, *Seattle, Past to Present* (Seattle: University of Washington Press, 1976), 12; Arthur

Denny, *Pioneer Days on Puget Sound*, 10–12; and Thomas Talbot Waterman, *Puget Sound Geography*, ed. Vi Hilbert, Jay Miller, and Zalmai Zahir (Seattle: Lushootseed Press, 2001), 119–27.

17. Thomas Prosch, *Chronological History*, 22–24; Watt, *Four Wagons West*, 30–32; and Emily Denny, *Blazing the Way*, 47–48.

18. Arthur Denny, *Pioneer Days on Puget Sound*, 10–12; Emily Denny, *Blazing the Way*, 49; and Archie Binns, *Northwest Gateway: The Story of the Port of Seattle* (Garden City, NY: Doubleday, Doran, and Co., 1941), 32–41.

19. Stuart M. Blumin, "Explaining the New Metropolis: Perception, Depiction, and Analysis in Mid–Nineteenth Century New York," *Journal of Urban History* 11, no. 1 (1984): 9–38; Burrows and Wallace, *Gotham*, 649–841.

20. For accounts of Knox County during this time, see Albert J. Perry, *History of Knox County, Illinois: Its Cities, Towns, and People* (Chicago: S. J. Clarke Publishing Co., 1912), 419–23, 447–49; and James E. Davis, *Frontier Illinois* (Bloomington: Indiana University Press, 1998), 331–33. For the Denny family's history in the area, see Arthur Armstrong Denny, "Reminiscences," Bancroft Collection, 5–8; and Sale, *Seattle, Past to Present*, 8–9, 17.

21. Albert Perry, *History of Knox County*, 5, 44; Richard White, *The Middle Ground: Indians, Empires, and Republics in the Great Lakes Region, 1650–1815* (New York: Cambridge University Press, 1991); J. Joseph Bauxar, "History of the Illinois Area," and Charles Callender, "Illinois," in *Handbook of North American Indians*, ed. William C. Sturtevant, vol. 15, *Northeast*, ed. Bruce G. Trigger (Washington: Smithsonian Institution, 1978), 594–601, 673–80.

22. Albert Perry, *History of Knox County*, 43–44, 447; Charles C. Chapman, *History of Knox County, Illinois* (Chicago: Blakely, Brown, and Marsh, Printers, 1878), 185–87; Rodney O. Davis, "The Frontier State, 1818–48," in *A Guide to the History of Illinois*, ed. John Hoffman (New York: Greenwood Press, 1991), 54; and Clarence B. Bagley, *History of Seattle from the Earliest Settlement to the Present Time*, vol. 2 (Chicago: S. J. Clarke, 1916), 824, 875.

23. Arthur Denny, *Pioneer Days on Puget Sound*, 13–14.

24. Ibid., 4–6, 8–9; Eugene E. Snyder, *Early Portland: Stump-Town Triumphant* (Portland, OR: Binfords and Mort, 1970), 70; and Emily Denny, *Blazing the Way*, 42.

25. Watt, *Four Wagons West*, 49–51, 60.

26. Eva Greenslit Anderson, *Chief Seattle* (Caldwell: Caxton Printers, 1943), 161; Emily Denny, *Blazing the Way*, 56; Carlson, "Chief Sealth," 26; Thomas Talbot Waterman, "The Geographical Names Used by the Indians of the Pacific Coast," *Geographical Review* 12 (1922): 192; personal communication with Thomas Speer, Duwamish Tribal Services.

27. Emily Denny, *Blazing the Way*, 57–58; interview with Walter Graham, February 1914, MOHAI MS Collection, folder 348; Arthur Denny, *Pioneer Days on Puget Sound*, 14; and Thomas Prosch, *Chronological History*, 26.

28. Wayne Suttles, "The Early Diffusion of the Potato among the Coast Salish," in *Coast Salish Essays*, 137–51; Thomas Prosch, *Chronological History*, 25–26; Arthur Denny, *Pioneer Days on Puget Sound*, 13; and Watt, *Four Wagons West*, 55.

29. Arthur Denny, *Pioneer Days on Puget Sound*, 17; Watt, *Four Wagons West*, 53, 64–65, 67; and Ruth Sehome Shelton, *Gram Ruth Sehome Shelton: The Wisdom of a Tulalip Elder* (Seattle: Lushootseed Press, 1995), 25–27.

30. Thomas Prosch, *Chronological History*, 28–29, 31, 41–42; Beaton, *City That Made Itself*, 21; and Watt, *Four Wagons West*, 70.

31. For examples of the various speculations, see Carlson, "Chief Sealth," 27; Thomas Prosch, *Chronological History*, 29; Bagley, *History of Seattle*, vol. 2, 27; and Watt, *Four Wagons West*, 70. Some modern-day Duwamish people see the naming of the city as a theft of indigenous cultural property, especially cutting in light of the dispossession they would later face. In personal communications with the author, anthropologist Jay Miller has suggested that Seeathl may have seen the naming as analogous to offering his name to a young descendant, thus ensuring that the name would live on. Meanwhile, present-day Duwamish tribal activist James Rasmussen has argued that Seeathl would in fact be proud of the city named after him; for that claim, see B. J. Bullert's documentary *Alki: Birthplace of Seattle* (Seattle: Southwest Seattle Historical Society and KCTS Television, 1997).

32. Bierwert, *Brushed by Cedar*, 43–44; Watt, *Four Wagons West*, 58–59.

33. Arthur Denny, *Pioneer Days on Puget Sound*, 19.

3 / Seattle Illahee

1. Philip J. Thomas, *Songs of the Pacific Northwest* (Saanichton, BC: Hancock House, 1979), 60–61. For accounts of the Fraser River gold rush, see R. Cole Harris, *The Resettlement of British Columbia: Essays on Colonialism and Geographical Change* (Vancouver: University of British Columbia Press, 1997), esp. 103–36; Andrea Laforet and Annie York, *Spuzzum: Fraser Canyon Histories, 1808–1939* (Vancouver: University of British Columbia Press, 1999); Daniel P. Marshall, "No Parallel: American Miner-Soldiers at War with the Nlaka'pamux of the Canadian West," in *Parallel Destinies: Canadian-American Relations West of the Rockies*, ed. John M. Findlay and Ken S. Coates (Seattle: University of Washington Press, 2002), 31–79; and Robert E. Ficken, *Unsettled Boundaries: Fraser Gold and the British-American Northwest* (Pullman: Washington State University Press, 2003).

2. David Kellogg to Vivian Carkeek, 20 May 1912, MOHAI MS Collection, folder 116.

3. "Story of Alonzo Russell," n.d. (1910s), MOHAI MS Collection, folder 526;

Caroline Leighton, *Life at Puget Sound, with Sketches of Travel in Washington Territory, British Columbia, Oregon, and California, 1865–1881* (Boston: Lee and Shepard, 1884), 39–40; and Dillis B. Ward, "From Salem, Oregon, to Seattle, Washington, in 1859," *Washington Historical Quarterly* 6 (1915): 100.

4. "The Christmas Times," *Seattle Times*, 14 December 1901; and Leighton, *Life at Puget Sound*, 41–42.

5. Cornelius H. Hanford, ed., *Seattle and Environs: 1852–1924* (Chicago: Pioneer Historical Publishing Co., 1924), 49.

6. David Kellogg to Vivian Carkeek, 20 May 1912; Jay Miller, *Lushootseed Culture*, 100–103. This was not an isolated event—Cornelius Hanford describes a similar initiation, of an indigenous man named Sampson, taking place in 1858 (*Seattle and Environs*, 142).

7. Seattle Historical Society interview with Louisa Boren Denny, n.d., MOHAI MS Collection, folder 258; Abbie Denny-Lindsley, "When Seattle Was an Indian Camp Forty-Five Years Ago," *Seattle P-I*, 15 April 1906; and Phoebe Goodell Judson, *A Pioneer's Search for an Ideal Home: A Book of Personal Memoirs* (Bellingham, WA: Union Printing, Binding, and Publishing Co., 1925), 188.

8. Bass, *Pigtail Days in Old Seattle*, 31; Arthur Denny, *Pioneer Days on Puget Sound*, 73; and Yvonne Prater, *Snoqualmie Pass: From Indian Trail to Interstate* (Seattle: The Mountaineers, 1981), 7–29.

9. For accounts of the "Puget Sound Indian War" (or the "Treaty War," as many Indian people call it), see J. A. Eckrom, *Remembered Drums: The Puget Sound Indian War* (Walla Walla, WA: Pioneer Press Books, 1989); and John Lutz, "Inventing an Indian War: Canadian Indians and American Settlers in the Pacific West, 1854–1864," *Journal of the West* 38, no. 3 (1998): 7–13.

10. Patricia Nelson Limerick, *The Legacy of Conquest: The Unbroken Past of the American West* (New York: Norton, 1987), 35–54.

11. Thomas Prosch, *Chronological History*, 32; Edith Sanderson Redfield, *Seattle Memories* (Boston: Lothrop, Lee, and Shepard Co., 1930), 31; John M. Swan narrative, 6–7, Bancroft Collection; "Adventures of William T. Ballou," 3, Bancroft Collection; and Waterman, "Geographical Names," 188; Thomas S. Phelps's map of Seattle, 1856, MSCUA negative UW4101.

12. Major J. Thomas Turner, "Reminiscences, 7 September 1914," MOHAI MS Collection, folder 106; Jane Fenton Kelly, "Trail of a Pioneer Family," n.d. (1910s), MOHAI MS Collection, folder 347; Redfield, *Seattle Memories*, 39; and J. G. Parker, "Puget Sound," 4, Bancroft Collection.

13. Thomas Prosch, *Chronological History*, 29; Thomas F. Gedosch, "A Note on the Dogfish Oil Industry of Washington Territory," *Pacific Northwest Quarterly* 59, no. 2 (1968): 100–102; Abbie Denny-Lindsley, "When Seattle Was an Indian Camp Forty-Five Years Ago," *Seattle P-I*, 15 April 1906; Catherine Blaine, "A Frontier Sketch" (n.p., n.d.), MSCUA; Sophie Frye Bass, *When Seattle Was a Village* (Seattle:

Lowman and Hanford, 1947), 44; and interview with Walter Graham, MOHAI MS Collection.

14. Thomas Prosch, *Chronological History*, 53; Brad Asher, *Beyond the Reservation: Indians, Settlers, and the Law in Washington Territory, 1853–1889* (Norman: University of Oklahoma Press, 1999), 107–53; David Blaine and Catherine Blaine, *Memoirs of Puget Sound: Early Seattle, 1853–1856,* ed. Richard A. Seiber (Fairfield, WA: Ye Galleon Press, 1978), 76–77.

15. Henry L. Yesler, "Henry Yesler and the Founding of Seattle," *Pacific Northwest Quarterly* 42 (1951): 274.

16. For a summary of the treaty process in Puget Sound, see Alexandra Harmon, *Indians in the Making: Ethnic Relations and Indian Identities around Puget Sound* (Berkeley and Los Angeles: University of California Press, 1998). For the details of the process in Seattle and central Puget Sound, see Furtwangler, *Answering Chief Seattle.*

17. Shelton, *Gram Ruth Sehome Shelton,* 26; Emily Denny, *Blazing the Way,* 67–68.

18. Michael T. Simmons to Isaac Ingalls Stevens, 27 December 1855, and Henry Yesler, David Phillips, C. C. Lewis, S. Samson Grow, and Thomas Mercer to C. H. Mason, 24 November 1855, Records of the Bureau of Indian Affairs, Western Washington Agency, NARA.

19. Hanford, *Seattle and Environs,* 148; William N. Bell, "Settlement of Seattle," Bancroft Collection; and Emily Denny, *Blazing the Way,* 374–75; "Historic Nisqually Chief Exonerated," *Seattle Times,* 11 December 2004.

20. "The Indian War!!" *Pioneer and Democrat,* 1 February 1856; Henry L. Yesler to Michael T. Simmons, 26 July 1856, Records of the Bureau of Indian Affairs, Western Washington Agency, NARA; George A. Paige to Michael T. Simmons, 23 January 1857, Records of the Bureau of Indian Affairs, Western Washington Agency, NARA; Commander S. S. Swarthout to Stevens, 31 August 1856, Records of the Bureau of Indian Affairs, Western Washington Agency, NARA.

21. George A. Paige to Michael T. Simmons, 30 November 1856, Records of the Bureau of Indian Affairs, Western Washington Agency, NARA; David S. Maynard to Michael T. Simmons, 19 September 1856, Records of the Bureau of Indian Affairs, Western Washington Agency, NARA; and M. Maloney, Capt. 4th Infantry at Muckleshoot, to Lt. Col. S. Casey, 9th Infantry, Commander of Puget Sound District at Fort Steilacoom, 24 November 1856, Records of the Bureau of Indian Affairs, Western Washington Agency, NARA.

22. George A. Paige to Isaac Ingalls Stevens, 6 November 1856, Records of the Bureau of Indian Affairs, Western Washington Agency, NARA; George A. Paige to Isaac Ingalls Stevens, 30 June 1857, Records of the Bureau of Indian Affairs, Western Washington Agency, NARA.

23. "Ordinances of the Town of Seattle," *Seattle Weekly Gazette*, 4 March 1865.

24. "Petition to the Honorable Arthur A. Denny, Delegate to Congress from Washington Territory," n.d., NARA, roll 909.

25. Arthur Denny, *Pioneer Days on Puget Sound*, 72–73.

26. For an account of the 1960s television show, see Walt Crowley, *Rites of Passage: A Memoir of the Sixties in Seattle* (Seattle: University of Washington Press, 1995), 260–61. For information on Asa Shinn Mercer, see Roger Conant, *Mercer's Belles: The Journal of a Reporter* (Seattle: University of Washington Press, 1960); and Lawrence M. Woods, *Asa Shinn Mercer: Western Promoter and Newspaperman, 1839–1917* (Spokane: Arthur H. Clark Co., 2003). For similar experiments with the importation of white women north of the border, see Adele Perry, *On the Edge of Empire: Gender, Race, and the Making of British Columbia, 1849–1871* (Toronto: University of Toronto Press, 2001).

27. Charles W. Smith, "Asa Shinn Mercer, Pioneer in Western Publicity," *Pacific Northwest Quarterly* 27 (1936): 355; *New York Times*, 26 January 1866; *Puget Sound Daily*, 2 June 1866.

28. Charles Prosch, *Reminiscences of Washington Territory: Scenes, Incidents, and Reflections of the Pioneer Period on Puget Sound* (Seattle: n.p., 1904), 118; N. M. Bogart, "Reminiscences of Early Pioneer Days," n.d., MOHAI MS Collection; Charles E. Roblin, Schedule of Unenrolled Indians, n.d. (1919), U.S. Department of the Interior, Office of Indian Affairs, NARA; Yesler, "Henry Yesler and the Founding of Seattle," 275; "Eldest Daughter of Henry Yesler Is Dead," *Seattle Times*, 12 February 1907; "Death of Yesler's Daughter, Julia," *Seattle P-I*, 17 February 1907; and Kathie Zetterberg and David Wilma, "Henry Yesler's Native American Daughter Julia Is Born on June 12, 1855," www.historylink.org.

29. Blaine and Blaine, *Memoirs of Puget Sound*, 120–21; Charles Prosch, *Reminiscences*, 27; Robin D. Sword, "The 'Saloon Crowd' and the 'Moral Darkness of Puget Sound,'" *Pacific Northwest Forum* 4, no. 1 (1991): 95–101.

30. W. W. Miller, "A Circular," *Washington Standard*, 21 September 1861; Asher, *Beyond the Reservation*, 63–68; Harmon, *Indians in the Making*, 77–78; and Charles Prosch, *Reminiscences*, 27. For analysis of similar laws throughout the American West, see Peggy Pascoe, "Race, Gender, and the Privileges of Property: On the Significance of Miscegenation Law in the U.S. West," in *Over the Edge: Remapping the American West*, ed. Valerie J. Matsumoto and Blake Allmendinger (Berkeley and Los Angeles: University of California Press, 1999), 215–30.

31. Morgan, *Skid Road*, 59–60; William C. Spiedel, *Sons of the Profits, or There's No Business Like Grow Business: The Seattle Story, 1851–1901* (Seattle: Nettle Creek Publishing Co., 1967), 112–14; Marjorie Rhodes, ed., *King County Censuses: 1870 U.S. Census and 1871 Territorial Census for King County, Washington Territory* (Seattle: Marjorie Rhodes, 1993), 33; and A. Atwood, *Glimpses in Pioneer Life on Puget Sound* (Seattle: Denny-Correll, 1903), 149.

32. Hilman F. Jones Papers (YS-26), box 1, file 28, Special Collections, Washington State Historical Society, Tacoma.

33. "The End of the Small-Pox," *Seattle Daily Intelligencer*, 16 January 1876; "Small-Pox," *Seattle Daily Intelligencer*, 29 December 1876.

34. "The Small-Pox Question," *Seattle Daily Intelligencer*, 30 December 1876; *Seattle Daily Intelligencer*, 14 March 1877.

35. *Daily Intelligencer*, 12 June 1877; "More on the Small-Pox," *Seattle Daily Intelligencer*, 25 May 1877; "Small-Pox Statistics," *Seattle Daily Intelligencer*, 30 July 1877; "Claimed to Be an Indian," *Seattle Daily Intelligencer*, 15 February 1878; "Small Pox—a Word of Caution," *Seattle Daily Intelligencer*, 19 February 1878; and "The Small-Pox Case," *Seattle Daily Intelligencer*, 20 February 1878. For similar patterns of prejudice facing other communities of color in the West, see Nayan Shah, *Contagious Divides: Epidemics and Race in San Francisco's Chinatown* (Berkeley and Los Angeles: University of California Press, 2001); and William Deverell, "Plague in Los Angeles: Ethnicity and Typicality," in Matsumoto and Allmendinger, eds., *Over the Edge*, 172–200.

36. For the history of fire in American cities, see Christine Meisner Rosen, *The Limits of Power: Great Fires and the Process of City Growth in America* (New York: Cambridge University Press, 1986); for a regional study, see Daniel E. Turbeville III, "Cities of Kindling: Geographical Implications of the Urban Fire Hazard on the Pacific Northwest Coast Frontier, 1851–1920" (Ph.D. diss., Simon Fraser University, 1986). Quotations come from "Forewarned, Forearmed," *Seattle Daily Intelligencer*, 15 May 1878; "Another Warning," *Seattle Daily Intelligencer*, 18 September 1878; and "A Nuisance," *Seattle Daily Intelligencer*, 9 May 1878.

37. "Seattle in Ashes," *Seattle Daily Intelligencer*, 27 July 1879; "A Big Blaze," *Seattle Daily Intelligencer*, 8 May 1878; "Made Room," *Seattle Daily Intelligencer*, 9 May 1878; and logbook, Thomas W. Prosch Papers, box 1, folder 4, MSCUA. For what remains the best overview of the political and cultural battles over whether Seattle would be an "open" or "closed" town, see Morgan, *Skid Road*.

38. Logbook, Thomas W. Prosch Papers, MSCUA.

4 / Mr. Glover's Imbricated City

1. "Birds-Eye View," *Seattle Daily Intelligencer*, 30 May 1878; and "A Beautiful View," *Seattle Daily Intelligencer*, 31 May 1878.

2. David Hamer, *New Towns in the New World: Images and Perceptions of the Nineteenth-Century Urban Frontier* (New York: Columbia University Press, 1990), 49. See also Reps, *Panoramas of Promise*.

3. Charles A. Kinnear, "Arrival of the George Kinnear Family on Puget Sound, and Early Recollections by C. A. Kinnear, One of the Children," n.d., MOHAI MS Collection.

4. Bates, Hess, and Hilbert, *Lushootseed Dictionary*, 78. For Puget Sound basketry traditions, see Nile Thompson and Carolyn Marr, *Crow's Shells: Artistic Basketry of Puget Sound* (Seattle: Dushuyay Publications, 1983).

5. For a snapshot portrayal of Seattle during this period, see David M. Buerge, *Seattle in the 1880s*, ed. Stuart R. Grover (Seattle: Historical Society of Seattle and King County, 1986).

6. Except where stated otherwise, the data given here come from the manuscript of the tenth census of the United States, NARA.

7. Redfield, *Seattle Memories*, 19.

8. Thomas Prosch, *Chronological History*, 287–88.

9. Mrs. E. E. Heg, "The Beginnings of Trinity Church, Seattle," *Seattle Churchman* 13, no. 2 (1900): 3–6; Atwood, *Glimpses in Pioneer Life*, 89–90.

10. King County Marriage Records, Puget Sound Branch, Washington State Archives, Bellevue.

11. Bass, *When Seattle Was a Village*, 23–25.

12. "A Wise Course," *Seattle Daily Intelligencer*, 13 May 1878.

13. "The Duwamish Road," *Seattle Daily Intelligencer*, 12 March 1878; "Duwamish Doings," *Seattle Daily Intelligencer*, 4 March 1880; and "The County Farm," *Seattle Daily Intelligencer*, 10 February 1877.

14. "Belltown," *Seattle Daily Intelligencer*, 22 March 1878; "A Skeleton Found," *Seattle Daily Intelligencer*, 21 August 1876; "Improvements near Lake Union," *Seattle Daily Intelligencer*, 15 May 1879; "Lake Union Suburb," *Seattle Daily Intelligencer*, 20 September 1879; "Salmon Bay," *Seattle Daily Intelligencer*, 12 November 1877; "Salmon Bay," *Seattle Daily Intelligencer*, 23 September 1879; and "A Choice Location," *Seattle Daily Intelligencer*, 9 April 1878.

15. Charles E. Roblin, Schedule of Unenrolled Indians, n.d. (1919), U.S. Department of the Interior, Office of Indian Affairs, NARA; J. A. Costello, *The Siwash: Their Life, Legends, and Tales* (Seattle: Calvert, 1895), 86–87; Real Property Assessment and Tax Rolls, Puget Sound Branch, Washington State Archives, Bellevue; Margaret Wandrey, *Four Bridges to Seattle: Old Ballard, 1853–1907* (Seattle: Wandrey, 1975), 21, 25, 82; Nile Thompson, "The Original Residents of Shilshole Bay," in *Passport to Ballard: The Centennial Story* (Seattle: Ballard News Tribune, 1998), 14; Paul Dorpat, "Indian Charlie," *Seattle Times*, 29 January 1984; and Waterman, "Geographical Names," 189.

16. "Indian Taxpayers," *Seattle Daily Intelligencer*, 3 December 1879. For detailed discussion of Dzakwoos and his family, see Jay Miller and Astrida R. Blukis Onat, *Winds, Waterways, and Weirs: Ethnographic Study of the Central Link Light Rail Corridor* (Seattle: BOAS, 2004), 78–85.

17. "Indian Taxpayers," *Seattle Daily Intelligencer*, 3 December 1879; Costello, *Siwash*, 86–87.

5 / City of the Changers

1. Interview with Ollie Wilbur by Lynn Larson, 26 May 1994, Alki/Transfer CSO Facilities Project Traditional Cultural Properties, MIT; Waterman, *Puget Sound Geography*, 23.

2. Amelia Sneatlum, recorded by Warren Snyder, 1955, and reprinted in Robin K. Wright, ed., *A Time of Gathering: Native Heritage in Washington State* (Seattle: University of Washington Press, 1991), 262.

3. The notion of "dispossession by degrees" comes from Jean M. O'Brien, *Dispossession by Degrees: Indian Land and Identity in Natick, Massachusetts, 1650–1790* (Cambridge: Cambridge University Press, 1997). One of O'Brien's primary arguments is that indigenous persistence (which in the case of the Natick involved staying in place, becoming individual landholders, and intermarrying with the non-Native population) ironically led to an erosion of corporate access to and use of traditional places. Although in a different place and time, the story of Seattle's indigenous people, and of the Duwamish Tribe in particular, seems to follow a similar pattern.

4. Rudyard Kipling, *From Sea to Sea and Other Sketches: Letters of Travel*, vol. 2 (Garden City, NY: Doubleday, Page, and Co., 1925), 93–94.

5. James R. Warren, *The Day Seattle Burned* (Seattle: J. R. Warren, 1989); and Colin E. Tweddell, "Historical and Ethnological Study of the Snohomish Indian People," in *Coast Salish and Western Washington Indians*, vol. 2 (New York: Garland Publishing, 1974), 552–53.

6. Orange Jacobs, *Memoirs of Orange Jacobs* (Seattle: Lowman and Hanford, 1908), 189–90.

7. "To-Day's Doings," *Seattle P-I*, 14 September 1883; "Jubilate" and "The Decorations," *Seattle P-I*, 15 September 1883; Kurt E. Armbruster, *Orphan Road: The Railroad Comes to Seattle, 1853–1911* (Pullman: Washington State University Press, 1999).

8. "Indians Burned Out," *Seattle Times*, 7 March 1893. According to anthropologist Jay Miller, tribal oral tradition claims that Watson was in fact an agent of the West Seattle Land Improvement Company. No documentary records that might confirm this allegation are known to exist.

9. Clay Eals, ed., *West Side Story* (Seattle: West Seattle Herald, 1987), 27, 94, 97; Bass, *When Seattle Was a Village*, 118–19; and interview with Harold Moses and

Gilbert King George by Lynn Larson, 22 June 1994, Alki/Transfer CSO Facilities Project Traditional Cultural Properties, MIT.

10. *Duwamish et al. vs. the United States of America, Consolidated Petition No. F-275* (Seattle: Argus Press, 1993), 683–87, 695, 701.

11. Miller and Onat, *Winds, Waterways, and Weirs*, 82–83.

12. "Indians Burned Out," *Seattle Times*, 7 March 1893; Army Corps of Engineers, Duwamish-Puyallup Surveys, 1907, Army Corps Archives, Seattle; Roblin, Schedule of Unenrolled Indians, n.d. (1919), U.S. Department of the Interior, Office of Indian Affairs, NARA.

13. Bass, *When Seattle Was a Village*, 118–19.

14. "Angeline Is No More," *Seattle P-I*, 1 June 1896; "Who Shall Bury Her?" *Seattle P-I*, 2 June 1896; "Angeline's Funeral," *Seattle P-I*, 5 June 1896; "Angeline's Funeral," *Seattle P-I*, 6 June 1896; and Mrs. Victor Zednick, "When I Was a Girl," *Seattle Times*, 19 January 1927.

15. "Poor Old Angeline," *Seattle P-I*, 2 August 1891; Henry L. Yesler, "The Daughter of Old Chief Seattle," *Pacific Magazine* 1, no. 3 (1889): 25–27; "Angeline Is No More," *Seattle P-I*, 31 May 1896; "The Last Indian Princess," *Northwest Magazine*, August 1896, 15; Edmond S. Meany, "Princess Angeline," *Seattle Argus*, 21 December 1901, 11–12; Thomas Prosch and C. T. Conover, comps., *Washington, the Evergreen State, and Seattle, Its Chief City* (Seattle: T. F. Kane, 1894); *One Hundred Views about Seattle, the Queen City* (Seattle: R. A. Reid, 1911); and "Seattle Historical Pageant Attracts Pioneer Interest," *Seattle Times*, 18 May 1930.

16. Mason Whitney, ed., *Magnolia: Memories and Milestones* (Seattle: Magnolia Community Club, 2000).

17. For accounts of Chesheeahud—whose name is spelled various ways—and Tleebuleetsa, see John Peabody Harrington, *The Papers of John Peabody Harrington in the Smithsonian Institution, 1907–1957*, ed. Elaine L. Miles (New York: Kraus International Publications, 1981), frame 0498; Edmond S. Meany, "The Last Lake Union Indians," *Seattle Times*, 11 June 1898; "Indian John in Hospital," *Seattle Times*, 8 February 1905; "Indian John Holds Potlatch," *Seattle P-I*, 29 May 1906; and Edmond S. Meany, "Story of Seattle's Nearest Indian Neighbors," *Seattle P-I*, 29 October 1905. For information on Hiram Gill, see Morgan, *Skid Road*, 169–81; and Sale, *Seattle: Past to Present*, 107–8, 118–19.

18. "Chief Seattle's Nephew Ruined by Gale," *Seattle P-I*, 6 January 1910; "Fund Is Started for Indian Billy," *Seattle P-I*, 7 January 1910; and "Members of Dying Race Whom Advance of Progress Crowds Off Seattle Waterfront," *Seattle P-I*, 11 May 1910.

19. S. A. Eliot, *Report upon the Conditions and Needs of the Indians of the Northwest Coast* (Washington: Government Printing Office, 1915), 21; *Duwamish et al. vs. United States*, 4; and Frank W. Porter III, "Without Reservation: Federal Indian

Policy and the Landless Tribes of Washington," in *State and Reservation: New Perspectives in Federal Indian Policy*, ed. George Pierre Castile and Robert L. Bee (Tucson: University of Arizona Press, 1992).

20. Applications for Enrollment and Allotment of Washington Indians, 1911–19, NARA, microfilm M1343, roll 3; "Lake Union John, Aged 90, Buried," *Seattle P-I*, 12 February 1910; and *Baist's Real Estate Atlas of Surveys of Seattle, Wash.* (Philadelphia: Baist, 1905), plate 14.

21. "Chief Seattle's Nephew Billy Ruined by Gale," *Seattle P-I*, 6 January 1910; "Fund Is Started for Indian Billy," *Seattle P-I*, 7 January 1910; "Help Comes for Old Indian Billy," *Seattle P-I*, 8 January 1910; Thompson, "Original Residents of Shilshole Bay," 15.

22. "Siwashes Again Seek the Streets," *Seattle P-I*, 31 May 1904; "Squaw Comes to Meet Mrs. Leary," *Seattle P-I*, 12 November 1907; "Mary Seattle Is Badly Hurt," *Seattle Times*, 15 April 1906; "Our Citizens of Yesterday," *Seattle Argus*, 22 December 1900; and Abbie Denny-Lindsley, "When Seattle Was an Indian Camp Forty-five Years Ago," *Seattle P-I*, 15 April 1906.

23. Waterman, "Geographical Names"; Edmond S. Meany Papers, MSCUA; Calhoun, Denny, and Ewing advertisement, *Seattle P-I*, 23 May 1909; "Thousand at Opening of the Licton Plat," *Seattle P-I*, 23 May 1909.

24. Don Sherwood, "Interpretive Essay: Licton Springs," Don Sherwood Collection, MSCUA; Paul Burch, "The Story of Licton Springs," *The Westerner* 9, no. 4 (1908): 19, 34.

25. Carl Abbott, "Footprints and Pathways: The Urban Imprint on the Pacific Northwest," in *Northwest Lands, Northwest Peoples: Readings in Environmental History*, ed. Dale D. Goble and Paul W. Hirt (Seattle: University of Washington Press, 1999), 113.

26. The finest treatment of Seattle's environmental history is Matthew W. Klingle, "Urban by Nature: An Environmental History of Seattle, 1880–1970" (Ph.D. diss., University of Washington, 2001). See also Mike Sato, *The Price of Taming a River: The Decline of Puget Sound's Duwamish/Green Waterway* (Seattle: The Mountaineers, 1997); Dick Paetze, *Pioneers and Partnerships: A History of the Port of Seattle* (Seattle: Port of Seattle, 1995); and Paul Dorpat and Genevieve McCoy, *Building Washington: A History of Washington State's Public Works* (Seattle: Tartu Publications, 1998).

27. Reginald Heber Thomson, with Grant H. Redford, *That Man Thomson* (Seattle: University of Washington Press, 1950), 106–8; and Hiram M. Chittenden, "Sentiment versus Utility in the Treatment of National Scenery," *Pacific Monthly* 23 (January 1910): 29–38.

28. Leonie Sandercock, *Towards Cosmopolis: Planning for Multicultural Cities* (Chichester, U.K.: John Wiley and Sons, 1998); Rose Simmons, "Old Angeline, the Princess of Seattle," *Overland Monthly* 20 (November 1892): 506.

29. Waterman, "Geographical Names," 476; M. J. Carter, "Lake Washington's New Beach Line," *Seattle Town Crier*, 14 April 1917.

30. Quoted in Sato, *Price of Taming a River*, 57; Meany, "Story of Seattle's Nearest Indian Neighbors," *Seattle P-I*, 29 October 1905.

31. Thomas Talbot Waterman, *Notes on the Ethnology of the Indians of Puget Sound* (New York: Heye Foundation, 1973), x.

32. Harrington, *Papers*, frames 344, 392, 409–12; Waterman, *Puget Sound Geography*, 23–34; and Ballard, *Mythology of Southern Puget Sound*, 35–41.

33. Interview with Art Williams by Lynn Larson, 3 May 1994, Alki/Transfer CSO Facilities Project Traditional Cultural Properties, MIT.

34. Ibid.; Cesare Marino, "History of Western Washington since 1846," in Suttles, ed., *Handbook of North American Indians*, 175; *Duwamish et al. vs. United States*, 701; Charles M. Buchanan, "The Rights of the Puget Sound Indians to Game and Fish," *Washington Historical Quarterly* 6, no. 2 (1916): 109–18; Bass, *Pigtail Days in Old Seattle*, 16; and Bass, *When Seattle Was a Village*, 118–19.

35. Wandrey, *Four Bridges to Seattle*, 154; Harrington, *Papers*, frame 344; Marian Smith, "Petroglyph Complexes," 315.

36. Harrington, *Papers*, frames 409–12; Don Sherwood, "Interpretive Essay: Alki Playground," Don Sherwood Collection, MSCUA.

37. Warren Snyder, *Southern Puget Sound Salish: Texts, Place Names, and Dictionary* (Sacramento: Sacramento Anthropological Society, 1968), 117–19; Patricia Slettvet Noel, *Muckleshoot Indian History* (Auburn, WA: Auburn School District, 1980); June M. Collins, "John Fornsby: The Personal Document of a Coast Salish Indian," in *Indians of the Urban Northwest*, ed. Marian W. Smith (New York: Columbia University Press, 1949); Russel Barsh, "Puget Sound Indian Demography, 1900–1920: Migration and Economic Integration," *Ethnohistory* 43 (1996): 65–97; and Webster and Stevens photograph, ca. 1911, of Suquamish tribal members waiting on Colman Dock after attempting to obtain land payments in Seattle, MOHAI 83.10.7,723.

38. Interview with Florence Wynn by Lynn Larson, 15 June 1994, Alki/Transfer CSO Facilities Project Traditional Cultural Properties, MIT; "Great-Granddaughter of Seattle Is Hostess at Her Home in Suquamish," *Seattle Times*, 29 November 1931; and Waterman, "Geographical Names," 188.

39. Marian Smith, *Puyallup-Nisqually*, 54.

40. Waterman, "Geographical Names," 188; Waterman, *Puget Sound Geography*, 23; Gedosch, "Note on the Dogfish Oil Industry"; and interview with Ollie Wilbur by Lynn Larson, 26 May 1994, Alki/Transfer CSO Facilities Project Traditional Cultural Properties, MIT.

41. Chittenden, "Sentiment versus Utility," 31; Marian Smith, *Puyallup-Nisqually*, 29.

6 / The Woven Coast

1. For descriptions of Seattle in 1900, see James R. Warren, "A Century of Business," *Puget Sound Business Journal*, 17 September 1999; and Richard C. Berner, *Seattle, 1900–1920: From Boomtown, Urban Turbulence, to Restoration* (Seattle: Charles Press, 1991). For the origins of Ballast Island, see J. Willis Sayre, *This City of Ours* (Seattle: Seattle School District, 1936), 69.

2. Manuscript of the twelfth census of the United States, NARA.

3. Viola Garfield, *Seattle's Totem Poles* (Bellevue, WA: Thistle Press, 1996), 9–31; undated handbill (probably 1900s) by Lowman and Hanford Co., MSCUA.

4. "Hop Pickers," *Seattle Daily Intelligencer*, 27 August 1878.

5. Larson and Lewarch, *Archaeology of West Point*, 10–12.

6. Costello, *Siwash*, 120; Abbie Denny-Lindsley, "When Seattle Was an Indian Camp, Forty-five Years Ago," *Seattle P-I*, 15 April 1906; Robert Galois, with Jay Powell and Gloria Cranmer Webster, *Kwakwaka'wakw Settlements, 1750–1920: A Geographical Gazetteer* (Vancouver: University of British Columbia Press, 1994), 55; "The Northern Indians," *Olympia Pioneer and Democrat*, 17 October 1856; and "Indian Difficulty on the Reserve," *Olympia Pioneer and Democrat*, 12 December 1856. See also Mike Vouri, "Raiders from the North: The Northern Indians and Northwest Washington in the 1850s," *Columbia* 11, no. 3 (1997): 24–35; and Lutz, "Inventing an Indian War."

7. For British Columbia Indians' participation in the hops industry, see John Lutz, "Work, Sex, and Death on the Great Thoroughfare: Annual Migrations of 'Canadian Indians' to the American Pacific Northwest," in *Parallel Destinies: Canadian-American Relations West of the Rockies*, ed. John M. Findlay and Ken Coates (Toronto: McGill-Queen's University Press, 2002), 80–103. For an excellent analysis of these migrations and their implications for Native identities (and perceptions of those identities), see Paige Raibmon, *Authentic Indians: Episodes of Encounter from the Late-Nineteenth-Century Northwest Coast* (Durham, NC: Duke University Press, 2005).

8. "Hop Pickers," *Seattle Daily Intelligencer*, 30 August 1879; *Seattle Daily Intelligencer*, 16 October 1876; and "Hop Picking," *Seattle Daily Intelligencer*, 4 September 1878.

9. Norman Kenny Luxton, *Tilikum: Luxton's Pacific Crossing* (Sidney, BC: Gray's Publishing, 1971), 40; Jacobs, *Memoirs*, 161; Ruth Kirk, *Tradition and Change on the Northwest Coast: The Makah, Nuu-chah-nulth, Southern Kwakiutl, and Nuxalk* (Seattle: University of Washington Press, 1986), 117.

10. *Annual Report of 1891*, 169, Department of Indian Affairs, BCA; Charles Nowell and Clellan J. Ford, *Smoke from Their Fires: The Life of a Kwakiutl Chief* (Hamden, CT: Archon Books, 1941), 132–33; *Annual Report of 1906*, 255, Depart-

ment of Indian Affairs, BCA; and *Annual Report of 1887*, 105, Department of Indian Affairs, BCA.

11. King County Death Records, Puget Sound Branch, Washington State Archives, Bellevue; *Annual Report of 1888*, 103, 114, Department of Indian Affairs, BCA; and *Annual Report of 1891*, 118, Department of Indian Affairs, BCA.

12. Nora Marks Dauenhauer, Haa Kusteyí, *Our Culture: Tlingit Life Stories* (Seattle: University of Washington Press, 1994), 13, 289–95; Thomas Fox Thornton, "Place and Being among the Tlingit" (Ph.D. diss., University of Washington, 1995); and Walter R. Goldschmidt, Haa Aaní, *Our Land: Tlingit and Haida Land Rights and Use* (Seattle: University of Washington Press, 1998).

13. Undated letter (1887?) from Daniel Quedessa to Kenneth G. Smith, Kenneth G. Smith Papers, MSCUA; *Annual Report of 1884*, 100, Department of Indian Affairs, BCA; *Annual Report of 1891*, xxxi, Department of Indian Affairs, BCA.

14. Arthur Wellington Clah, Diary, 1859–1909, entry for 31 August 1899, National Archives of Canada, Ottawa; Philip Drucker, *The Northern and Central Nootkan Tribes*, Bureau of American Ethnology Bulletin 144 (Washington: Smithsonian Institution, 1951), 13–14.

15. Charles Moser, *Reminiscences of the West Coast of Vancouver Island* (Victoria: Acme Press, 1926), 143; Colonel John W. Foulkes, "Jesus Will Save an Irishman," in *American Life Histories: Manuscripts from the Federal Writers' Project, 1936–1940* (Washington: Library of Congress, 1998); Elizabeth Colson, *The Makah Indians: A Study of an Indian Tribe in Modern American Society* (Minneapolis: University of Minnesota Press, 1953), 159–67; and Daniel Quedessa to Kenneth G. Smith, 1 November 1915, Kenneth G. Smith Papers, MSCUA.

16. Warren Snyder, *Southern Puget Sound Salish*, 107; interview with Art Williams by Lynn Larson, 3 May 1994, Alki/Transfer CSO Facilities Project Traditional Cultural Properties, MIT.

17. Garfield, *Seattle's Totem Poles*, 9. For the role of totem and mortuary poles in traditional Tlingit society, see George Thornton Emmons and Frederica de Laguna, *The Tlingit Indians* (Seattle: University of Washington Press, 1991), 193–96.

18. There have been many accounts—often differing—of this event. For a balanced synthesis of the various versions, see Garfield, *Seattle's Totem Poles*.

19. William J. Lampton, "The Totem Pole," *Seattle P-I*, 3 September 1899.

20. Thomas Prosch, *Chronological History*, 205–6; and Ted C. Hinckley, *The Americanization of Alaska, 1867–1897* (Palo Alto, CA: Pacific Books, 1972). See also Kathryn Morse, *The Nature of Gold: An Environmental History of the Klondike Gold Rush* (Seattle: University of Washington Press, 2003).

21. Douglas Cole, *Captured Heritage: The Scramble for Northwest Coast Artifacts* (Seattle: University of Washington Press, 1985); Ted C. Hinckley, "The Inside Passage: A Popular Gilded Age Tour," *Pacific Northwest Quarterly* 56, no. 2 (1965): 67–74; *Alaska: "Our Frontier Wonderland"* (Seattle: Alaska Bureau, Seattle Chamber of

Commerce, 1915); John Muir, *Travels in Alaska* (New York: Houghton Mifflin, 1915), 276; and Kate C. Duncan, *1001 Curious Things: Ye Olde Curiosity Shop and Native American Art* (Seattle: University of Washington Press, 2000), 175–81. See also Raibmon, *Authentic Indians,* for discussion of the "curio" trade.

22. John R. Swanton, "Explanation of the Seattle Totem Pole," *Journal of American Folklore* 11 (1905): 108–10; postcard from C. H. Ober to Myra H. Ober, dated 10 January 1901, Postcard Collection, MSCUA; and Agnes Lockhart Hughes, "Totem Poles," *Seattle Patriarch,* 16 November 1907. For examples of urban imperial identities from the European context, see Felix Driver and David Gilbert, eds., *Imperial Cities: Landscape, Display, and Identity* (Manchester: Manchester University Press, 1999).

23. This story has been recounted a number of times in various local books and newspapers. See, e.g., E. G. Blaine, "The Famous Totem Pole of Seattle: How It Was Procured, and the Fun It Caused," *Northwest Magazine* 20, no. 6 (1902): 1–2; and Eleanor Shaw, "The Case of the 'Stolen' Totem," *Seattle P-I,* 15 February 1974.

24. *A.-Y.-P. News,* 7 July 1906; "A.-Y.-P. Vividly Portrays the Redman," *Seattle Times,* 29 August 1909; "E. S. Curtis Here to Handle Exhibit," *Seattle Times,* 28 May 1909; and "Five-Foot Board Hewn by an Indian to Be Exhibited," *Seattle P-I,* 2 May 1909.

25. "Space Is Needed on Pay Streak," *Seattle P-I,* 21 March 1909; "Eskimos Come Out to Exhibit at 1909 Fair," *Seattle P-I,* 19 September 1908; "Columbia, Eskimo Belle, Will Hold Receptions," *Seattle Times,* 29 August 1909; "Eskimo Colony for the AYP to Catch Fish in Hood Canal All Winter," *Seattle Times,* 4 October 1908; "Shows Stages of Indians' Progress," *Seattle P-I,* 24 August 1909; and "Two Performers with Cheyenne Bill's Show," *Seattle Times,* 14 July 1909. For the racial and imperial narratives of world's fairs, see Robert W. Rydell, *All the World's a Fair: Visions of Empire at American International Expositions, 1876–1916* (Chicago: University of Chicago Press, 1984).

26. "Eskimo Deserts Reindeer at Fair," *Seattle Times,* 13 June 1909; L. G. Moses, *Wild West Shows and the Images of American Indians* (Albuquerque: University of New Mexico Press, 1996); "Miss Columbia Wins Contest," *Seattle P-I,* 19 August 1909; and "Three Famous Brothers in Alaska Indian Tribe," *Seattle Times,* 10 October 1909.

27. "Neah Bay Indians Seek Whale Contract," *Seattle Times,* 1 August 1909; "Johns Challenges Taholah," *Seattle Times,* 18 April 1909; "A.-Y.-P. Vividly Portrays the Redman," *Seattle Times,* 29 August 1909; and Harmon, *Indians in the Making,* 152.

28. Peter Murray, *The Devil and Mr. Duncan* (Victoria: Sono Nis Press, 1985); Michael E. Jarboe, "Education in the New Metlakatla, Alaska Mission Settlement" (Ph.D. diss., University of Washington, 1983); John A. Dunn and Arnold Booth,

"Tsimshian of Metlakatla, Alaska," in Suttles, ed., *Handbook of North American Indians*, 294–97; Jean Usher, *William Duncan of Metlakatla: A Victorian Missionary in British Columbia* (Ottawa: National Museum of Canada, 1974); "Alaska Women Prepare Exhibit," *Seattle P-I*, 13 May 1909; "Red Men's Band to Play at Fair," *Seattle P-I*, 6 September 1909; and Jay Miller and Carol M. Eastman, *The Tsimshian and Their Neighbors of the North Pacific Coast* (Seattle: University of Washington Press, 1984).

29. "Red Men Revel in Real Races," *Seattle Times*, 7 September 1909; "Painted Warriors at Fair," *Seattle Times*, 16 July 1909; and "Sioux Greets Red Brother at AYPE," *Seattle Star*, 16 July 1909.

30. "Indian Life on Seattle Streets," *Seattle P-I*, 10 December 1905; Nina Alberta Arndt, "Seeing Seattle: The Metropolis of the Great Northwest," *Overland Monthly*, 2d ser., 52 (1908): 68; "Indians Returning from Hop Fields," *Seattle P-I*, 1 October 1906; and *Annual Report for 1906*, 255, Department of Indian Affairs, BCA.

31. "Indian Life on Seattle Streets," *Seattle P-I*, 10 December 1905.

32. "Indian Baskets, Rare Works of Art by Aborigines of Washington and Alaska," *Seattle P-I*, 22 July 1900; Robert C. Nesbit, *"He Built Seattle": A Biography of Judge Thomas Burke* (Seattle: University of Washington Press, 1961), 407; and Helen Elizabeth Vogt, *Charlie Frye and His Times* (Seattle: Peanut Butter Publishing, 1997), 71. See also Ruth B. Phillips, *Trading Identities: The Souvenir in Native North American Art, 1700–1900* (Seattle: University of Washington Press, 1998); and Shepard Krech III and Barbara A. Hail, eds., *Collecting Native America, 1870–1960* (Washington: Smithsonian Institution Press, 1999).

33. Edward Sapir, *Nootka Texts* (Philadelphia: Linguistic Society of America, 1939); J. V. Powell, *Quileute Dictionary* (Moscow: University of Idaho, 1976); Timothy Montler, "Saanich, North Straits Salish" (M.A. thesis, University of Victoria, 1968); David M. Grubb, *A Practical Writing System and Short Dictionary of Kwakw'ala* (Ottawa: National Museum of Canada, 1977); and Gillian L. Story, *Tlingit Verb Dictionary* (Fairbanks: University of Alaska Native Language Center, 1973).

7 / The Changers, Changed

1. For an overview of the life of Seeathl, see Furtwangler, *Answering Chief Seattle*. For a highly melodramatic account of his funeral, see C. M. Scammon, "Old Seattle and His Tribe," *Overland Monthly* 4, no. 4 (April 1870): 297–302.

2. "To Honor Memory of Old Chief Seattle," *Seattle Times*, 25 August 1911; "Service at Grave of Seattle Prove [*sic*] Most Enthusiastic," *Seattle Times*, 27 August 1911; "Fund Started in Memory of Chief Seattle," *Seattle P-I*, 26 January 1938; and "Chief Seattle Memorial," *Seattle P-I*, 25 May 1938.

3. Edmond S. Meany, "At Chief Seattle's Grave," printed in University of Washington *Daily* for Junior Day, 12 May 1911, Chief Seattle pamphlet file, MSCUA.

4. Florence Reynolds, *Chief Seattle: The Rugged Old Indian after Whom the Metropolis of the Northwest Was Named* (n.p., 1922), Chief Seattle pamphlet file, MSCUA; T. M. Crepar, *Legend of Seattle and Suquamish* (Seattle: Grettner-Diers Printing Co., 1928), Chief Seattle pamphlet file, MSCUA.

5. "Hyas Tyee Comes to Reign over Carnival Crowds of Seattle," *Seattle Times*, 17 July 1912.

6. "Potlatch President Greeting Hyas Tyee," *Seattle Times*, 18 July 1912; "Hyas Tyee Comes to Reign over Carnival Crowds of Seattle," *Seattle Times*, 17 July 1912; and "Riches and Glory of North Shown in Great Parade," *Seattle P-I*, 18 July 1912.

7. Stephen V. Ward, *Selling Places: The Marketing and Promotion of Towns and Cities, 1850–2000* (London: Routledge, 1998), esp. 9–28; Potlatch brochure, 1912, Edmond S. Meany Papers, box 20, folder 7, MSCUA.

8. Kathleen Mooney, "Social Distance and Exchange: The Coast Salish Case," *Ethnology* 15, no. 4 (1976): 323–46; Jay Miller, *Lushootseed Culture*, 27; Waterman, *Notes on the Ethnology of the Indians of Puget Sound*, 76–78; and Shelton, *Gram Ruth Sehome Shelton*, 1–5.

9. Douglas Cole and Ira Chaikin, *An Iron Hand upon the People: The Law against the Potlatch on the Northwest Coast* (Toronto: Douglas and McIntyre, 1990); Christopher Bracken, *The Potlatch Papers: A Colonial Case History* (Chicago: University of Chicago Press, 1997).

10. "Portland Heralded Golden Age of City," *Seattle Times*, 19 July 1911; Potlatch brochure, 1912; Puget Sound Traction, Light, and Power Company advertisement, *Seattle P-I*, 20 July 1912; "Chinook Chorus High Honor to Tyee," *Seattle Times*, 20 July 1912; "Liner Potlatch to be Launched Tomorrow," *Seattle Times*, 17 July 1912; "Tomorrow's Potlatch Program," *Seattle Times*, 16 July 1912; and "Tyee, Plain Citizen Again, Regrets Swift Passing of His Reign," *Seattle Times*, 21 July 1912.

11. Cheasty's Haberdashery advertisement, *Seattle P-I*, 15 July 1912; "Tilikums and Alaska Day Pageant," *Seattle Times*, 17 July 1912; "War Canoe and Its Crew Score Big Hit," *Seattle Times*, 18 July 1912; and "Personnel of the Tilikums," *Seattle Times*, 21 July 1912.

12. "Ikht Tribe Wins Tilikums' Fight for Membership," *Seattle P-I*, 28 May 1913; postcard dated 27 March 1917, Postcard Collection, MSCUA. For other groups whose rituals involved impersonating Native people, see Philip J. Deloria, *Playing Indian* (New Haven: Yale University Press, 1998).

13. "Potlatch President Greeting Hyas Tyee," *Seattle Times*, 18 July 1912; "Hyas Tyee Comes to Reign over Carnival Crowds of Seattle," *Seattle Times*, 17 July 1912; and "Riches and Glory of North Shown in Great Parade," *Seattle P-I*, 18 July 1912.

14. "I.W.W. Denounced by Head of Navy, Attack Soldiers and Sailors," *Seattle Times*, 18 July 1913; "Three Soldiers Assaulted by Mob, Saved by Police," *Seattle P-I*,

18 July 1913; "Anarchy in Seattle Stamped Out When Sailors Get Busy," *Seattle Times*, 19 July 1913; "1914 Potlatch Starts with Key Ceremony," *Seattle Times*, 15 July 1914; and "Tilikums, New, Old, to Discuss Potlatch Plans," *Seattle Times*, 19 August 1934.

15. "Descendants of Pioneers Celebrate," *Seattle P-I*, 13 November 1938.

16. Thomas Prosch, *Chronological History*, 214; "Roll of Pioneers," *Seattle Times* or *P-I*, undated clipping (but likely 1893), Clarence B. Bagley Scrapbooks, vol. 1, 143, MSCUA.

17. Arthur Denny, *Pioneer Days on Puget Sound*, 3, 76–77; Denny narrative, Bancroft Collection; and "The City's Birthday," *Seattle P-I*, 13 May 1893.

18. Major J. Thomas Turner, "Reminiscences, 7 September 1914," MOHAI MS Collection, folder 106; Charles A. Kinnear, "Arrival of the George Kinnear Family on Puget Sound, and Early Recollections by C. A. Kinnear, One of the Children," n.d., MOHAI MS Collection; and Redfield, *Seattle Memories*, frontispiece.

19. Henry's poems can be found in Charles Prosch, *Reminiscences*, 126–28.

20. "The Pioneers," *Seattle Patriarch*, 7 June 1913; David M. Wrobel, *Promised Lands: Promotion, Memory, and the Creation of the American West* (Lawrence: University Press of Kansas, 2002).

21. Emily Denny, *Blazing the Way*, 114–15, 141–42; Emily Inez Denny, "Chapter 13—Miss Denny's Chapter," n.d., MOHAI MS Collection, folder 271.

22. Bass, *Pigtail Days in Old Seattle*, 46, 84; Bass, *When Seattle Was a Village*, 117–18; and Watt, *Four Wagons West*, 377.

23. Emily Denny, *Blazing the Way*, 381. This kind of analysis of local pioneer-newcomer conflicts was first explored by Alexandra Harmon in *Indians in the Making*, esp. 145–47.

24. For an overview of Meany's life and work, see George A. Frykman, *Seattle's Historian and Promoter: The Life of Edmond Stephen Meany* (Pullman: Washington State University Press, 1998). For examples of Meany's documentation of local Indians, see "The Last Lake Union Indians," *Seattle Times*, 11 June 1898; and "The Story of Seattle's Nearest Indian Neighbors," *Seattle P-I*, 29 October 1905. For numerous examples of his participation in high school pageants, Potlatches, the AYPE, and "Indian" naming, see Meany's extensive correspondence files in his collected papers at the University of Washington.

25. "Address by Judge C. H. Hanford on the occasion of unveiling historical tablet at the foot of Cherry St., Seattle, November 13 1905," MOHAI MS Collection, folder 298; Hanford, *Seattle and Environs*, 23.

26. David Kellogg to Vivian Carkeek, ca. 1912, MOHAI MS Collection, folder 116; "75 Candles on Cake Will Tell Seattle's Age," *Seattle P-I*, 13 November 1926; and David Kellogg, "The Making of a Medicine Man," 20 May 1912, MOHAI MS Collection, folder 116.

27. Abbie Denny-Lindsley, "When Seattle Was an Indian Camp Forty-five Years Ago," *Seattle P-I*, 15 April 1906; W. T. Dovell, "The Pathfinders," *Washington*

Historical Quarterly 1, no. 1 (1906): 47; and "Pioneers Honor City's Founders at West Seattle," *Seattle Times*, 16 November 1938.

28. For discussion of these powerful cultural dynamics, see David M. Wrobel, *The End of American Exceptionalism: Frontier Anxiety from the Old West to the New Deal* (Lawrence: University Press of Kansas, 1993); and Michael Kammen, *Mystic Chords of Memory: The Transformation of Tradition in American Culture* (New York: Knopf, 1991).

29. "Indians in Canoes Beaten by Whites," *Seattle P-I*, 22 July 1911; "Chief Seattle to Be Honored," *Seattle Times*, 12 November 1936; and "Pioneers Honor City's Founders at West Seattle," *Seattle Times*, 16 November 1938.

30. For examples of Native participation in Chief Seattle Days, see "To Honor Memory of Old Chief Seattle," *Seattle Times*, 25 August 1911; "Service at Grave of Chief Seattle Prove [*sic*] Most Enthusiastic," *Seattle Times*, 27 August 1911; and "Palefaces in Yearly Homage at Grave of Chief Seattle," *Seattle Times*, 2 August 1935. For one example of alternative historical consciousness from the South— the story of a slave rebellion—see James Sidbury, *Ploughshares into Swords: Race, Rebellion, and Identity in Gabriel's Virginia, 1730–1810* (Cambridge: Cambridge University Press, 1997). For speculations on the "intimate remembrances" of Seeathl in local Indian communities, see Bierwert, "Remembering Chief Seattle."

31. Shelton, *Gram Ruth Sehome Shelton*, 66.

32. Harriet Shelton Williams, "Indian Potlatch," *Seattle P-I*, 10 August 1939.

8 / On the Cusp of Past and Future

1. Marian W. Smith, ed., *Indians of the Urban Northwest* (New York: Columbia University Press, 1949), viii, 4.

2. Ibid., 6.

3. Richard C. Berner, *Seattle, 1921–1940: From Boom to Bust* (Seattle: Charles Press, 1992); Rolf Knight, *Indians at Work: An Informal History of Native Indian Labour in British Columbia, 1858–1930* (Vancouver: New Star Books, 1978); and Dauenhauer, Haa Kusteyí, *Our Culture*, 691–95.

4. Except where noted otherwise, data in this chapter come from the manuscript of the fifteenth census of the United States, NARA.

5. Lynn Moen, ed., *Voices of Ballard: Immigrant Stories from the Vanishing Generation* (Seattle: Nordic Heritage Museum, 2001), 163–65, 174–79.

6. Richard Hugo, *The Real West Marginal Way: A Poet's Autobiography*, ed. Ripley S. Hugo, Lois M. Welch, and James Welch (New York: W. W. Norton, 1986), 8, 11; and Donald Francis Roy, "Hooverville: A Study of a Community of Homeless Men in Seattle" (M.A. thesis, University of Washington, 1935), 12, 25, 83.

7. *Polk's Seattle (Washington) City Directory*, vol. 44 (Seattle: R. L. Polk and Co., 1930), 823; Colson, *Makah Indians*, 168.

8. Interview with Diane Vendiola by Will Sarvis, 10 September 2001, Anacortes Museum; Bob Santos, *Humbows, Not Hot Dogs! Memoirs of a Savvy Asian American Activist* (Seattle: International Examiner Press, 2002), 35. For Seattle's Filipino history, see Dorothy Fujita-Rony, *American Workers, Colonial Power: Philippine Seattle and the Transpacific West, 1919–1941* (Berkeley and Los Angeles: University of California Press, 2003).

9. Totem poles and other forms of Northwest Coast art marking the approaches to the city are described in James M. Rupp and Mary Randlett, *Art in Seattle's Public Places: An Illustrated Guide* (Seattle: University of Washington Press, 1992), 162, 255. See also "City Totem Pole Gone to Happy Hunting Ground," *Seattle Times*, 2 May 1966. Numerous photographs of the Totem Pole Motel and other examples of "Indian" roadside art on the Pacific Highway can be found in the collection of the Museum of History and Industry.

10. "On with the New," *Seattle Argus*, 22 July 1939; *Seattle Argus*, 12 November 1938; "Heap Big Fuss; Use Store-Bought Paint on Totem Pole, Quit Talking, Say Indians," *Seattle Daily Times*, 21 July 1938; "At Long Last! Indians to Get Famed Totem," *Seattle P-I*, 9 December 1939; Aldona Jonaitis, "Totem Poles and the Indian New Deal," *Canadian Journal of Native Studies* 2 (1989): 237–52; and "Replica of Famous Old Landmark Arrives Safely from Alaska," *Seattle P-I*, 18 April 1940.

11. Bryden Turner, "105, and History Lives for Jimmy John," *Nanaimo (BC) Times*, 7 May 1981; Shirl Ramsay, "A Visit with Jimmy John: Master Carver," *Victoria (BC) Daily Colonist*, 1 July 1979; Reg Ashwell, "Captain Jack's Inside House-Posts," *Victoria (BC) Daily Colonist*, 12 August 1974; Gregory Roberts, "A Crisp Assessment of Fish and Chips," *Seattle P-I*, 29 May 1998; and Hilary Stewart, *Looking at Totem Poles* (Vancouver: Douglas and McIntyre, 1993), 117.

12. For the accounts of "old-timers," see Ross Anderson, "Gritty Last Stand of 'Old Seattle': The 1930s," *Seattle Times*, 29 July 2001. For one historian's perspective on the 1930s, and an explanation of the nostalgia they engender, see Sale, *Seattle, Past to Present*, 136–44.

13. John Dos Passos, *The 42nd Parallel* (New York: Harper and Brothers Publishers, 1930), 75.

9 / Urban Renewal in Indian Territory

1. Richard Simmons, "Indians Invade Fort Lawton," *Seattle P-I*, 9 March 1970; "Army Disrupts Indian Claim on Fort Lawton," *Seattle P-I*, 9 March 1970; and

"Indian 'Attack' on Fort Lawton Fascinates World Press," *Seattle Times*, 9 March 1970.

2. Richard C. Berner, *Seattle Transformed: World War II to Cold War* (Seattle: Charles Press, 1999), 44–47. A 1947 poem protesting the plane's name can be found in John M. Rich, *Chief Seattle's Unanswered Challenge: Spoken on the Wild Forest Threshold of the City That Bears His Name, 1854* (Seattle: Lowman and Hanford, 1947), 51–53. For the effects of wartime mobilization on the West more broadly, see Gerald D. Nash, *American West Transformed: The Impact of the Second World War* (Lincoln: University of Nebraska Press, 1990).

3. Lewis Kamb, "Adeline Skultka Garcia, 1923–2004: Activist Changed Life for Urban Indians," *Seattle P-I*, 28 February 2004. For discussions of Indians in the Second World War, see Alison R. Bernstein, *American Indians and World War II: Toward a New Era in Indian Affairs* (Norman: University of Oklahoma Press, 1991); Jere Bishop Franco, *Crossing the Pond: The Native American Effort in World War II* (Denton: University of North Texas Press, 1999); and Kenneth William Townsend, *World War II and the American Indian* (Albuquerque: University of New Mexico Press, 2000).

4. Bahr, Chadwick, and Stauss, "Discrimination against Urban Indians in Seattle"; interview with Marilyn Bentz by Teresa BrownWolf Powers, n.d. (2000), videotape, American Indian Studies Center Library, University of Washington.

5. Morgan, *Skid Road*, 9; Cathy Duchamp, "The Urban Indian Experience," KUOW National Public Radio, 13 January 2004, transcripts at www.kuow.org; Skid Road Study Committee, *Report* (Seattle: Council of Planning Affiliates, 1969), not paginated.

6. Karen Tranberg Hansen, "American Indians and Work in Seattle: Associations, Ethnicity, and Class" (Ph.D. diss., University of Washington, 1979), 93–98; interview with Adeline Garcia by Teresa BrownWolf Powers, 24 May 2000, videotape, American Indian Studies Center Library, University of Washington; interview with Lillian Chapelle by Teresa BrownWolf Powers, n.d. (2000), videotape, American Indian Studies Center Library, University of Washington.

7. "Indian Women's Organization Grows," *Northwest Indian News*, February 1959; *Indian Center News*, 21 February 1962.

8. Gail Paul, "Dream of Permanent Home Inspires Summer Activity at 'Indian Center,'" *Indian Center News*, 8 September 1962; interview with Mary Jo Butterfield by Teresa BrownWolf Powers, 11 May 2001, videotape, American Indian Studies Center Library, University of Washington.

9. *Indian Center News*, March 1971; interview with Adeline Garcia; and interview with Mary Jo Butterfield.

10. Ramona Bennett lecture, 6 December 2000, videotape, American Indian Studies Center Library, University of Washington; "North American Indian Benefit Ball," *Indian Center News*, 7 April 1961; "Indian Center Picnic," *Indian*

Center News, 16 September 1961; "Indians Perform for Audubon Society," *Indian Center News*, February 1967; and "Successful Seventh Annual Salmon Bake," *Indian Center News*, September 1967.

11. "Pearl Warren Discusses Urban Indian Problems before Senate Subcommittee," *Indian Center News*, January 1968; "National Indian Urban Consultation Organizes in Seattle," *Indian Center News*, February 1968; interview with Letoy Eike by Teresa BrownWolf Powers, 29 August 2000, videotape, American Indian Studies Center Library, University of Washington; Maxine Cushing Gray, "Buck-Passing on Longhouse Led to Ft. Lawton Affair," *Seattle Argus*, 13 March 1970; and Rupp and Randlett, *Art in Seattle's Public Places*, 161.

12. Santos, *Humbows, Not Hot Dogs!* 35, 56–60; and "A Brief History of the United Indians of All Tribes Foundation," Pamphlet Files, MSCUA.

13. See Paul Chaat Smith and Robert Warrior, *Like a Hurricane: The Indian Movement from Alcatraz to Wounded Knee* (New York: New Press, 1996); Adam Fortunate Eagle, *Heart of the Rock: The Indian Invasion of Alcatraz* (Norman: University of Oklahoma Press, 2002); and Stephen E. Cornell, *The Return of the Native: American Indian Political Resurgence* (New York: Oxford University Press, 1988).

14. Don Hannula, "Indian Picket Line Remains at Ft. Lawton," *Seattle Times*, 11 March 1970; Jerry Bergman, "Indians Begin 2nd Week of Picketing," *Seattle Times*, 17 March 1970; Richard Simmons, "MP's Arrest 77 Indians at Lawton," *Seattle P-I*, 16 March 1970; Don Hannula, "Indians Again Try to Occupy Fort Lawton; 80 Detained," *Seattle Times*, 2 April 1970; Don Hannula, "Message from Sky: 'Fort, Give Up,'" *Seattle Times*, 19 March 1970; Derek Creisler, *Princess of the Powwow* (Seattle: Running Colors Productions, 1987); and "United Indians of All Tribes Use Invasion of Fort Lawton in Effort to Get Support for All-Indian Multiservice and Educational Center," *Indian Center News*, April 1970.

15. Bahr, Chadwick, and Stauss, "Discrimination against Urban Indians in Seattle," 6; Don Hannula, "Indian Picket Line Remains at Ft. Lawton," *Seattle Times*, 11 March 1970; "Indians Seek Immediate Use of 16 Ft. Lawton Buildings," *Seattle Times*, 14 March 1970; "Indians Want Nixon Powwow," *Seattle Times*, 16 March 1970; "A Brief History of the United Indians of All Tribes Foundation," Pamphlet Files, MSCUA; "Seattle Human Rights Commission Says Claim of Indians Must Not Be Ignored," *Seattle Medium*, 12 November 1970; "City, Indians Agree on Lawton Lease Plan," *Seattle Times*, 15 November 1971; Hilda Bryant, "A Proud Day for the Indians—Big Cultural Arts Center Opens Here," *Seattle P-I*, 12 May 1977; Brenda Dunn, "The Indian Arts Center That Nobody Thought Would Happen," *Seattle Weekly*, 18 May 1977; and interview with Arlene Red Elk by Teresa BrownWolf Powers, 18 May 2000, videotape, American Indian Studies Center Library, University of Washington.

16. Guy Monthan and Doris Monthan, "Daybreak Star Center," *American Indian Art* 3, no. 3 (Summer 1978): 28–34.

17. Santos, *Humbows, Not Hot Dogs!* 64–67; interview with Diane Vendiola by Will Sarvis, 10 September 2001, Anacortes Museum; interview with Marilyn Bentz; and *Indian Center News*, March 1971. For similar tensions elsewhere, see Smith and Warrior, *Like a Hurricane;* and Loretta Fowler, *Shared Symbols, Contested Meanings: Gros Ventre Culture and History, 1778–1984* (Ithaca: Cornell University Press, 1987).

18. Lewis Kamb, "Adeline Skultka Garcia, 1923–2004: Activist Changed Life for Urban Indians," *Seattle P-I*, 28 February 2004; and Jacqueline R. Swanson, "American Indian Women's Service League: The Role of Indian and Alaska Native Women in Establishing Seattle's Contemporary Indian Community," unpublished research paper in author's possession.

19. Diane Shamash, ed., *In Public: Seattle, 1991* (Seattle: Seattle Arts Commission, 1991), 40.

20. Regina Hackett, "Heap of Birds' 'In Public' Work Is Set Up," *Seattle P-I*, 15 May 1991; Laurie Olin, *Breath on the Mirror: Seattle's Skid Road Community* (n.p., 1972), 33.

21. Frank J. Clancy, *Doctor Come Quickly* (Seattle: Superior Publishing, 1950), 108; Morgan, *Skid Road*, 9; Jeffrey Lewis Dann, "A Study of an Indian Tavern on Skid Road" (M.A. thesis, University of Washington, 1967), 41, 44, 55; and interview with Bill Regan by Coll Thrush and Dana Cox, 6 December 1998, Oral History Collection, Northwest Lesbian and Gay History Museum Project Archives, Seattle. For other communities of Pioneer Square and Skid Road, see Paul De Barros, *Jackson Street After Hours: The Roots of Jazz in Seattle* (Seattle: Sasquatch Books, 1993); Don Paulson, with Roger Simpson, *An Evening at the Garden of Allah: A Gay Cabaret in Seattle* (New York: Columbia University Press, 1996); and Ron Chew, ed., *Reflections of Seattle's Chinese Americans: The First 100 Years* (Seattle: University of Washington Press, 1994).

22. Morgan, *Skid Road*, 9; Dann, "Study of an Indian Tavern," 5, 24, 27, 36–37, 43–66, 75–84, 129; Jackie Swanson, personal communication.

23. Morgan, *Skid Road*, 9; Dann, "Study of an Indian Tavern," 5, 24, 27, 36–37, 43–66, 75–84, 129; John Graham and Company, *Pioneer Square Redevelopment* (Seattle: n.p., 1966); "Skid Road Shelter Program Quietly Ends," *Seattle Times*, 1 April 1976; and Olin, *Breath on the Mirror*, 14.

24. John Graham and Company, *Pioneer Square Redevelopment*. See also Sohyun Park Lee, "From Redevelopment to Preservation: Downtown Planning in Post-war Seattle" (Ph.D. diss., University of Washington, 2001).

25. "More Police Promised for Pioneer Square Area," *Seattle Times*, 12 June 1969; James P. Spradley, *You Owe Yourself a Drunk: An Ethnography of Urban Nomads* (Boston: Little, Brown and Co., 1970), 142; John Graham and Company, *Pioneer Square Redevelopment*; "Seattle's Success Story Recycling Skid Row," *Phoenix Gazette*, 14 June 1978; and David Hamer, *History in Urban Places: The*

Historic Districts of the United States (Columbus: Ohio State University Press, 1998), 94.

26. The ordinances in question are nos. 98552, 98868, 102901, and 103655. Joseph P. Churchill, "Skid Row in Transition" (M.A. thesis, University of Washington, 1976), 19–22; Skid Road Study Committee, *Report*; Skid Road Community Council, *Changes in Downtown Seattle: 1960–1974* (Seattle: Skid Road Community Council, 1974), 1; and "Skid Road Shelter Program Quietly Ends," *Seattle Times,* 1 April 1976. For background on SRO hotels, see Charles Hoch and Robert A. Slayton, *New Homeless and Old: Community and the Skid Row Hotel* (Philadelphia: Temple University Press, 1989); and Paul Groth, *Living Downtown: The History of Residential Hotels in the United States* (Berkeley and Los Angeles: University of California Press, 1994). For the politics of Seattle's downtown streets, see Timothy A. Gibson, *Securing the Spectacular City: The Politics of Revitalization and Homelessness in Downtown Seattle* (Lanham, MD: Lexington Books, 2004).

27. Skid Road Study Committee, *Report*; Rupp and Randlett, *Art in Seattle's Public Places,* 5, 23, 296; and Nard Jones, *Seattle* (Garden City, NY: Doubleday, 1972), 266.

28. J. A. Correa, "The City," *Northwest Indian News,* February/March 1972; Olin, *Breath on the Mirror,* 28, 32; and Earle Thompson, "Injun Blues," *Seattle Real Change,* February 1999.

29. David Horsey, "Is It Really Art?" *Seattle P-I,* 28 July 1991; Ben Jacklet, "A Hard Life: A Week in the Life of Some of Seattle's Urban Indians," *Seattle Stranger,* 9 October 1997.

30. Interview with Marilyn Bentz.

31. Cathy Duchamp, "The Urban Indian Experience," KUOW National Public Radio, 13 January 2004, transcripts at www.kuow.org.

32. "Equality in Seattle Is Indians' Message," *Seattle P-I,* 12 March 1970; Brenda Dunn, "The Indian Arts Center That Nobody Thought Would Happen," *Seattle Weekly,* 18 May 1977; David A. Fahrenthold, "People's Lodge Draws Foes," *Seattle Times,* 13 July 1998; and James Bush, "Edifice Complex," *Seattle Weekly,* 29 January 1999, 15.

33. Bernie Whitebear, "My Brother the Eagle Knows the Truth," *Seattle Times,* 19 November 1998.

10 / The Returning Hosts

1. Alki Women's Improvement Club, Centennial Revue program, Badcon Collection, MOHAI; "Original City Charter Shown," *Seattle P-I,* 13 November 1951; "Alki Landing Reenacted; Throng to See M'Arthur," *Seattle P-I,* 13 November 1951;

and William Schulze, "Landing at Alki Reenacted, and 'Capsule' Buried," *Seattle P-I*, 14 November 1951.

2. "Congratulates Seattle; Sounds Warning on Foreign Aggression," *Seattle P-I*, 14 November 1951. Ted Best recalled the impact of the national broadcast in a 1955 issue of the West Seattle Commercial Club newsletter, Badcon Collection, MOHAI. For connections between frontier mythology and Cold War ideology, see Richard Slotkin, *Gunfighter Nation: The Myth of the Frontier in Twentieth-Century America* (New York: Atheneum, 1992); and Richard Drinnon, *Facing West: The Metaphysics of Indian-Hating and Empire-Building* (Minneapolis: University of Minnesota Press, 1980).

3. Dorothy Hart, "A Look Forward," *Seattle P-I*, 11 November 1951.

4. Murray Morgan, *Century 21: The Story of the Seattle World's Fair, 1962* (Seattle: Acme Press, 1963); Don Duncan, *Meet Me at the Center* (Seattle: Seattle Center Foundation, 1992); and *Official Guide Book: Seattle World's Fair, 1962* (Seattle: Acme Publications, 1962). See also John M. Findlay, *Magic Lands: Western Cityscapes and American Culture after 1940* (Berkeley and Los Angeles: University of California Press, 1992).

5. Ernest Callenbach, *Ecotopia: The Notebooks and Reports of William Weston* (Berkeley: Banyan Tree Books, 1975).

6. See Klingle, "Urban by Nature"; and Sale, *Seattle, Past to Present*.

7. For overviews of 1970s reworkings of the speech, see Bierwert, "Remembering Chief Seattle"; and Furtwangler, *Answering Chief Seattle*.

8. Thomas Berry, *The Dream of the Earth* (San Francisco: Sierra Club Books, 1988), 173.

9. "Nine of Ten Netted: METRO Perturbed as Indians Block Salmon Spawning Run," *Seattle Times*, 20 September 1963.

10. Interview with Gilbert King George, MIT; "A Brief History of the United Indians of All Tribes Foundation," Pamphlet Files, MSCUA; interview with Bernice White by Coll Thrush and Warren King George, 25 June 2004, Green River Project, MIT; and "Informing Our Fellow Citizens," *Indian Center News*, 2 November 1965.

11. For one example, see American Friends Service Committee, *Uncommon Controversy: Fishing Rights of Muckleshoot, Puyallup, and Nisqually Indians* (Seattle: University of Washington Press, 1972). The text of the 1987 church apology can be found at the website of the Washington Association of Churches, www.thewac.org/Apology%201987.htm.

12. Lee Moriwaki, "Indian Fishermen's Worries Could Sink West Seattle Marina Project," *Seattle Times*, 20 August 1982; Brad O'Connor, "Sports-Fishing Preserve Carved Out of Elliott Bay," *Seattle P-I*, 2 October 1988; and "Protecting a Steelhead Run: Muckleshoots Set Fine Conservation Example," *Seattle Times*, 25 January 1989.

13. Richard Seven, "A Snarly Problem in Ship Canal," *Seattle Times*, 8 October 1987; Peter Lewis, "Marina Plan Gets Its Permit, but Tribes Pledge Court Fight," *Seattle Times*, 25 July 1987; Robert T. Nelson, "Permit Is Reissued for Marina," *Seattle Times*, 17 March 1988; Steve Miletich, "Tribes Win Halt to Work on Magnolia Bluff Marina," *Seattle P-I*, 2 July 1988; and Gil Bailey, "Magnolia Marina Agreement," *Seattle P-I*, 10 November 1989. For the listing of local salmon runs under the Endangered Species Act, see Klingle, "Urban by Nature." For the sea lion hunt, see M. L. Lyke, "Tribe's Sea Lion Hunt Adds to Saga," *Seattle P-I*, 30 June 1997.

14. Lewis Kamb, "Boldt Ruling's Effects Felt around the World," *Seattle P-I*, 12 February 2004; and Erik Lacitis, "We 'Have No Culture Left,'" *Seattle Times*, 17 July 1976.

15. Fred Brack, "Port Charged with 'Razing' Unique Site," *Seattle P-I*, 13 July 1976; "Artifacts to Delay Port Plan 3 Years," *Seattle Times*, 24 February 1977; Don Page, "Diggin' the Dirt along Duwamish," *Seattle P-I*, 13 March 1977; and Erik Lacitis, "No Single Culprit in Duwamish Probe," *Seattle Times*, 28 July 1976.

16. Erik Lacitis, "We 'Have No Culture Left,'" *Seattle Times*, 17 July 1976; Terry Tafoya, "Minority Voices: Indian 'Roots' Uncovered on Duwamish," *Seattle P-I*, 26 February 1977; "Uncovering Seattle's Hidden History," *Seattle P-I*, 22 February 1977; and Pablo Lopez, "Archaeologists Dug Up Artifacts That Could Help Duwamish Tribe," *Seattle P-I*, 7 June 1986.

17. Solveig Torvik, "A History at West Point," *Seattle P-I*, 8 May 1994; Dee Norton, "Artifacts Found; Trade Center Work Suspended," *Seattle Times*, 5 February 1998; Dee Norton, "Duwamish Complain of Snub over Artifacts," *Seattle Times*, 6 February 1998; Suky Hutton, "Construction Unearths Duwamish Remains," *On Indian Land*, Spring 1998; and Alex Tizon, "Work Resumes at World Trade Center Site Where Bones Were Found," *Seattle Times*, 25 February 1998.

18. Hector Castro and Mike Barber, "After Decades, Duwamish Tribe Wins Federal Recognition," *Seattle P-I*, 20 January 2001; Bernard McGhee, "Duwamish Tribe Wins Recognition," *Seattle Times*, 20 January 2001; Bureau of Indian Affairs, "BIA Issues Final Determination on the Recognition of the Duwamish Tribal Organization," news release, 19 January 2001; Sara Jean Green, "Chief Seattle's Tribe Clings to Its Identity," *Seattle Times*, 18 June 2001; and Susan Gilmore, "Duwamish Denied Tribal Status," *Seattle Times*, 29 September 2001.

19. Stuart Eskenazi, "Settling Seattle Again: Founding Families Pay Tribute to Duwamish Tribe's Support," *Seattle Times*, 14 November 2001.

20. Jerry Large, "Interpretation of History Depends on Perspective," *Seattle Times*, 18 November 2001; "Seattle Marks 150th Anniversary in Pouring Rain," www .komotv.com, 13 November 2001; Paul Shukovsky, "Ballard Locks' Creation Left Tribe High and Dry," *Seattle P-I*, 24 November 2001; and D. Parvaz, "Duwamish Share Lessons of the Water with Others: Canoe Paddle a Tribute to Harmony with White Settlers," *Seattle P-I*, 29 August 2002.

21. Pioneer Association of the State of Washington, "A Petition to Support Recognition of the Duwamish Indians as a Tribe," 18 June 1988, reprinted at www.historylink.org; Paul Shukovsky, "Tribal Fate in Hands of a Few Federal Employees," *Seattle P-I*, 24 November 2001; Stuart Eskenazi, "Reversal of Tribe's Status Blasted," *Seattle Times*, 11 January 2002; Stuart Eskenazi, "Duwamish Tribe's Recognition Hangs on a Small Technicality," *Seattle Times*, 5 March 2002; Paul Shukovsky, "Religious Leaders Back Recognition for Duwamish Tribe," *Seattle P-I*, 14 March 2002; Paul Shukovsky, "Decision Is Death Knell for Duwamish," *Seattle P-I*, 11 May 2002; Stuart Eskenazi, "Duwamish Mull Next Move," *Seattle Times*, 14 May 2002; and Paul Shukovsky, "Duwamish Will Take Their Case for Recognition to Congress," *Seattle P-I*, 9 July 2002.

22. Sara Jean Green, "Chief Seattle's Tribe Clings to Its Identity," *Seattle Times*, 18 June 2001. For additional discussion of the Duwamish case within the broader context of "nonrecognized" indigenous peoples, see Bruce Granville Miller, *Invisible Indigenes: The Politics of Nonrecognition* (Lincoln: University of Nebraska Press, 2002), 94–97.

23. *Seattle, Her Faults and Her Virtues* (ca. 1925), quoted in Carlos A. Schwantes, *The Pacific Northwest: An Interpretive History* (Lincoln: University of Nebraska Press, 1996), 1.

24. Lynda V. Mapes, "Bones Unearthed; Reburial Carries Hefty Price," *Seattle Times*, 19 October 2002.

25. Peter H. Jackson, "The Love Song of J. Timothy Eyman," *Seattle Weekly*, 31 January 2002, 24; Sherman Alexie, "Rapid Transit," *Seattle Stranger*, 14 November 2002, 17; *Seattle Weekly*, 28 May 2003; and "Life and Times of Seattle," *Seattle Times*, 16 November 2001.

26. Emmett Watson, *Digressions of a Native Son* (Seattle: Pacific Institute, 1982); Emmett Watson, *My Life in Print* (Seattle: Lesser Seattle Publishing, 1993); and Fred Moody, *Seattle and the Demons of Ambition* (New York: St. Martin's Press, 2003), 24, 91, 106, 252, 279.

27. Robert Ferrigno, "Kiss My Tan Line: How Californians Saved Seattle," www.slate.com, 1 November 1996; and Julia Sommerfeld, "Our Social Dis-Ease," *Seattle Times* magazine section, 13 February 2005.

28. Sara Jean Green, "Duwamish Site May Be Sacred, but It's Slated for Development," *Seattle Times*, 4 September 2001; and Eric Mathison, "Hill Rich in Heritage Preserved," *Highline Times*, 23 June 2004.

29. Lisa Stiffler, "Park Gives Little Salmon a Refuge," *Seattle P-I*, 4 June 2001; and Caitlin Cleary, "New Park Sprouts on Old Waste Site," *Seattle Times*, 4 June 2001.

30. Daniel K. Richter, *Facing East from Indian Country: A Native History of Early America* (Cambridge, MA: Harvard University Press, 2001), 10.

31. Ibid.

An Atlas of Indigenous Seattle

1. Waterman, "Geographical Names," 186.

2. Ibid., 178, 186.

3. Puget Sound Geography, eds. Vi Hilbert, Jay Miller, and Zalmai Zahir (Seattle: Lushootseed Press, 2001).

4. For coverage of Harrington's life and work, see the special issue of *Anthropological Linguistics* (33, no. 4, Winter 1991) devoted to his legacy. Discussion of Harrington's time in Seattle and an index to the field notes used in this atlas can found in Miles, *Papers.*

5. *Cadastral Survey Field Notes and Plats for Oregon and Washington* (Denver: U.S. Department of the Interior, Bureau of Land Management, 1982); *Duwamish et al. vs. United States,* exhibit W-2; Erna Gunther, *Ethnobotany of Western Washington: The Knowledge and Use of Indigenous Plants by Native Americans* (Seattle: University of Washington Press, 1945).

6. Waterman, "Geographical Names," 178.

7. See, e.g., Harvey Manning and Penny Manning, *Walks and Hikes on the Beaches around Puget Sound* (Seattle: The Mountaineers, 1995).

8. Thompson, "Original Residents of Shilshole Bay," 10.

9. Jay Wells, U.S. Army Corps of Engineers, personal communication.

10. Marian Smith, *Puyallup-Nisqually,* 69; Miller and Onat, *Winds, Waterways, and Weirs,* 75–82.

11. Warren Snyder, *Southern Puget Sound Salish,* 131.

12. Emily Denny, *Blazing the Way,* 137–39; Gordon R. Newell, *Westward to Alki: The Story of David and Louisa Denny* (Seattle: Superior Publishing Co., 1977), 83–84, 89–90.

13. For the full report of the excavation, see Larson and Lewarch, *Archaeology of West Point.*

14. George Vancouver, *A Voyage of Discovery to the North Pacific ocean, and round the world; in which the coast of north-west America has been carefully examined and accurately surveyed* (London: J. Stockdale, 1801), 512–13.

15. For this genre of stories, see Ballard, *Mythology of Southern Puget Sound.*

16. Arthur Denny, *Pioneer Days on Puget Sound,* 17; Mary McWilliams, *Seattle Water Department History, 1854–1954* (Seattle: Dogwood Press, 1955), 4–6.

17. Bass, *Pig-Tail Days in Old Seattle,* 37; Emily Denny, *Blazing the Way,* 9.

18. Waterman, "Geographical Names," 188.

19. Bass, *Pig-Tail Days in Old Seattle,* 152.

20. Marian Smith, *Puyallup-Nisqually,* 135.

21. Ibid., 59; Jay Miller, *Lushootseed Culture,* 11–12.

22. Marian Smith, "Petroglyph Complexes," 315.

23. *Duwamish et al. vs. United States*, 697.

24. See Sarah K. Campbell, *The Duwamish No. 1 Site: A Lower Puget Sound Shell Midden* (Seattle: University of Washington Institute for Environmental Studies, Office of Public Archaeology, 1981); and *The Duwamish No. 1 Site: 1986 Data Recovery* (Seattle: BOAS, 1987).

25. Marian Smith, *Puyallup-Nisqually*, 127; William W. Elmendorf, *The Structure of Twana Culture* (Pullman: Washington State University, 1960), 51.

26. "Duwamish Duck Marsh of Century Ago Has Developed into Seattle's 'Golden Shore,'" *Seattle Business* 33 (1949): 2.

27. Warren Snyder, *Southern Puget Sound Salish*, 131.

28. Nile Robert Thompson and C. Dale Sproat, "The Use of Oral Literature to Provide Community Health Education on the Southern Northwest Coast," *American Indian Culture and Research Journal* 28, no. 3 (2004): 15–16.

29. Interview with Florence "Dosie" Starr Wynn, Alki/Transfer CSO Facilities Project Traditional Cultural Properties, MIT.

30. Ballard, *Mythology of Southern Puget Sound*, 55–64. Detailed discussion of the many versions of this epic can be found in Miller and Onat, *Winds, Waterways, and Weirs*.

31. Ballard, *Mythology of Southern Puget Sound*, 64.

32. Ibid., 60.

33. Ibid., 121–22; interview with Ellen Bena Williams, Alki/Transfer CSO Facilities Project Traditional Cultural Properties, MIT.

34. Marian Smith, *Puyallup-Nisqually*, 68.

35. Ibid., 57, 62.

36. Waterman, *Puget Sound Geography*, 19.

37. In his *Notes on the Ethnology of the Indians of Puget Sound*, Waterman describes the process: "'Indian red' (ochre) . . . is dug from the ground, kneaded by the women into lumps, and baked. The lumps are then broken open and the reddest portions picked out. These are pounded up as fine as flour, and mixed with salmon eggs. . . . This combination gives a beautiful dull red, which seems to adhere to a surface almost as well as our commercial paints, though it has no gloss" (47).

38. There was a Suquamish site with a similar name west of Gorst: šábdup 'drying place'.

39. Bass, *Pig-Tail Days in Old Seattle*, 152.

40. For discussion of the boulder, see Maria Dolan and Kathryn True, *Nature in the City: Seattle* (Seattle: The Mountaineers Books, 2003), 243–44.

41. Marian Smith, *Puyallup-Nisqually*, 70; Hermann Haeberlin and Erna Gunther, *The Indians of Puget Sound* (Seattle: University of Washington Press, 1930), 75.

BIBLIOGRAPHY

Abbott, Carl. "Footprints and Pathways: The Urban Imprint on the Pacific Northwest." In *Northwest Lands, Northwest Peoples: Readings in Environmental History*, edited by Dale D. Goble and Paul W. Hirt, 111–24. Seattle: University of Washington Press, 1999.

Alaska: "Our Frontier Wonderland." Seattle: Alaska Bureau, Seattle Chamber of Commerce, 1915.

Alexie, Sherman. *Indian Killer*. New York: Atlantic Monthly Press, 1996.

American Friends Service Committee. *Uncommon Controversy: Fishing Rights of Muckleshoot, Puyallup, and Nisqually Indians*. Seattle: University of Washington Press, 1972.

American Indian Culture and Research Journal 22, no. 4 (1998), special issue devoted to urban Indian issues and literatures.

Anderson, Eva Greenslit. *Chief Seattle*. Caldwell: Caxton Printers, 1943.

Armbruster, Kurt E. *Orphan Road: The Railroad Comes to Seattle, 1853–1911*. Pullman: Washington State University Press, 1999.

Asher, Brad. *Beyond the Reservation: Indians, Settlers, and the Law in Washington Territory, 1853–1889*. Norman: University of Oklahoma Press, 1999.

Atwood, A. *Glimpses in Pioneer Life on Puget Sound*. Seattle: Denny-Correll, 1903.

Bagley, Clarence B. "Chief Seattle and Angeline." *Washington Historical Quarterly* 22, no. 4 (1931): 243–75.

———. *History of King County, Washington*. Chicago: S. J. Clarke, 1929.

———. *History of Seattle from the Earliest Settlement to the Present Time*. 3 vols. Chicago: S. J. Clarke, 1916.

Bahr, Howard M., Bruce A. Chadwick, and Joseph H. Stauss. "Discrimination against Urban Indians in Seattle." *Indian Historian* 5, no. 4 (1972): 4–11.

Baillargeon, Emily. "Seattle Now: A Letter." *New England Review* 20, no. 2 (1999): 147–56.

Baist's Real Estate Atlas of Surveys of Seattle, Wash. Philadelphia: Baist, 1905.

Ballard, Arthur C. *Mythology of Southern Puget Sound.* Seattle: University of Washington Press, 1929.

———. *Some Tales of the Southern Puget Sound Salish.* Seattle: University of Washington Press, 1927.

Barsh, Russel. "Puget Sound Indian Demography, 1900–1920: Migration and Economic Integration." *Ethnohistory* 43 (1996): 65–97.

Bass, Sophie Frye. *Pigtail Days in Old Seattle.* Portland, OR: Metropolitan Press, 1937.

———. *When Seattle Was a Village.* Seattle: Lowman and Hanford, 1947.

Basso, Keith H. *Wisdom Sits in Places: Landscape and Language among the Western Apache.* Albuquerque: University of New Mexico Press, 1996.

Bates, Dawn, Thom Hess, and Vi Hilbert. *Lushootseed Dictionary.* Seattle: University of Washington Press, 1994.

Bauxar, J. Joseph. "History of the Illinois Area." In *Handbook of North American Indians,* edited by William C. Sturtevant, vol. 15, *Northeast,* edited by Bruce G. Trigger, 594–601. Washington: Smithsonian Institution, 1978.

Beaton, Welford. *The City That Made Itself: A Literary and Pictorial Record of the Building of Seattle.* Seattle: Terminal Publishing Co., 1914.

Bergland, Renée. *The National Uncanny: Indian Ghosts and American Subjects.* Hanover, NH: University Press of New England, 2000.

Berkhofer, Robert F., Jr. *The White Man's Indian: Images of the American Indian from Columbus to the Present.* New York: Knopf, 1978.

Berner, Richard C. *Seattle, 1900–1920: From Boomtown, Urban Turbulence, to Restoration.* Seattle: Charles Press, 1991.

———. *Seattle, 1921–1940: From Boom to Bust.* Seattle: Charles Press, 1992.

———. *Seattle Transformed: World War II to Cold War.* Seattle: Charles Press, 1999.

Bernstein, Alison R. *American Indians and World War II: Toward a New Era in Indian Affairs.* Norman: University of Oklahoma Press, 1991.

Berry, Thomas. *The Dream of the Earth.* San Francisco: Sierra Club Books, 1988.

Bierwert, Crisca. *Brushed by Cedar, Living by the River: Coast Salish Figures of Power.* Tucson: University of Arizona Press, 1999.

———. "Remembering Chief Seattle: Reversing Cultural Studies of a Vanishing American." *American Indian Quarterly* 22, no. 3 (1998): 280–307.

Binns, Archie. *Northwest Gateway: The Story of the Port of Seattle.* Garden City, NY: Doubleday, Doran, and Company, 1941.

Blaine, David, and Catherine Blaine. *Memoirs of Puget Sound: Early Seattle,*

1853–1856. Edited by Richard A. Seiber. Fairfield, WA: Ye Galleon Press, 1978.

Blaine, E. G. "The Famous Totem Pole of Seattle: How It Was Procured, and the Fun It Caused." *Northwest Magazine* 20, no. 6 (1902): 1–2.

Blumin, Stuart M. "Explaining the New Metropolis: Perception, Depiction, and Analysis in Mid–Nineteenth Century New York." *Journal of Urban History* 11, no. 1 (1984): 9–38.

Bolyai, John Zoltan. "The Seattle Diphtheria Epidemic of 1972–1973 and Its Relationship to Diphtheria among North American Native Americans." M.P.H. thesis, University of Washington, 1974.

Boyd, Robert. *The Coming of the Spirit of Pestilence: Introduced Infectious Diseases and Population Decline among Northwest Coast Indians, 1774–1874.* Seattle: University of Washington Press, 1999.

Bracken, Christopher. *The Potlatch Papers: A Colonial Case History.* Chicago: University of Chicago Press, 1997.

Brechin, Gray. *Imperial San Francisco: Urban Power, Earthly Ruin.* Berkeley and Los Angeles: University of California Press, 1999.

Brown, Kate. "Gridded Lives: Why Kazakhstan and Montana Are Nearly the Same Place." *American Historical Review* 106, no. 1 (2001): 17–48.

Buchanan, Charles M. "The Rights of the Puget Sound Indians to Game and Fish." *Washington Historical Quarterly* 6, no. 2 (1916): 109–18.

Buerge, David M. *Seattle in the 1880s.* Edited by Stuart R. Grover. Seattle: Historical Society of Seattle and King County, 1986.

Burch, Paul. "The Story of Licton Springs." *The Westerner* 9, no. 4 (1908): 19, 34.

Burrows, Edwin G., and Mike Wallace. *Gotham: A History of New York City to 1898.* New York: Oxford University Press, 1999.

Bussell, C. B. *Tide Lands: Their Story.* Seattle: n.p., 1906.

Cadastral Survey Field Notes and Plats for Oregon and Washington. Denver: U.S. Department of the Interior, Bureau of Land Management, 1982.

Cady, Jack. *Street: A Novel.* New York: St. Martin's Press, 1994.

Callenbach, Ernest. *Ecotopia: The Notebooks and Reports of William Weston.* Berkeley: Banyan Tree Books, 1975.

Callender, Charles. "Illinois." In *Handbook of North American Indians,* edited by William C. Sturtevant, vol. 15, *Northeast,* edited by Bruce G. Trigger, 673–80. Washington: Smithsonian Institution, 1978.

Campbell, Sarah K. *The Duwamish No. 1 Site: A Lower Puget Sound Shell Midden.* Seattle: University of Washington Institute for Environmental Studies, Office of Public Archaeology, 1981.

Carlson, Frank. "Chief Sealth." M.A. thesis, University of Washington, 1903.

Carpenter, Cecelia Svinth. *Fort Nisqually: A Documented History of Indian and British Interaction*. Tacoma, WA: Tahoma Research Services, 1986.

Carter, Paul. *The Road to Botany Bay: An Exploration of Landscape and History*. Chicago: University of Chicago Press, 1987.

Chadwick, Bruce A., and Joseph H. Stauss. "The Assimilation of American Indians into Urban Society: The Seattle Case." *Human Organization* 34, no. 4 (1975): 359–69.

Chadwick, Bruce A., Joseph Stauss, Howard M. Bahr, and Lowell K. Halverson. "Confrontation with the Law: The Case of the American Indians in Seattle." *Phylon* 37, no. 2 (1976): 163–71.

Chambers, Andrew Jackson. *Recollections*. N.p., 1947. Copy available in Special Collections, University of Washington Libraries.

Chapman, Charles C. *History of Knox County, Illinois*. Chicago: Blakely, Brown, and Marsh, Printers, 1878.

Chew, Ron, ed. *Reflections of Seattle's Chinese Americans: The First 100 Years*. Seattle: University of Washington Press, 1994.

Chittenden, Hiram M. "Sentiment versus Utility in the Treatment of National Scenery." *Pacific Monthly* 23 (January 1910): 29–38.

Churchill, Joseph P. "Skid Row in Transition." M.A. thesis, University of Washington, 1976.

Clancy, Frank J. *Doctor Come Quickly*. Seattle: Superior Publishing, 1950.

Clayton, Daniel W. *Islands of Truth: The Imperial Fashioning of Vancouver Island*. Vancouver: University of British Columbia Press, 2000.

Cole, Douglas. *Captured Heritage: The Scramble for Northwest Coast Artifacts*. Seattle: University of Washington Press, 1985.

Cole, Douglas, and Ira Chaikin. *An Iron Hand upon the People: The Law against the Potlatch on the Northwest Coast*. Toronto: Douglas and McIntyre, 1990.

Collins, June M. "John Fornsby: The Personal Document of a Coast Salish Indian." In *Indians of the Urban Northwest*, edited by Marian W. Smith, 287–342. New York: Columbia University Press, 1949.

Colson, Elizabeth. *The Makah Indians: A Study of an Indian Tribe in Modern American Society*. Minneapolis: University of Minnesota Press, 1953.

Conant, Roger. *Mercer's Belles: The Journal of a Reporter*. Seattle: University of Washington Press, 1960.

Cornell, Stephen E. *The Return of the Native: American Indian Political Resurgence*. New York: Oxford University Press, 1988.

Costello, J. A. *The Siwash: Their Life, Legends, and Tales*. Seattle: Calvert, 1895.

Cotterill, George F. *Climax of a World Quest: The Story of Puget Sound, the Modern Mediterranean of the Pacific.* Seattle: Olympic Publishing Co., 1928.

Creisler, Derek. *Princess of the Powwow.* Seattle: Running Colors Productions, 1987.

Cronon, William. *Nature's Metropolis: Chicago and the Great West.* New York: W. W. Norton, 1991.

Crowley, Walt. *Rites of Passage: A Memoir of the Sixties in Seattle.* Seattle: University of Washington Press, 1995.

Dann, Jeffrey Lewis. "A Study of an Indian Tavern on Skid Road." M.A. thesis, University of Washington, 1967.

Danziger, Edmund. *Survival and Regeneration: Detroit's American Indian Community.* Detroit: Wayne State University, 1991.

Dauenhauer, Nora Marks. Haa Kusteyí, *Our Culture: Tlingit Life Stories.* Seattle: University of Washington Press, 1994.

Davis, James E. *Frontier Illinois.* Bloomington: Indiana University Press, 1998.

Davis, Rodney O. "The Frontier State, 1818–48." In *A Guide to the History of Illinois,* edited by John Hoffman, 49–62. New York: Greenwood Press, 1991.

Dawson, Michael. *Selling British Columbia: Tourism and Consumer Culture, 1890–1970.* Vancouver: University of British Columbia Press, 2004.

De Barros, Paul. *Jackson Street After Hours: The Roots of Jazz in Seattle.* Seattle: Sasquatch Books, 1993.

Deloria, Philip J. *Playing Indian.* New Haven: Yale University Press, 1998.

Dening, Greg. *Islands and Beaches: Discourse on a Silent Land, Marquesas, 1774–1880.* Honolulu: University of Hawaii Press, 1980.

Denny, Arthur Armstrong. *Pioneer Days on Puget Sound.* Seattle: C. B. Bagley, Printer, 1888.

Denny, Emily Inez. *Blazing the Way; or, True Stories, Songs, and Sketches of Puget Sound and Other Pioneers.* Seattle: Rainier Printing Co., 1909.

Deverell, William. "Plague in Los Angeles: Ethnicity and Typicality." In *Over the Edge: Remapping the American West,* edited by Valerie J. Matsumoto and Blake Allmendinger, 172–200. Berkeley and Los Angeles: University of California Press, 1999.

Dilworth, Leah. *Imagining Indians in the Southwest: Persistent Visions of a Primitive Past.* Washington: Smithsonian Institution, 1996.

Dippie, Brian W. *The Vanishing American: White Attitudes and U.S. Indian Policy.* Lawrence: University Press of Kansas, 1982.

Dolan, Maria, and Kathryn True. *Nature in the City: Seattle.* Seattle: The Mountaineers Books, 2003.

Dorpat, Paul, and Genevieve McCoy. *Building Washington: A History of Washington State's Public Works*. Seattle: Tartu Publications, 1998.

Dos Passos, John. *The 42nd Parallel*. New York: Harper and Brothers Publishers, 1930.

Dovell, W. T. "The Pathfinders." *Washington Historical Quarterly* 1, no. 1 (1906): 47–50.

Drinnon, Richard. *Facing West: The Metaphysics of Indian-Hating and Empire-Building*. Minneapolis: University of Minnesota Press, 1980.

Driver, Felix, and David Gilbert, eds. *Imperial Cities: Landscape, Display, and Identity*. Manchester: Manchester University Press, 1999.

Drucker, Philip. *The Northern and Central Nootkan Tribes*. Bureau of American Ethnology Bulletin 144. Washington: Smithsonian Institution, 1951.

Duncan, Don. *Meet Me at the Center*. Seattle: Seattle Center Foundation, 1992.

Duncan, Kate C. *1001 Curious Things: Ye Olde Curiosity Shop and Native American Art*. Seattle: University of Washington Press, 2000.

Dunn, John A., and Arnold Booth. "Tsimshian of Metlakatla, Alaska." In *Handbook of North American Indians*, edited by William C. Sturtevant, vol. 7, *Northwest Coast*, edited by Wayne M. Suttles, 294–97. Washington: Smithsonian Institution, 1991.

Duwamish et al. vs. the United States of America, Consolidated Petition No. F-275. Seattle: Argus Press, 1993.

The Duwamish No. 1 Site: 1986 Data Recovery. Seattle: BOAS, 1987.

Eals, Clay, ed. *West Side Story*. Seattle: West Seattle Herald, 1987.

Eckrom, J. A. *Remembered Drums: The Puget Sound Indian War*. Walla Walla, WA: Pioneer Press Books, 1989.

Egan, Timothy. *The Good Rain: Across Time and Terrain in the Pacific Northwest*. New York: Vintage Books, 1990.

Eliot, S. A. *Report upon the Conditions and Needs of the Indians of the Northwest Coast*. Washington: Government Printing Office, 1915.

Elmendorf, William W. *The Structure of Twana Culture*. Pullman: Washington State University, 1960.

Emmons, George Thornton, and Frederica de Laguna. *The Tlingit Indians*. Seattle: University of Washington Press, 1991.

Faragher, John Mack, ed. *Rereading Frederick Jackson Turner: The Significance of the Frontier in American History and Other Essays*. New York: H. Holt, 1994.

Ficken, Robert E. *Unsettled Boundaries: Fraser Gold and the British-American Northwest*. Pullman: Washington State University Press, 2003.

Findlay, John M. *Magic Lands: Western Cityscapes and American Culture after 1940*. Berkeley and Los Angeles: University of California Press, 1992.

Fixico, Donald L. *The Urban Indian Experience in America*. Albuquerque: University of New Mexico Press, 2000.

Fortunate Eagle, Adam. *Heart of the Rock: The Indian Invasion of Alcatraz*. Norman: University of Oklahoma Press, 2002.

Foulkes, Colonel John W. "Jesus Will Save an Irishman." In *American Life Histories: Manuscripts from the Federal Writers' Project, 1936–1940*. Washington: Library of Congress, 1998.

Fowler, Loretta. *Shared Symbols, Contested Meanings: Gros Ventre Culture and History, 1778–1984*. Ithaca: Cornell University Press, 1987.

Franco, Jere Bishop. *Crossing the Pond: The Native American Effort in World War II*. Denton: University of North Texas Press, 1999.

Frykman, George A. *Seattle's Historian and Promoter: The Life of Edmond Stephen Meany*. Pullman: Washington State University Press, 1998.

Fujita-Rony, Dorothy. *American Workers, Colonial Power: Philippine Seattle and the Transpacific West, 1919–1941*. Berkeley and Los Angeles: University of California Press, 2003.

Furtwangler, Albert. *Answering Chief Seattle*. Seattle: University of Washington Press, 1997.

Galois, Robert, with Jay Powell and Gloria Cranmer Webster. *Kwakwaka'wakw Settlements, 1750–1920: A Geographical Gazetteer*. Vancouver: University of British Columbia Press, 1994.

Garfield, Viola. *Seattle's Totem Poles*. Bellevue, WA: Thistle Press, 1996.

Gedosch, Thomas F. "A Note on the Dogfish Oil Industry of Washington Territory." *Pacific Northwest Quarterly* 59, no. 2 (1968): 100–102.

Gibbs, George. *A Dictionary of the Niskwalli Indian Language—Western Washington*. Contributions to North American Ethnology, vol. 1. Washington: Department of the Interior, 1877.

Gibson, Timothy A. *Securing the Spectacular City: The Politics of Revitalization and Homelessness in Downtown Seattle*. Lanham, MD: Lexington Books, 2004.

Goldschmidt, Walter R. *Haa Aaní, Our Land: Tlingit and Haida Land Rights and Use*. Seattle: University of Washington Press, 1998.

Gould, Stephen Jay. "The Creation Myths of Cooperstown." In *Bully for Brontosaurus: Reflections in Natural History*, by Stephen Jay Gould, 42–58. New York: W. W. Norton, 1991.

Grant, Frederick James. *History of Seattle, Washington*. New York: American, 1891.

Groth, Paul. *Living Downtown: The History of Residential Hotels in the United States.* Berkeley and Los Angeles: University of California Press, 1994.

Grubb, David M. *A Practical Writing System and Short Dictionary of Kwakw'ala.* Ottawa: National Museum of Canada, 1977.

Gunther, Erna. *Ethnobotany of Western Washington: The Knowledge and Use of Indigenous Plants by Native Americans.* Seattle: University of Washington Press, 1945.

Haas, Lisbeth. *Conquests and Historical Identities in California, 1769–1936.* Berkeley and Los Angeles: University of California Press, 1995.

Haeberlin, Hermann, and Erna Gunther. *The Indians of Puget Sound.* Seattle: University of Washington Press, 1930.

Hamer, David. *History in Urban Places: The Historic Districts of the United States.* Columbus: Ohio State University Press, 1998.

———. *New Towns in the New World: Images and Perceptions of the Nineteenth-Century Urban Frontier.* New York: Columbia University Press, 1990.

Hancock, Samuel. *The Narrative of Samuel Hancock, 1845–1860.* New York: R. M. McBride and Co., 1927.

Hanford, Cornelius H., ed. *Seattle and Environs: 1852–1924.* Chicago: Pioneer Historical Publishing Co., 1924.

Hansen, Karen Tranberg. "American Indians and Work in Seattle: Associations, Ethnicity, and Class." Ph.D. diss., University of Washington, 1979.

Harmon, Alexandra. *Indians in the Making: Ethnic Relations and Indian Identities around Puget Sound.* Berkeley and Los Angeles: University of California Press, 1998.

Harrington, John Peabody. *The Papers of John Peabody Harrington in the Smithsonian Institution, 1907–1957.* Edited by Elaine L. Miles. New York: Kraus International Publications, 1981.

Harris, R. Cole. "How Did Colonialism Dispossess? Comments from an Edge of Empire." *Annals of the Association of American Geographers* 94, no. 1 (2004): 165–82.

———. *The Resettlement of British Columbia: Essays on Colonialism and Geographical Change.* Vancouver: University of British Columbia Press, 1997.

Hayden, Dolores. *The Power of Place: Urban Landscapes as Public History.* Cambridge, MA: MIT Press, 1995.

Heg, Mrs. E. E. "The Beginnings of Trinity Church, Seattle." *Seattle Churchman* 13, no. 2 (1900): 3–6.

Hilbert, Vi. "When Chief Seattle Spoke." In *A Time of Gathering: Native*

Heritage in Washington State, edited by Robin K. Wright, 259–66. Seattle: University of Washington Press, 1991.

Hinckley, Ted C. *The Americanization of Alaska, 1867–1897.* Palo Alto, CA: Pacific Books, 1972.

———. "The Inside Passage: A Popular Gilded Age Tour." *Pacific Northwest Quarterly* 56, no. 2 (1965): 67–74.

Hoch, Charles, and Robert A. Slayton. *New Homeless and Old: Community and the Skid Row Hotel.* Philadelphia: Temple University Press, 1989.

Hoffman, John, ed. *A Guide to the History of Illinois.* New York: Greenwood Press, 1991.

Holloway, Maria Aurora. "Illness Perception and Knowledge among Seattle Urban Indians." M.Nur. thesis, University of Washington, 1974.

Hudson, Travis, Janice Timbrook, and Melissa Rempe, eds. *Tomol: Chumash Watercraft as Described in the Ethnographic Notes of John P. Harrington.* Santa Barbara, CA: Ballena Press/Santa Barbara Museum of Natural History, 1978.

Hugo, Richard. *The Real West Marginal Way: A Poet's Autobiography.* Edited by Ripley S. Hugo, Lois M. Welch, and James Welch. New York: W. W. Norton, 1986.

Jackson, Deborah Davis. *Our Elders Lived It: American Indian Identity in the City.* DeKalb: Northern Illinois University Press, 2002.

Jacobs, Orange. *Memoirs of Orange Jacobs.* Seattle: Lowman and Hanford, 1908.

Jarboe, Michael E. "Education in the New Metlakatla, Alaska Mission Settlement." Ph.D. diss., University of Washington, 1983.

John Graham and Company. *Pioneer Square Redevelopment.* Seattle: n.p., 1966.

Jonaitis, Aldona. "Totem Poles and the Indian New Deal." *Canadian Journal of Native Studies* 2 (1989): 237–52.

Jones, Nard. *Seattle.* Garden City, NY: Doubleday, 1972.

Judson, Phoebe Goodell. *A Pioneer's Search for an Ideal Home: A Book of Personal Memoirs.* Bellingham, WA: Union Printing, Binding, and Publishing Co., 1925.

Kaiser, Rudolf. "Chief Seattle's Speech(es): American Origins and European Reception." In *Recovering the Word: Essays on Native American Literature,* edited by Brian Swann and Arnold Krupat, 497–536. Berkeley and Los Angeles: University of California Press, 1987.

Kammen, Michael. *Mystic Chords of Memory: The Transformation of Tradition in American Culture.* New York: Knopf, 1991.

Kipling, Rudyard. *From Sea to Sea and Other Sketches: Letters of Travel.* Garden City, NY: Doubleday, Page, and Co., 1925.

Kirk, Ruth. *Tradition and Change on the Northwest Coast: The Makah, Nuu-chah-nulth, Southern Kwakiutl, and Nuxalk.* Seattle: University of Washington Press, 1986.

Kittredge, William. *The Nature of Generosity.* New York: Alfred A. Knopf, 2000.

Klein, Kerwin Lee. *Frontiers of Historical Imagination: Narrating the European Conquest of Native America, 1890–1990.* Berkeley and Los Angeles: University of California Press, 1997.

Klingle, Matthew W. "Urban by Nature: An Environmental History of Seattle, 1880–1970." Ph.D. diss., University of Washington, 2001.

Knight, Rolf. *Indians at Work: An Informal History of Native Indian Labour in British Columbia, 1858–1930.* Vancouver: New Star Books, 1978.

Krech, Shepard, III, and Barbara A. Hail, eds. *Collecting Native America, 1870–1960.* Washington: Smithsonian Institution Press, 1999.

Krouse, S. A. "Kinship and Identity: Mixed Bloods in Urban Indian Communities." *American Indian Culture and Research Journal* 23, no. 2 (1999): 73–89.

Kruckeberg, Arthur. *A Natural History of Puget Sound Country.* Seattle: University of Washington Press, 1991.

Kuipers, Aert H. "Salish Etymological Dictionary." *University of Montana Occasional Papers in Linguistics* 16 (2002).

Laforet, Andrea, and Annie York. *Spuzzum: Fraser Canyon Histories, 1808–1939.* Vancouver: University of British Columbia Press, 1999.

Larson, Lynn L., and Dennis E. Lewarch, eds. *The Archaeology of West Point, Seattle, Washington: 4,000 Years of Hunter-Fisher-Gatherer Land Use in Southern Puget Sound.* Seattle: Larson Anthropological/Archaeological Services, 1995.

Lee, Sohyun Park. "From Redevelopment to Preservation: Downtown Planning in Post-war Seattle." Ph.D. diss., University of Washington, 2001.

Leighton, Caroline. *Life at Puget Sound, with Sketches of Travel in Washington Territory, British Columbia, Oregon, and California, 1865–1881.* Boston: Lee and Shepard, 1884.

Limerick, Patricia Nelson. *The Legacy of Conquest: The Unbroken Past of the American West.* New York: Norton, 1987.

Lind, Carol. *Western Gothic.* Seattle: Lind, 1983.

Low, Denise. "Contemporary Reinventions of Chief Seattle: Variant Texts of Chief Seattle's 1854 Speech." *American Indian Quarterly* 19, no. 3 (1995): 407–22.

Lutz, John. "Inventing an Indian War: Canadian Indians and American Settlers in the Pacific West, 1854–1864." *Journal of the West* 38, no. 3 (1998): 7–13.

———. "Work, Sex, and Death on the Great Thoroughfare: Annual Migrations of 'Canadian Indians' to the American Pacific Northwest." In *Parallel Destinies: Canadian-American Relations West of the Rockies,* edited by John M. Findlay and Ken Coates, 80–103. Toronto: McGill-Queen's University Press, 2002.

Luxton, Norman Kenny. *Tilikum: Luxton's Pacific Crossing.* Sidney, BC: Gray's Publishing, 1971.

Manning, Harvey, and Penny Manning. *Walks and Hikes on the Beaches around Puget Sound.* Seattle: The Mountaineers, 1995.

Marino, Cesare. "History of Western Washington since 1846." In *Handbook of North American Indians,* edited by William C. Sturtevant, vol. 7, *Northwest Coast,* edited by Wayne M. Suttles, 169–79. Washington: Smithsonian Institution, 1991.

Marshall, Daniel P. "No Parallel: American Miner-Soldiers at War with the Nlaka'pamux of the Canadian West." In *Parallel Destinies: Canadian-American Relations West of the Rockies,* edited by John M. Findlay and Ken S. Coates, 31–79. Seattle: University of Washington Press, 2002.

McElroy, Colleen J. *Traveling Music: Poems.* Ashland, OR: Story Line Press, 1998.

McWilliams, Mary. *Seattle Water Department History, 1854–1954.* Seattle: Dogwood Press, 1955.

Meany, Edmond S., ed. "Diary of Wilkes in the Northwest." *Washington Historical Quarterly* 17 (1926): 137–56.

———, ed. *Vancouver's Discovery of Puget Sound.* New York: Macmillan, 1907.

Miller, Bruce Granville. *Invisible Indigenes: The Politics of Nonrecognition.* Lincoln: University of Nebraska Press, 2002.

Miller, Jay. *Lushootseed Culture and the Shamanic Odyssey: An Anchored Radiance.* Lincoln: University of Nebraska Press, 1999.

Miller, Jay, and Carol M. Eastman. *The Tsimshian and Their Neighbors of the North Pacific Coast.* Seattle: University of Washington Press, 1984.

Miller, Jay, and Astrida R. Blukis Onat. *Winds, Waterways, and Weirs: Ethnographic Study of the Central Link Light Rail Corridor.* Seattle: BOAS, 2004.

Milner, Clyde A., II, Carol A. O'Connor, and Martha Sandweiss, eds. *The*

Oxford History of the American West. New York: Oxford University Press, 1996.

Moehring, Eugene P. *Urbanism and Empire in the Far West, 1840–1890*. Reno: University of Nevada Press, 2004.

Moen, Lynn, ed. *Voices of Ballard: Immigrant Stories from the Vanishing Generation*. Seattle: Nordic Heritage Museum, 2001.

Monthan, Guy, and Doris Monthan. "Daybreak Star Center." *American Indian Art* 3, no. 3 (Summer 1978): 28–34.

Montler, Timothy. "Saanich, North Straits Salish." M.A. thesis, University of Victoria, 1968.

Moody, Fred. *Seattle and the Demons of Ambition*. New York: St. Martin's Press, 2003.

Mooney, Kathleen. "Social Distance and Exchange: The Coast Salish Case." *Ethnology* 15, no. 4 (1976): 323–46.

Morgan, Murray. *Century 21: The Story of the Seattle World's Fair, 1962*. Seattle: Acme Press, 1963.

———. *Skid Road: An Informal Portrait of Seattle*. New York: Viking Press, 1951.

Morse, Kathryn. *The Nature of Gold: An Environmental History of the Klondike Gold Rush*. Seattle: University of Washington Press, 2003.

Moser, Charles. *Reminiscences of the West Coast of Vancouver Island*. Victoria: Acme Press, 1926.

Moses, L. G. *Wild West Shows and the Images of American Indians*. Albuquerque: University of New Mexico Press, 1996.

Muir, John. *Travels in Alaska*. New York: Houghton Mifflin, 1915.

Murray, Peter. *The Devil and Mr. Duncan*. Victoria: Sono Nis Press, 1985.

Nash, Gerald D. *American West Transformed: The Impact of the Second World War*. Lincoln: University of Nebraska Press, 1990.

Nelson, Charles M. "Prehistory of the Puget Sound Region." In *Handbook of North American Indians*, edited by William C. Sturtevant, vol. 7, *Northwest Coast*, edited by Wayne Suttles, 481–84. Washington: Smithsonian Institution, 1990.

Nesbit, Robert C. *"He Built Seattle": A Biography of Judge Thomas Burke*. Seattle: University of Washington Press, 1961.

Newell, Gordon R. *Westward to Alki: The Story of David and Louisa Denny*. Seattle: Superior Publishing Co., 1977.

Noel, Patricia Slettvet. *Muckleshoot Indian History*. Auburn, WA: Auburn School District, 1980.

Nowell, Charles, and Clellan J. Ford. *Smoke from Their Fires: The Life of a Kwakiutl Chief.* Hamden, CT: Archon Books, 1941.

O'Brien, Jean M. *Dispossession by Degrees: Indian Land and Identity in Natick, Massachusetts, 1650–1790.* Cambridge: Cambridge University Press, 1997.

Official Guide Book: Seattle World's Fair, 1962. Seattle: Acme Publications, 1962.

Olin, Laurie. *Breath on the Mirror: Seattle's Skid Road Community.* N.p., 1972.

One Hundred Views about Seattle, the Queen City. Seattle: R. A. Reid, 1911.

Paetze, Dick. *Pioneers and Partnerships: A History of the Port of Seattle.* Seattle: Port of Seattle, 1995.

Pascoe, Peggy. "Race, Gender, and the Privileges of Property: On the Significance of Miscegenation Law in the U.S. West." In *Over the Edge: Remapping the American West,* edited by Valerie J. Matsumoto and Blake Allmendinger, 215–30. Berkeley and Los Angeles: University of California Press, 1999.

Paulson, Don, with Roger Simpson. *An Evening at the Garden of Allah: A Gay Cabaret in Seattle.* New York: Columbia University Press, 1996.

Perry, Adele. *On the Edge of Empire: Gender, Race, and the Making of British Columbia, 1849–1871.* Toronto: University of Toronto Press, 2001.

Perry, Albert J. *History of Knox County, Illinois: Its Cities, Towns, and People.* Chicago: S. J. Clarke Publishing Co., 1912.

Philbrick, Nathaniel. *Sea of Glory: America's Voyage of Discovery, the U.S. Exploring Expedition, 1838–1842.* New York: Viking, 2003.

Phillips, Ruth B. *Trading Identities: The Souvenir in Native North American Art, 1700–1900.* Seattle: University of Washington Press, 1998.

Polk's Seattle (Washington) City Directory. Vol. 44. Seattle: R. L. Polk and Co., 1930.

Porter, Frank W., III. "Without Reservation: Federal Indian Policy and the Landless Tribes of Washington." In *State and Reservation: New Perspectives in Federal Indian Policy,* edited by George Pierre Castile and Robert L. Bee, 110–35. Tucson: University of Arizona Press, 1992.

Powell, J. V. *Quileute Dictionary.* Moscow: University of Idaho, 1976.

Prater, Yvonne. *Snoqualmie Pass: From Indian Trail to Interstate.* Seattle: The Mountaineers, 1981.

Prosch, Charles. *Reminiscences of Washington Territory: Scenes, Incidents, and Reflections of the Pioneer Period on Puget Sound.* Seattle: n.p., 1904.

Prosch, Thomas W. *Chronological History of Seattle from 1850 to 1897.* Seattle: n.p., 1900.

Prosch, Thomas W., and C. T. Conover, comps. *Washington, the Evergreen State, and Seattle, Its Chief City*. Seattle: T. F. Kane, 1894.

Raban, Jonathan. *Hunting Mr. Heartbreak: A Discovery of America*. New York: Edward Burlingame Books, 1991.

Raibmon, Paige. *Authentic Indians: Episodes of Encounter from the Late-Nineteenth-Century Northwest Coast*. Durham, NC: Duke University Press, 2005.

Redfield, Edith Sanderson. *Seattle Memories*. Boston: Lothrop, Lee, and Shepard Co., 1930.

Reps, John W. *Panoramas of Promise: Pacific Northwest Towns and Cities in Nineteenth-Century Lithographs*. Pullman: Washington State University Press, 1984.

Rhodes, Marjorie, ed. *King County Censuses: 1870 U.S. Census and 1871 Territorial Census for King County, Washington Territory*. Seattle: Marjorie Rhodes, 1993.

Rich, John M. *Chief Seattle's Unanswered Challenge: Spoken on the Wild Forest Threshold of the City That Bears His Name, 1854*. Seattle: Lowman and Hanford, 1947.

Richardson, Judith. *Possessions: The History and Uses of Haunting in the Hudson Valley*. Cambridge, MA: Harvard University Press, 2003.

Richter, Daniel K. *Facing East from Indian Country: A Native History of Early America*. Cambridge, MA: Harvard University Press, 2001.

Robbins, Tom. *Still Life with Woodpecker*. New York: Bantam Books, 1980.

Ronda, James P. "Coboway's Tale: A Story of Power and Places along the Columbia." In *Power and Place in the North American West*, edited by John M. Findlay and Richard White, 3–22. Seattle: University of Washington Press, 1999.

Rosen, Christine Meisner. *The Limits of Power: Great Fires and the Process of City Growth in America*. New York: Cambridge University Press, 1986.

Rosenthal, Nicholas. "Repositioning Indianness: Native American Organizations in Portland, Oregon, 1959–1975." *Pacific Historical Review* 71, no. 3 (2002): 415–38.

Roy, Donald Francis. "Hooverville: A Study of a Community of Homeless Men in Seattle." M.A. thesis, University of Washington, 1935.

Rupp, James M., and Mary Randlett. *Art in Seattle's Public Places: An Illustrated Guide*. Seattle: University of Washington Press, 1992.

Rydell, Robert W. *All the World's a Fair: Visions of Empire at American International Expositions, 1876–1916*. Chicago: University of Chicago Press, 1984.

Sale, Roger. *Seattle, Past to Present*. Seattle: University of Washington Press, 1976.

Salmonson, Jessica Amanda. *The Mysterious Doom and Other Ghostly Tales of the Pacific Northwest*. Seattle: Sasquatch Books, 1992.

Sandercock, Leonie. *Towards Cosmopolis: Planning for Multicultural Cities*. Chichester, U.K.: John Wiley and Sons, 1998.

Santos, Bob. *Humbows, Not Hot Dogs! Memoirs of a Savvy Asian American Activist*. Seattle: International Examiner Press, 2002.

Sapir, Edward. *Nootka Texts*. Philadelphia: Linguistic Society of America, 1939.

Sato, Mike. *The Price of Taming a River: The Decline of Puget Sound's Duwamish/Green Waterway*. Seattle: The Mountaineers, 1997.

Sayre, J. Willis. *This City of Ours*. Seattle: Seattle School District, 1936.

Scammon, C. M. "Old Seattle and His Tribe." *Overland Monthly* 4, no. 4 (April 1870): 297–302.

Schmitt, Jean-Claude. *Ghosts in the Middle Ages: The Living and the Dead in Medieval Society*. Translated by Teresa Lavender Fagan. Chicago: University of Chicago Press, 1998.

Schwantes, Carlos A. *The Pacific Northwest: An Interpretive History*. Lincoln: University of Nebraska Press, 1996.

Shah, Nayan. *Contagious Divides: Epidemics and Race in San Francisco's Chinatown*. Berkeley and Los Angeles: University of California Press, 2001.

Shamash, Diane, ed. *In Public: Seattle, 1991*. Seattle: Seattle Arts Commission, 1991.

Shelton, Ruth Sehome. *Gram Ruth Sehome Shelton: The Wisdom of a Tulalip Elder*. Seattle: Lushootseed Press, 1995.

Shoemaker, Nancy. "Urban Indians and Ethnic Choices: American Indian Organizations in Minneapolis, 1920–1950." *Western Historical Quarterly* 19, no. 4 (1988): 431–47.

Sidbury, James. *Ploughshares into Swords: Race, Rebellion, and Identity in Gabriel's Virginia, 1730–1810*. Cambridge: Cambridge University Press, 1997.

Simmons, Rose. "Old Angeline, the Princess of Seattle." *Overland Monthly* 20 (November 1892): 506.

Skid Road Community Council. *Changes in Downtown Seattle: 1960–1974*. Seattle: Skid Road Community Council, 1974.

Skid Road Study Committee. *Report*. Seattle: Council of Planning Affiliates, 1969.

Slotkin, Richard. *Gunfighter Nation: The Myth of the Frontier in Twentieth-Century America*. New York: Atheneum, 1992.

Smith, Charles W. "Asa Shinn Mercer, Pioneer in Western Publicity." *Pacific Northwest Quarterly* 27 (1936): 352–67.

Smith, Henry Nash. *Virgin Land: The American West as Symbol and Myth.* New York: Vintage Books, 1957.

Smith, Marian W., ed. *Indians of the Urban Northwest.* New York: Columbia University Press, 1949.

———. "Petroglyph Complexes in the History of the Columbia-Fraser Region." *Southwest Journal of Anthropology* 2, no. 3 (1946): 315–49.

———. *The Puyallup-Nisqually.* New York: Columbia University Press, 1940.

Smith, Paul Chaat, and Robert Warrior. *Like a Hurricane: The Indian Movement from Alcatraz to Wounded Knee.* New York: New Press, 1996.

Snyder, Eugene E. *Early Portland: Stump-Town Triumphant.* Portland, OR: Binfords and Mort, 1970.

Snyder, Warren. *Southern Puget Sound Salish: Texts, Place Names, and Dictionary.* Sacramento: Sacramento Anthropological Society, 1968.

Sorkin, Alan L. *The Urban American Indian.* Lexington, MA: Lexington Books, 1978.

Spiedel, William C. *Sons of the Profits, or There's No Business Like Grow Business: The Seattle Story, 1851–1901.* Seattle: Nettle Creek Publishing Co., 1967.

Spradley, James P. *You Owe Yourself a Drunk: An Ethnography of Urban Nomads.* Boston: Little, Brown and Co., 1970.

Stanbury, W. T. *Success and Failure: Indians in Urban Society.* Vancouver: University of British Columbia Press, 1975.

Stewart, Hilary. *Looking at Totem Poles.* Vancouver: Douglas and McIntyre, 1993.

Story, Gillian L. *Tlingit Verb Dictionary.* Fairbanks: University of Alaska Native Language Center, 1973.

Sugarman, Jonathan R., and David C. Grossman. "Trauma among American Indians in an Urban Community." *Public Health Reports* 111, no. 4 (1996): 321–28.

Suttles, Wayne M. "The Early Diffusion of the Potato among the Coast Salish." In *Coast Salish Essays,* by Wayne M. Suttles, 137–51. Seattle: University of Washington Press; Vancouver: Talonbooks, 1987.

———. "Northwest Coast Linguistic History—a View from the Coast." In *Coast Salish Essays,* by Wayne M. Suttles, 265–81. Seattle: University of Washington Press; Vancouver: Talonbooks, 1987.

———. "Persistence of Intervillage Ties among the Coast Salish." In *Coast Salish Essays,* by Wayne M. Suttles, 209–30. Seattle: University of Washington Press; Vancouver: Talonbooks, 1987.

Swanton, John R. "Explanation of the Seattle Totem Pole." *Journal of American Folklore* 11 (1905): 108–10.

Sword, Robin D. "The 'Saloon Crowd' and the 'Moral Darkness of Puget Sound.'" *Pacific Northwest Forum* 4, no. 1 (1991): 95–101.

Thomas, Philip J. *Songs of the Pacific Northwest*. Saanichton, BC: Hancock House, 1979.

Thompson, Nile. "The Original Residents of Shilshole Bay." In *Passport to Ballard: The Centennial Story*, 10–16. Seattle: Ballard News Tribune, 1998.

———. *A Preliminary Dictionary of the Twana Language*. Shelton, WA: Twana Language Project, Skokomish Indian Tribe, 1979.

Thompson, Nile, and Carolyn Marr. *Crow's Shells: Artistic Basketry of Puget Sound*. Seattle: Dushuyay Publications, 1983.

Thompson, Nile, and C. Dale Sproat. "The Use of Oral Literature to Provide Community Health Education on the Southern Northwest Coast." *American Indian Culture and Research Journal* 28, no. 3 (2004): 1–28.

Thomson, Reginald Heber, with Grant H. Redford. *That Man Thomson*. Seattle: University of Washington Press, 1950.

Thornton, Russell, Gary D. Sandefur, and Harold G. Grasmick. *The Urbanization of American Indians: A Critical Bibliography*. Bloomington: Indiana University Press, 1982.

Thornton, Thomas Fox. "Place and Being among the Tlingit." Ph.D. diss., University of Washington, 1995.

Thrush, Coll-Peter. "Creation Stories: Rethinking the Founding of Seattle." In *More Voices, New Stories: King County, Washington's First 150 Years*, edited by Mary C. Wright, 34–49. Seattle: Pacific Northwest Historians Guild, 2002.

Tolmie, William Fraser. *The Journals of William Fraser Tolmie: Physician and Fur Trader*. Vancouver: Mitchell Press, 1963.

Townsend, Kenneth William. *World War II and the American Indian*. Albuquerque: University of New Mexico Press, 2000.

Tuan, Yi-Fu. *Space and Place: The Perspective of Experience*. Minneapolis: University of Minnesota Press, 1977.

Turbeville, Daniel E., III. "Cities of Kindling: Geographical Implications of the Urban Fire Hazard on the Pacific Northwest Coast Frontier, 1851–1920." Ph.D. diss., Simon Fraser University, 1986.

Tweddell, Colin E. "Historical and Ethnological Study of the Snohomish Indian People." In *Coast Salish and Western Washington Indians*, vol. 2, 475–694. New York: Garland Publishing, 1974.

Usher, Jean. *William Duncan of Metlakatla: A Victorian Missionary in British Columbia*. Ottawa: National Museum of Canada, 1974.

Vancouver, George. *A Voyage of Discovery to the North Pacific ocean, and round the world; in which the coast of north-west America has been carefully examined and accurately surveyed*. London: J. Stockdale, 1801.

Vogt, Helen Elizabeth. *Charlie Frye and His Times*. Seattle: Peanut Butter Publishing, 1997.

Vouri, Mike. "Raiders from the North: The Northern Indians and Northwest Washington in the 1850s." *Columbia* 11, no. 3 (1997): 24–35.

Wade, Richard C. *The Urban Frontier: The Rise of Western Cities, 1790–1830*. Cambridge, MA: Harvard University Press, 1959.

Wandrey, Margaret. *Four Bridges to Seattle: Old Ballard, 1853–1907*. Seattle: Wandrey, 1975.

Ward, Dillis B. "From Salem, Oregon, to Seattle, Washington, in 1859." *Washington Historical Quarterly* 6 (1915): 100–116.

Ward, Stephen V. *Selling Places: The Marketing and Promotion of Towns and Cities, 1850–2000*. London: Routledge, 1998.

Warren, James R. *The Day Seattle Burned*. Seattle: J. R. Warren, 1989.

Waterman, Thomas Talbot. "The Geographical Names Used by the Indians of the Pacific Coast." *Geographical Review* 12 (1922): 175–94.

———. *Notes on the Ethnology of the Indians of Puget Sound*. New York: Heye Foundation, 1973.

———. *Puget Sound Geography*. Edited by Vi Hilbert, Jay Miller, and Zalmai Zahir. Seattle: Lushootseed Press, 2001.

Watson, Emmett. *Digressions of a Native Son*. Seattle: Pacific Institute, 1982.

———. *My Life in Print*. Seattle: Lesser Seattle Publishing, 1993.

Watt, Roberta Frye. *Four Wagons West: The Story of Seattle*. Portland, OR: Metropolitan Press, 1931.

Weibel-Orlando, Joan. *Indian Country, L.A.: Maintaining Ethnic Community in Complex Society*. Urbana: University of Illinois Press, 1991.

White, Richard. *The Middle Ground: Indians, Empires, and Republics in the Great Lakes Region, 1650–1815*. New York: Cambridge University Press, 1991.

Whitney, Mason, ed. *Magnolia: Memories and Milestones*. Seattle: Magnolia Community Club, 2000.

Wilkes, Charles. *Narrative of the United States Exploring Expedition during the Years 1838, 1839, 1840, 1841, and 1842*. 5 vols. New York: G. P. Putnam, 1844.

Williams, Larry E., Bruce A. Chadwick, and Howard M. Bahr. "Antecedents of Self-Reported Arrest for Indian Americans in Seattle." *Phylon* 40, no. 3 (1979): 243–52.

Wolf, Eric R. *Europe and People without History.* Berkeley and Los Angeles: University of California Press, 1982.

Woods, Lawrence M. *Asa Shinn Mercer: Western Promoter and Newspaperman, 1839–1917.* Spokane: Arthur H. Clark Co., 2003.

Wright, Robin K., ed. *A Time of Gathering: Native Heritage in Washington State.* Seattle: University of Washington Press, 1991.

Wrobel, David M. *The End of American Exceptionalism: Frontier Anxiety from the Old West to the New Deal.* Lawrence: University Press of Kansas, 1993.

———. *Promised Lands: Promotion, Memory, and the Creation of the American West.* Lawrence: University Press of Kansas, 2002.

Yesler, Henry L. "The Daughter of Old Chief Seattle." *Pacific Magazine* 1, no. 3 (1889): 25–27.

———. "Henry Yesler and the Founding of Seattle." *Pacific Northwest Quarterly* 42 (1951): 271–76.

Newspapers

A.-Y.-P. News (Seattle)
Highline Times (Burien and Sea-Tac, WA)
Indian Center News (Seattle)
Nanaimo (BC) Times
New York Times
Northwest Indian News (Federal Way, WA)
Olympia Pioneer and Democrat
On Indian Land (Seattle)
Puget Sound Business Journal (Bellevue, WA)
Puget Sound Daily
Seattle Argus
Seattle Business
Seattle Daily Intelligencer
Seattle Daily Times
Seattle Medium
Seattle Patriarch
Seattle Post-Intelligencer (*P-I*)
Seattle Real Change

Seattle Star
Seattle Stranger
Seattle Times
Seattle Town Crier
Seattle Weekly
Seattle Weekly Gazette
Victoria (BC) Daily Colonist
Washington Standard (Olympia, WA)

Videotape Recordings

Bennett, Ramona. Lecture, 6 December 2000. American Indian Studies Center Library, University of Washington.

Bullert, B. J. *Alki: Birthplace of Seattle*. Seattle: Southwest Seattle Historical Society and KCTS Television, 1997.

Powers, Teresa BrownWolf. Interviews with members of the American Indian Women's Service League. American Indian Studies Center Library, University of Washington.

Websites

Central Pacific Railroad Museum, cprr.org/Museum.

HistoryLink, www.historylink.org.

KOMO-4 Television, Seattle, www.komotv.com.

KUOW National Public Radio, Seattle, www.kuow.org.

Slate magazine, www.slate.com.

Washington Association of Churches, www.thewac.org.

Unpublished Manuscripts

Bancroft, Hubert Howe. Narratives of and interviews with early settlers, 1878. Originals at Bancroft Library, Berkeley, California; uncataloged microfilm copies at University of Washington, cited as Bancroft Collection.

Clah, Arthur Wellington. Diary, 1859–1909. National Archives of Canada, Ottawa.

Sarvis, Will. Interview with Diane Vendiola, 10 September 2001. Anacortes Museum.

Swanson, Jacqueline R. "American Indian Women's Service League: The Role of Indian and Alaska Native Women in Establishing Seattle's Contemporary Indian Community." Unpublished research paper in author's possession.

Waterman, Thomas Talbot. "Puget Sound Geography." 1920. Photocopy of original at University of Washington.

Archival Collections

Army Corps Archives, Seattle. Duwamish-Puyallup Surveys.

British Columbia Archives (BCA), Victoria. Annual Reports, Department of Indian Affairs.

Burke Museum of Natural History and Culture, University of Washington. Accession Records.

Manuscripts, Special Collections, and University Archives (MSCUA), University of Washington. Clarence B. Bagley Scrapbooks. Edmond S. Meany Papers. Pamphlet Files. Postcard Collection. Thomas W. Prosch Papers. Don Sherwood Collection. Kenneth G. Smith Papers.

Muckleshoot Indian Tribe Archives (MIT), Auburn, WA. Alki/Transfer CSO Facilities Project Traditional Cultural Properties. Green River Project.

Museum of History and Industry (MOHAI), Seattle. Manuscript Collection. Badcon Collection.

National Archives and Records Administration (NARA), Pacific Northwest Region. Records of the Bureau of Indian Affairs, Western Washington Agency. United States Census.

National Archives of Canada, Ottawa.

Northwest Lesbian and Gay History Museum Project Archives, Seattle. Oral History Collection.

Oregon Historical Society, Portland. Scrapbooks.

Puget Sound Branch, Washington State Archives, Bellevue. King County Death Records. King County Marriage Records. Real Property Assessment and Tax Rolls.

Washington State Historical Society, Tacoma. Hilman F. Jones Papers.

INDEX

Indigenous community affiliations of individuals are given where known; these affiliations do not imply tribal enrollment or other legal status, nor does lack of listed affiliation necessarily imply non-Indian status.

theft and installation of, 113–15; and tourism, 116–17; destruction and replacement of, 158–59

Chief Seattle Club, 181

Chief Seattle Day, 126–27, 148–49

Chief Seattle Speech, 180, 182, 198, 227; as ghost story, 5–7; revival of, in 1970s, 187–88. *See also* Seeathl

Chinatown, 155

Chinese (people), 47, 64–65, 75, 108, 165, 175

Chinook Jargon, 49; in place names, 30, 126, 203; use by Indians, 112, 148, 167; use by non-Indians, 36, 40, 43, 44, 49, 54, 64–65, 123; use by Tilikums of Elttaes, 130, 133. *See also* Cheechako

Chittenden, Hiram M., 95, 104

Choctaw (people), 153, 167

Christianity, 43, 73, 120–21, 188, 190

Christopher, John and Bridget, 73

Clah, Arthur Wellington (Tsimshian), 111

Class: as explanation for racial conflict, 50, 143–44; connected to "Indian vices," 61; relations between high-class Duwamish and settler elite, 35, 42, 73; and effects of Great Fire, 81–82; Indians as markers of white class status, 124, 155. *See also* "Curios"; Intermarriage/"miscegenation"; "Squaw men"

Clayton, Daniel W., 22

Collins, Luther, 29, 49, 53

Collins, Patsy, 160–61

Columbia (Labrador Inuit woman), 120

Columbia City (neighborhood), 77

Colville (people), 157, 165

Commodities: Indians purchasing consumer goods in Seattle, 44–45, 107, 108, 150; Indian food vendors, 70. *See also* "Curios"

Conklin, Ann ("Mother Damnable"), 47, 54

Conservation: effects of laws on indigenous peoples, 99–100, 189

Correa, J. A., 178

Cotterill, George, 19

Cowichan (people), 110

Cowlitz (people), 164

Crab John (Shilshoolabsh), 88

Crepar, T. M., 128

Cross, Alice (Duwamish), 233

Crow, Joseph, 61

Crown Hill (neighborhood), 154

"Curios" (Native objects sold as souvenirs), 115, 124, 160. *See also* Baskets; Totem poles

Cultus Charley (Duwamish), 54

Cumming, Bill, 160–61

Curley (Duwamish; also known as Old Duwampsh Curley), 29, 47, 52, 54, 229; as "father-in-law" of Henry Yesler, 57

Curtis, Edward S., 118

Darling family, 153–54

Davis, Ed (Snoqualmie), 85

Davis, Harvey (Choctaw) and Nellie, 167, 172

Davis, Jennie John (Hachooabsh/Suquamish), 84, 98, 210

Day/Night (art), 173–74, 179–80

Daybreak Star Cultural Center, 171–72, 174, 181, 182

Deeds, Jan, 200

Dening, Greg, 16

Denny, Arthur, 33, 35, 45, 47, 53, 55, 228; and decision to come to Puget Sound, 27; finds site for Seattle, 36–38; advocates laws against race-mixing, 59; writes memoirs, 138–39

WEYERHAEUSER ENVIRONMENTAL BOOKS

WEYERHAEUSER ENVIRONMENTAL CLASSICS